ROUTLEDGE LIBRARY EDITIONS:
WORLD EMPIRES

Volume 16

EMPIRE AND COMMERCE
IN AFRICA

EMPIRE AND COMMERCE IN AFRICA

A Study in Economic Imperialism

LEONARD WOOLF

LONDON AND NEW YORK

This edition published by Routledge/Thoemmes Press in 1998

This edition first published in 2018
by Routledge
2 Park Square, Milton Park, Abingdon, Oxon OX14 4RN

and by Routledge
711 Third Avenue, New York, NY 10017

Routledge is an imprint of the Taylor & Francis Group, an informa business

© 1998 Routledge

British Library Cataloguing in Publication Data
A catalogue record for this book is available from the British Library

ISBN: 978-1-138-47911-1 (Set)
ISBN: 978-1-351-00226-4 (Set) (ebk)
ISBN: 978-1-138-49609-5 (Volume 16) (hbk)
ISBN: 978-1-351-02238-5 (Volume 16) (ebk)

Publisher's Note
The publisher has gone to great lengths to ensure the quality of this reprint but points out that some imperfections in the original copies may be apparent.

Disclaimer
The publisher has made every effort to trace copyright holders and would welcome correspondence from those they have been unable to trace.

EMPIRE AND COMMERCE
IN AFRICA

A Study in Economic Imperialism

Leonard Woolf

With a new Introduction by
Peter Cain
Sheffield Hallam University

ROUTLEDGE/THOEMMES PRESS

This edition published by Routledge/Thoemmes Press, 1998

Routledge/Thoemmes Press
11 New Fetter Lane
London EC4P 4EE

Reprinted 1999

The Empire and its Critics, 1899–1939
8 Volumes : ISBN 0 415 17945 9

© Routledge, 1998

This is a reprint of the 1920 edition

Routledge / Thoemmes Press is a joint imprint
of Routledge Ltd. and Thoemmes Ltd.

British Library Cataloguing-in-Publication Data
A CIP record of this set is available from the British Library

Publisher's Note

The publisher has gone to great lengths to ensure the
quality of this reprint but points out that some
imperfections in the original book may be apparent.

This book is printed on acid-free paper, sewn, and
cased in a durable buckram cloth.

INTRODUCTION

The First World War had a dramatic effect upon the fortunes of the Labour party in Britain. At the 1918 election, the party became a serious contender for power for the first time. Its position was also strengthened by an influx of radical liberals dissatisfied with Lloyd George's conduct of the war, a group which counted J. A. Hobson, E. D. Morel and H. N. Brailsford amongst their number. These radical intellectuals had a marked effect upon many aspects of Labour policy formation in the 1920s, especially foreign and imperial policy. Much of the thinking behind the latter was hammered out in the early 1920s by Morel and by Leonard Woolf (1880–1969). At this time, Woolf was honorary secretary of the party's advisory committee on international and imperial affairs, and *Empire and Commerce in Africa*, published first in 1920, was actually written at the request of the Labour Research Department.

Woolf was born into a well-to-do Reform Jewish community (his father was a prominent barrister) and he read classics at Cambridge where he met Lytton Strachey, J. M. Keynes and other members of what became known as the Bloomsbury Group. Between 1904 and 1912 he served as a civil servant in Ceylon, Sri Lanka, leaving the service to marry the novelist Virginia Stephen, daughter of Sir Leslie Stephen, whose fame under her married name far outstripped that of her husband. With Virginia, Woolf founded the famous Hogarth Press in the 1920s and he also acted as joint editor of the *Political Quarterly* between 1931 and 1958. He maintained a strong interest in international affairs and promoted the idea of international government throughout his long life; his thinking on these issues had a considerable influence on major figures in inter-war politics such as Arthur Henderson.

Radical attacks on imperialism were sometimes long on theory and short on the evidence necessary to back them up. What most distinguishes *Empire and Commerce in Africa* from the other radical documents in this collection is the extent of the material on which the argument is based. It is undoubtedly a 'weighty tome', the result of a long period of meticulous research, and it demonstrates a familiarity with an impressive range of sources from across western Europe. There is a detailed account of the Italian fiasco in Abyssinia (Ethiopia), of the French empire in Algeria and Tunisia and of Leopold's acquisition of the Congo. Indeed, the book has rather more to say about French imperialism in Africa than about British and the only aspect of the latter which receives extended coverage is the expansion into East Africa in the 1890s. Woolf recognized that Britain and other powers were pursuing an imperialist policy in China and had acquired an empire in South East Asia, an area of which he had first-hand experience; but he chose to concentrate on Africa because, like Morel and for similar reasons, he saw it as the central problem of imperialism in his time. His study was, therefore, largely confined to the so-called 'formal' empire. Moreover, the very thoroughness of his research limited his scope considerably and meant that even his coverage of Africa was patchy: he left the British occupation of Egypt out of his account because 'to deal with it adequately would require a volume in itself' (p. 115). Nonetheless, despite its heavyweight appearance, the book is compellingly written and is sustained by a wit and an irony which act as masks for Woolf's contempt and indignation at what he believed to be the crimes and follies of Europeans in Africa.

In an analysis which helped to shape attitudes to imperialism for more than one generation of radicals and socialists, Woolf dated the beginnings of modern imperialism in the early 1880s. Before then, Western penetration had been haphazard with only occasional interventions by European states in crises. After 1880, governments actively pursued an imperialist policy in Africa in the belief that, firstly, it was now the state's duty to promote the economic well-being of its subjects and, secondly, that imperialism offered the chance of considerable economic gains. The key turning point was the negotiations which ended with Leopold, King of the Belgians, installed in the Congo: this was the signal for 'the nations of Europe ... to fall upon Africa like a pack of snarling, tearing, quarrelling jackals' (p. 44). From the perspective of the 1920s, Woolf argued that the economic gains had so far proved delusive; that the impact on the Africans themselves had been disastrous; and that the possession of

African territory had not added anything significant to the military might of the imperial powers and had probably increased their vulnerability to attack. As for the last of these, Woolf felt, as did Morel and Brailsford, that the continuous jostling for territory between the powers, all convinced of the necessity of imperialism to their own well-being as nations, had undoubtedly contributed to the antagonisms which lay behind the First World War and might soon spark another worldwide conflict unless drastic changes in colonial policy were undertaken quickly.

Africa had failed to provide the Europeans with wealth and power, both of which had proved a 'mirage of politics and economics' (p. 137). But what had been costly to the African and to the average man on the Clapham omnibus was profitable to a 'small group of persons, the financiers, traders and capitalists who are seeking particular economic ends in Africa' (p. 319). These men were the moving force behind speculative enterprises like the Imperial British East Africa Company which had used the illusions of the age to persuade governments to open up African territory for them and who, when they ran into difficulties, trafficked in the same illusions to persuade the state to step in, take control and relieve them of both their responsibilities and their financial embarrassments. Yet Woolf was willing to grant that even Sir William Mackinnon, the begetter of the IBEAC, was prey to the same illusions he had so carefully manipulated and had genuinely believed that his pursuit of profit in Uganda brought benefits to Britain and to Africa. The chapter on East Africa, written in an ironic style which sometimes bears a striking resemblance to Veblen's, provides an excellent example of Hobson's contention that 'finance is the governor of the imperial engine', focusing the energies of other imperialist forces and spurring them to action. Yet, like Morel and unlike Hobson and Brailsford, at no point does Woolf make an attempt to link the machinations of financiers and traders in Africa with faults in the structures of the European economies which sponsored them. There is no talk of underconsumption or oversaving, and the domestic scene, which shaped the forces of economic imperialism in Africa which Woolf so vividly described, remains no more than a shadowy background presence.

Woolf felt that the war had been brutal enough to force the European publics to shed their illusions about imperialism and to make it possible for a new policy to be pursued in Africa. He agreed that Germany was unfit to hold colonies, but so were all the other powers. He distrusted the emerging idea of mandates because it might prove simply to be a cover for old-fashioned exploitation by other powers who had simply carved up Germany's empire amongst themselves. Hence he argued for genuine international government of colonies, supervised by a League of Nations with real powers and capable of ensuring that Africans retained their land, their culture and their right to free trade and the 'open door'. In this endeavour, Woolf was close to Morel whose practical proposals for the reform of colonial economic management he strongly supported, and the ideas they put forward became an important part of Labour's international policy heritage between the wars.

There is a brief biography of Woolf in the *Dictionary of National Biography, 1961–70* (1981) and a much more substantial one by Margaret Cole in J. M. Bellamy and John Saville (eds.), *Dictionary of Labour Biography*, vol. 5 (1979). In his old age, Woolf also wrote a multi-volume autobiography. His other works on imperialism include *Economic Imperialism* (1925) and *Imperialism and Civilisation* (1928). His work for the Labour party on imperial matters is discussed in P. S. Gupta, *Imperialism and the British Labour Movement, 1914–1964* (1975), esp. pp. 31–5, 73–8. There is also a broader study of his political career and opinions by Duncan Wilson, *Leonard Woolf: A Political Biography* (1979).

Peter Cain
Sheffield Hallam University, 1998

EMPIRE & COMMERCE IN AFRICA

A STUDY IN ECONOMIC IMPERIALISM

BY

LEONARD WOOLF

"Si j'avais à soutenir le droit que nous avons eu de rendre les nègres esclaves, je dirais : les peuples d'Europe ayant exterminé ceux de l'Amérique, ont dû mettre en esclavage ceux de l'Afrique pour s'en servir à défricher tant de terres. Ceux dont il s'agit sont noirs des pieds à la tête ; ils ont le nez si écrasé qu'il est presque impossible de les plaindre. On ne peut se mettre dans l'esprit que Dieu, qui est un être très sage, ait mis une âme, surtout une âme bonne, dans un corps tout noir."—MONTESQUIEU, *Esprit des lois*.

PUBLISHED BY THE LABOUR RESEARCH DEPARTMENT, 34 ECCLESTON SQUARE, WEST-MINSTER; AND BY GEORGE ALLEN AND UNWIN, LIMITED, 40 MUSEUM STREET, LONDON, WC.1.

NOTE

I HAVE to thank Miss Alix Sargent-Florence, who has given me valuable help in research for Part II. of this book,

The volume was written as a Report for a Committee of the Labour Research Department.

CONTENTS

PART I.—INTERNATIONAL ECONOMIC POLICY

CHAP.   PAGE
I. INTRODUCTORY 3
II. THE STATE'S RANGE OF ECONOMIC ACTION . . . 13
III. THE ECONOMIC IMPERIALISM OF EUROPE . . . 21
IV. SCOPE OF THE ENQUIRY 48

PART II.—ECONOMIC IMPERIALISM IN AFRICA

I. EUROPE AND AFRICA 53
II. MEDITERRANEAN AFRICA: ALGERIA 69
III. MEDITERRANEAN AFRICA: TUNIS 79
IV. MEDITERRANEAN AFRICA: TUNIS AND TRIPOLI . . 114
V. ABYSSINIA AND THE NILE 138
VI. ZANZIBAR AND EAST AFRICA 228
VII. THE BELGIAN CONGO 303

PART III.—REFLECTIONS AND CONCLUSIONS

I. THE EFFECTS OF ECONOMIC IMPERIALISM . . . 315
II. THE FUTURE OF AFRICA 352
INDEX 369

MAPS

I. THE PARTITION OF AFRICA IN 1880 52
II. THE PARTITION OF AFRICA IN 1914 52
III. ETHIOPIAN AND EAST AFRICA 138
IV. ETHIOPIAN AFRICA, 1894 AND 1900 170
V. THE TERRITORY OF THE SULTAN OF ZANZIBAR IN 1886 AND 1890 175

Ce chien est à moi, disoient ces pauvres enfants ; c'est là ma place au soleil : voilà le commencement et l'image de l'usurpation de toute la terre.—PASCAL, *Pensées*.

PART I

INTERNATIONAL ECONOMIC POLICY

CHAPTER I

INTRODUCTORY

MOST people, if, for a moment, they shut their eyes and allow their memory to steal away out of their habitual control of it and rummage in the past, will find that suddenly a very vivid picture of their first "lessons" rises before them. No historian, no publicist, and certainly no writer or reader in any subject of what is aptly called controversial politics, should ever begin his task without five minutes' ceremonial of this kind. Practically every page of this book will be concerned with political subjects so controversial that no gentleman can discuss them with any one who does not believe exactly the things which he believes, and remain a gentleman. Every writer naturally wants his reader to behave like a gentleman towards him, that is to listen to what he says at least with an air of respect. That is why I would beg my reader to go through this brief ceremony, and to recall his or her first lessons, whether at the proverbial mother's knee or, more probably, at a kindergarten table under the worried eye of a most ill-informed lady. After pot-hooks and hangers he was taught to write, and in the process he made acquaintance for the first time with generalizations about man. His mother or his teacher impressed these generalizations upon him as true, and, if he be candid with himself, he will admit that to this day his belief in them is more unquestioning and more deep than in almost any other facts. No one ever learns to question the statement that evil communications corrupt good manners, and nobody ever acts upon his belief. Another generalization—and it is one which I should like to get into my reader's head at once as a perpetually recurring air or theme or rhythm running through every page and chapter of this book—was that man differs essentially from the animals because he acts according to reason. Man is infinitely above the beasts because he is self-conscious, because he reasons and acts on reason, because through his reason he is able to control his destiny. We believe these generalizations as passionately and as unquestioningly as that evil communications corrupt

3

good manners, and perhaps with very much the same effect. People who go to Wagner's operas often hold in their hands little explanatory books, in which the airs or tunes or themes are picked out and printed, as, for instance, Siegfried's theme or Wotan's or Brynhilde's, and the listener who has not got these running in his head, so that he can pick them out and recognize them, is not supposed to be able fully to appreciate the meaning of the music as a whole. In every book there are, or ought to be, similar themes of thought, and the writer ought to pick them out and print them in his introductory chapter. No reader of this book will be able to appreciate its meaning who has not running in his head the generalizations given above, in which he almost certainly believes deeply and firmly.

The subject of this book is Policy and Commerce, or, as I propose to call it, international economic policy. If we can imagine the race of bees suddenly endowed with man's peculiar gift of reason, the first step which it would take would undoubtedly be to appoint a Royal Commission of Bees to report upon the manner in which Man, the only other reasoning animal, organizes the human hive. There can be no doubt that, if the Commission of Bees began its enquiries in the year 1917, it would immediately see the immense and almost overwhelming importance in the economy of the human hive which is played to-day by the State. If man controls his destiny by the use of his reason, it has led him to decide that it can only be controlled effectively and happily through the organization of mankind in States. And if the Royal Commission of Bees treated its enquiry historically, it would report with amazement upon the enormous change in the form and importance of the State which has taken place in recent years. The State is one of the most ancient of man's institutions, with an unbroken history of evolution stretching far back to times which are the twilight between mythology and history. Its chief attributes have, from the earliest times, been power and mystery, and of all human contrivances and abstractions it has always attracted to itself the most violent love, superstition, and hatred. Its age and its power may be recognized from the fact that time has swept away whole civilizations with all their marks and memorials except those of the State, cut in hieroglyphics upon stone obelisks. But the State like all human institutions, to the almost universal dismay of man himself, changes. The change is usually so slow as to be almost imperceptible to each generation, so that the vast majority in each generation, to whom progress is extremely distasteful and discomforting because it implies change, can console themselves with the belief that, whatever else has been improved, the State at least has remained unalterably the same. Unfortunately, however, the pace at which men themselves and their lives change sometimes quickens, and then they can no longer delude themselves that even their God and their State have remained unchanged. Such a quickening in the pace of the evolution of European man occurred somewhere about the year 1790, and it has had the most profound effect upon the State.

This book is not a treatise upon either the nature or the theory of the State. But it will deal throughout with policy, and policy is at least the instrument of a State's action. While I do not therefore wish to be led aside down any alluring and winding path of theory, it is necessary, in order to explain the scope and object of the book, to say something about the nature of the State and its growth during the last 125 years. The State, as we know it to-day, is a growth of very recent years : in its present form and with its present attributes it did not exist even in 1820. No doubt all the elements of its present form existed in the eighteenth-century State, but an embryo is not the same as an adult, nor a tadpole the same as a frog. All historians agree that the three strongest currents in European evolution during the last century were those of democracy, of nationalism, and of industrialism. It is these three currents which have been mainly responsible for the immense modifications in the structure and sphere of the State. Before the nineteenth century the State was a kind of vested interest, the personal preserve or estate of a particular family or families. The national power, organized or fashioned into an instrument for gain, or sharpened into a weapon for defence or offence by legislation and administration, was first vested in the hands of the king, and later in those of a few noble families. Occasionally a few city merchants were admitted to some share in the monopoly, and helped to shape national policy by imposing upon the unsound system of internal economy, devised by and for the landowners, a still more unsound system of foreign trade. The conception of the State as the whole nation organized for certain ends did not exist in practice, though it can be traced in the writings of publicists who, because they foresaw and foretold the trend of human development, seemed to their contemporaries to be either criminal or lunatic.

The old view of the State as a vested interest has not become extinct, but it has almost succumbed to the combined poisons of democracy, nationalism, and industrialism. Society was violently inoculated with these poisons, first in the democratic movement which centred in the French Revolution, secondly in the Napoleonic Wars, and thirdly through the industrial revolution. The old State and the ancient depositaries of power and policy have been forced to modify their methods, and even their views, in order to avoid complete destruction. In order to adjust itself to, and so far as possible nullify, the currents of democracy and nationalism, the State has abandoned the claim to be a personal preserve and prerogative, and has emerged as the Nation organized for national interests. The function of the eighteenth-century State was mainly power and government; that of the nineteenth century professes to be the attainment of "the greatest good of the greatest number," or "the realization of the best life," or the materialization of a mysterious and sacred "general will." Interacting upon these conceptions, the industrial revolution has come with irresistible force and swung the State into an orbit where its range and velocity have been immeasurably increased. Before 1790 life was for the most part slow, local, inefficient, uneconomic : in the last century it has been enormously speeded up, it has become national, it has been industrialized and commercialized. The State has not escaped this tendency to apply the standards of industry and commerce to all the departments of human life. Nobody in the eighteenth century thought of asking whether the State was efficient, for the main functions of the State were not economic : to-day, despite the enormous increase of nationalistic patriotism, we instinctively regard the State as a kind of super-joint-stock-company.[1] As an economic instrument the value of the organized national power could not escape the attention of the industrial age.

This book will be largely concerned with the examination of facts which prove the statement in the last sentence and paragraph. It will show how, in one sphere at any rate, our generation, permeated with the ideas and standards of industrialism and commercialism, has come to regard the main function of the State as the pursuit of national economic interests by means of organized national power. I do not propose, therefore, in this place to labour the point, but I will leave the reader to ponder over one little proof. If we wish to get a clear view of what any generation considers to be the work and ideals of State action, we should go to the writings and speeches of those men to whom have been entrusted the control

---

[1] This statement may appear to some people exaggerated. Reflection on the leading articles in the daily press, on the pages of *Hansard*, and on the works of serious political philosophers will confirm the generalization. There is an interesting confirmation of it in Sidgwick's *Elements of Politics*, p. 517. Sidgwick was not a particularly commercially-minded man, and yet he instinctively makes even the question of local and sectional government depend principally on commercial considerations. "The expense," he writes, "of paving and lighting the streets of a town should be thrown on those who reside in it . . . for though the resulting advantages will be partly shared by travellers and persons who make a temporary sojourn in the town, this will only be the case to a minor extent, and its effect seems fairly compensated by the contributions which such persons will indirectly make to the material prosperity of the town by their purchases from innkeepers, shopkeepers, etc." Thus Sidgwick instinctively applies to the State the commercial standard that it is wrong to allow any person to profit by anything unless you make him pay for it, or, as he puts it elsewhere, "the primary ground for establishing local organs of government" is "the principle that those who profit by any governmental expenditure should at the same time bear the burden of it, and exercise financial control over it " (p. 526).

of such action and the direction of State policy. They will show us what, in the opinion of the chief actors or rather engineers, were the objects and motives which at any particular moment set in motion the great engine of national power. Now in 1895 the British nation, through its electors, entrusted the direction of the State to a Conservative Government in which one of the most important and powerful Ministers was Mr. Joseph Chamberlain, Secretary of State for the Colonies. In 1896 the Birmingham Chamber of Commerce gave a banquet to Mr. Chamberlain, who made a speech in reply to the toast of " Her Majesty's Ministers." In that speech Mr. Chamberlain gives a very clear exposition of what he considered to be the main function of the State and the chief duty of the Ministry.

" From the moment that we accepted and entered upon the duties of office," he said, " our most important duty, our most absorbing care, has been not the party legislation which occupies probably the largest part of our public discussions, but the development and the maintenance of that vast agricultural, manufacturing, and commercial enterprise upon which the welfare and even the existence of our great population depends. Now, I think, gentlemen, that you may safely give the widest interpretation to the statement that I have just made. All the great offices of State are occupied with commercial affairs. The Foreign Office and the Colonial Office are chiefly engaged in finding new markets and in defending old ones. The War Office and Admiralty are mostly occupied in preparations for the defence of these markets and for the protection of our commerce. The Boards of Agriculture and of Trade are entirely concerned with those two great branches of industry. Even the Education Department bases its claims to the public money upon the necessity of keeping our people well to the front in the commercial competition which they have to sustain ; and the Home Office finds the largest scope for its activity in the protection of the life and health, and in the promotion of the comfort of, the vast army of manual labourers who are engaged in those industries. Therefore it is not too much to say that commerce is the greatest of all political interests, and that that Government deserves most the popular approval which does most to increase our trade and to settle it on a firm foundation."

It is clear that in the opinion of this Minister, who for many years took the first part in the direction of policy, the national economic interests are the primary concern of the State, and the whole machinery of government and Government Offices should be mainly directed to the promotion of the commercial interests of the nation. Is it altogether an exaggeration to say that Mr. Chamberlain's conception of the State in this speech approximates more nearly to a super-joint-stock-company than to a " City of God " ? The applause of his audience showed that they shared his political vision, and with him had travelled far from the Greek, who, in thinking of the policy of his own State, fixed his eyes upon the vision of that city which is laid up in Heaven as a pattern " for him who desires to see it." [1]   Some allowance must, of course, be made for the fact that the Greek was a philosopher, while the Minister was a politician addressing a company of commercial gentlemen who were his hosts.   But the same view of the functions of the State can be found in all Mr. Chamberlain's speeches during the '90's ; and that they were endorsed by the electorate is shown by the fact that he and the Government to which he belonged were returned to power in 1902.

It will be observed that in form Mr. Chamberlain's words were a statement of facts.   In reality they were a statement of policy. The State, he said, *is* an organisation for the pursuit of the economic ends of nations ; Government Offices and Ministers *are* the instruments of that pursuit ; " commerce *is* the greatest of all political interests."   The minister was, however, in reality stating the formula of his own and his hearers' policy ; and policy is a question not so much of facts as of beliefs and ideals.   The neglect of this truth or truism causes so much political folly and misery, and is the begetter of so much false history, that it is necessary to deal with it here at some length.   History is presented to us as a record of events or facts, and the practical statesman, whenever any political problem has to be solved by us, exhorts us to fix our eyes not upon theories or ideals, but upon facts.   Commercial rivalry between nations, the struggle for markets, tariffs, armaments, and war, are the kind of facts which humanity is continually being exhorted to contemplate, if not with satisfaction, at least with resignation.   Call a political evil a fact and it is immediately invested with a kind of holiness which belongs to things which must remain eternally the same.   Nearly every political evil, from slavery and torture to the subjection of women and war, has at some time or other been consecrated as a fact by contemporaries. Since most men are by nature pessimistic conservatives, it is the evils and not the goods which are particularly singled out for this consecration ; and politicians, statesmen, and historians represent the horrible story of man's political development which they call history, as almost entirely determined by the " logic of events " or the " logic of facts."   But in history there is no logic of events and no logic of facts, there is only a logic of men's beliefs and ideals.

Let us test the truth of this by applying it to the particular problem of history and politics with which I am concerned in this book—Power, Policy, and Commerce.   The general problem may be stated as follows :   We find ourselves living here in a world

[1] Ἐν οὐρανῷ ἴσως παράδειγμα ἀνάκειται τῷ βουλομένῳ ὁρᾶν, Plato, *Republic IX.* 592 b.

of States. The sphere of the State's internal and external action has in the last century increased enormously, until to-day there is hardly any department of individual life and activity which is not subjected to State control or interference. External policy, with which I am concerned, is from one point of view the instrument of the State's action in its relations with other States. All these are no doubt facts, but is there any logic of these facts in the sense that their existence is inevitable, or that, because they exist, certain other facts must inevitably exist? The answer to the question will depend upon whether, after all, man is a reasoning animal and is capable by his reason of determining his destiny.

Policy, I have said, is the instrument of a State's action. But policy is determined by our beliefs and our ideals: it represents our view of what we want the State to be, and what we want the State to do in the world of States. Thus the State is what we want it to be and believe it to be, and there is here no logic of facts, but a logic of beliefs and desires. Mr. Chamberlain's State and his Government Offices and his Secretaries of State and his Policy will all be of a particular kind, because he believes that the promotion of commercial interests is the greatest of political interests, the chief function of the State. Here there is a logic of Mr. Chamberlain's belief and desire, no logic of facts. The builders and controllers of the Ottoman Empire believed that the greatest of political interests was an unlimited supply of slaves and concubines.[1] That belief and desire determined the nature of the Ottoman State, determined the policy of the Ottoman people, and determined the fate of millions of individuals living between the Persian Gulf and the Danube. The Ottoman Empire and its history differed from the British Empire and its history, because the Turk believed and wanted the State to be or to do one thing, and Mr. Chamberlain and other Britons believed and wanted the State to be or to do something else. The Turkish State sacked city after city to supply its citizens with concubines: the British State in a few years added 2,600,000 square miles to its territory in order to supply its citizens with free markets.[2] That is the logic, not of events, but of beliefs and desires.

Man's past was caused by what men desired and believed: the future will be caused by what we desire and believe. Hence the enormous and increasing importance of our desires and beliefs with regard to the State and policy. For policy is a kind of immaterial tissue of communal desires and beliefs, woven out of what we desire and believe the State to be, and what we desire and believe that the State can attain for us in its relations with other States. Policy

[1] See *The Turkish Empire*, by Lord Eversley.
[2] See Mr. Chamberlain's speech quoted above, and also the speech delivered by him in the House of Commons on March 20, 1893.

is thus a means or instrument for certain ends, and its action will depend both upon the ends and upon the means adopted for attaining those ends. In this book I shall be dealing with Policy and Commerce, which is only part of the larger question of what man wishes the State to be and to attain. But the part is sufficiently large and important to claim the exercise of man's reason upon it, if it be still true that he proposes to control his destiny through his reason. Nowhere has the growth of the State's sphere of action been so great, or linked with such tremendous upheaval, as in the sphere of international economic policy. Nowhere have the desires and beliefs implied in the view that " commerce is the greatest of political interests " become more universal than in the region of external or foreign policy. There is no statesman or writer in any European country to-day who would contest the political axiom that the power of the State can be and should be used upon the world outside the State for the economic purposes of the world within the State. It is almost impossible to visualize the total effect which the acceptance of this axiom in the last sixty years has had upon the world. It has turned whole nations into armies, and industry and commerce into weapons of economic war. It has caused more bloodshed than ever religion or dynasties caused in an equal number of years, when gods and kings, rather than commerce, were the " greatest of political interests." It was the chief cause of the war which we have just been fighting, and which in Asia men already talk of as the first act in the passing of the civilization of Europe. It has proved infinitely stronger than the other two great currents in nineteenth-century history, democracy and nationalism, for everywhere in Europe democratic have yielded to economic ideals, and nationalism, wherever it has appeared, has applied itself most violently to economic ends. Within Europe the form and method of national commerce and industry have been moulded by it, and it has built the barriers and set the limits of all international intercourse. These are only some of its more beneficent results upon the lives of Europeans, but its effects have been almost more violent outside Europe. For it has converted the whole of Africa and Asia into mere appendages of the European State, and the history of those two continents, the lives which men live in Nigeria or Abyssinia, in India and Siam and China, are largely determined by the conviction of Europeans that " commerce is the greatest of European political interests."

It is a safe prophecy that the importance of international economic policy will not decrease, but will increase, during the next fifty years, and that the history of the twentieth century will be very largely determined by the international economic policy which follows the war. It would be foolish to attempt to prejudge the question whether that policy will be moulded only by passion and instinct, or whether it is amenable to the control of reason. But if policy and man's destiny are in any way to be subject to the control of his reason, then certainly we want to know what external economic ends we desire the State to pursue, which of those ends the State can attain, and what means are available for their attainment. But that knowledge is not possible for any one who has not undertaken the preliminary task of ascertaining what have been the ends previously desired and pursued, and what have been the actual results of the pursuit. That is the angle from which I propose to approach the whole subject of economic policy. At first sight it may appear to some that the enquiry is unnecessary, because there exist already an immense number of books upon different parts of the subject. Any library catalogue will furnish a melancholy proof of the existence of those books, and it would be presumptuous to question the value and importance of many of them. There is, however, no presumption in maintaining the truth, namely, that there has been no adequate attempt to treat the subject from exactly the angle of vision put forward in this chapter. One of the chief reasons for the inadequacy is, I believe, the fact that writers on the subject of policy have not clearly seen and taken steps to guard against a difficulty peculiar to the subject. That difficulty comes from patriotism and the prejudices of policy itself. Nearly all history is patriotic and therefore unreliable : for instance, a very little investigation will reveal the fact that the French account of British economic policy is diametrically the opposite of the British account, and the British account of French economic policy is diametrically the opposite of the French account. Now the British writer almost invariably adopts without enquiry the British account, and the French writer adopts the French account. That is largely due to the method of approach to the subject : the British writer approaches the subject by asking what effect upon Britain has British policy had, while the French writer asks what effect has French economic policy had upon France ; or the British Imperialist looks at the policy of Imperialism and sees that it is good—for Britain, while the Free Trader looks at the policy of protectionism, and sees that it is bad—for Britain. The man is a fool who deceives himself by the belief that he is exempt from the universal fate of human beings to be governed by prejudice and preconception : for every political writer should be able to say with Reland, "Every day I become more and more convinced that the world wishes to be deceived and to be governed by prejudice." [1] The distortions and deceptions of preconceived opinions about policies, and of the prejudices of patriotism, will certainly leave their decipherable marks upon the pages of this book : but

[1] "Qui quotidie magis magisque experior mundum decipi velle et praeconceptis opinionibus regi," Reland, *De Religione Mohammedica*.

an attempt can at least be made to guard against them by approaching the subject with one's eyes open, and from a direction which is against the wind of prejudice.   What we want to know is, first, whether British history or French history is true, whether the French or the British account of British policy is true, and whether the British or French account of French policy is true.   Secondly, we should be concerned not so much with the question of what British policy has effected for Britain, or French policy for France, as with the question what these policies have effected and will effect for the world of States and its inhabitants.   Lastly—and this is perhaps the hardest of his tasks—the political enquirer should attempt to guard against the attitude of defence of, or attack against, particular policies.   He should try to forget that men have ever wrangled over the rightness or wrongness of "Imperialism" and "Little-Englandism," of "Protectionism" and "Free-Trade," for his concern should be not with the "-isms" and catch-words of party politics, which are saturated with the prejudices of policy, but with the meaning of men's political desires and beliefs, and their influence upon the past and the future of mankind.   This volume will certainly not live up to these intentions and resolutions, but, at any rate, before it was written it intended to be an experiment upon such lines in one particular division of the subject of policy.

CHAPTER II

POLICY is the formula of man's beliefs and desires with regard to the use of the State's power. But while men exist and occasionally attempt to express clearly what they want and believe politically, man is an abstraction which is deprived of even the limited power of expression possessed by men. Therefore policy, in the sense of a formula of man's political beliefs and ideals, is unexpressed, and it must be either deduced from his political actions or sought for in formulae offered by, and accepted from, representative men or statesmen. That is the method by which I propose to define the limits and divisions of the State's range of economic action, as they have appeared in international economic policy, which is the formula of man's beliefs and desires with regard to the use of the State's power for economic ends. In this chapter I shall be concerned only with the preliminary task of mapping out these limits and divisions.

In the first place, it must be observed that we shall be concerned with two things, the ends and the means of international economic policy. For such policy proposes to use the State's power for certain political and economic ends, and to do so by the use of certain specific political means. There is no difficulty in answering the question what those ends are. When Mr. Chamberlain stated that " commerce is the greatest of all political interests," and that " that Government deserves most the popular approval which does most to increase our trade and to settle it on a firm foundation," he was stating in the clearest terms, and with the approval of his audience, the ends of international economic policy. Words unfortunately mean what they say, and statesmen forget that the logic of beliefs and desires, not of events, is merciless. If we act upon the belief that commerce is the greatest of all political interests, it means that we shall make the ultimate end of State action not the intellectual, moral, or artistic activities of its citizens, but their material, commercial, and industrial prosperity. The chief aim of

State action and organization becomes the promotion of industry and commerce, and, as Mr. Chamberlain saw with more logic than many people who have the same political desires and beliefs, the State educates its citizens mainly in order to keep them " to the front in the commercial competition," and protects their " life and health " mainly in order to provide a " vast army of manual labourers."

We live in an industrial and a commercial age in which the main standard of value for every department of life is accepted to be material profit. Hence the view of the object of State action, so clearly expressed by Mr. Chamberlain, is also expressed or implicitly accepted by all the statesmen of great European nations throughout the nineteenth century. For it must be remembered that no men have ever been more sincere and devoted adherents of the maxim that " commerce is the greatest of political interests " than the leaders and followers in the great individualist and free-trade movement of the middle of last century. Neither Bright nor Cobden would have disagreed with Mr. Chamberlain's statement that " that Government deserves most the popular approval which does most to increase our trade and to settle it on a firm foundation"; they would only have disagreed with him over the means to be adopted for attaining this end. Hence we can say without exaggeration that it has become a universally accepted political axiom among Europeans that the chief object of each State's policy should be directed to further the economic interests of its own citizens.

It is of immense importance to see that so many men and nations, so bitterly opposed in their policies and beliefs, agree in their conviction as to what is the ultimate end of the State and political action. The end of government, of State action or inaction, of national organization or disorganization, is the economic interests of the citizens of our own State. The measure of economic interests is the largeness or smallness of trade. These desires and beliefs underlie nearly all the political and economic thought and action of the nineteenth century. In fact, they have their roots in an even older age. For they were born in the theory and practice of Mercantilism. Mercantilism " regarded world-economy relations as a means of enriching the national economy group. Each state should sell as much as possible to foreign countries, and buy as little as possible from them, so that its national wealth might be increased through a large excess of exports over imports. Commercial treaties were regarded as a means of taking advantage of other nations, and to be desired only by politically powerful countries and feared by all others." [1] Here we have the first clear realization and statement of this formula of State action, namely, that the

---

[1] *Economic Protectionism*, by Josef Grunzel, p. 7.

power and organization of the individual State should be directed against the world outside the State for the economic purposes of the world within the State.   And now turn from the old mercantilists to their most bitter opponents, the individualists and free-traders.   " Their tendency," says a recent writer, " to think of trade as the ultimate goal of national policy was one that Cobden and his school unconsciously inherited from the exponents of the system they attacked." [1]   That is the literal truth.   There was no difference between Cobden and his opponents over the ends of political action, there was only a disagreement as to the right means for attaining those ends.   The policies of free-trade, non-interference, anti-imperialism, and peace, were recommended to the British people as the surest means of attaining material, i.e. industrial and commercial, prosperity.   To the mid-Victorian radical and democrat the " Real and Substantial " national interests were " Commercial interests," and since commercial interests could be best attained by the operation of enlightened self-interest, the whole duty of the State was to keep the ring, nationally and internationally, and allow competition and enlightened self-interest to perform their beneficent work of money-making, whether in Manchester or Birmingham, Paris or Berlin, the opium trade in China or the gin-traffic in West Africa.

   And now look again from the desires and beliefs of the Manchester school to those of the political schools which succeeded them in the latter part of the nineteenth century.   The outstanding feature of that period is the intensive growth of industrial and commercial organization.   The big factory, the Trust and Kartel and Syndicate, the multiple shop, are all symptoms of this development.   Vast and complicated organizations were considered to be necessary for industrial and commercial efficiency.   But men who believed this and were themselves manufacturers and traders could not overlook the possibility of using the power and organization of the State for economic ends.   If trade and industry were the ultimate goals of national policy, the golden goal might surely be attained more effectively by an active and aggressive use of the national power and organization than by a policy of passivism and pacificism. The Mr. Chamberlain of the '90's, whom we have already quoted,

---

[1] *The Commonwealth of Nations*, edited by L. Curtis, p. 308.   Two quotations in this book are of interest as showing the historical growth of this axiom of policy. Burke (*An Examination of the Commercial Principles of the Late Negotiations*) writes in 1762 : " There is no situation in which Wealth is not Strength, and in which Commerce is not Wealth.   If Commerce is our Object, we know, and in all other Cases we can at best only guess, what we acquire."   Whately (*The Regulations lately made concerning the Colonies*) writes in 1765 : " Happily for this country the Real and Substantial, and those are the Commercial Interests of Great Britain, are now preferred to every other Consideration."   That " happily " has been echoed and endorsed by the nineteenth century : will it be echoed and endorsed by the twentieth after its recent experiences ?

is in this country the spokesman of this new tendency, but everywhere in Europe the change was felt with increasing force. The Germans tell us that free-trade policy gave place to Macht- and Weltpolitik in the '80's. "Ein neues Zeitalter des Merkantilismus ist angebrochen," [1] a new era of Mercantilism has broken out in the world, they exclaimed with some satisfaction and complacency, and that perhaps is the best description of the new orientation. For it points out its most marked characteristic, namely, that it is an old policy under a new name and adapted to modern conditions. And it was based upon the conception of the ends of State action handed down in unbroken succession from the Mercantilists, through Burke and Whately, and Bright and Cobden, to the Imperialists and Little Englanders of our day, the conception that "the Real and Substantial" national interests are commercial interests, that commerce is the greatest of political interests, that the true sphere of policy is to use the power and organization of the State upon the world outside the State for the economic ends of the world within the State.

I have insisted upon this almost universal acceptance of the same end of national policy by so many "packs and sets of great ones," because it seems to me a legitimate assumption that the ultimate end which man aims at politically will have some small influence upon his fate and political development. A man may of course aim at a star and fall into a ditch, but, if man has any control of his destiny, we should hardly recommend him either to aim at a star if his object is to fall into a ditch, or to fling himself into a ditch in an effort to reach the stars. If whole nations, possessed of the vast and impersonal power which comes from modern numbers, modern machinery, and modern organization, act upon the maxim that commerce is the greatest of political interests, they cannot but produce a different world from that which men will create who believe that war or kings or concubines or religion or truth or peace are the greatest of political interests. I have already given some proof of the assertion that Europe has almost universally accepted the principle of policy that the power of the State should be used upon the world outside the State for the economic purposes of the world within the State. Detailed proofs will occur again and again in the pages which follow. But one word is necessary here to many persons who will immediately dissent from this interpretation of the modern statesman's and citizen's view of State action. They will accuse us of placing the cart before the horse, of confusing means with ends. Modern policy, they will say, has aimed at economic ends, but only to use them as means for other and higher ends. Thus Mr. Arthur Greenwood in an

---

[1] Max Gering in *Handels- und Machtpolitik* (1900), pp. 14 and 34.

excellent little book,[1] designed to instruct the uninitiated in the problems of international relations, writes thus of Mr. Chamberlain's twentieth-century campaign for the reintroduction of a " Colonial system " :

And much of the flood of argument was used to show the free-traders, on the one hand, that they would be better off under a protective tariff, and the protectionists on the other that they were better off with the system of free imports. But Mr. Chamberlain's motive was political. Rightly or wrongly, he believed that fiscal charges were called for in what he considered to be the best interests of the nation and the Empire. The economic results were not to him ends in themselves, but means for the realization of imperial power and prestige. The tariff was an economic instrument to be wielded for political purposes, a weapon with which to gain state ends in the sphere of international politics.

There is in Mr. Greenwood's exposition an element of truth, but also an element of confusion. It is true that Mr. Chamberlain's motive for desiring Colonial Preference was political [2] rather than economic, in the sense that he recommended it as a weapon or means for the realization of imperial power and prestige. But it is wrong to argue that, therefore, Mr. Chamberlain did not regard national economic interests as the ultimate ends of policy. The question is whether Mr. Chamberlain regarded " imperial power and prestige " as the ultimate ends of national policy, or whether he really looked upon them only as means for the realization of other and more important ends. Now statesmen and nations are not always logical, clear, or consistent in their desires and beliefs. It is the commonest thing for human beings to shirk or confuse the issue as to whether something which they desire and aim at is to them an ultimate end or merely valuable as the means for realizing some other end. The man who desires money as a means for the realization of leisure and pleasure ends as a miser who desires money because it is money. It is possible that the Chamberlain of 1904 had come to believe that " imperial power and prestige " were ends in themselves : certainly some of his fellow-imperialists in all countries, and particularly Germany, have written and spoken as if Empire was to be desired simply because it is Empire. But that was most certainly not the view of the Chamberlain of 1896, who

[1] *An Introduction to the Study of International Relations*, by A. J. Grant, Arthur Greenwood, etc., p. 80 (Macmillan, 1916).

[2] It may be pointed out that the mere fact that we call something a " political end " implies that it is not an ultimate national end, but a means for attaining something else of national value. A political end, in Mr. Greenwood's sense, is only a weapon or instrument of international policy. But policy is no more than a tariff, an " end in itself " ; policy aims at realizing some further national good. So, too, Empire and prestige are desirable not because they are Empire and prestige, but only because, and if they produce, certain political goods.

told the leaders of the Empire's commerce assembled in London that " I believe that the toast of Empire would have carried with it all that is meant by Commerce and Empire, because, gentlemen, the Empire, to parody a celebrated expression, is commerce." [1] Nor was it the opinion of the Chamberlain of 1894 who said to the people of Birmingham :

Give me the demand for more goods and then I will undertake to give plenty of employment in making the goods ; and the only thing, in my opinion, that the Government can do in order to meet this great difficulty that we are considering is so to arrange its policy that every inducement shall be given to the demand ; that new markets shall be created, and that old markets shall be effectually developed. You are aware that some of my opponents please themselves occasionally by finding names for me, and among other names lately they have been calling me a Jingo. I am no more a Jingo than you are. But for the reasons and arguments I have put before you to-night, I am convinced that it is a necessity, as well as a duty, for us to uphold the dominion and empire which we now possess. For these reasons among others I would never lose the hold which we now have over our great Indian dependency—by far the greatest and most valuable of all the customers we have or ever shall have in this country. For the same reasons I approve of the continued occupation of Egypt ; and for the same reasons I have urged upon this Government, and upon previous Governments, the necessity for using every legitimate opportunity to extend our influence and control in that great African continent which is now being opened up to civilization and to commerce.[2]

The Chamberlain of 1894 and 1896, it will be observed, regarded imperial power and prestige as definite means to economic ends, the provision of markets and customers, because he held that commerce, not empire and prestige, was the greatest of political interests. It is possible, as I have said, that a nation or a man who begins by seeking Empire as a means to commerce may end by acquiring a taste for Empire " in itself," just as many persons who begin to drink beer as a means of quenching thirst end by acquiring a taste for beer " in itself." That, however, does not affect the truth of the generalization that the main and ultimate end of policy during the last fifty years has been economic interests, commercial, industrial, and financial. What I propose to do in this book is to examine the results of this view that the power and organization of the State should be used upon the world outside the State in order to promote the economic interests of the world inside the State. For that purpose it is unnecessary at present to say anything more about the ends of this international economic

---

[1] Speech to the Congress of the Chambers of Commerce of the Empire, London, June 10, 1896.
[2] Speech at Birmingham, January 22, 1894.

policy. In the modern world there is little, if any, difference of opinion over those ends. Where men have during the last fifty years been divided is in the question of the best means for realizing the ends of international economic policy. The means advocated and employed fall roughly into three classes, and for the purposes of enquiry it is necessary to keep distinct the three different spheres in which these three classes of means are and can be used. The three classes may be shortly defined as follows :

1. *Economic Imperialism.* — Under this term I include the international economic policy of the European States, of the U.S.A., and latterly of Japan, in the unexploited and non-Europeanized territories of the world. The policy of Economic Imperialism includes colonial policy and the acquisition by the Europeanized State of exploitable territory, the policy of spheres of influence, and the policy of obtaining economic control through other political means. These various kinds of policy are all distinguished by one important characteristic ; they all aim at using the power and organization of the European form of State in the economic interests of its inhabitants in lands where the European form of State has not developed. I call it imperialism because the policy always implies either the extension of the State's territory by conquest or occupation, or the application of its dominion or some form of political control to peoples who are not its citizens. I qualify it with the word economic because the motives of this imperialism are not defence nor prestige nor conquest nor the "spread of civilization," but the profit of the citizens, or of some citizens, of the European State.

2. *Protectionism and its Opposite.*—The characteristic of this form of policy is the use of fiscal and other administrative measures which directly or indirectly affect the commerce, industry, or finance of the citizens of two or more States. When the motive for the adoption of such measures by a State is the economic interests of its citizens, they become part of the State's international economic policy.

3. *Other Forms.*—There are certain other varieties of international economic policy, *e.g.* peaceful penetration under State influence or control, which do not fall within either of the first two classes. They require, therefore, to be dealt with separately.

It will be noticed that these three divisions are not entirely exclusive. For instance, a colonial policy which falls within the first class, Economic Imperialism, may include within it a protective policy which really falls under the second class. Nevertheless, the international economic policy of the modern State may rightly be said, roughly, to fall into these three well-marked divisions. If we are to understand what we wish our State to attain for us economically by international policy, we must know what have been the past policies of States in these three divisions, and what actually they have attained. The State's range of action is, however, so wide, and the facts with regard to it are so obscure and complicated, that it is impossible in a single volume adequately to cover the three fields of economic policy. Consequently I propose in this book to enquire into the nature and results only of Economic Imperialism, and to leave for a future volume the enquiry and discussion of the other two kinds of policy.

CHAPTER III

THE ECONOMIC IMPERIALISM OF EUROPE

THE problem which Europeans have not faced, but which, if they are to control their destiny, they must face is that of the results of their communal desires, beliefs, and actions. Civilization may be defined with some truth as the process of gaining control over one's environment. But environment may be mental and moral, as well as physical. Europe in the last century gained control over its physical environment with a rapidity and to a degree never attained before in any place or age. To dominate the earth, to ride the winds, and to harness fire and water are great and valuable achievements, but their greatness and value also depend upon whether the world's passions and beliefs are harnessed and under control. Some people seem to think that a maniac with a modern revolver in his hand is a nobler spectacle than a maniac with bow and arrow from the Stone Age. Perhaps he is, but at least it cannot be denied that he is infinitely more dangerous. So, too, the uncontrolled passions of fifty million men and women armed with twelve-inch guns and aeroplanes may be a finer thing to contemplate than the blind instincts of five thousand savages armed with tomahawks, but national passions firing off twelve-inch guns are more dangerous to humanity than tribal instinct directing a tomahawk. It is only because from our schooldays history is represented falsely to us as the logic of events rather than the logic of men's beliefs and desires that we are not driven—by fear, if by nothing else—to consider continually the possible results of national and communal beliefs and desires.

The beliefs and desires which produced the economic imperialism of the last half of the nineteenth century are no new phenomenon in the world. History is full of examples of organized States attempting, for economic ends, to conquer or to control politically the peoples of less highly organized States. But the world and its inhabitants change, and when old passions and beliefs reappear in new environments, they acquire a new nature and produce new results. The imperialism of our day is different, both in its nature

21

and its effects, from that of tribes and peoples who moved like the swallows in blind migrations : it is different from the imperialism of old kings and conquerors ; and it is different even from the imperialism which immediately preceded it in the seventeenth and eighteenth centuries. It is necessary to say something about this difference and the causes of it, because only in that way can we give an idea of the general nature of the policy which we propose to investigate.

The most striking difference comes from the singleness and purity of motive for the policy, and of the keener consciousness of what the motive was. The part played by Europe in the world during the last hundred years has been that of a political octopus. States have stretched out from Europe the tentacles of their political power and organization, and have grasped or enmeshed practically the whole of Asia, Africa, and Australia, together with all the islands of all the oceans. History records no other movement of conquest and dominion which can equal this in volume and extent. And the nearer we get to 1914, the more single becomes the economic purpose in this movement, and the more conscious of this economic motive become those who direct it. Imperialism before 1800 was always partly religious, partly dynastic, partly economic, and partly sentimental. In the first part of the nineteenth century the beliefs and desires which caused European States to lay their hands or the weight of their political pressure upon Africa and Asia were still often neither commercial nor industrial nor financial. The modern onslaught of the European State upon Asia and Africa began in 1830 when France entered Algeria. The immediate cause was not economic, but sentimental and strategic. These inhabitants of Africa were subjected to the power and organization of the French State, first, because in 1827 the Dey of Algiers had struck one of its officers in the face with a fly-whisk ; secondly, because the French Government wished to show the world and its own citizens that France had now sufficiently recovered from the Napoleonic wars to think and act imperially ; thirdly, because the possession of the coast of Algeria was a counter in that strategic game called "the Mediterranean question."[1] Similarly, the completion of the subjection of India to a European State was mainly the result of strategic impulse, and the old sentimental instinct towards empire. The British State[2] extended its Indian

[1] Wellington, for instance, regarded the whole of the Algerian question from the point of view of " maintaining the *status quo* in the Mediterranean."

[2] We are not accustomed to speak of the British State, but it is an aid to clear thinking to call things what they are. When we say that India became a part of the British Empire, the statement is so conveniently vague that it may mean anything. When we say that the system of the British State was extended to several hundred million Indians, we lay stress in our words upon the real meaning of this phenomenon.

Empire because a State feels so often that, in order to hold what it has, it must take what it has not. Or, if we look to China, we see again how small a part in the first half of the nineteenth century commerce played in the policy of European States towards Asia and Africa. The sole interests of Europeans in China were economic, for it was still too far off for Chinese territory to affect the strategy or Chinese insults the honour of Europe. Hence, since the European State was concerned more with strategy and prestige than with commerce, the economic interests of Europeans were left for long to the merchants, and there was no Chinese policy in the Foreign Offices of the Powers. But the current of beliefs and desires was already setting towards economic imperialism. As early as 1833 the British merchants at Canton were demanding that the British State should apply its power to enforcing in China their claim that they had a right to trade with the people who did not want to trade with them. The Opium War and the Treaty of Nanking of 1842 were the beginning of the policy of using the power and organization of the European State upon the world outside the State in China. The statements of Sir Henry Pottinger, our plenipotentiary, show very clearly how the older principles of State policy and action were giving place to the dictates of an economic policy. Just as an insolent fly-whisk had brought the French fleet and the French State to Algiers, so, too, the British fleet and the British State were brought to China " to enforce reparation for past injuries and insults." But, " furthermore," we had come " to compel the Chinese to abandon their policy of exclusion and their attitude of superiority towards other civilised nations." [1] Many nations besides the Chinese adopt " an attitude of superiority towards other civilized nations," and it is notoriously difficult to eradicate this national feeling, even by the use of the overwhelming power of a modern European State. We must accept the British plenipotentiary's word that the eradication of the Chinese attitude of superiority was a motive of British policy, but it should also be observed that the other motive was to compel the Chinese to abandon their policy of exclusion, and that exclusion was essentially commercial and economic. And as soon as one examines the actual terms of the Treaty of Nanking, one perceives that the British plenipotentiary had, perhaps wisely, neglected to exact any provisions which would have compelled the Chinese not to feel superior to Europeans, and had confined himself to exacting clauses which compelled the Chinese to promote the economic interests of Britons. Thus the first application of the European State's power and organization to the Far East, even in 1842, was in effect directed to promote the economic interests of Europeans.

[1] *Anglo-Chinese Commerce and Diplomacy*, by A. J. Sargent, pp. 58-86 (1907).

In 1850 the forces which produced the imperialism of our own time were already in motion, but they were not yet in undisputed control of policy. Thus the Jingoism of Lord Beaconsfield and his party was sentimental rather than utilitarian,[1] and it had its roots in their " attitude of superiority towards other civilized nations," rather than in a determination to exploit commercially uncivilized nations. Empire to Disraeli and his followers was not Commerce, but imperial pomp and circumstance and titles, dominion and war, ships and men and money too. It was a policy conceived in terms of Power and Prestige rather than of money-making and markets. It was in the ninth decade of the nineteenth century that economic imperialism fully and finally established itself. In the great States of Europe, now completely industrialized, political power had passed from the hands of birth into the hands of wealth, and the political ideals of rule and power and prestige gave way to those of commerce, industry, and finance. After 1880 [2] European policy is dominated by rival imperialisms, colonial policies, spheres of influence, commercial treaties, markets, and tariffs. And wherever these European States use their power and organization outside Europe in relation to Asiatic or African peoples, the motives of policy become more and more clearly recognized and proclaimed as economic ends. The second part of this volume will furnish proof of this statement at least in one division of policy, but, since some people will certainly feel inclined to deny the truth of the generalization, it is necessary here briefly to bring forward the facts which prove it from a rather wider field.

Between 1880 and 1914 the States of Britain, France, and Germany each acquired an immense colonial empire outside Europe. These empires were empires in the literal sense of the word : they were founded by conquest, sometimes openly acknowledged, and sometimes disguised under various synonyms for civilization. The territories acquired were incorporated, usually against the wishes of their inhabitants, in the European State, and the inhabitants were subjected to the autocratic rule of the European State. The territory acquired by the British State in this way was about 3¼

---

[1] See an interesting passage in *L'Angleterre et l'Impérialisme*, by Victor Bérard (1900), in which the Jingoism of Disraeli is compared with the Imperialism of Chamberlain : " Le *jingoisme* et l'*impérialisme* à sa façon ne sont pas choses identiques ni seulement comparables. En réalité, le jingoïsme était *tory* et cet impérialisme est radical. Le jingoïsme, à son origine, n'avait été que l'explosion bravache des colères de John Bull. . . . Le jingoïsme, simple rodomontade patriotique, fut satisfait quand Lord Beaconsfield lui rapporta de Berlin ' la paix avec l'honneur ' : J. Chamberlain et les impérialistes de sa bande proclament ouvertement que ' la guerre avec le profit ' est le plus cher de leurs désirs. Leur impérialisme est radical, c'est-à-dire, avant tout, utilitaire " (pp. 65 and 66).

[2] The change from the Imperialism of Disraeli to that of economic imperialism was noticed by Gladstone. " Jingoism," he said to Dilke in 1887, " is stronger than ever. It is no longer war fever, but earth hunger " (*Life of Dilke*, vol. ii. p. 256).

million square miles, and the population subjected to its rule was about 46 million.   The French State acquired 4 million square miles, and a population of over 50 million; the German State 1 million square miles, and a population of 15 million.   The policy which led to the acquisition of this empire by Britain was the policy of Mr. Chamberlain and his followers.   The motives have been sufficiently illustrated above from the declarations of Mr. Chamberlain himself.   They were purely economic.   In conquering the unexploited portions of Asia and Africa we were "pegging out claims for posterity,"[1] and the claims of posterity were for more markets.   And the reasons which this school of policy gave for our "never losing the hold which we now have" over "our great Indian dependency" and over Egypt were the same, namely, the provision of markets and customers for the European citizens of the British State.   Now, if we turn to France, we find that in that country, too, the creation of a colonial empire was the work of a political party with definite and imperial and colonial aims.   A French writer upon colonial affairs, an imperialist, and a man of sound and moderate judgments, M. E. Fallot, has pointed out that the first colonial acquisitions of France after the revolution were not the result of any conscious plan : they were fortuitous and occasional, the acts of a Government to which the people remained indifferent.   But it is not the same with the colonial policy of the Republic for which Gambetta, Jules Ferry,[2] and Barthélemy Saint-Hilaire were responsible.   That policy was the result of a political plan carefully studied, applied methodically in the face of great difficulties, and finally realized with complete success.[3]   Those who urged this "politique coloniale" upon the French people with such persistence and success gave as their reasons for the necessity of "expansion" precisely the same political motives as the imperialists of Britain.   The ends of the French "politique coloniale" were mainly economic, and where the Englishmen made "provision for markets" in Asia and Africa the Frenchman talked of the necessity for colonies as "débouchés à nos produits."   If anything, the economic nature of the new imperialism was recognized or admitted earlier in France than in Britain.   This is shown by the motives for the French Tonkin expedition which was almost the prelude to the imperial activities of the Republic and which was the first act in the partition or domination of China for economic ends by the European States.

[1] Lord Rosebery's phrase, but quoted with approval by Mr. Chamberlain in the House of Commons, March 20, 1893, with regard to Uganda.

[2] See Appendix to this chapter.

[3] E. Fallot, *L'Avenir colonial de la France*, 1901, p. 482: "Dans la persévérance de son effort, il est impossible de méconnaître l'exécution d'un plan politique mûrement étudié, appliqué avec méthode en dépit de difficultés sans nombre, et finalement réalisé avec un succès complet."

Jules Ferry, the minister responsible for this expedition, at the time repeatedly defended his action by urging that the possession of Tonkin would assure to the French the navigation of the Red River, and that, thanks to that magnificent natural highway ("magnifique voie naturelle") they would be able to penetrate into China and secure for themselves the commercial monopoly of the Western Provinces of China.[1]

It is true that particularly between 1880 and 1890 the partisans of the "politique coloniale" put forward motives, which were not economic, for their imperialism. In those early days it was pointed out, for instance, that France had to carry out in Algeria her mission of civilization ("remplir notre mission civilisatrice"). But the desire for and belief in Europe's mission of civilization in Asia and Africa rapidly lost its position as a motive for policy in the last decade of the century. Already in 1885 a distinguished French writer and politician [2] had written : "Voilà comment nous avons su remplir en Algérie notre ' mission civilisatrice.' . . . Nous, nous avons su ' apprendre aux Arabes qu'à boire de l'absinthe et à pisser debout.' " Not many writers or politicians put the matter quite as baldly or affirmatively as that : the European's disillusionment with his own civilizing mission is shown more often by his negative attitude towards it. After 1890 it is extremely rare to find any authoritative imperialist recommending imperialism as a duty : the stress is laid upon economic necessity and commercial profit. Thus, even the Englishman, Sir F. D. Lugard, an expert in these matters—for he added an immense territory to the British Empire—writes in 1893 that "the scramble for Africa . . . was due to the growing commercial rivalry, which brought home to civilized nations the vital necessity of securing the only remaining fields for industrial enterprise and expansion." "It is well then to realise," he continues, "that it is for our advantage—and not alone at the dictates of duty—that we have undertaken responsibilities in East Africa. It is in order to foster the growth of the trade of this country, and to find an outlet for our manufactures and our surplus energy, that our far-seeing statesmen and our commercial men advocate colonial expansion. . . . I do not believe that in these days our national policy is based on motives of philanthropy only." [3] And Sir F. D. Lugard shows what, in his view, were the relative importance of the " dictates of duty," the motives

---

[1] See Yves Guyot, *Lettres sur la politique coloniale*, 1885, p. 300. Guyot points out that Ferry's " magnifique voie naturelle " was more often than not unnavigable from floods or drought. This book of Guyot's which was written in the first flush of the " politique coloniale," and is a most witty attack upon it, shows very clearly what a large part economic motives played in the policy.

[2] Yves Guyot, *Lettres sur la politique coloniale*, p. 217.

[3] *The Rise of our East African Empire*, by Captain F. D. Lugard, 1893, pp. 379-382.

of philanthropy, and economic motives, by saying practically nothing more about duty and philanthropy, but devoting whole chapters to the economic advantages which the inhabitants of Britain will derive from the subjection of Uganda to the British State. So, too, when a well-known French writer has to sum up in 1904 the causes of the French " mouvement colonial," he forgets to mention the " mission civilisatrice," and puts it all down to " vital necessity," the universal competition, and the struggle for national existence. " Ce n'est qu'après 1870," writes M. Jean Darcy, " lorsque la France vaincue et mutilée eut pansé ses plaies, que notre mouvement colonial prit une réelle ampleur. On parut alors comprendre que, de nos jours, l'expansion d'une race hors de ses frontières est la condition de sa durée, la forme moderne de la lutte pour la vie, et que, dans ce temps de concurrence universelle, qui n'avance pas recule, et qui recule est submergé par le flot." [1]

There was another kind of belief and desire which had more influence upon French than upon British Imperialism, and which at, first sight appears to be unconnected with commerce. The French imperialist of the '80's believed that the acquisition of territory in Asia and Africa was a necessity for the French State in order to provide an outlet, not only for its goods, but for its " surplus population." Hence Frenchmen desired territory for the foundation of a " New France," just as Germans desired it for the foundation of a " New Germany," and French and German " colonial " writers and politicians drew a distinction between the " colonies d'exploitation," or " Handelskolonien," and the "colonie de peuplement," or " Bauernkolonien." The first were tropical lands in which the European could not.live and multiply, but were desirable as " débouchés à nos produits," possessions to be exploited in the commercial interests of France or Germany : the second were places where the climate made it possible for the European to make a home and a settlement. There are two points which deserve remark in connection with this. In the first place, the reason why these beliefs and desires played a greater part in the colonial policies of France and Germany than in that of Britain was because by 1880 Britain already had in Australia and Canada sufficient inhabitable territory to absorb not only the surplus, but the whole population of the British Isles. It was impossible to raise in England a cry for land for emigration when Australia, New Zealand, and Canada were crying aloud for immigrants. But France, whose " colonies had only served to involve her in wars, and whose wars had only served to lose her her colonies," and Germany, who had never had any colonies even to lose, were in a different situation ; and many Frenchmen and Germans turned their eyes towards Asia and Africa as outlets for surplus populations.

[1] Jean Darcy, *Cent Années de rivalité coloniale*, 1904, p. 21.

It is true that this motive of French and German imperialism does not belong wholly to economic imperialism. There is a "natural" desire among Britons, Frenchmen, and Germans to increase the number of Britons, Frenchmen, and Germans respectively in the world, and perhaps to decrease the number of non-Britons, non-Frenchmen, and non-Germans respectively. This desire is partly sentimental, and partly founded upon the belief of all nations that their citizens are the salt and others the scum of the earth. The tendency to desire a high birth-rate and a low death-rate within one's own State, and a low birth-rate and high death-rate in other States, is also connected with the policy of power. For every living German is a potential soldier, and every unborn or dead Frenchman leaves a blank space in a French regiment. All these non-economic beliefs and desires had their share in forming the policy of Empire as an outlet for surplus population. And yet even behind this policy the economic motives show more strongly and persistently than the sentimental and the military. The arguments of those who urged it invariably in the end come back from nationalism and patriotism to trade and commerce. The "New France" and the "Greater Germany" which are at first seen in a vision as carrying, after the manner of the colónists of ancient Greece, into the lands of barbarians a spark from the altar of French and German culture, or, more prosaically, as providing a reservoir for the French and German armies, are always finally recommended as nationally desirable, just like the *colonie d'exploitation*, as "outlets for our goods." For a million Frenchmen in Africa, or a million Germans in the Pacific, would appear to provide better customers and a surer market for their mother-countries than a million naked savages.

As the century waned, and imperialism became more and more economic, the "surplus population" argument and motive was more and more rarely used. In France it was dropped almost entirely, and even in Germany its appeal became obviously weaker. There were several reasons for this. Even the logic of events could not make colonies a vital necessity for absorbing a surplus population which did not exist. The absence of a surplus population in France became in the last years of the nineteenth century unconcealable, and, as soon as Germany acquired an Empire outside Europe, Germans ceased to emigrate. Thus the French authorities estimated that New Caledonia, which had been in the possession of France since 1851, was capable of containing and maintaining a million French colonists. As the surplus population of France would not go there of its free will, the French Government in its early years made a valiant attempt to colonize it with that part of the surplus population which was found in French jails, and which could be sent to New Caledonia whether it liked it or not. Even this experiment was not very encouraging, for the convicts after forty years had only produced a population of 9914, while the free civil population was 8141. Thus forty years' colonization of New Caledonia had produced a French population of 18,055, of whom over half were of penal origin, and the colony was still in need of 981,945 persons from the surplus population of France. And when in 1894, we are told, M. Feillet became Governor, he saw that what New Caledonia wanted was free emigration from France, and instituted a system of settling colonists on the land. In five years he succeeded in settling 400 families, or 1200 persons, a result which the French historian calls " un début encourageant " ; [1] but the population was still only about 20,000, and New Caledonia was still looking eagerly for 980,000 immigrants. At this rate of increase it will take about two thousand five hundred years for France to colonize New Caledonia.

France had already been in possession of New Caledonia for thirty years when the new storm of imperialism broke upon her and she started to " carve out " her new empire. At that time, too, she had already been in possession of Algeria for fifty years. The area of New Caledonia is 7200 square miles, that of Algeria is 1,119,416 square miles. In Algeria the greatest efforts had been made to attract the surplus population of France. In those fifty years the French Government had succeeded in amassing in Algeria a French population of 233,000, of whom, however, nearly 130,000 were military, Government employees, or concessionaires. In fifty years, therefore, the surplus population of France had contributed to Algeria 25,000 families. " If," wrote Yves Guyot in 1885, " one desired to represent allegorically the cost in population of these 25,000 colonists settled in Algeria, each would be sitting on four corpses and guarded by two soldiers. Such is the result of our colonizing efforts in Algeria when simply and plainly stated and stripped of conventional and official phraseology." [2] It is a curious commentary upon the springs of political desires and beliefs and the motives of political actions that, despite the fact that in 1881

[1] E. Fallot, L'Avenir colonial, pp. 248-251.
[2] Lettres sur la politique coloniale, p. 38. Guyot reckoned that the gross total of troops employed by France during fifty-four years of occupation had been 2,160,000 men, and the mortality had been 100,000 men. The efforts to colonize Algeria were hardly more successful after Guyot's book was written. By 1901 the European population was 655,637, but of this only 364,000 were French by birth : in 1911 the European population was 752,043. Even M. Fallot, who takes a very different view of this question from Guyot's, has to admit : " Certes l'Algérie a coûté cher à la France. On n'estime pas à moins de 3 milliards et demi ou 4 milliards les sommes qui y ont été dépensées." It should be added that other authorities estimate the cost of acquisition of Algeria by France at a very much higher figure than M. Fallot, e.g. J. Scott Keltie in The Partition of Africa (1893), p. 96, writes : " Algeria has, no doubt, prospered greatly under French rule, though it will be long ere France is able to recoup herself for the outlay of the £150,000,000 sterling which its conquest has cost her."

the French State was vainly trying to colonize these two possessions, the belief that new territory was necessary for the surplus population of France, and the desire for lands in Africa and Asia to be filled with French emigrants, were certainly powerful enough to provide some stimulus to the new imperialism. But, eventually, facts make some impression even upon nations, and the fact that France was unable to populate the colonies which she possessed did eventually cause a waning and languishing in the national desire for new colonies as an outlet for population.

It was natural that in Germany, where the population was towards the end of the century increasing faster than in France, the motive of creating a Greater, and still German, Germany did not lose its appeal quite so completely. In 1885 when 171,000 Germans emigrated, it was at least reasonable for Germans to desire some territory where these emigrants might go and still remain citizens of the German State. But by 1898 the stream of emigration had fallen to 22,921, and it never subsequently in any year has exceeded 32,000. Thus this non-economic motive for imperialism lost its hold even in Germany. And in Germany as well as in France another cause was operating to make the end of colonial policy not colonization, but economic exploitation. There is no doubt that the "colonial parties" in those two countries, whose policy led in the '80's to the scramble for African and Asiatic territories, had vague and erroneous ideas of the nature of the empire which they were conquering. This was particularly true of Africa, the mystery of whose forests and lakes and rivers was only just being revealed to Europeans. Undoubtedly a vision of "many goodly states and kingdoms" swam before the eyes of patriots, who dreamed dreams of German or French Australias and Canadas rising by the side of great rivers, or in the tropical forests of Asia and Africa. No one is more liable than the stern realist to be carried away by his own visions, and these followers of the logic of facts forgot or overlooked one of the few facts whose logic is inexorable, malaria and climate. The French acquired hundreds of thousands of square miles of land in Africa, only to find that they could provide little but graves for the Frenchmen that went there, and that in the matter of graves "'tis all one to lie in St. Innocent's Church-Yard, as in the Sands of Egypt." "Les partisans de la 'politique coloniale,'" wrote the anti-imperialist, "parlent pompeusement de notre 'empire africain.' Il n'y manque qu'une chose, c'est de pouvoir y vivre." And the German, too, found that the one thing that he could not do with his African Empire was to live in it, in the waterless deserts of South-West Africa, the sun and fever of Togoland, and the Cameroons, and East Africa. Thus, although by 1913 Germany had acquired a colonial empire of 1,134,239 square miles, it only contained a population of 18,500 living Germans.   In view of these facts it is not surprising that the force of the " surplus population " motive lost its hold in Germany as it had done in France.

Nowhere, in fact, is the economic nature of modern imperialism shown more clearly than in the history of Germany.   The German has a brutal habit of saying what he thinks, and of calling spades spades.   In German trade is not a synonym for Christianity, nor finance for civilization.   Already in the '70's German writers were insisting upon the necessity of colonies for the protection and fostering of German trade.   Innumerable schemes were put forward in newspapers and books and pamphlets for founding colonies in every part of the world.   This was part of the same current of beliefs and desires which was also gathering strength in France and Britain, and which finally burst out into the economic imperialism of the '80's in all three countries.   It was only the passion of Germans for dotting their i's and crossing their t's which made the nature of their beliefs and desires plain in those early years.   This kind of propaganda culminated in Fabri's well-known book, *Bedarf Deutschland der Kolonien ?* which was published in 1879.   Fabri answered his question in the affirmative for economic reasons, and proposed the foundation of " Handelskolonien " in Samoa, New Guinea, North Borneo, Formosa, Madagascar, and Central Africa.   A strong and definite German policy of economic imperialism sprang directly from Fabri and his book.   The important thing to notice is that this policy was not only pressed upon the Government for economic reasons, but, as in the case of French and British imperialism, its chief support came from certain strong financial and commercial interests.

The close connection between colonial policy and commercial interests began in Germany even before Fabri.   In 1871 a proposal was put about that Samoa should be taken as a naval station and colony.   The proposal was certainly not unconnected with the large Hamburg firm of Godeffroy which " was all-powerful in Samoa."   At that time the Government was indisposed to imperialist adventure, and nothing came of the idea beyond the visit of German warships and the signing of treaties with the natives in 1876, 1877, and 1879.   But in 1878 there was a development most significant of the future.   The Godeffroy firm was in difficulties, and proposed or threatened to sell its interests to the London firm of Baring.   The firm of Godeffroy was one of the earliest to realize that financial difficulties can be made the first stepping-stone towards Empire.   The method of converting bankruptcy into lucrative imperialism has since become a commonplace of colonial policy,[1] but this early example, though unsuccessful, is illuminating.

---

[1] For an example, drawn from France, see p. 210.   In that case the French financial and commercial interests behind the Compagnie Impériale des Chemins

Godeffroy appealed to German patriotism not to allow him to sell patriotically his interests in Samoa to a British firm. He looked to German patriots to invest five million marks in a German Trading and Plantation Company which would relieve him of his South Sea interests. But the security offered by Herr Godeffroy was insufficient to induce German patriotism to invest more than one million marks; and one million marks was insufficient to induce Herr Godeffroy's patriotism to part with his interests. He then conceived the idea of appealing to the patriotism of the German Government by floating a new Company to take over his interests, and of inducing the Government to guarantee a 4½ per cent dividend for twenty years. In this way the interests of Herr Godeffroy, of German trade and finance, and of imperialism, would be all promoted, and the financial difficulties of Herr Godeffroy would become the first stepping-stone to a German colony in Samoa. At that time the German Government was Bismarck, and Bismarck was by no means favourable to "colonial policies" and economic imperialism. But no man can be more resourceful than a patriotic financier in financial difficulties. Herr Godeffroy went to a well-known financier, von Hansemann, Director of the Diskontogesellschaft, who was a friend of Geheimrat von Kusserow of the German Foreign Office, and of the banker von Bleichröder,[1] who was Bismarck's financial adviser. Herr Godeffroy talked von Hansemann over to his scheme; von Hansemann talked over the Geheimrat and the banker; the Geheimrat and the banker talked over Bismarck. And Bismarck was talked over because Herr Godeffroy could, as it

de Fer éthiopiens pursued precisely the same policy as the Godeffroy firm. Being in financial difficulties, they used the threat of selling their interests to British financiers as a lever whereby they forced the French Government to subsidize or guarantee the French financiers, the first step towards the superimposition of political control upon financial exploitation, as the Negus Menelik of Abyssinia was quick to perceive. A similar example from British history is the attempt of the British East Africa Company to use the threat of impending bankruptcy, and the resignation of its interests to German traders and financiers as the lever for getting a subsidy from the British Government, see p. 294.

[1] These three men are continually cropping up in the story of German colonial and imperialist policy; see, for instance, Zimmermann, *Geschichte der deutschen Kolonial-politik*, pp. 14, 18 ff., 20, 21, 39, 55 ff., 62, 64, 81, 95 ff., 98, 100, 116, 120, 125, 135, 173, 190, 222, 208. See, too, 35 *infra*. Geheimrat von Kusserow was a very highly-placed diplomatic and Foreign Office official. In 1874, after serving in the London embassy, he was appointed to a post in the German Foreign Office where questions of overseas commercial relations were entrusted to him. He prepared in 1884 the official memorandum which went fully into the whole question of Germany acquiring colonies and was laid before Bismarck. It was Bismarck's orders on this memorandum which finally inaugurated Germany's entrance into Africa as a colonial power. Bleichröder is often referred to in the pages of Dr. Busch, whose diary shows the kind of influence which he might be expected to exercise over the Chancellor. It may be recalled that Bleichröder once gave Bismarck a birthday present consisting of "a pipe-rack in carved oak, and seven long cherrywood pipes with painted porcelain bowls representing game, together with two large vases containing azaleas in blossom."

happened, offer a *quid pro quo*. At that moment Bismarck was anxious to get his protection proposals accepted among the trading interests, particularly in the Hanse towns. The firm of Godeffroy strenuously supported these proposals, and did very much to obtain for them the support of the Hanse traders and financiers. In return, the Government proposed in the Reichstag to guarantee the dividend of 4½ per cent to the new company for twenty years. Unfortunately for Herr Godeffroy he had forgotten to talk over the Reichstag, and the proposal was rejected.[1] So, for the moment, the German Government failed to step into Samoa over the financial corpse of J. C. Godeffroy & Son by the process through which that Government between 1880 and 1890 stepped into East Africa over the financial corpse of the Deutsch-Östafrikanische Gesellschaft, or through which the British Government stepped into East Africa and Uganda over the financial corpse of the British East Africa Company, or through which, in 1902, the French Government all but succeeded in stepping into Abyssinia over the financial corpse of the Compagnie Impériale des Chemins de Fer éthiopiens. It should, however, be remarked that the firm of J. C. Godeffroy was not as moribund as it appeared to be in 1878. It continued through its Bismarckian manager, Theodor Weber, to be " all-powerful " in Samoa, and its influence and machinations led finally to the treaties and annexations of 1899 and 1900.[2]

The close connection between the colonial policy and commercial interests is very clear in this case of Samoa. It is no less clear in the developments which followed upon the publication of Fabri's book. A few facts will prove this. Fabri immediately became one of the leading exponents of imperialist policy. He was joined in his propaganda and schemes by the Hamburg wholesale merchant and shipper, C. Woermann. The firm of Woermann and the Woermann Line were in process of becoming a dominating German commercial and financial interest in Africa. In 1880 Woermann joined Fabri in founding the Westdeutsche Verein für Kolonisation und Export, which started a plantation enterprise in the Cameroons, where a Woermann had already in 1868 made a commercial settlement. Fabri himself was in the early '80's working with von Maltzan, the founder of the Kolonialverein, which was a powerful influence in spreading imperialist and colonial ideas. The methods of this Association are admirably explained in the advice given to von Maltzan by two prominent imperialists. "Make yourself," wrote

---

[1] For an account of these transactions see A. Zimmermann, *Geschichte der deutschen Kolonialpolitik*, 1914, pp. 17-21.

[2] For an account of the activities of Weber and Godeffroy & Son, from the British and anti-German point of view, see *The New Pacific*, by C. B. Fletcher (1917). Reference may also be made to *A Lady's Cruise in a French Man-of-War*, by Miss Gordon-Cumming (1882), Stevenson's *A Footnote to History* (1892), and Dr. George Brown's *Autobiography*.

Gustav Freytag, " a focus for the wishes and interests of our traders on unappropriated coast lands (of Africa) . . . undismayed by occasional failure of endeavour, . . . and I am convinced that the day will come when suddenly and unawares a German warship will produce a *fait accompli* there, where the Association shall have prepared the ground." And Prince Hohenlohe in advising the establishment by the Association of "Handelsstationen" with State guarantee, wrote : " Naturally the Association must work in close harmony with the large Hamburg and Bremen firms." [1] It would take too long to unravel and explain the complicated relations between the various propagandist Associations and commercial companies, between the literary and political imperialist agitators like Fabri, von Maltzan, and Prince Hohenlohe, the traders and financiers like Woermann of Hamburg and Lüderitz of Bremen, and the explorers like Peters and the Dernhardts. But these three groups in Germany, just as in Britain and France, were working closely together.[2] Their policy was that described in the quotation from Freytag, and their motives were almost entirely economic. They aimed at starting commercial and financial enterprises in " unappropriated countries," and then at the appropriate moment, through the pressure of a public opinion which they themselves had created at home, to force the hand of the Government to send a " German warship " and thus present the world with the *fait accompli* of economic imperialism.

In 1880 Bismarck was the German equivalent of a Little Englander.[3] By 1885 the imperialists, explorers, and traders had forced his hand and converted him ostensibly to a policy of imperialism. His policy and his imperialism were purely economic. The causes of this conversion and the facts connected with it throw great light upon the general motives of modern imperialism. First of all, let us examine the immediate influences within Germany which were brought to bear upon Bismarck. They were commercial and financial. Bismarck's change of policy was actually shown by his extending the power and rule of the German State to four places in Africa, South-West Africa, the Cameroons, Togoland, and East Africa. Now in South-West Africa the immediate impulse came from Lüderitz, the Bremen merchant, who after a

---

[1] See A. Zimmermann, *op. cit.* pp. 28-33.

[2] The kind of interconnection is shown by the foundation in 1884 by Dr. Peters of the Gesellschaft für deutsche Kolonisation, which was at one time intended to work in co-operation with the Kolonialverein. Peters was also the agent of the Commercial Company, the Deutsch-Ostafrikanische Gesellschaft.

[3] Bismarck's attitude up to 1880 can best be given in his own words in 1871 : " I do not want colonies at all. Their only use is to provide sinecures. That is all England at present gets out of her colonies, and Spain too. And as for us Germans, colonies would be exactly like the silks and sables of the Polish nobleman who had no shirt to wear under them" (Busch, *Bismarck*, translation (1898), vol. i. p. 552).

year's hard work at last in 1883 obtained official backing from the Chancellor for his enterprise. And it is significant that the financial backing of the German West African Company, which took over Lüderitz's newly acquired interests in 1885, came from the financiers Hansemann and Bleichröder, to whose connection with German colonial policy we have previously had to refer. In the Cameroons the impulse came from Woermann, the Hamburg trader and ally of Fabri, who, in 1884, laid before Bismarck, at the Chancellor's request, a memorandum suggesting steps to be taken for protecting German commercial interests in the Cameroons. This memorandum formed the basis of Bismarck's instructions to the Nachtigal expedition which acquired the Cameroons for Germany. In Togoland Woermann again was chiefly responsible, for, as soon as Bismarck's consent to the occupation of South-West Africa became known, Woermann despatched an agent to prepare the way for similar action in Togoland, and in 1885 similar action followed. In East Africa the course of events was even more illuminating. In 1884 Dr. Peters the explorer arrived in Zanzibar with the intention of obtaining certain "concessions" on the coast. The German consul, acting on direct orders from Bismarck, refused him all Government protection or encouragement. He then turned to the business firms, and from them, e.g. Hansing & Co., he obtained every assistance. Owing to their help he succeeded in making various treaties with the natives for concessions of land. He then returned to Berlin and, now heavily backed by the commercial interests, betook himself to that same Geheimrat von Kusserow of the Foreign Office who had proved so useful to Herr Godeffroy in his financial difficulties. Peters and the German traders in East Africa found no more difficulty in talking over von Kusserow than had Herr Godeffroy in the case of Samoa. And von Kusserow once more talked over Bismarck, this time, it is said, by his glowing account of East Africa. The result was a charter for Peters' Deutsch-Ostafrikanische Gesellschaft.

Thus the immediate impulse which caused the German State to lay its hand upon islands in the Pacific, upon Togoland and the Cameroons, and South-West and East Africa, came from trade and finance, from the Godeffroys, Woermanns, Lüderitz's, and Hansings. In Germany these traders, shippers, and financiers prepared the ground by working upon public opinion through their agents, the agitators, politicians, and civil servants, like Fabri, Hohenlohe, von Maltzan, and von Kusserow; in Africa they prepared the ground by working upon the natives through their agents, the explorers, like Dr. Peters and Flegel. But the economic impulse is shown not only in these subterranean workings and interconnections: it is shown just as clearly in the words and actions by which Bismarck expressed the new policy of the German State. For the preliminary step to Bismarck's public change of policy was his circular to the senates of the Hanse towns asking for their recommendations with respect to the difficulties and interests of firms operating in Africa.[1] In other words, the Chancellor consulted only economic interests and thought only of economic motives. And when he had determined upon his new policy and publicly announced it, he showed that it was the policy of the flag following and protecting trade, and that the centre of it was the German trader (der deutsche Kaufman). "It is not possible," he said in 1884, "to conquer oversea territories by men-of-war or to take possession of them without further ceremony. Nevertheless the German trader wherever he has settled will be protected, and wherever he has assumed possession of territory there the Administration will follow him, as England has continually done." And in the Reichstag, on June 26, 1884, he made his policy and objects even more plain: "Our purpose is therefore to found not provinces but commercial enterprises: but it is also our purpose that these enterprises in their highest development shall acquire a sovereignty, a commercial sovereignty resting ultimately upon the support of the German Empire and standing under its protection, and that we shall protect them not only against the attacks of their immediate neighbours, but also against any harms or harassings which may come from other European Powers."

Practically the whole of contemporary and historical German opinion agrees that the new colonial policy of Germany in the '80's was due to economic beliefs and desires. An historian like A. Zimmermann, looking back in 1914, writes [2] that Germany's need for colonies arose from a need for assuring to herself markets in which she could buy and sell in a world rapidly narrowing through protection and commercial competition. He agrees, therefore, with a contemporary like Fabri, who wrote in 1882 to von Maltzan: "Fiscal reforms and other similar legislation may be necessary, but all these represent only financial alterations of the national property, while our enterprises overseas have in view the increase of Germany's productive power, the raising of the national income, etc." We have seen that Bismarck had for long shown no sympathy for the current of opinion represented by Fabri, but that suddenly between 1880 and 1884 he yielded, accepted the view of economic imperialism, and reversed his policy. The wider causes of this conversion are not without importance. Bismarck was not a man to yield easily to clamour or agitation, whether of democrats, catholics, socialists, or traders and financiers. No statesman

---

[1] This action of Bismarck followed immediately upon protests of the firm of Woermann that German interests in West Africa were being threatened by England, Portugal, and Spain, and upon the Anglo-French treaty of June 28, 1882; see Zimmermann, op. cit. 54.

[2] Op. cit. Preface.

could be more unmalleable when he liked to the backstairs influences of the von Hansemanns and von Kusserows of the world, or more contemptuous of the kind of propaganda which takes the form of a National Association for establishing the millennium, abolishing poverty, or more often filling somebody's pocket. He was one of those rare statesmen who never allow an agitation to force his hand until he has himself decided to open it for a reason of his own, undreamt of by the agitators. On the face of it, it was Woermann, Lüderitz, and their open and secret agents who converted the Chancellor to economic imperialism ; in reality it was another German, Leopold I. of Belgium, who combined the business of a monarch with the profession of knight-errant of Christian civilization, and the profession of a crusader with the business of an extremely shady company promoter. For the proper appreciation of the extra-European policies of the Great Powers in the last twenty years of the nineteenth century it is essential to understand the part played by Leopold in loosing modern economic imperialism into Africa.

In 1880 a conscious policy of economic imperialism hardly existed. The European traders and financiers competed on the coasts of Africa, and up and down the length of Asia, with little or no help and interference from their own Governments. The European State had not yet been impelled by economic motives and interests to penetrate either continent, and its power was nowhere used or its sovereignty extended over the inhabitants and territory of Asia or Africa in order to promote the economic interests of its European subjects. Africa was unpartitioned, and in Asia only India and a few other places were under European dominion. But certain dates and facts are significant. Between 1874 and 1877 Stanley accomplished his famous journey in Africa. In 1878 Leopold of Belgium received Stanley in Brussels. In the same year the King formed in Brussels the " Comité d'Études du Haut Congo." This was an international Committee for the purposes of science and exploration. A year later the Committee was converted into the "Association Internationale du Congo." The Association was still ostensibly international, and to the outside world seemed to have the same laudable and disinterested objects as the Committee. In reality a tremendous change had come over the Association and the objects of its royal founder. Mr. Stanley entered its service and proceeded to the Congo in 1879 to found " stations," and to make treaties with the native chiefs in the name of the Association. In 1880 the first station was established at Vivi, and in 1880 the Association became a purely Belgian enterprise. This event, acting upon desires and beliefs, ready to turn in this direction or that, was the small act, like the pressing of a button or the turning of a screw, which set in motion the

terrific forces of national policies, which swung Europe into the
road of Empire and the bitter rivalries of economic imperialism,
which filled Asia and Africa with the explorers, the soldiers and
administrators, the traders and capitalists, the missionaries, the law,
order, drunkenness, religion, exploitation, and efficiency of Europe.

In 1880 it became clear to those with knowledge that the objects
of the Association had become economic, that the head of the
Belgian State, through his lieutenant Stanley, his stations, and his
treaties, was proceeding to acquire direct control of African territory
for exclusively Belgian commercial and economic interests. A
tremor ran through the political and commercial circles of Europe,
and, as so often happens, it was immediately felt very distinctly
in that sensitive organism, the British Empire. The British Government was among the first to take alarm, among the first to make
a move in the immense game of imperialism which followed. After
considerable and unobtrusive negotiations we signed in 1884 that
curious and abortive Anglo-Portuguese treaty which was designed to
counter the Belgian move by subjecting the Congo to the dominion of
our small but hereditary ally, Portugal. It was, perhaps, not unnatural that both Germany and France should suspect the purity of
motive in our diplomacy and policy which led up to the signing of
this treaty. By it we recognized the claims of our ally to territory
upon which the eyes of the whole world had lately been turned.
The tales of its wonders and riches and heathen savages had already
made the mouths of traders and missionaries water. When Germany, France, and the United States learnt that the British Foreign
Office had very quietly made arrangements for putting this Eldorado
of rubber, precious metals, and savage souls—or, at any rate, the
key to this Eldorado—into the hands of Portugal, they were exceedingly perturbed. The claims of Portugal to this immense and
undefined territory which we so suddenly supported rested upon
the solitary fact that a Portuguese, Diogo Cam, had four hundred
years previously discovered the mouth of the Congo. The titles
upon which most Empires are claimed and possessed would not
bear very close scrutiny, but even imperialists admitted that the
claim of Portugal was thin, and the view of the British Government
was shown by the fact that, after signing in London on February
26, 1884, the Treaty which was to hand over this territory to
Portugal, ten months later they had decided not to ratify the
arrangement, and at Berlin, on December 16, 1884, they signed
another Treaty handing over the territory to some one else. Moreover the moral title of the British *protégé* was certainly no stronger
than the legal title. There is no exaggeration in the following
judgement of an English historian [1] whose bias is certainly not

[1] J. Holland Rose, *The Development of the European Nations* (5th edit. 1915),
p. 547.

towards anti-imperialism : " The Portuguese officials were notoriously inefficient and generally corrupt ; while the customs system of that State was such as to fetter the activities of trade with shackles of a truly mediaeval type." In fact, the ordinary view of Portugal's moral right to empire is well represented by the view of that expert in imperialism, Cecil Rhodes, expressed only a few years after this attempt of the British Government to enlarge the Portuguese African Empire, that the duty of expropriating Portugal from the colonial territory which she actually held was imposed upon us as a measure of international utility.[1]

Frenchmen and Germans have been practically unanimous in their view of British policy with regard to the Congo and the Anglo-Portuguese treaty between 1882 and 1884. They were convinced that the British Government, as soon as it realized the economic motives and objects of Leopold, conceived the plan of substituting Portugal for Belgium, with the knowledge that Portuguese policy was peculiarly susceptible to British influence and pressure, and with the intention of ultimately succeeding to the African possessions of its " faithful ally." French historians, in particular, have found confirmation of this view in the agitation some years later of Rhodes, and sections of the Johannesburg and London Press, over our " duty " to expropriate Portugal. It must always be remembered that the subsequent dealings of the British Government with the Portuguese colonies appear in a very different light to the foreign critic from that in which they are shown by British writers to British readers. Five years after we had attempted to instal Portugal in the Congo on the West Coast of Africa we were denying her claim to the hinterland of Mozambique on the East Coast, and claiming the territory for ourselves. The English historian's account of these transactions is that about 1889 the British South Africa Company "subjected the Portuguese territories south of the Zambezi to a searching scrutiny on the part of these merchant adventurers who laid hands, on behalf of Great Britain, on all territories where the Portuguese could not prove claims supported by occupation or ruling influence," and the Englishman adds that " the strongest temptation existed to ignore Portuguese claims on the Pungwe River and push a way down to the sea at Beira ; but a spirit of justice prevailed, and no real transgression of Portuguese rights was sanctioned by the British Government, or indeed

[1] This view of Rhodes was enunciated, it should be remembered, at a time when British imperialists were very seriously concerned with the signs of sickness and decadence in the remnants of the Portuguese Empire, and were urging that it would be for the good of the world, of Portugal, and of Africa, if these remnants were absorbed in the British Empire. French imperialists and French historians have, perhaps not unnaturally, taken a cynical view of this exhibition of British altruism ; see, for instance, an amusing and interesting account of the proposals and negotiations for the disposal of the Portuguese colonies in *La Conquête de l'Afrique*, by J. Darcy (1900), pp. 108-209, and particularly pp. 188-190.

attempted by the Company."[1]   Unfortunately, neither the Portuguese nor the Frenchman sees so comfortable or high-minded a picture in the events of 1890. The French historian maintains that the Portuguese claims were good, that it was only when the British Government, under pressure from the British South African Company, issued an ultimatum to her unfortunate "ally," that Portugal bowed to the inevitable in the shape of superior force and withdrew her just claims, and finally that the feeling in Portugal was so embittered that leagues were formed all over the country to boycott British goods. According to the French view this was a partially successful attempt on the part of Britain to perform its duty of expropriating Portugal : when it became obvious later that we could not single-handed accomplish what remained of our task, we undertook those curious negotiations in 1898 and 1899 which at one time resulted in an agreement between Germany and ourselves for the partition of the Portuguese colonies. Thus the foreigner's account of British policy between 1889 and 1899 confirms the foreigner in his belief with regard to the British policy of 1882–84.[2]

It would be unwise for any one anxious to escape from the bias of patriotism and the prejudices of policy either to accept entirely, or to dismiss entirely, the German and French account of the Anglo-Portuguese transactions of 1882–84. It is improbable, we may safely say, that the Foreign Office under Mr. Gladstone and Lord Granville, and, a fortiori, the Liberal Government of the time, had quite so definite, sinister, and long-sighted a scheme as French history exposes to the moral and patriotic indignation of Frenchmen. A Machiavelli and a Bismarck are dark stars which have never appeared, and never could appear, in the galaxy of British statesmanship : they and their policies can only exist among men who are cynical enough to call a spade a spade, and immoral enough to admit to themselves, or even to other people, the logic and consequences of their beliefs and desires. And of all British statesmen, Professor Gladstone, as Bismarck used to call him, was the least Bismarckian. We may, therefore, dismiss entirely the possibility that any responsible member of the British Government or Foreign Office in 1884, in so suddenly deciding to make a present to Portugal of a large, undefined territory on the west coast of Africa, had any

[1] Sir H. H. Johnston, *History of the Colonization of Africa by Alien Races* (1899), p. 59.

[2] See generally Darcy, *La Conquête de l'Afrique*, referred to above. For the events of 1890 see Darcy (p. 149), who maintains that the figures of British trade with Portugal prove that the boycott was effective, the British share of the total Portuguese commerce falling from 39 per cent in 1889 to 34 per cent in 1890, and 27 per cent in 1897. For the negotiations for the partition of the Portuguese colonies between Germany and Britain, and the visit of Rhodes to Berlin in 1899, see Lemonon, *L'Europe et la politique britannique* (1911), pp. 167-169. For the subsequent negotiations see Prince Lichnowsky's *My London Mission*.

conscious intention of acquiring it subsequently for the British Empire. Only the extraordinary ignorance among foreigners of the British character and politics could lead any one to suppose that the minds of British statesmen work like that.

On the other hand, it is not possible to accept entirely the view of British historians that the motives of British policy with regard to the treaty were purely philanthropic and altruistic. It is admitted that the decision to place Portugal in possession of the key to the Congo region was determined by the operations of King Leopold and Mr. Stanley. No one now pretends that Portugal had any right to possess that territory. That she would have been one of the worst possible trustees of a region so rich in economic treasures is shown by the fact that our Government's action was immediately strongly opposed by English commercial and industrial interests, and also by the agitation a few years later for the entire expropriation of Portugal in Africa. We shall therefore not be very far from the truth if we reconstruct the motives of the British policy on the following lines. The operations of King Leopold and his "Association Internationale du Congo" were very disquieting. The international "great philanthropic enterprise" had suddenly become national and commercial. The suspicion [1] that the King had in view territorial acquisition on behalf of Belgium, and that the partition of Africa had begun, became almost a certainty. To hand over to Belgium and her King—whose practice was as sharp as his wits— one of the richest lands of Africa was to take a leap in the dark. Belgium had no shadow of a claim to the Congo. On the other hand, Diogo Cam, a Portuguese, had discovered the mouth of that river in the fourteenth century, and in the nineteenth century Portugal, though not a model for colonial administration, was at least susceptible of British influence. Even with States and Kingdoms and Foreign Policy, men prefer to bear the ills they have than to fly to others that they know not of. On these principles, we may imagine, our Foreign Office preferred to see Portugal rather than King Leopold at the mouth of the Congo. Hence the Anglo-Portuguese treaty. Unfortunately, France and Germany were more

---

[1] It is not easy to say when these suspicions definitely arose, but it is significant that Sir Bartle Frere, who was the British representative on King Leopold's Association, was withdrawn before 1880 and his place taken by Mr. Sandford of the U.S.A. According to British historians, Stanley had always been under the impression that the final protectorate of the Congo region would be British, and when he gave up the governorship of the Congo in 1883, he did certainly press for the intervention of Britain. (See Johnston, *Colonization of Africa*, pp. 224-230, and Darcy, *Cent Années de Rivalité Coloniale* (1904), pp. 324-340.) This statement with regard to Stanley's motives must be taken with some reserve. It should be added that the suspicions of Leopold's philanthropy were not confined to Britain. The expedition of de Brazza in 1879 from Gabun, when he anticipated Stanley in reaching the Congo at Stanley Pool, had the definite object, successfully accomplished, of protecting "French interests" against the Belgian enterprise.

suspicious of Britain and Portugal than of Leopold and Belgium, and by refusing to recognize our treaty they caused us to abandon it and to take part in that curious Conference at Berlin, which was the sign that King Leopold had won an Empire, and that economic imperialism had begun with the partition of Africa.

This long analysis has not been merely an irrelevant excrescence upon our argument. We were led into it, it will be remembered, by the necessity of finding some adequate reason for the sudden conversion of Bismarck between 1880 and 1884 to economic imperialism. Bismarck, of course, was well acquainted with every move in the game which Leopold [1] and Stanley were playing in Africa, and also with the Anglo-Portuguese negotiations. In the events of 1881–84 he took a leading part behind the scenes. It was to him that Leopold applied for protection when Stanley gave up the governorship of the Congo in 1883, and pressed for British intervention. It was his joining with France in protest against the Anglo-Portuguese treaty which finally decided the British Government to abandon it. Lastly, it was at his initiative, and on his invitation, that the Congo Conference met in Berlin in 1884. The fact that the part played by him in these transactions coincided with his change of policy is most significant. The British Government saw in the operations of Leopold the beginning of the partition of Africa, and of an attempt to use the power and organization of a European State to acquire outside Europe exclusive commercial advantages. The French Government agreed with the British in its view of the trend of affairs in Africa. It is unlikely that the meaning of all this escaped Bismarck. At any rate, the British reply to Leopold was the Anglo-Portuguese negotiations of 1880–84, the protectorates over the Oil Rivers, Bechuanaland, and Lagos in 1884, and the acquisition of Burma and the territory between Lagos and Rio del Rey (Nigeria) in 1885. The answer of France was just as clear: the French historian, M. A. Rambaud, in his Life of Jules Ferry remarks that "France, through her possessions in Gabun and the occupations outlined by her explorers, found herself in very direct contact with the turbulent Association." The result of that contact, as M. Rambaud points out, was felt as early as 1879 when the French Chambers voted 100,000 francs for a new de Brazza mission, and, apparently considering that imperialism was educational rather than economic, placed the mission under the direction of the Minister of Public Instruction, Jules Ferry. Between 1879 and 1882 took place the race for empire between de Brazza on behalf of France and Stanley on behalf of Leopold and Belgium, a struggle from

[1] When the explorer Rohlfs told Bismarck that Leopold had said to him in 1883, "There is nothing that would give me greater pleasure than to see Germany take over the whole Congo enterprise," Bismarck's comment was: "That's all very well, but the King is playing a game of hide and seek with us" (C. Günther, *Gerhard Rohlfs*, 1912, p. 327).

which each of the rivals emerged with a substantial prize. When de Brazza returned to France in 1882 he had in his pocket treaties with the native chiefs which gave France a protectorate over the vast territory stretching along the Congo (from Brazzaville) and the Oubanghi : the French Chambers ratified the treaties, and voted 1,275,000 francs (increased in 1884 to two millions) for the organization of this new empire, and in 1885, when the Ministry of Public Instruction handed the territory over to the Ministère de la marine et des colonies, France had added 300,000 square miles to her possessions at a cost of 2,155,000 francs.[1] Such was the French answer to Leopold in the immediate vicinity of the Congo : elsewhere it also showed itself in a similar policy, in the annexations and organization of colonies on the Ivory and Somali Coasts, 1884, in the invasion of Tunis, 1881, and the Tonkin expedition, 1883. Bismarck's reply was precisely similar to that of the British and the French : it consisted in the official recognition of Lüderitz, 1883, the protectorate over South-West Africa, 1884, and the acquisition of the Cameroons and Togoland, 1885. These were the signs of his change of policy. They came at the same time and were due to the same causes as the similar acts of the British and French States. They were due to the fact that Leopold and his International Association had let loose a flood of economic and political beliefs and desires. The scramble for Asia and Africa and Pacific Islands had begun, and Bismarck, with some reluctance, had decided that the German Empire could not entirely stand aside from the scramble. And thus the age of economic imperialism broke out over the world.

There is no irony quite so bitter as the irony of history. When the diplomatists had met in the Congo Conference in Berlin and had signed the Final Act, contemporaries saw in it the beginning of a new era of colonial administration, a kind of African and Asiatic millennium based upon international co-operation, equal rights for all men, nations, and races, and the banishment of all commercial competition. Here, they exclaimed, you see how Europe, out of the wisdom of its Christian civilization, has created in the heart of Africa " a great Mediterranean State, open commercially to all nations, and yet withdrawn politically from their competitions. At the same time there have been laid down the bases of an economic legislation applicable to the central zone of the African continent, but destined in fact to a wider application. This system, inspired by the most liberal ideas, which removes every thought of selfish exploitation, will protect at the same time both the natives and Europeans in their relations with the colonizing Powers : it provides a sanction for the principles of religious and civil liberty, of loyal and pacific commerce, and openly breaks with the obsolete traditions

---

[1] See A. Rambaud, *Jules Ferry* (1903), p. 276.

of the old colonial system." [1] Such were some men's hopes and visions in 1884: the future was the exact opposite of what they hoped for, and their millennium was shattered by their own Messiah. The next generation saw the Final Act of the Congo Conference become a mockery, one more tool of imperialist ambitions and competition. It saw the " great Mediterranean State " and the " great philanthropic enterprise " become an administrative abomination, an empire based upon commercial monopoly in the interests of a few Europeans and ruthless exploitation of the African. It saw the nations of Europe, as soon as the doors of the Conference closed, fall upon Africa like a pack of snarling, tearing, quarrelling jackals. And when Africa in a few years had been completely divided up amid a yapping and yelping of mutual recrimination, it saw the same pack take itself off to Asia to quarrel and fight over Siam, and Persia, and Tonkin, and Manchuria, and Shantung, and the Yangtse Valley, and the Philippine Islands, and Samoa. It was not " the most liberal principles " which inspired the new era, nor " religious and civil liberty," nor " loyal and pacific commerce," nor the " protection of both natives and Europeans " ; it was something older, simpler, more " real," hunger, the " accursed hunger for gold." The German was more correct when he exclaimed : " Ein neues Zeitalter des Merkantilismus ist angebrochen."

The preceding pages will have given a general idea of the nature of economic imperialism. The " neues Zeitalter " which dawned in 1884 did not share M. Banning's beliefs and desires : it had its own vision, and, like all eras and generations, its history was determined and fashioned by its vision. Its beliefs and desires were those of economic imperialism. Its objects were economic. Its main impulse was the determination to use the power and the machinery of the European State for economic ends in Asia and Africa. But the historian cannot leave his task when he has given a general diagnosis of the beliefs and desires which have moulded history. He must enquire curiously into the details of results ; he must follow the trail of beliefs as the springs of actions and track desires to their ends in failure or success. So we, too, stand now only at the beginning of our search and problem. We must follow this vision of King Leopold, of the Godeffroys and Goldies and Lugards and Gambettas and Ferrys, into the labyrinths of African forests and the details of African history. We see their determination to use the power and machinery of the European State for economic ends : we want to know for our own guidance how and with what effect they proceeded to carry out their determination. It will be no easy task, for we must attempt to track the effects of King Leopold's beliefs and desires not only

[1] *Le Partage politique de l'Afrique,* by E. Banning (1888), p. 5.

in the Chancelleries of Europe and the policies of Great Powers, but in the Exchanges and markets and counting-houses and factories, and in the life and fate of a single African negro. We want, in fact, to know what exactly the ends were for which the power and machinery of the State were to be used, and since the ends were economic, what their economic worth has proved to be. We must enquire what the economic worth of the ends actually attained by the action of European States in Asia and Africa has been, and also what it was expected to be by those who set in motion the policies of economic imperialism. At the same time we must enquire what the different means were which were adopted by the different policies for attaining the ends, and how far they were shown by history to be adapted to the attainment of the ends desired. No one can give an answer to these questions by a cursory glance over historical text-books, or even by an intuition based on patriotism. Our enquiry must take the form of a plunge into the details of African and Asiatic history, of Blue Books, and Statistics.

The European State has gone to Nigeria, the Cameroons, and the French Congo, to Tonkin, the Yangtse Valley, and Kiao-Chau, impelled by certain economic beliefs and desires. Only by turning back the pages of history with some care and minuteness can we discover exactly what in each case those desires and beliefs were. Then when we have done this, we must again look forward and with the same care and minuteness examine the economic results to see whether they have confirmed the beliefs and fulfilled the desires. We shall be concerned with the details of history, trade, industry, and finance. And details too often become merely the fog of history which is used to obscure from human beings the inevitable consequences of their own thoughts and actions. Our enquiry will be useless unless we manage to maintain through these details some vision of the problem as a whole. The real vision is one of millions of Europeans suddenly applying to millions of Asiatics and Africans the power and machinery of the modern European State. The problem and the enquiry cannot be confined to a question only of economic ends and means. On the coasts, in the forests, and along the rivers of Africa, State meets State, and the effect of the clash of those meetings falls both socially and economically on the populations of those States far off in Europe. Those populations through their policy, their desires and beliefs, are sowing in African forests, but they reap sometimes in European cities, and sometimes even upon European battle-fields. We cannot therefore ignore the possibility that by sowing dragons' teeth in Africa we may reap a most bloody crop of armed men in Europe as well as a most lucrative rubber crop in Africa. In other words, we cannot isolate the question of what we desire to get in Africa and Asia from what we desire to get in London,

Paris, and Berlin. But further, it is not possible entirely to leave out of the vision, much as we may wish to do so, the millions of Africans and Asiatics to whom the power and machinery of the modern European State is being applied for economic ends. The effects of that application are themselves economic and social and political, and they therefore have a reflex economic, social, and political effect upon the populations of the European State. We cannot isolate the question of what we want to get in Africa and Asia entirely from the question of what we want the African and Asiatic to get.

APPENDIX TO CHAPTER III. PART I

THE POLICY OF ECONOMIC IMPERIALISM AS DESCRIBED BY JULES FERRY

ON March 30, 1885, the cabinet of Jules Ferry fell. Ferry, who more than any other man was responsible for the colonial and imperialist policy of France in the '80's, defended his policy in a speech delivered in the French Chamber on July 28, 1885, when the vote of credit for Madagascar was under discussion. That speech gives the fullest account of the motives and objects of his general policy. M. A. Rambaud in his Life of Ferry (pages 389 and ff.) gives the following résumé of, and extracts from, the speech which I have translated :

" He did not deny that those of his enterprises which had been considered the most bold or even rash had been influenced, just as the Chambers' decisions, by the necessity of obtaining certain compensations, or of redeeming certain failures. Certainly the acquisition of Cyprus by England had influenced our expedition to Tunis ; the encroachments of the Belgian Association our action on the Congo ; the loss of Egypt our conquest of Tonkin.

" But beyond these European, international considerations, what had been the motives of his policy ? Since the loss of colonies of settlement, such as Canada by the treaty of 1763, and Louisiana ceded to the United States by Bonaparte, there no longer existed any such colonies on the globe, so rapid had been the English acquisitions. The only place where it remained possible to make acquisitions was in the tropics. It was no longer possible to seek outlets for a French emigration which no doubt had not taken place ; it was a question of finding outlets for our industries, exports, and capital (*débouchés pour nos industries, nos exportations, nos capitaux*). That was an absolute necessity, since Europe was closing itself to Europe ; to Europe, too, North America was being closed by covering itself with almost prohibitive tariffs ; South America was beginning to organize itself industrially ; at many other points we remained in competition with English industry, which itself was complaining of the competition of German industry daily growing more active. That was why France had to expand in West Africa, on the Congo, in Madagascar. At the same time it was not among these half-savage peoples that we would find an adequate market for placing our products. At this moment of history the acquisition of Tonkin was more valuable, and its value resided less in Tonkin itself than in the fact that, thanks to the Treaty of Tien-Tsin, we became the neighbours of a nation of 400 million men, perhaps of 400 million consumers ' who are not poor blacks like the inhabitants of equatorial Africa, populations without wants because their life is altogether rudimentary.' Tonkin brought us in contact with ' one of the most advanced and richest peoples of the world, which, by an inevitable evolution, hastened by recent events, is rapidly entering the orbit of commercial exchange with the Western peoples.'

" ' There is a new form of colonization: it is that which is adapted to peoples which have either a mass of disposable capital or an excess of manufactures. And that is the modern, existing form, the most widespread, and the most fruitful. . . . It is clear that a country which allows a large stream of emigration to leave it is not a fortunate country, and it is no insult to France . . . to remark that of all the countries of Europe she has the fewest emigrants. But that is not the only interest in colonization. Colonies are for rich countries one of the most lucrative methods of investing capital. . . . Oh, yes, for the capitalists. But is it a matter of indifference to us that the total capital should increase by intelligent investments ? Is it not to the interest of labour that capital should be abundant ? I say that France which is glutted with capital . . . and which has exported considerable quantities abroad—one can estimate them at thousands of millions—has an interest in looking at this side of the colonial question. . . . It is the same question as that of outlets for our manufactures. . . . The remark has been made, and in fact there are many proofs in the economic history of modern peoples, that the bond subsisting between a mother-country which manufactures and colonies founded by her is sufficient to ensure that economic predominance accompanies and follows, in some sort, the political predominance.' . . .

" Colonies had for France another use besides that of giving scope for her energy and capital. With steamships capable of carrying only fourteen days' supply of coal in their bunkers, it is necessary to have upon all the seas harbours for revictualling, places of shelter, ports for defensive and provisioning purposes."

CHAPTER IV

THE problem of which the general terms have been outlined in the previous chapter is a political, social, and economic one. The subject is vast, and could only be dealt with in a vast work of many volumes. Some one some day, when all the flames of prejudice and passion have died down, and when all the facts material to a full judgement have been forgotten and lost, will attempt the task, and will write across another page of history the words which universally sum up the result of historical science and political speculation : " too late." He will have to trace and to track the career of economic imperialism and of the European State over the whole world outside Europe. We can conceive his writing a wonderful new Odyssey in which the wanderers are States and nations, the characters national beliefs, desires, forlorn hopes, ambitions, greeds, and ideals, the background not men and cities, but races and continents. But the world must wait for the full Odyssey of Europe's imperial passions. Here it is possible to deal only with a single episode. In other words, I propose in this book to limit the enquiry, and in this chapter to define its limitations.

Part II. of this volume will be devoted to Africa. My main object will be to answer a question : What do we desire to attain, particularly economically, in Africa, and how far is it attainable through policy ? Or the same question can, perhaps, be better stated thus : What has been the result and what the lessons of the application of the power and machinery of the European State to Africa ? With this object in view, I propose first to take a preliminary survey of the African ground and problem. I shall then in some detail examine the history of the past, endeavouring to trace what exactly were the beliefs and desires which impelled the European States to enter with their power and organization the different regions of Africa. I shall then examine the results obtained in this attempt to act upon these national beliefs and desires. The examination will mainly be confined to the African policy of the three Great Powers, Britain, France, and Germany. I shall endeavour to discover what that policy has been and what it has attained. Its attainments cannot be measured merely in square miles of territory or in millions of population or even in the statistics of commerce and industry ; these material results and achievements must be weighed against such elusive "imponderables" as civilization and barbarism, and the deadly flickering of racial passion and national ambitions. Finally, in the light of this examination, I shall try to consider what in the future we want the European State to do in Africa, and how our policy can be used to attain what we desire.

PART II
ECONOMIC IMPERIALISM IN AFRICA

THE
PARTITION of AFRICA
IN 1880

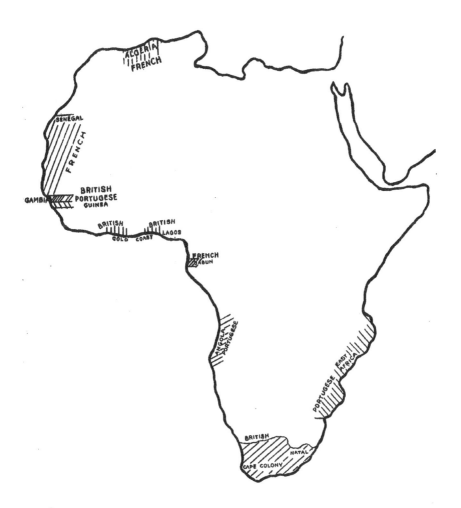

THE
PARTITION OF AFRICA
IN 1914

CHAPTER I

AFRICA is one of the finest fields for the study of economic imperialism, of the interaction between European policy and commerce in non-European countries. The European State first laid its hand with determination upon the African continent only eighty-eight years ago. But the determination in this first movement of imperialism was fitful, and for another forty years very little of Africa was even known to Europeans. Then suddenly the whole continent was, in the course of a few years, thrown open to the action of European States. Economic imperialism was given full rein, and in the history of the last forty or fifty years we can follow the effects of policy pursued with the greatest freedom and determination. It is a peculiarly fine field for study, not only because the actions and reactions are crowded into the space of a few years which do not outspan the memory of many now living. The African policy of European States was more conscious, more open and unabashed, and less complicated and obscured by ancient traditions, vested interests, proprieties, and political expediencies, than has been the case in other continents. Thus we shall not be worried to any great extent, as we should be in Asia, by being compelled to pick our way carefully through the tortuous subterfuges of diplomacy. In Africa, for the most part, Germany, France, and Britain took what they wanted openly, and the territories and peoples, which they took by the right of conquest, they incorporated openly and at once within their empires. In the Ottoman Empire, Persia, Siam, and China, the real nature of the application of the European State's power for economic ends is continually concealed under the most intricate systems of diplomatic fictions. We have sovereign States which are no longer States or sovereign, independent rulers who are neither rulers nor independent, a network of " protectorates," " spheres of influence," " perpetual leases," " peaceful penetration," " concessions," " diplomatic pressure " or " advice," all of which are designed to conceal the powerful, but often clumsy, movements of that Leviathan, the European State, in its encroachments upon Asia. The causes of this difference in European policy in Africa and Asia are not without interest, but they can here only briefly be indicated. In Asia, the European State, in order to further its economic interests, had to destroy a political and social system which even the European realizes as a " civilization " of sorts, and which the Asiatic sometimes stubbornly regards as just as civilized as, or even more civilized than, European civilization. The European State very soon found that it is no simple matter to apply force to so weak but highly developed a civilization as that of China. Japan again showed that if trodden on violently even the non-European worm may turn. The mere age of Eastern institutions and civilization protected them, for old nations, like old men, have a curious power of passive resistance, and the natural conservatism of imperialists made them unwilling openly to disturb anything quite so old and venerable as China. Further, the relations of the European States to one another in Asia were, by the nineteenth century, already both old and complicated. All these facts made an open application of the State's power by means of a frontal attack upon the East both difficult and dangerous, and the historian who desires to trace the causes and effects of desires and beliefs of economic imperialism in Turkey and China will not be able to tell a simple or straightforward story. But in Africa there was no old or intricate civilization to resist the European, and the gulf between the African and the European is so immense that it has been accepted as a postulate, not only of policy but of morality, that for the good of the world the " uncivilized " must be placed openly and completely in the power and under the government of the " civilized." There was therefore nothing either to resist the force or to disturb the conscience of the European when once he had got the belief that he ought to subdue and govern the African and had conceived the desire to acquire the African's territory. Occasionally, as in Abyssinia, Uganda, and Dahomey, the African had developed an organization of government which the European had to recognize as a " kind of civilization," but it was always so " barbarous and cruel " that it had to be destroyed by force, and in all Africa only the Abyssinian proved capable of successfully meeting force by force. At the same time the situation, as between the different States of Europe, was simplified, because the greater part of the continent had never before been opened to them, and therefore there were few complications of ancient policies and vested interests. It is true that the question whether Africans should be ruled by Frenchmen, Germans, Englishmen, Portuguese, Belgians, or Italians has caused the most difficult and dangerous international situations, but the policy pursued in nearly all cases, and by all the States concerned, has been comparatively simple and direct. It is the policy of grab.

Thus the history of the last ninety years in Africa offers in simplest and clearest form the facts and effects of a policy of economic imperialism. The facts and effects will be examined in the following chapters : in this chapter I propose to fix, if possible in broadest outline, a picture of what has actually happened in Africa in those ninety years. First, for a brief moment, we must go back to the year 1815, which for all international questions is the beginning of the modern era. The 11½ million square miles of Africa formed no part of the great world settlement after the Napoleonic wars. The European State had scarcely penetrated anywhere into the continent. On the whole northern coast Europe had no footing at all, for Turkey is not a part of Europe. The whole of the west coast was "independent" except for the following minute European claims or encroachments :

1. FRANCE possessed the Senegal coast from Cape Blanco to the Gambia, but had nowhere penetrated inland except for a short distance along the Senegal River.

2. BRITAIN had possession of small patches of territory on the Gambia and the Gold Coast and in Sierra Leone.

3. PORTUGAL claimed territory stretching from what is now the southern boundary of French Congo down to Cape Frio, but she actually occupied only a few places on the coast in what is now Angola. She also possessed the Cape Verde Islands and a small extent of territory in Portuguese Guinea.

4. SPAIN held Fernando Po, and DENMARK and HOLLAND a few stations on the coast.[1]

In the whole of the rest of Africa there were only two places where the European State had set foot. In the south Britain occupied 120,000 square miles of territory in her Cape Colony, and on the east coast Portugal had an undefined claim to a strip of the coast between Lourenço Marques and Cape Delgado. Thus in 1815 Europe's claims to African territory amounted to considerably less than 500,000 square miles, or one twenty-third of the entire continent, and probably not one twenty-third of this one twenty-third was actually occupied or administered. Between 1815 and 1880 the real penetration of Africa by the European State began, but it was, as we have said, vague, spasmodic, and, for the most part, feeble. The actual acquisitions of territory during this period were as follows :

1. FRANCE in 1830 began the conquest of Algeria. It was completed by 1841. In 1854 General Faidherbe was sent as Governor-General to Senegal, and under his active administration the territory occupied by France was considerably increased. In

[1] See J. Scott Keltie, *The Partition of Africa*, pp. 88-94.

1868 a protectorate was established over Porto Novo on the Dahomey Coast,[1] but no steps were taken to extend it. The foundations of the empire of the French Congo were laid in 1842 when a foothold was obtained in Gabun, and in the '60's there followed some extension of the French possessions inland. Finally, on the Somali Coast, France in 1862 purchased Obock from the Sultan of Tajura, but no attempt was made to make the occupation effective.

2. BRITAIN slightly extended her hold upon Sierra Leone and the Gold Coast, and in 1861 acquired Lagos. The acquisition of Walfish Bay, although it was declared British in 1878, really belongs to the period of economic imperialism after 1880. The chief acquisitions between 1815 and 1880 had been in South Africa, where the northern boundary had been pushed back until it was formed by the Orange River, the Orange Free State, the Transvaal, and Portuguese East Africa. The territory in the possession of Britain in 1880 was roughly 250,000 square miles.

Thus in the fifty years between 1830 and 1880 the only important acquisitions by European States were Algeria and the British occupation of some 130,000 square miles in South Africa. By the Algerian adventure France had established a vague claim to an area estimated at over 1,000,000 square miles, but in 1880 not 10 per cent of the entire continent was effectively subject to the European State. In the next twenty years the whole of the remainder of the continent, except Morocco and Tripoli, was seized and divided up among the European States, and by far the greater part of the process was actually completed in the ten years following 1880. The final absorption of Morocco, Tripoli, and Egypt by France, Italy, and Britain leaves Abyssinia to-day the only African territory which is even nominally independent of Europe.

It is extremely important that the reader of this book should have in his mind a clear idea of the general chronology and extent of this partition of Africa. The annexed tables have been prepared with a view to providing a clear picture of the steps in the process of the absorption of a continent by the European State. They give, first, in detail the African claims or possessions in 1815, in 1880, in 1890, and in 1914. Secondly, they give the total claims or possessions at the same four dates. The figures of population and area must be accepted with caution, particularly for the years 1815 and 1880, because the occupation of territory was still at that time usually vague and ineffective, and most of the claims to possession were of the most indefinite kind. But the figures are sufficiently accurate for our purpose, which is to impress upon the mind of the reader a general picture of the political relationship of Africa to Europe at these four dates. There are one or two important facts

---

[1] British writers deny this; see J. Scott Keltie, *The Partition of Africa*, p. 100; but compare Sir H. H. Johnston, *The Colonization of Africa*, p. 125.

revealed by these tables which deserve attention. In 1815 the only important holding by a European State is in the south, namely, the British occupation of Cape Colony. It was a strategic possession, won by a European State from a European State in the course of a European war. The importance of the Cape in 1815 lay not in Africa, but in Asia. All the other claims and possessions at the beginning of the nineteenth century were small, vague, and undefined. Thus in 1815 the European State had not realized that it had any African interests in Africa : the value of Africa, except as a reservoir of slaves, appeared to consist solely in its lying to port of a vessel sailing from Europe to Asia. The next sixty-five years saw scarcely any fundamental change in Europe's attitude. It is true that in the tables the extent occupied or claimed by European States rises from 500,000 square miles to over 1 million square miles, an increase of 100 per cent. But the increase is due almost entirely to the French occupation of Algeria. The occupation was a most significant event, but in itself it had little connection with the imperialism of later times. As we shall see in the next chapter, it belonged essentially to a school of ideas and policy which was already by 1880 an anachronism, but which continued to exercise the maleficent attraction and influence which always attach to dead ideas. The conquest of Algeria by France in 1830 brought the northern coast of Africa within the immediate orbit of European policy, and into the scales of the European balance of power. Henceforth Africa, between Port Said and Tangier, lay within the European system, with its *status quo*, its alliances, and its policy of power. The effect of the desires and beliefs which sent France to Algiers persisted in this region of Africa long after they were as dead as the men who felt and thought them. To say they were the beliefs and desires of men like Metternich and Wellington and Talleyrand and Auguste - Jules - Armand - Marie, Prince de Polignac, is to show more effectively than one could in many paragraphs of explanation how completely different they were from the desires and beliefs of men like Jules Ferry, Cecil Rhodes, Joseph Chamberlain, Herr Krupp, Herr Woermann, and Prince Bernhard von Bülow. To Charles X., de Polignac, and Wellington the Algerian question immediately presented itself as part of "the Mediterranean question," of "the Eastern question," of the European "Balance of Power" and "*status quo*," of questions, in fact, which were all mistily and mystically connected with ideas of political and military strategy. The idea that commerce is the greatest of political interests could not possibly have penetrated even to the fringe of Wellington's mind : to him strategy was so obviously the greatest of political interests, and all the statesmen and kings of Europe agreed with him. The northern coast of Africa, therefore, in 1830 became drawn into the circle of European strategy in its widest sense, a strategy of which the most marked characteristic was that it was concerned, always and only, with the balance of power within Europe. By 1880 the world was no longer Europe, and Europe had become only a part of the world. This ancient school of "European" policy had lost the little meaning and actuality which it had ever possessed, and it was only kept alive by the fact that the last of its great adherents, Bismarck, was one of those rare geniuses who are able to force the world into the shape which they believe or desire it to possess. But it is important to note that, although after 1880 European statesmanship dealt with the rest of Africa in the light of new political and national ideas, the older policy of Wellington and de Polignac has never entirely lost its hold upon the northern coast. The statesmen who played for and won and lost Egypt, Tunis, Tripoli, and Morocco all believed that commerce was the greatest of political interests, and on the Niger, the Congo, and the Zambezi they put their beliefs into practice : but in Egypt, Tunis, Tripoli, and Morocco their economic imperialism was never pure ; it was always mixed with considerations of European strategy and alliances and the balance of power. The northern coast, having fallen within the European system in 1830, never succeeded entirely in freeing itself from the network of historical and political formulae which constitute that system. This fact makes the history of the northern coast very different from that of the rest of Africa ; and the philosophic historian must note with a melancholy smile how in the twentieth century, although economic forces played strongly upon the chief actors at Algeciras and in the Agadir incident, the spirit of the dead statesmanship of Metternich, Wellington, and de Polignac seemed to haunt and to "possess" Prince Bülow and M. Delcassé, Herr Kiderlen-Wächter and Sir Edward Grey.

But we must return to the period 1815–80. The increase in the territory dominated by the European State was due entirely to the French conquest of Algeria in the north, and to the extension of the British colony in the south. There was no change upon the western and eastern coasts of Africa. The years 1880–90 reversed the history of 1815–80. The area into which the European State had penetrated rose from 1 million square miles to 6 million square miles. But the increase in the north and south was negligible. In the north, which we have seen to lie within the circle of European politics, only Egypt fell to a European State, and it is significant that even here an attempt was made to conceal the fact that a change in political sovereignty had taken place. In the south the extent of territory affected was still smaller, so that out of the 5 million square miles appropriated during these ten years in Africa only half a million lay in the extreme north and extreme south. On the other hand, the whole of the western and eastern coasts were seized and divided up among the predatory States of Europe. Now it is only on her western and eastern coasts that Africa is undiluted Africa; in the north she is half-European, and in the extreme south she is, or at least was, one of the key positions in world strategy. These figures reflect the fact that the purely African interests of Europe in the continent only became clear to Europeans between 1880 and 1890, and dominated the policy of those ten years. Those interests were economic; they lay almost entirely on the west and east within the tropical zone· of Africa, and the strategic, the " European," and the " world " interests, in the north and the south, were forgotten and neglected.

The period 1890-1914 again shows a change in the nature of Europe's penetration into Africa. On the east and west coasts, the claims of posterity had been fully pegged out by the different States. The increase in territory appropriated was therefore caused by extension of existing possessions on the coast into the hinterlands.· In fact in these regions the States were occupied not in acquiring new possessions, but in rounding off their previous conquests, and in converting spheres of interest into full colonial dominion. And, since in tropical Africa there was nothing left for Europe to do but attempt to digest what she had swallowed, those who still had cravings for " expansion " and for economic imperialism had to turn once more to the only remaining places where it was possible to expand, the north and the south. Consequently the history of our last period, 1890-1914, reverts to that of our first, 1815-80, the penetration of France into the north by the acquisition of Tunis and Morocco, and the penetration of the south by Britain through the conquest or absorption of Rhodesia, the Transvaal, and the Orange Free State.

Thus the complete partition of Africa (with the doubtful exception of Abyssinia) and its subjection to the full dominion of European States has now been fulfilled. In the following chapters I shall attempt to trace in some detail the more important lines of policy pursued in different cases. The reader, however, before passing on to these details, should bear in mind the actual extents of territory acquired by the different States in the different regions of Africa. The following tables give the facts in their simplest form:

[TABLE I.

THE EUROPEAN STATE IN AFRICA

TABLE I.—1815

Territory acquired.	Extent acquired.	Acquired by
NORTHERN COAST	Nil	..
WEST COAST—		
Senegal	Small	France
Gambia	Small	Britain
Guinea	Small	Portugal
Sierra Leone	Small	Britain
Gold Coast	Small	Britain
Angola	Undefined	Portugal
SOUTH—		
Cape Colony	120,000 sq. miles	Britain
EAST COAST—		
Portuguese East Africa . . .	Undefined	Portugal
Total about 500,000 sq. miles.		

TABLE II.—1880

Territory acquired.	Extent acquired.	Acquired by
NORTHERN COAST—		
Algeria	Undefined	France
WEST COAST—		
Senegal	Small	France
Gambia	Small	Britain
Guinea	Small	Portugal
Gold Coast	Small	Britain
Lagos	Small	Britain
Gabun	Small	France
Sierra Leone	Small	Britain
Angola	Undefined	Portugal
SOUTH—		
Cape Colony, etc.	250,000 sq. miles	Britain
EAST COAST—		
Portuguese East Africa . . .	Undefined	Portugal
Total extent claimed about 1,000,000 sq. miles.		

TABLE III.—1890

Territory acquired.	Population.	Estimated Area, square miles.	Acquired by	* Date and Treaty of Final Settlement or Acquisition.
NORTHERN COAST—				
Algeria	5,600,000	1,100,000	France	1890. Agreement, Aug. 5, between France and Britain
Tunis	1,800,000	46,000	France	1881. Occupation begun
Egypt	11,300,000	400,000	Britain	1882. Occupation begun
Total .	18,700,000	1,546,000		
WEST COAST—				
Cape Bogudor to Cape Blanco	200,000	75,000	Spain	1885. Jan. 9, Notification
Senegal .	1,250,000	74,000	France	1889. Arrangement between France and Britain, Aug. 10
Gambia .	146,000	4,000	Britain	1889. Arrangement between France and Britain, Aug. 10
Portuguese Guinea	400,000	14,000	Portugal	1886. Agreement, France and Portugal, May 12
French Guinea	1,737,350	92,000	France	1889. Arrangement, Aug. 10
Sierra Leone	1,000,000	34,000	Britain	1889. Arrangement, Aug. 10
Ivory Coast	1,216,000	120,000	France	1889. Arrangement, Aug. 10
Gold Coast	857,000	40,000	Britain	1889. Arrangement, Aug. 10
Togoland	1,000,000	33,000	Germany	1890. Agreement, Britain and Germany, July 1
Porto Novo	?	?	France	1890. Arrangement, France and Dahomey, Oct. 3
Lagos	?	?	Britain	1889. Arrangement, Aug. 10
Nigeria	?	Undefined	Britain	1890. Notification of Protectorate, June 5
				1890. Agreement, France and Britain, Aug. 5, Germany and Britain, July 1
Cameroon	3,500,000	295,000	Germany	1884. Notification of Protectorate, Oct. 15
				1885. Arrangement, Germany and Britain, April-June; Protocol, Germany and France, Dec. 24
French Congo	?	?	France	1885. Protocol, France and Germany, Dec. 24
				1886. Convention, France and Portugal, May 12
				1884-5. Treaties of recognition
Congo Free State	15,000,000	802,000	Belgium	1885. Convention, Portugal and International Association, Feb. 14
Angola .	5,000,000	480,000	Portugal	1886. Convention, Portugal and France, May 12; Declaration, Portugal and Germany, Dec. 30

TALBE III.—1890 (Continued)

Territory acquired.	Population.	Estimated Area, square miles.	Acquired by	Date and Treaty of Final Settlement or Acquisition.
German South-West Africa	120,000	322,000	Germany	1884. Declaration of Protectorate, Aug. 10 1886. Agreement, Germany and Portugal, Dec. 30
Estimated	33,000,000	2,500,000		
SOUTH—				
Cape Colony	2,460,000	220,000	Britain	British before 1880
Natal	1,190,000	35,000	Britain	Do.
Basutoland	350,000	10,000	Britain	Do.
British Bechuanaland	99,000	51,000	Britain	1885. Order in Council and Proclamation, Sept. 29 and 30
British South Africa Company	?	?	Britain	1889. Charter, Oct. 29
EAST COAST—				
Portuguese East Africa	3,200,000	300,000	Portugal	1886. Declaration, Portugal and Germany
Madagascar, etc.	3,153,000	226,000	France	1890. Declaration, France and Britain, Aug. 5; and France and Germany, July 1
German East Africa	7,645,000	384,000	Germany	1885. Notification, March 6 1886. Declaration, Germany and Portugal, Dec. 30 1890. Agreement, Germany and Britain, July 1
British East Africa	4,000,000 (?)	246,000	Britain	1888. Charter, British East Africa Company 1890. Agreement, Britain and Germany
Italian Somaliland	300,000	131,000	Italy	1889. Notification, Protectorate
British Somaliland	300,000 (?)	68,000	Britain	1884. Protectorate 1888. Exchange Notes, Britain and France, Feb. 2 and 9
French Somaliland	200,000	46,000	France	1889. Order in Council 1888. Exchange Notes, France and Britain
Eritrea	280,000	60,000	Italy	1888. Treaties with Sultans
Estimated	19,000,000	1,450,000		

TABLE IV.—1914

Territory Acquired.	Estimated Population.	Estimated Extent, square miles.	Acquired by	Date of Acquisition.	Date of Treaties, etc., governing Final Settlement.
NORTHERN COAST—					
Egypt	11,300,000	400,000	Britain	1882	1899. See Table III.
Soudan	2,000,000	1,000,000	Britain	1898	Declaration between France and Britain, March 21
Tripoli	1,000,000	900,000	Italy	1912	1912. Treaty of Ouchy, Oct.
Tunis	1,800,000	46,300	France	1881	1896 and 1897. Treaties with various Powers
Algeria	5,600,000	1,100,000	France	1830	See Table III.
Morocco	7,000,000	190,000	France	1904–1912	1912. Convention between Germany and France, Nov. 4
Total, Northern Coast	28,700,000	3,636,000			
WEST COAST—					
Cape Bogador to Cape Blanco	200,000	75,000	Spain	1885	1889. Notification, Jan. 9
Senegal	1,250,000	74,000	France	1783, 1880–1889 [1]	1898. Arrangement between France and Britain, Aug. 10
Upper Senegal and Niger	5,000,000 (?)	837,000	France	1893–1898	1906. Convention between France and Britain, June 14 1906. Convention between France and Britain, May 29 1906. Agreement between France and Britain, May 29–July 19
Gambia	146,000	4,000	Britain	Begun before 1880	1889. Arrangement between France and Britain, Aug. 4 1904. Convention between France and Britain, April 8
Portuguese Guinea	400,000	14,000	Portugal	Begun before 1880	1886. Agreement between Britain and Portugal, May 12
French Guinea	1,737,000	92,600	France	1880–1889	1889. Arrangement between Britain and France, Aug. 10
Sierra Leone	1,000,000	34,000	Britain	Begun before 1880	1904. Exchange of Notes between Britain and France, March 22–April 5

[1] Final.

TABLE IV.—1914 (*Continued*)

Territory Acquired.	Estimated Population.	Estimated Extent, square miles.	Acquired by.	Date of Acquisition.	Date of Treaties, etc., governing Final Settlement.
Ivory Coast	1,216,000	120,000	France	1880–1889	1889. Arrangement between Britain and France, Aug. 10
Gold Coast and Ashanti, etc.	1,503,000	80,000	Britain	Begun before 1880 Completed 1901	1889. Arrangement between Britain and France, Aug. 10. 1890. Agreement between Britain and Germany, July 1. 1905. Exchange of Notes between Britain and France, May 11–May 15
Togoland	1,000,000	33,000	Germany	1884	1894. Agreement between Britain and Germany, July 1. 1904. Exchange of Notes between Britain and Germany, June 25
Dahomey	878,000	38,000	France	1892	1898. Convention between France and Britain, June 14. 1906. Agreement between France and Britain, Oct. 19
Sahara	450,000 (?)	1,000,000 (?)	France	1890–1899	1890. Declaration between France and Britain, Aug. 5. 1899. Declaration between France and Britain, March 21
Southern Nigeria	8,000,000	77,880	Britain	Completed 1899	1890. Agreement between France and Britain, Aug. 5. 1890. Agreement between Britain and Germany, July 1. 1898. Convention between Britain and France, June 14. 1906. Agreement between Britain and France, Oct. 19
Northern Nigeria	9,000,000	256,000	Britain	Completed 1899	1898. Convention between Britain and France, June 14. 1906. Convention between Britain and France, May 29

TABLE IV.—1914 (*Continued*)

Territory acquired	Estimated Population.	Estimated Extent, square miles.	Acquired by	Date of Acquisition.	Date of Treaties, etc., governing Final Settlement.
Cameroon	3,500,000	295,000	Germany	1884	1884. Notification of Protectorate by Germany, Oct. 15 1885. Arrangement between Germany and Britain, April-June 1885. Protocol, Germany and France, Dec. 24 1912. Convention between Germany and France, Nov. 4
French Congo	9,000,000	513,000	France	1885–1912	1898. Declaration between France and Britain, June 14 1908. Convention between France and Germany, April 18 1912. Convention between France and Germany, Nov. 4
Belgian Congo	15,000,000	802,000	Belgium	1884–1885	1884–1885. Treaties of recognition
Angola	5,000,000	480,000	Portugal	Begun before 1880	See Table III
German South-West Africa	120,000	322,000	Germany	1884	See Table III
Total, West Coast	64,400,000	5,147,480			
SOUTH AFRICA—					
Cape of Good Hope (including Bechuanaland)	2,560,000	276,000	Britain	Before 1800	
Natal	1,190,000	35,290	Britain	Before 1800	
Basutoland	350,000	10,300	Britain	Before 1800	
Transvaal	1,686,000	110,426	Britain	1902	1902. Treaty of Vereeniging, May 31
Orange Free State	528,000	50,389	Britain	1902	
Bechuanaland Protectorate	126,000	275,000	Britain	1885–1891	1891. Order in Council of May 9
Rhodesia	1,750,000	450,000	Britain	1889–1900	Various notifications and agreements
Total, South Africa	8,190,000	1,207,405			

TABLE IV.—1914 (Continued)

Territory acquired.	Estimated Population.	Estimated Extent, square miles.	Acquired by	Date of Acquisition.	Date of Treaties, etc., governing Final Settlement.
EAST COAST—					
Portuguese East Africa .	3,200,000	300,000	Portugal	Before 1880	1886. Declaration between Portugal and Germany, Dec. 30
Madagascar	3,153,000	226,000	France	1890–1896	1890. Declaration between France and Britain, Aug. 15; France and Germany, Nov. 17
					1896. Law of Aug. 6 declaring French Colony
German East Africa .	7,645,000	384,000	Germany	1885	See Table III
British East Africa .	4,000,000	246,822	Britain	1888	See Table III
Uganda	2,500,000	121,437	Britain	1894–1896	1894. Notification of Protectorate, June 18
					1907. Agreement between Britain and Ethiopia, Dec. 6
Italian Somaliland .	300,000	131,000	Italy	1889	1889. Notification of Protectorate, Nov. 19
British Somaliland .	300,000	68,000	Britain	1884	See Table III
French Somaliland .	208,000	46,300	France	1880–1885	See Table III
Eritrea	280,000	60,000	Italy	1888	1898–1907. Various treaties between Britain and Italy
					1908. Convention between Italy and Abyssinia
Total, East Coast .	21,586,000	1,583,559			

TABLE V

THE PARTITION OF AFRICA IN 1815, 1880, 1890, AND 1914. TOTAL AFRICAN POPULATION AND TERRITORY IN HANDS OF EUROPEAN STATES

	1815		1880		1890		1914	
	Population	Area, square miles.	Population	Area, square miles.	Population	Area, square miles.	Population	Area, square miles.
Northern Coast	..	..	(?)	(?)	18,700,000	1,546,300	28,700,000	3,636,000
West Coast	(?)		(?)	(?)	33,000,000	2,500,000	64,400,000	5,147,480
South	(?)	120,000 (?)	2,000,000	250,000	3,875,000	491,000	8,190,000	1,207,405
East Coast	(?)	(?)	(?)	(?)	19,086,000	1,461,000	21,586,000	1,583,559
	3,000,000 (?)	500,000 (?)	10,000,000 (?)	1,000,000 (?)	74,661,000	5,998,300	122,876,000	11,574,444

TABLE VI

THE PARTITION OF AFRICA IN 1914

	Extent acquired in square miles.				Number of square miles of African Possessions to 1000 Home Inhabitants.[1]	Number of Home Inhabitants per square mile of African possessions.[1]
	North Africa.	Central Africa, East and West Coasts.	South Africa.	Total.		
France	1,336,300	2,946,900	...	4,283,200	108	9
Britain	1,400,000	888,139	1,207,405	3,495,544	77	13
Germany	...	1,031,000	...	1,031,000	16	63
Italy	900,000	191,000	...	1,091,000	31	33
Belgium	...	800,000	...	800,000	107	9
Portugal	...	780,000	...	780,000	130	7
Spain	...	75,000	...	75,000	3	266
	3,636,300	6,712,039	1,207,405	11,555,744		

[1] I have borrowed the idea of the two last columns in this table from *Problems of the Peace*, by W. H. Dawson (1918), p. 216. Mr. Dawson's tables and statistics are different, being prepared for a wider field than that of Africa, but the idea of representing statistically the ratio of home population to colonial empire is his. The facts revealed by these statistics are significant, and deserve study.

CHAPTER II

THE science of civilization, if it existed, would like all sciences consist mainly in the tracing of cause and effect. The subject of this book is visionary and probably non-existent, for it is this science of civilization. I am concerned, therefore, with causes and effects, and I find my data in the quicksands of history. The causes which I desire to study are the desires and beliefs of Europeans which pass under the name of policy, and the effects which I hope to trace are the results of the action and reaction of these desires and beliefs within the continent of Africa. The chapters in Part I. have established the fact that there have been operating in the world certain desires and beliefs which can be accurately defined as the policy of economic imperialism. But policy, which represents the desires and beliefs of communities, is just as complex as the beliefs, motives, and intentions which determine the actions of individuals. Consequently, if we wish to trace with any certainty the effects of this policy of economic imperialism in Africa, we must attempt first to disentangle its manifestations from the complex of national beliefs and desires which determined the action of European States in Africa. We must start by tracing in the details of African history the broad divisions of policy. Very little acquaintance with that history will convince any one that policy, and therefore economic imperialism, worked geographically in four clearly marked divisions, although, naturally, since these geographical divisions meet and touch one another at certain points, so too the policies operating within them meet and react upon each other at the same points. The geographical divisions are :

(A) Mediterranean Africa, which includes (1) Algiers, Tunis, Morocco, and Tripoli ; and (2) Egypt and Abyssinia.[1]

(B) The East Coast.

(C) The West Coast.

(D) South Africa.

[1] Abyssinia belongs, both by geographical position and policy, partly to (A) and partly to (B).

I propose to trace in some of these divisions the main lines of policy and so to be in a position to estimate the force and effect of the desires and beliefs of economic imperialism. And I shall begin with Algeria.

It is one of the most difficult things in the world to apply one's imagination to historical facts, and yet, without imagination, those facts are meaningless. We accept as an historical fact the state-ment, for instance, that in 1829 Algeria was nominally subject to Turkey, and that in 1830 it passed into French hands : we leave it as such passive in our minds where it has no more meaning to us than the perhaps equally true statement that $a+b=x$. It is necessary that people should exercise their imaginations upon these bare and formulary statements of history, for in no other way is it possible to grasp the real meaning which underlies the formula.

Up to 1830 the northern coast of Africa, from Egypt to Morocco, was nominally subject to the Ottoman Empire. But the sovereignty of the Sultan was purely nominal, and the whole region was really governed and administered as a number of independent Muhammadan States. In Egypt ruled the powerful and ambitious viceroy of the Sultan, Mehemet-Ali, who was a terror rather than an obedient servant to the Sublime Porte. Tripoli, Algeria, and Tunis, the three Regencies, were ruled by deys or beys who had completely thrown off all dependence upon Turkey. Suddenly, in 1830, France, a European State, landed an army in Algeria, conquered the country, overturned the rule of the deys, and sub-jected the population to the rule and administration of France. That is the bare formula, in " a's," and " b's " and " x's," presented to us by the history books ; but, stated thus, the facts are as strange, fortuitous, and meaningless as an isolated flash of lightning : if he is to understand them, the reader must somehow manage to translate them through his imagination into realities and facts which live. For what could be more curious than the bare fact of this sudden incursion of a European " State " into Muhammadan Africa in the nineteenth century ? A State does not act from " blind," physical causes like the lightning ; the State is indis-tinguishable from the men who compose or govern nations, and its actions are their actions. The French State which entered Algeria in 1830 was Frenchmen. Viewed in this light the facts take on a meaning and life of their own, but they become at the same time more curious, more in need of imagination and explanation, than the historical formula. For what beliefs and desires sent these French-men of 1830, in the midst of peace, out of their everyday life of love and business, into the sands of Africa ? They were not impelled to move there blindly like the tides or lightning : they went there presumably as reasoning men who " control their destiny by reason," because they believed and desired certain things with regard to

" France," " Algeria," the " Mediterranean," " Europe." If we are to understand the causes and effects of economic imperialism and European policy in Africa, we must understand who these Frenchmen were who started the nineteenth-century conquest of Africa. Were they the French nation or only some Frenchmen ? With what desires and beliefs did they descend upon Algeria, and how did the succeeding years confirm those beliefs and satisfy the desires ?

When we come to examine the period of economic imperialism proper which began in 1880 we shall find that politicians and historians often maintain that the incorporation of pieces of Africa in the dominions of European States was the result of the " imperative demand " of public opinion in the imperialist nation. The policy and the action which was its manifestation are represented almost as great, blind, physical movements or processes, like the silting up of the mouth of a river or the erosion of a coast. The partition of Africa thus assumes the aspect of a movement not within the control of individual human beings, and all responsibility is smoothed away by the easy explanation that all this is the " logic of events." The conquest of Algeria is immediately distinguished from later imperialist movements because no one has ever been able even to pretend that there was any demand for it in the French nation. The policy was purely that of a Government composed of a king and a few statesmen and army officers : the French people were indifferent or actually hostile to it : [1] its success was immediately followed by revolution, the deposition of the king, and the fall of the Government. Indeed, such is the irony rather than the logic of facts that when the messenger arrived in France hot-haste to give to Charles X. the good news of the final success of the French arms, and to present to him the captured banners of the Algerian, he found no Charles X. to receive the news or the trophies ; and the new Government, in view of the popular indifference or hostility

---

[1] See Le Marchand, *L'Europe et la Conquête d'Alger* (1913), and Darcy, *Cent Années de rivalité coloniale*, 1904, p. 161 ff. The opinions of deputies and politicians, quoted by M. Darcy, show the widespread parliamentary opposition both to the conquest and retention of Algiers. " It would have been a good thing," it was said in the Chamber, " if we had never conquered Algiers." M. Passy, rapporteur du budget de la guerre, said : " The possession of Algiers is dangerous and onerous : I would gladly exchange it for a village on the Rhine." M. Dupin, another minister, speaking on the vote of credit for Algeria in 1834, declared that " colonization was an absurdity, and that they ought to hasten the moment of freeing France from a burden which she could not and would not bear for long." Talleyrand " had always condemned the Algerian expedition," and " would have joyfully seized any opportunity of throwing overboard that unlucky conquest." Among the supporters of Louis-Philippe, only " the old soldier," Marshal Soult, was enthusiastic for the conquest and its retention, and his reasons are illuminating : " By our predominance in the Mediterranean, and by setting foot in the East, we can become the controllers of the cradle of the world." The world, one may remark, is slow to understand what these " old soldiers " mean by their desire to control its cradle.

towards the Algerian adventure, considered it politic quietly to
suppress both the messenger and his banners.

The expedition to Algeria was the work entirely of the French
King, Charles X., and of the small circle of ministers and soldiers
who surrounded him. The history of the desires and beliefs which
constituted these men's policy is most instructive, by reason both
of their differences from, and resemblances to, the motives and causes
of the later imperialism. There existed an " Algerian question "
long before 1830. It was one of those international " questions "
which, on the face of them, would appear to the plain man simple,
but which had become entangled in the complicated desires and
beliefs of statesmanship. To Marshal Soult, as we have seen, the
Algerian question was connected with a desire " to control the
cradle of the world," and nothing is simple to men who think in
terms of, or desire, " the control of the cradle of the world." It
is necessary, however, to begin by attempting to translate the
terms and desires of kings and marshals into the language of ordinary
men. When this is done, the Algerian question seems to consist in
the problem of suppressing piracy on the coast of Algeria. The
subjects of the Dey of Algeria had for years preyed upon the
commerce and shipping of Europeans in the Mediterranean.
Throughout the first twenty-seven years of the nineteenth century
the European Powers were faced intermittently with the problem
of suppressing this piracy. Occasionally active measures were
taken by one or other of these Powers to exert pressure upon the
Algerians and their Dey, either by threats or protest, or occasionally,
as when Lord Exmouth bombarded the Algerians in 1816, by force
of arms. But after 1815 for many years the statesmen of Europe
were extraordinarily tender of something called by them the *status
quo*, or the Balance of Power, and any isolated action by any
State, even the threatening or bombardment of a Dey, might upset
the *status quo*, or the Balance of Power. Hence the pirates and
their truculent Dey, who was well informed as to the domestic
relations of the Christian Powers in Europe, knew that they had
little to fear from the isolated action of France or Britain beyond
an occasional bombardment, and, as the Dey himself remarked,
all that one had to do after a bombardment was to replace the
right way up the cannons which had been overturned in the forts.
On the other hand, although concerted action was from time to time
discussed, it had always been found impossible. With regard to
this failure of the Powers to act together, it should be noted that it
provides an interesting example of that fact to which attention
was drawn on page 11 that history which is patriotic is unreliable,
and that the French account of British policy will be found again
and again diametrically to contradict the British account. The
question of concerted international action to put down piracy in

the Mediterranean finds no place in British histories; in French histories it attains considerable prominence. The French historian maintains [1] that the failure of the Great Powers to take common action against the pirates was due entirely to Britain, and that it was actually a part of British policy to maintain piracy in the Mediterranean. M. Darcy, for instance, states that while the commerce of other nations suffered severely from the Algerian corsairs, the merchant-ships of Britain had "nothing to fear from these *corsaires barbaresques*, who had every interest in respecting them." He finds confirmation of this view in the reports of French consuls that British agents sold boats and munitions to the pirates. He quotes the statement of Lord Castlereagh to Bernstorff, that "the destruction of the Regencies . . . would inevitably result in the creation, upon the coast of Africa, of States united to France, which would destroy our influence in the Mediterranean, and in consequence would ruin our commerce ": and he notes with evident satisfaction Bernstorff's remark in relating this anecdote : "I could not resist expressing to the English minister my surprise at an admission which so well expressed the selfishness of English policy : England demands urgently the abolition of the black slave-trade, but refuses to do anything to prevent every kind of torture which the whites have to bear in Africa." "That," drily remarks the French historian, "was not a point of view peculiar to Lord Castlereagh."

The "question" of piracy and Algeria, though intermittent, did not become acute until 1827. It is unnecessary here to trace in detail the events of the three years' quarrel between France and the Dey, which led eventually to the conquest of Algeria. For our purpose all that is necessary is to draw attention to the salient points which throw light upon the later policy of economic imperialism. The first point to remember is that the quarrel consisted of two distinct parts. There was first the general question of piracy, and particular complaints of piratical action which France had to make against the Algerians. But, if France had a cause of complaint against the Dey and his government, the Dey had, or thought he had, a cause of complaint against France. The Dey's grievance shows the curious difference between the position of Europe towards Africa in 1830, as compared with that position in the period of economic imperialism after 1880. In the later period, as is well known, the acquisition of dominion in Africa and Asia frequently followed a process of economic penetration of non-European territory by the subjects of a European State. This economic penetration often took the form of converting the "uncivilized" administration into a debtor of the European Power or its subjects. Economic imperialism frequently worked through a

[1] *E.g.* Darcy, *Cent Années de rivalité coloniale*, pp. 43-47.

process whereby Europeans first obtained this kind of economic stake in the country, and political penetration followed in order to protect the economic interests. For example, both Turkey and Morocco were heavily in debt to Europeans, and this debt was both the excuse and the opportunity for political penetration. Now it is interesting to observe that in Algeria in 1830 the conditions were entirely reversed—and they led, almost providentially, to precisely the same result. In 1881 the Bey of Tunis was heavily in debt to France, and his indebtedness by the "logic of events" led to the French conquest of Tunis : in 1827 the Dey of Algeria was the creditor of France, and French indebtedness, presumably by the same logic of events, led directly to the French conquest of Algeria. It seems to be as fatal for a Dey to be a creditor as it is for a Bey to be a debtor to Europe. It is worth while recording briefly the story of the Dey's fatal money transactions, because it is not generally available to English readers.

In the early years of the nineteenth century there existed a firm of Algerian subjects, the Bacri. These African financiers lent money to Europeans just as in later years Europeans lent money to Africans. During the Napoleonic wars the French Government made considerable use of the financial accommodations offered by the Bacri, and borrowed a considerable sum of money from them to pay for the supplies of the army operating in Africa. After the war the money was not paid, and the debt due by a civilized Power to an "uncivilized" financier apparently has the same tendency to mount up automatically as in later years was often the case with the debts of "uncivilized" Powers to civilized financiers. At any rate the Bacri maintained that the French debt which had amounted to 7 million francs in 1800 had risen to 13 million by 1815. Again, there is a curious kind of looking-glass resemblance between the transactions of 1827 and the financial undercurrents of a later imperialism. In later times the European States have often taken upon themselves the duty of seeing that uncivilized or semi-civilized Powers met their financial obligations to Europeans. The Dey, Hussein, of Algeria, foolishly as the event proved, attempted in 1827 to pursue precisely the same policy with regard to the civilized Government of France : in fact, by a financial transaction, the details of which are not important, he became the assignee of the money due to the Bacri. There came a moment when the Dey, like other creditors, began to press for payment, and when France, like most debtors, appeared to be dilatory in complying. According to the French account, and there is no reason to doubt it, the French Government was quite willing to pay what it actually owed, and it appointed a Government commission—on which Algeria was naturally not represented [1]—to determine what was

---

[1] Civilized Powers in later times improved upon this procedure. When the

the Government debt. By 1827 this Commission was appointed, and it was only the necessary formalities of a civilized system of Government offices and a Treasury which delayed the payment to the Dey of what was due to him. Unfortunately the Dey was unacquainted with and could not be made to understand the formalities and delays incidental to a European system of Government, which are always particularly noticeable in those cases in which the Government has to pay money. He had more than once forcibly expressed his opinion to the French Consul at Algiers, M. Deval, that if France admitted the debt all she had to do was to pay the money. M. Deval's attempts to explain European systems of accountancy and administration only exasperated Hussein, and at an audience in 1827 the exasperation reached such a pitch that the Dey of Algeria struck the French consul in the face with his fly-whisk. That blow cost Hussein not only 13 million francs, but his kingdom, for by losing his temper he had converted the Algerian question from one of piracy to one of national " honour," a change most ominous for the independence of Algeria. But the European State's sense of honour was as unintelligible to Hussein as its system of keeping accounts and paying its debts.

France now had two excuses for intervention in Algeria, one personal, the affront to her honour, and the other piracy, which was a common international concern of all the States of Europe. The idea of using these excuses for conquering Algeria immediately occurred to Charles X. and his Ministers, and was discussed in the King's Council in 1827. For three years the French Government hesitated to take any more decisive act towards a conquest than the declaration of a somewhat ineffective blockade of the Algerian coast, and the cause of this hesitation shows very clearly the desires and beliefs underlying Charles X.'s policy of imperialism. The king and his ministers knew that any attempt on their part to establish French domination on the coast of Africa would incur the hostility and opposition of Britain as disturbing the " status quo and Balance of Power in the Mediterranean." On the other hand, it was precisely this disturbance of the status-quo and Balance of Power which the French Government really desired. Under analysis the beliefs underlying the policy of Charles X. will be found to be two : first, that the possession of Algeria by France would increase the strategic power of France and decrease that of Britain in the Mediterranean; second, that its conquest would, in the words of a French historian, assure him the " triumph . . . of seeing the ancient banner with the fleur-de-lis float over the ramparts of Algiers." In other words, the Algerian question, both

---

debtors were uncivilized and the creditors civilized, such Commissions were composed of the creditors, and the debtors were not represented, e.g. see the facts given below with regard to the Commission financière in Tunis.

for France and Britain, was, in 1830, not economic, but strategic and sentimental.

That these were the desires and beliefs of 1830 may be shown briefly by a few facts. The student who has any knowledge of the diplomatic and historical records of later imperialist enterprises will be astonished in reading the documents of 1827–30 to see that economic considerations hardly ever seemed to occur to the statesmen of France and Britain. It is true that the Englishmen occasionally referred vaguely to the injury which would result to British commerce if Algeria passed into French hands. But there is only one solitary recorded instance, which we have found, in which a French statesman put forward an economic argument for the acquisition of Algeria. In a council held by Charles X., as early as October 1827, the whole question of conquering Algeria was discussed in a memorandum read to the Council by the Minister or War, M. de Clermont-Tonnerre. The discussion turned almost entirely upon strategy and prestige, but for one moment the Minister of War referred to economics. In his memorandum " he set out all the advantages which France might derive from the conquest of a fertile country whose mountains contained mines." [1] This solitary and striking excursion into the beliefs of economic imperialism shows that M. de Clermont-Tonnerre was ahead of his times.

This is negative evidence ; positive evidence is contained in a most illuminating memorandum,[2] in which in 1830 Louis-Philippe issued his general instructions to Talleyrand on his proceeding as ambassador to London. The new king reviewed the past and future of the Algerian policy, and, in doing so, made perfectly clear what to contemporaries seemed the motives of that policy. They were strategic and had to do only with the *status quo* and the Balance of Power. France and England, the king explains, are in disagreement over " certain particular questions which touch upon the actual distribution of power in the world. It is to England's interest that the *status quo* should be observed absolutely, it is to France's interest that it should be modified. Affairs in the East, the insurrection in Greece, and the Algerian expedition have raised the large question of the distribution of power in the Mediterranean. . . . The policy of France could not be doubtful on this occasion despite the fact that the Government then in power (*i.e.* of Charles X.) scarcely represented national tendencies and interests. . . . In fact, France has a pressing interest in diminishing the predominance of England in a sea which is hers, and in which England has not even coastal territory." The king, after touching on the Greek question, continues : " The Algerian enterprise may have even more advantageous results for our future on the sea.

[1] E. Le Marchand, *L'Europe et la Conquête d'Alger*, p. 94.
[2] See Darcy, *Cents Années de rivalité coloniale*, p. 38.

On these two questions . . . the interests and policy of France are the opposite of those of England."

Such was the French point of view. The beliefs and desires of the English statesmen and journalists were no less exclusively concerned with the catchwords of power and the elusive phrases of strategy and high policy. It was the persistent diplomatic opposition and threat of war from the British Cabinet which for three years caused Charles X. and his ministers to hesitate over their scheme of landing an army in Algeria. Wellington, Lord Aberdeen, and their ambassador in Paris, Lord Stuart of Rothesay, again and again put the British point of view quite plainly to the king and M. de Polignac. They pressed for an official assurance that under no circumstances would France seek territorial possession or aggrandisement on the coast of Africa. " If she did," said Lord Aberdeen in 1830, owing to the geographical position, " she would be upsetting the equilibrium existing between the riverain Powers on the Mediterranean." " How can you expect us," said that strange ambassador, Lord Stuart, to M. de Polignac, " not to feel anxiety when we see France, a contracting party to the Congress of Vienna, destroying with her own hands the equilibrium of the Mediterranean ? " " We are more interested than any other Power in maintaining the *status quo* in the Mediterranean," said Wellington. There were thunder and threats from Printing-House Square and from Downing Street, as it became more and more certain that the French king was making up his mind to re-habilitate the imperialist glory of France and to upset the equilibrium of the Mediterranean. " Every one is convinced," wrote *The Times* on May 23, 1830, " that the French Government cannot seriously think of forming colonies on the coast of Africa . . . for a war would break out between France and England, and the first result of the war would be for France the loss of her new colonies." The ultimatum in *The Times* was, as is so often the case, followed by an ultimatum from the British Government. War seemed to be inevitable, especially when the French Minister of Marine told the British Ambassador in Paris that " La France se f . . . l'Angleterre," adding hastily, " I need not point out to you that this language is not diplomatic : it is a conversation between Lord Stuart and Baron d'Haussez, and not an interview between the Ambassador of England and le Ministre de la Marine de France." The truth was that the Government of Charles X. was tottering in France, and to men in the position of the king and his ministers the possibility of a European war seemed a trifle or even a relief. So, on May 25, the French army sailed from Toulon : the Dey and Algeria were conquered, the Balance of Power was upset, the *status quo* disturbed, the equilibrium of the Mediterranean destroyed. Charles X. was driven from his throne to seek retirement in England.

The threats and the thunder died down in London. France had acquired her first African possession, and the relations of France and Britain settled down into a condition of increased hostility and opposition. Of the British opposition the French historian of the twentieth century writes : " One cannot but see in it one of those irrational outbursts which so often lead the English people to consider as a personal offence any successful enterprise of one of their neighbours, any maritime and colonial success won by a foreign flag."

CHAPTER III

THE facts given in the preceding pages allow us to see what were the beliefs and desires which sent the French into Algeria. What we have seen is curious and not altogether consistent with the kind of picture of historical events which the patriotic historian draws for us. Algeria and the Algerians were subjected to the French State because a few persons controlling the French Government desired to diminish "the predominance of Britain" in the Mediterranean, to upset something which they called the Balance of Power and the equilibrium in that sea. History was made here because these men believed certain things, acted upon their beliefs, and followed their desires: there was no "logic of events," no circumstances inevitably compelling men and nations along a particular path. It is amusing to notice that the patriotic historian in his passion for seeing man the helpless victim of "facts" and "circumstances," himself unable through his ideas and desires to affect his own fate or his environment, simply disregards in Algeria the aims and motives of Charles X., de Polignac, Louis-Philippe, Lord Aberdeen, and Wellington, and solemnly assures us that all this was the "logic of events." In order to do this, M. Fallot[1] has to forget all the discussions in Charles X.'s Council, all the negotiations between London and Paris, Paris and St. Petersburg, Paris, London, and Constantinople; he can then safely inform his French readers that when the French army disembarked on the African coast in 1830, its sole object was "to avenge the outrage inflicted three years before by the Dey of Algiers on our consul." Having got the French army into Algiers for this solitary object, it is easy for him to show that, although the object is attained, man and his armies are so entangled in the iron power of "circumstances" that it was impossible ever to get the army out again. "But," he continues, "when the Turkish sovereign had signed the capitulation, France understood that she owed to

[1] *L'Avenir colonial*, p. 388.

79

Europe the suppression of the nest of pirates, . . . and this necessitated the maintenance of the occupation. . . . The partisans of
the policy of 'restricted occupation,' as it was then called,
represented indeed the opinion of the mass of the nation. But "
—note the triumphant conclusion—" the logic of events showed
soon the impossibility of this solution and the necessity of choosing
between evacuation . . . and conquest of the whole country.
. . . Circumstances imposed the second alternative."

This comfortable view of history, which relieves man of all
responsibility for his thoughts and actions, falsifies the past and
jeopardizes the future. It is almost incredible that, although nine-
tenths of the happiness and miseries of mankind have been caused
because men held certain beliefs or followed certain desires, historians and their dupes, taking this fatalistic view of M. Fallot,
hardly ever pause to consider what actually were the results of the
beliefs and desires which have made history. Nobody ever asks
how the future dealt with Charles X.'s desire to upset the equilibrium
of the Mediterranean, or with Wellington's belief that the maintenance of that equilibrium was so vital that England should
declare war rather than allow France permanently to acquire Algeria.
Perhaps it is reverence for the reputation of the great men who
are dead which prevents historians from examining history from
this, the only important and useful angle. For, as soon as one
examines the Algerian expedition from it, one finds that the beliefs
and desires of the king and statesmen, which caused the subjection
of Algeria to the French State, were founded upon nothing but
illusions and hallucinations. It is utterly impossible for any one
to point to a single fact or event in the history of Europe subsequent
to 1830 which shows that the possession of Algeria by France had
any effect at all upon the Balance of Power or the equilibrium in
the Mediterranean. There is nothing to show that, either in war
or in peace, at any moment the power of France was increased or
that of Britain diminished. We were on the point of fighting
France in 1830 because of the terrible things which would happen
to the British Empire if the *status quo* in the Mediterranean was
destroyed : the *status quo* was destroyed, and nothing happened
at all. The possession of Algeria has had no effect upon the power,
the policy, or the strategy of France or England, or of any other
nation of Europe. If history proves anything, it proves that the
status quo, the Balance of Power, and the equilibrium in the Mediterranean, which shaped the policy of Charles X. and of the British
Government and the history of Algeria and France, were simply
words, and had no relation to existing facts or to future realities.

It will be noticed that these terms and ideas, the " *status quo*,"
" Balance of Power," and " equilibrium," which formed the content
of the beliefs and motives of the statesmen of 1830, are extremely

vague. If you try to grasp their exact meaning, they have a way of slipping from you into a kind of mist of historical and political associations. But one thing is quite clear, namely, that they all refer not to a policy of co-operation, alliance, or friendliness, nor to an economic policy or a policy of commerce and mercantile shipping, but to a policy of power. The French statesmen went to Algeria, and the British statesmen tried to prevent their going there, because both believed that in some way or other the possession of Algeria would affect the relative power of France and Britain. Hence the policy was strictly strategic, but strategic in the broadest sense, for when Charles X. and Wellington thought of Algeria as conferring power, they meant not power in the narrow military sense, but a kind of combination of military, political, and diplomatic power for offence.

This policy of power was, as I have said, founded upon illusion, and the proof is that there is no single event in the subsequent history of Europe which shows that the events of 1830 altered in any respect the relative power of Britain and France in the Mediterranean, or anywhere else. But there is another proof which is even more relevant to the object of my enquiry. As soon as Algeria was safely in the hands of France, the statesmen of both France and Britain almost entirely forgot the objects with which France had gone to Algeria. Frenchmen, it is true, maintain that the success of the Algerian adventure was never forgiven by English statesmen, and that for half a century and more it remained a settled part of English policy to thwart France in every possible way on the northern coast of Africa. There is some truth in this allegation, but it is much more important to observe that, although the result of the colonial policy of Charles X. was to increase the permanent hostility of France and Britain, yet there is no instance after 1830 in which any British statesman found or alleged that the possession of Algeria by France was specifically diminishing the *power* of Britain. Nor is there any instance in which a French statesman specifically treated the possession of Algeria as a means of increasing the *power* of France relatively to Britain. In other words, once France had seized Algeria, and the time had arrived for putting into practice the beliefs, and attaining the objects, underlying Charles X.'s policy, the whole policy of power was abandoned and forgotten on both sides. What took its place was the policy of economic imperialism. Gradually French statesmen and imperialists, having forgotten the effect which Algeria was to have upon the *status quo* and the Balance of Power, began to talk of the economic importance of that possession to France. Thus Algeria, which in 1830 was to have been a weapon for upsetting the Balance of Power in the Mediterranean, was by 1880 regarded almost entirely as a weapon against British trade. The statesmen no longer pretended to talk of its importance in terms of strategy and power, but in terms of economics, as a market, a field for French enterprise, *débouché à nos produits*.

This change in the French and British view of the importance of Algeria is only a particular instance of the change from the old European policy of power to the modern policy of economic imperialism. I have stressed the point because no one can understand the significance of European policy in northern Africa after 1830 who does not bear in mind that this change took place, and yet that in this particular part of Africa the beliefs and desires underlying the old policy continued to exist and to affect the minds and actions of statesmen. The curious thing is that the old policy continued to influence statesmanship only with regard to new adventures, not with regard to territory which they had already acquired, and where alone they could put their beliefs and desires to the test of acting upon them.

The history of the acquisition of Tunis, which, after Algeria, was the next point of penetration, shows how by 1880 the real and active motives of policy were those of economic imperialism, and yet the chimeras of the old policy of power continued to buzz in the brains and the speeches of statesmen. Nothing could be more different than the conditions in Tunis in 1880 and those in Algeria in 1830. It is true that in 1830 there was a Dey ruling in Algeria, and in 1880 there was a Bey ruling in Tunis; that in 1831 the French State, owing to a military expedition, ruled over the Dey, and in 1881 the French State, by similar means, came to rule over the Bey. But there the resemblance ends. If we turn to a French historian who believes that the French acquisition of Tunis was "inevitable," a legitimate cause of glory, power, and profit for France, of civilization for the Tunisians, and of manifold blessings for the rest of the world, we shall see quite clearly the conditions of economic imperialism which the beliefs and desires of Frenchmen had created in Tunis between 1830 and 1880.

The absorption of Algeria by France made an immense difference to Tunis and its Bey. The Muhammadan, "semi-civilized" Power found itself a neighbour, possessing a common boundary, with a great, European, Christian Power. M. D'Estournelles de Constant begins his book by remarking that these circumstances were inevitably fatal to the Beys of Tunis: he takes the fatalistic view of history universal among imperialists, that Frenchmen, Deys, and Beys are all helpless victims of the inevitable logic of events. But the facts which he himself then records only prove that Frenchmen—and Deys and Beys—are the victims of their own desires and beliefs. Let us examine those facts.[1]

[1] The facts here given will be found (except where otherwise stated) in *La Politique française en Tunisie*, by D'Estournelles de Constant (1891), and *Cent*

The presence of the French State upon its border did not for some time have any marked effect upon the kingdom of the Beys. The causes of this were two. The first fruits of the Algerian expedition were not encouraging, and were not calculated to make further colonial adventures popular. Then came the year of revolution in 1848 and the flowering of beliefs and desires which were the antithesis of imperialism. The flowering, profuse in France, matured in that curious phenomenon, the presence of Algerian and negro deputies in the French Chamber. · Their presence testified to the reawakened desire in Frenchmen for Liberty, Equality, Fraternity : and while those principles were leading Frenchmen to proclaim for the moment the doctrine of "Africa for the Africans" and "Algeria for the Algerians," it was natural that the doctrine of "Tunis for the French" found, also for the moment, few adherents.

But towards 1860 new doctrines and desires began to make their presence visible in Tunis. They were economic. The first visible effect of a common boundary between Tunis and a European, Christian, civilized State was that financiers, traders, and manufacturers flowed over it into the kingdom of the Bey. These Frenchmen were not moved thither by the logic of events, but by certain quite simple and legitimate desires, desires for economic advantages and profit. The effect of their presence is already visible in the curious incidents of 1857. In that year the Bey ruling in Tunis was Muhammad. His subjects were Muhammadans. Now, according to the barbarous notions of Muhammad and his Muhammadans, blasphemy and adultery are crimes for which the appropriate punishment is death. A Jew, who had blasphemed in the public street, was charged with the offence before the civil and religious court of Tunis, found guilty, and condemned to death. The Bey confirmed the sentence, and the Jew's head was cut off. This incident, as M. de Constant points out with sympathy and seriousness, caused considerable emotion among the Europeans in Tunis, for if the Bey, with a motion of his hand, could decapitate a Jew for blasphemy, there was no knowing that the same might not happen at any moment to the heads of Christians. And another incident showed that the danger was not imaginary. A young Italian was convicted of adultery with a Muhammadan woman : the lady was sewn up in a sack and thrown into a lake, and the Christian was handed over to the executioner. But this was too much for the Great Powers of Europe : their consuls succeeded, as

---

Années de rivalité coloniale, by J. Darcy. I have purposely chosen M. de Constant and M. Darcy as my authorities for the facts because they are fervid supporters of the policy of imperialism, and their evidence is therefore unimpeachable. If I had chosen M. Yves Guyot, it might have been said that his facts and his views were due to the bias of anti-imperialism.

M. de Constant puts it, in "making the Bey blush for his barbarity." Under their pressure he signed a kind of declaration of the rights of Jews and Christians in Tunis, and at a solemn ceremony in his palace, before the ulemas, the representatives of the Great Powers, four admirals and sixty French naval officers, he swore to observe the new constitution. "Tunis," we read, "was *en fête*, and Europe applauded" the adhesion of the Bey to the principles of European civilization. To mark the occasion, the Emperor Napoleon sent Muhammad the grand cordon of the Legion of Honour. But Muhammad's blush was not only moral; it turned out to be also economic. "On his side the Bey," as M. de Constant naïvely puts it, "showed his gratitude for all the interest which was taken in him. Léon Roches (the French consul) obtained from him important advantages for our countrymen." Those advantages were economic: a monopoly of the telegraphic service in Tunis was given to the French administration; a concession for restoring an ancient aqueduct and for supplying Tunis with water was given to a French engineer. But the Bey's gratitude was not confined solely to France and Frenchmen. Mr. Wood, the English consul, "in the absence of the French consul from Tunis," obtained several concessions from Muhammad, among which the most valuable was that for the construction, by an English Company, of a railway from Tunis to Goleta. Thus in 1857 the battle for concessions by diplomatic pressure had already begun in Tunis, and the battle for concessions is another name for, or one phase of, economic imperialism.[1]

In 1860, the historians tell us, the signs of decay and ruin were already visible in Tunis, and the intervention of a European State had already become inevitable. As soon as the facts are examined, the causes of the decay are found to be not moral nor political, but economic. There had descended upon Tunis and its Bey a swarm of European financiers, speculators, and traders. "They were attracted by the odour of decay," says M. de Constant, but the facts which he himself records show that they were themselves rather the causes of the odour and the decay. The Arabs said that they pursued and settled upon the country like "flies swarming upon a wounded ass," and M. de Constant admits the applicability of the simile. When Dr. Nachtigal visited Tunis he found that "the administration was entirely in the hands of European speculators and money-lenders." The methods of these men, and the effects of their methods, are described by M. de Constant and other

---

[1] There is an interesting example in M. de Constant's history of the bias of the patriotic historian. In his account of these negotiations for concessions he says of the concessions to the French that the Bey "showed his gratitude," and that the French consul "obtained" certain advantages; when he has to tell of the similar concessions to the English, he remarks that the English consul "wrung them (*en arracher*) from the Bey." See *La Politique française en Tunisie*, p. 27.

French historians. They lent money to the Bey on ruinous terms. In payment of interest, or on even flimsier pretexts, they extorted concessions from him for cultivating immense stretches of territory, or for opening up unexplored mines. In return for these concessions they promised to transform the country, to cover it with gold : and their promises were so dazzling that they contrived to " make the concessionaire appear the benefactor and the Bey his debtor." The result was that the Bey added to the concession privileges such as exemption from taxation. The concession hunter then betook himself to Paris and floated a Company. Sometimes the Company and its creator returned to Tunis and built a few sheds or scratched the surface of the earth : more often they took no steps at all to exploit their concession. But for the Bey the end was always the same. The Company presented him with a bill, a demand for indemnity against losses sustained in attempting to exploit the concession. And the Bey paid, because the claim was always made on the ground that the enterprise had failed owing to the insecurity of the country for which the Government was responsible.[1] For the days of the rule of a Bey are numbered, if he has as neighbour a great, Christian, European Power, and admits that his own country is insecure for the operations of Paris and London joint-stock companies. So the Bey of Tunis paid.

The Bey of Tunis paid the speculators, the money-lenders, and the joint-stock companies of Paris, London, and Rome. But by the logic of events and economics it was the people of Tunis who really paid. There was only one source of revenue for a Bey who is pouring money into the bottomless pit of the money-markets of a Christian and civilized Europe: it was his own "Arabs." The people of Tunis were taxed and taxed again : economically the country was bled white,[2] and that was what the Arabs meant when they said that the harbingers of economic imperialism were swarming upon the country " like flies upon a wounded ass." The agents of the Bey were " insatiable " : they went up and down the land wringing the last piece of money and the last grain of corn from a population already reduced to starvation by taxation. The tax-gatherer combined his office with that of torturer, and a man suspected of concealing grain, which the logic of events and the laws of economics required to pass through the hands of the Bey into the money-market of Paris, was beaten until he acknowledged the power of facts, fate, and finance. And this state of things immediately set working one of those vicious circles which confirm the historian in his belief that man is helpless in the grip of inevitable " facts." Starvation, the tax-collector, and his bastinado at last reduced the population to a chronic state of revolt. Insurrec-

[1] D'Estournelles de Constant, *op. cit.* pp. 64 and 65.
[2] *Idem, op. cit.* p. 43.

tions were continually flaring up all over the country, and the tortures and barbarities, with which the uncivilized government of the Bey endeavoured to suppress them, only added to the disorder throughout the country. Thus, in order to pay the civilized financier and concessionaire, the uncivilized Bey was driving his people into insurrection, and was therefore creating the " insecurity of the country " which again became the grounds for further payments and indemnities to the concessionaires. The more he paid the more disorder he created, and the more disorder the more he had to pay.

I shall have again to refer to this question of " disorder " and the part which it played in the process by which the French State was led inevitably to conquer Tunis. For the moment it is necessary to return to finance and economics. From 1837 to 1873 the Regency of Tunis was happy in the possession of a very remarkable servant of state, Mustapha khaznadar. During those thirty-five years Beys came and Beys went, but Mustapha khaznadar remained Prime Minister of Tunis. In 1863 Mustapha, now in his twenty-fifth year of office, was chief counsellor to a Bey called Sidi-Saddok. The debts of Sidi-Saddok to concessionaires and European financiers amounted to 28,000,000 francs. The khaznadar conceived the brilliant, but not entirely original, idea of paying off the old debt by contracting a new one. The interest payable to the swarm of old creditors was at the rate of at least 13 per cent : the khaznadar represented to his master that, by going into the money-market in Paris, he could borrow a lump sum at half that rate of interest, and so effect what in civilized countries might be called an extremely clever conversion of the public debt. Sidi-Saddok was overjoyed at the news, and his joy was still greater when he heard that a loan of 35,000,000 francs had been floated by the bankers of Paris. He imagined, not unnaturally, that he would soon be the happy possessor of 35,000,000 francs with which to pay off once and for all the horde of financial gentlemen who were swarming over Tunis, and which would still leave him a substantial balance for objects of personal expenditure which are never wanting to Beys. Unfortunately Sidi-Saddok was ignorant of the ways in which the higher finance of civilized Europe works. Of the 35,000,000 francs which he had expected he received exactly 5,640,914 : but naturally he had to pay interest, not on the 5, but on the 35 million. The result, therefore, of this clever " conversion " was that the Bey's debt leapt at a bound from 28 to 60 million francs. The Bey paid once more, and the people of Tunis paid the Bey, for the taxes had to be doubled to keep pace with the doubled debt. The loan of 1863 was followed in due course by a violent insurrection in 1864, which, as we shall see later, became a subject of European and international complications. For the moment, however, the

Bey succeeded in suppressing his rebellious subjects, but his financial difficulties increased. He followed the old road to ruin which so many debtors have trodden, and appealed once more to the financiers of Paris. This time the good financiers floated a loan for him of 25,000,000 francs, but by the inevitable logic of economics the terms of his second loan were less favourable than those of his first. Only a very small part of the loan came to him in the form of cash : a very large part had to be taken by him in the form of armaments manufactured in France. Thus 2½ million francs came to him in the shape of a frigate for the Tunisian fleet which did not exist, and one million in the form of ancient cannons.[1] for the Tunisian army which was in a state of revolt. The guarantee of this loan was the Tunisian Customs revenue, and, as he was now deprived of this source of revenue, the Bey had to increase the direct exactions from his own people. From 1865 to 1867 the " disorder " in Tunis also increased. Sidi-Saddok became more and more barbarous in his methods of suppressing rebels and of raising the money required by the European shareholders. He took to hanging or poisoning large numbers of the richer of his subjects, and then confiscating their property to the State, and in 1867 the number of these victims was so great that, as the French historian informs us, " at this moment a feeling of horror seized upon the European population of Tunis. In truth the Bey's time has passed (*le bey n'est vraiement plus de son temps*), and people asked what would become of the Regency if it remained without control in his hands. The intervention of Europe was inevitable. . . ."

But this question of the " intervention of Europe " was not a simple one. To any one who rejects the " inevitable " theory of history, the theory of the " logic of facts," the disorders in Tunis in 1867 were the direct cause of the economic desires and beliefs of Europeans. Those beliefs and desires caused the concessionaires and money-lenders of Paris, Rome, and London to " exploit " the Bey and Tunis : the " exploitation " of the Bey caused the Bey to exploit his subjects : and the exploitation of his subjects caused those subjects to rebel, and rebellion caused " disorder." But intervention—and this was well recognized even in 1865—would give to the subjects of the European Power which intervened increased opportunities of " exploitation." Economic imperialism, in its full and final form, was just stirring the consciousness of Frenchmen, Italians, and Englishmen. The possibility of using the power of the European State to promote in Tunis those economic interests which had themselves caused the " disorders " was dimly recognized. Hence France, Britain, and Italy jealously watched

---

[1] These cannons were guaranteed to be " rifled " ; they proved indeed to be rifled, but rifled outside ! For the facts given above see D'Estournelles de Constant, pp. 32-43.

one another's actions in Tunis. France always claimed a special position in the Regency for two reasons : first, because the Bey owed more money to Frenchmen than to Englishmen or Italians, and secondly, because Algeria adjoined Tunis and "disorder" in Tunis might spread across the boundary. These desires, jealousies, and suspicions are reflected in the attitude and intrigues of the representatives of France, Britain, and Italy in Tunis, M. Roches (and his successors M. Botmiliau and M. Roustan), Mr. Wood, and Signor Pinna. We have already seen how, as early as 1857, the French and English consuls inaugurated a policy of competing against one another in extracting from the Bey valuable concessions for their respective nationals. This policy continued, and in later years, as we shall see, M. Pinna joined in on behalf of Italians and Italy. At the same time the three consuls wove around the Bey a network of diplomatic intrigues and hostilities in which, for the most part, the Englishman and Italian presented a more or less united front against the Frenchman. The details of this struggle cannot be given here : it must be sufficient to record that, from 1860 to 1878, every action or proposal of the French consul was certain to meet with the opposition of the English, the Italian or both, and *vice versa*.

The international hostilities engendered by these conditions were not confined to the consuls and the consulates. They overflowed into the Chanceries of Europe. The loudest cry for intervention to suppress the "disorder" came from France, where the Bey's debts were most heavy and most numerous. The reason given for this cry was, however, usually not the debts, but the danger to Algeria. And then one of those curious international incidents happened which seem so natural to the patriotic historian, but which is apt to provide an ethical puzzle to the enquirer who tries to keep his mind clear from national bias and prejudices. In the '60's France knew that she could not intervene herself even to suppress the "disorder" under the jealous eyes of Britain and Italy.[1] Yet the terrible conditions of 1864 and 1865, when the Regency was devastated by insurrection, starvation, disease, and the tax-collectors, roused an almost overwhelming demand for the suppression of the disorders. Now, it must be remembered that nominally and according to the strict interpretation of the Law of Nations Tunis was still part of the Turkish Empire. The Porte had always maintained that its suzerainty over the Regencies had not lapsed, and Great Britain at least once, namely in 1835, had

---

[1] See Darcy, *Cent Années*, p. 195, "England remained for long intractable on the principle of French intervention. For the question of Tunis, it was said in London, there can be no other solution than the maintenance of the *status quo*, for on the day which saw Tunis and Bizerta united with Algeria, the freedom of the Mediterranean would be at the discretion of France."

supported this contention.[1] The phantom rights of Turkey were, in fact, used as a convenient bulwark against French intervention. But phantom rights can sometimes, at convenient moments and for special purposes, materialize ; and in 1864 such a materialization presented itself as a method for suppressing disorder and at the same time for keeping France out of Tunis. M. Darcy states that Mr. Wood, the English consul, travelled through Tunis organizing " manifestations in honour of the Sultan " in the villages. This was followed by the Sultan assembling troops and ships, and announcing that he proposed to land a force in his Regency and put down the disorders. And here arises the ethical puzzle. For France apparently preferred the disorders to continue in Tunis rather than that they should be suppressed by its legal suzerain. " The Cabinet of the Tuileries immediately sent a corps of observation to Tebessa, and warned the Porte that, if it persisted in its plans, our soldiers would be in Tunis before those of the Porte. . . . The Porte gave way, and renounced its idea of intervention." [2] Happily, the French historian tells us, the danger of Turkish intervention and the suppression of the disorders were thus prevented : and yet the same historian, when he comes to tell us how, sixteen years later, France intervened to suppress the disorders, of which in 1864 she had refused to allow the suppression, calmly remarks : " Such a situation could not last indefinitely. The moment approached when the state of anarchy and decomposition, in which the Regency was struggling, was to end in a foreign intervention, and every day's delay increased the risk for us of seeing ourselves anticipated. Besides, even our interests in the material security of our possessions in Algeria demanded that we should destroy at our doors a hot-bed of unrest and intrigues . . . which the Government of the Bey was unable to suppress." [3]

Thus, to sum up the situation in 1865, the subjects of the French, British, and Italian States were the ultimate cause of the disorders in Tunis by their economic and financial exploitation of the Bey. This exploitation was carried on under the protection and encouragement of the official representatives of the respective States. The French State was seeking to use the disorders as a pretext for intervention, was being prevented from doing so by Britain and Italy, and was at the same time preventing, by the threat of armed force, any attempt on the part of the legal suzerain of Tunis to put an end to the anarchy. In this way the three Great and civilized Powers were at one in their determination not to allow

---

[1] Darcy, *op. cit.* p. 193.

[2] Darcy, *op. cit.* p. 194, and D'Estournelles de Constant, *La Politique française en Tunisie,* p. 40.

[3] See Darcy, *op. cit.* p. 196. M. de Constant takes the same view, see *La Politique française,* p. 40.

any intervention for the purpose of ending the devastation of the country, and the impoverishment, starvation, and massacre of its uncivilized inhabitants. Nevertheless they were able to agree upon intervention, and a joint intervention to protect the economic and financial interests of their subjects, who had obtained concessions and lent money to the Bey. The details of this transaction are not unimportant as an early example of the objects and methods of economic imperialism.

The creditors of the Bey fell into two classes. There were first the Parisian financiers who had negotiated the loans of 1863 and 1865 described above. These were State loans issued on the security of the Customs revenue. The second class of creditor consisted of a number of French, British, and Italian concession-aires, traders, and financiers, to whom individually the Bey owed money. There was no special hypothecation or security for these debts, and it was in order to pay them off and convert them that the loan of 1863 had been floated in Paris. As we saw, the loan was floated, but the money necessary for paying off the old debts never reached the Bey. These miscellaneous creditors, of whom the majority were French subjects, being without any special security and being creditors, not of the State, but of the Bey of Tunis, were in an inferior position financially to the Paris financiers. On the other hand, being resident in Tunis, their opportunities for intrigue and "pressure" were superior, and, supported by their respective consuls, they began to use those opportunities for the purpose of placing themselves upon an equality with the bankers of Paris. The intrigues were long and complicated, but in 1868 they resulted in the "conversion" of the local and miscellaneous debt into a uniform loan secured upon the Customs revenue, which was already the security for the Paris loan. Naturally, an outcry arose from the Paris money market, and now "pressure" was put by the French consul upon the Bey's Government, this time on behalf of the Paris creditors. This pressure was resisted by the consuls of Britain and Italy, the two States whose subjects were not interested in the Paris loan. The French consul was for the moment successful, and an agreement was arrived at between France and Tunis to "constitute a Commission charged with the collection of the revenues of the Regency, and with ensuring its division among the State creditors."

This time a cry went up from London and Rome and Florence, from Mr. Wood and from Signor Pinna. A fierce campaign opened in the French and Italian press. France, which had been intimidated from intervening on the plea of "disorder," now appeared to be entering Tunis by the back door of a "Financial Commission," with powers of controlling the revenue and protecting the economic interests of her own subjects under the significant title of "*State*

creditors." If there was to be intervention, even financial intervention, the British and Italians argued, it must be a joint international
intervention, and not individual action by a single nation. When,
therefore, the decree embodying the Franco-Tunisian agreement
was published, " Britain and Italy refused flatly to recognize it,"
and " pressure " of a diplomatic nature was once more, and successfully, applied to the unfortunate Bey.[1] Sidi-Saddok, swinging
violently from the Scylla of France to the Charybdis of Britain and
Italy, promptly repudiated his agreement. M. Botmiliau, the French
representative, lowered the French flag, and broke off official
relations with the Tunisian Government, and for a moment it
looked as if Tunis, supported by Italy and Britain, would receive
an ultimatum from France. But in 1868, midway between the
Luxemburg affair and the Franco-Prussian war, the European
situation was too threatening for France to allow even the Imperial
Government to run the risk of war with Italy and Britain over
Tunis. So the French Government bowed gracefully behind the
appropriate diplomatic forms to the inevitable, and on July 9,
1869, an International Financial Commission was constituted,
sanctioning the joint intervention of France, Britain, and Italy
to rehabilitate the finances and protect the economic interests of
their subjects in Tunis. M. Pinna also took the opportunity of
extracting from the Bey certain important economic privileges for
his nationals and a valuable lead-mining concession for an Italian
company.[2]

Thus Europe had at last been compelled to intervene, and the
finances of Tunis were now subjected to control in the economic
interests of Europeans. The control was a curious species of
international government. The Financial Commission consisted
of two Committees, one—the Executive Committee—composed of
two Tunisians and a Frenchmen, the other—the Committee of
Control—composed of two Italian, two British, and two French
subjects. Statesmen are never tired of insisting upon the
unworkability of any form of international government ; and
there is some reason for their conviction, because whenever they
themselves resort to international control, they set up a form of
government which could not possibly work, whether it was national
or international.[3] As in Egypt, so in Tunis those responsible
for introducing the International Financial Commission divided
the responsibility and control between two Committees whose

---

[1] French historians maintain that that remarkable Prime Minister, the khaznadar Mustapha, was working hand in glove with the British and Italian consuls,
while pretending to favour the French agreement, and that the victory of Mr.
Wood and Signor Pinna over their French colleague was due to his intrigues and
secret support.

[2] See D'Estournelles de Constant, op. cit. pp. 48-53.

[3] See on this point The Future of Constantinople, by Leonard Woolf, pp. 28-35.

powers and functions were ill-defined. Innumerable difficulties were naturally the result, but it is significant that, despite the handicap with which it had been unnecessarily endowed at birth, this international organ was by no means a failure. M. de Constant, who regards it with the hostile eye of a patriotic Frenchman, is yet compelled to recognize what it achieved in the following words : " It put off for ten years the necessity of a foreign occupation . . . it reconstituted as well as it could an administration which was very valuable to us ; it re-established in a country devastated by corruption whatever order and honesty we found there later."

Unfortunately—or fortunately, according as one regards the matter from the point of view of a patriotic Frenchman or a patriotic Tunisian—it was too late for even the International Commission to save Tunis. It must always be remembered that the Commission was constituted primarily to protect the economic interests of the European creditors. Even in the re-establishment of the Tunisian finances it kept this object loyally and steadfastly in view. Having taken a survey of the financial situation, it established the fact that the floating debt amounted to no less than 160,000,000 francs, and the interest annually payable to 19,000,000 francs. The Government, therefore, had to be treated as a bankrupt, and a composition with the creditors reduced the debt to 125,000,000 francs, and the interest at 5 per cent to 6,000,000. Even to pay this sum annually practically the entire revenue of the country had to be hypothecated as security for the European creditors. The revenues left to the Government for carrying on the administration consisted, for the most part, of taxes in kind, levied upon nomad tribes in the interior, and their collection was only possible by means of military expeditions against the tax-payers. In other words, the European financiers were given a first mortgage upon Tunis, and out of the revenue which remained after they had been paid—namely, nothing —the Bey had to establish an orderly government in the place of chaos and anarchy—on pain of occupation by a European Power. The result is admirably summed up by M. de Constant, who remarks that after 1870 Tunis was in the position of the horse which would have become accustomed not to eat had it not unfortunately died first from hunger.

We now approach the last act in the absorption of Tunis by a European State, and, as we approach nearer to the final scene of 1881, the motives and policies of economic imperialism in its most complete form come more and more into the forefront of the picture. The period 1870–80 is notable for a more conscious and determined struggle by the three interested States, France, Italy, and Britain, to employ the political and diplomatic powers of the State for promoting the economic interests of their subjects in Tunis. At the same time there is a constant series of threats and counter-threats of " intervention " from France and Italy. I propose to trace these operations in some detail, but, before doing so, it is necessary to make clear the influence which the European international situation exercised during this period upon policy on the northern coast of Africa. Immediately after the Franco-Prussian war France was not in a position to embark on any adventures. At the same time the national movement in Italy began to show signs of overflowing the boundaries of Italy, and of creating a strong current towards " expansion " and imperialism. Finance, trade, and strategy united to beckon some Italians across the Mediterranean to Tunis and Bizerta. These two events produced a curious diplomatic situation. For Britain had always been hostile to the idea of French intervention or occupation, and had used Italian co-operation to combat the growth of French " influence " in Tunis. But the vision of Italy in Tunis was no less distasteful to British traders and statesmen than that of a French protectorate : in fact French historians maintain that British statesmen were determined that, if Bizerta had to pass into the possession of a European Power, it should not pass into the hands of a Power which also occupied Sicily. Thus at the very moment when the economic beliefs and desires were gathering strength to mould policy in Tunis, we find the old ghosts of Wellington's and de Polignac's policy—the equilibrium of the Mediterranean and the *status quo* and the Balance of Power—rising in the brain, and distracting and complicating the manœuvres, of European statesmanship. The earliest hint of this new development came in 1871, when, for the first time in the diplomatic history of Tunis, British diplomacy supported France against its own ally, Italy. The action of Italy was, it is true, in this case extravagant, for M. Pinna had taken advantage of the embarrassments of France to exact from the Bey an immense number of privileges and concessions for Italian subjects. The Bey, supported not only by the French but also by the English consul, resisted the demands ; whereupon the matter rose into the higher altitudes of international policy. Italy threatened a " naval demonstration," and it required the combined protests or counsels of the British and French Governments at Florence to prevent an Italian fleet sailing to the coast of Africa.

But the international struggle in Tunis during the decade following 1870 turned principally round the question of " concessions," and here we can observe in operation for the first time one of the most characteristic methods of economic imperialism. The political power—and behind the political the military power— of the three Great States is used against each other and the Bey to further the economic interests of their subjects by exacting economic privileges, monopolies, and concessions. Then, again, these economic interests are themselves used as a pretext for acquiring political control over the country, and the political control is again used for promoting economic interests. Thus a vicious circle is formed in which political and diplomatic pressure is followed by economic penetration, the economic penetration necessitates further political action, that action ensures more penetration, and so on until the time is ripe for the pressure to become a military expedition, and the penetration a protectorate. We have already seen how Italy and M. Pinna attempted in 1871 to start an Italian circle, and how Britain joined France to prevent Italian economic concessions taking the first step towards conversion into an Italian protectorate. Britain and Mr. Wood were not, however, neglectful of the economic interests of Britons : in 1871 the English consul, in protecting the Bey from the economic demands of Italy, improved the occasion by obtaining from Sidi-Saddok a confirmation of the Tunis-Goleta railway concession which had lapsed. He followed up this success by extracting in 1874 another concession for an English Company, namely, the construction of a railway between Tunis and Algeria. The beliefs and desires operating behind these actions can best be shown by quoting M. de Constant's comment upon this railway concession. "Fortunately," he remarks, "the company did not find the capital ; otherwise British interests, which were practically non-existent, would have become superior to those of France in the Regency. A rival administration would have ruled in the north of the country right up to our frontier, and would in consequence have justified a foreign interference in the affairs of Tunis. Not only our influence with the Bey, but our dominion in northern Africa, would have profoundly felt the consequences of this interference."

This interaction of penetration, politics, and power only came to a head after 1878. The end of Tunisian independence was preceded by the great diplomatic transformation scene of the Berlin Congress. The Congress was brilliantly staged, and the world watched all the great statesmen standing on one another's shoulders and juggling with the powers and peoples of Europe. Some of the juggling was done openly before the world's eyes, and some in secret. Diplomacy yields up its secrets reluctantly, and it is not possible even in 1918 to say with certainty what happened in the *coulisses* of the congress of 1878. But it seems pretty clear that at some time or other M. Waddington and Lord Salisbury and Bismarck got together into a corner and did some juggling with Tunis and its Bey. The account of these transactions usually adopted by British writers [1] is that Bismarck instigated France to "seize" Tunis ;

[1] Thus Lord Newton in his *Life of Lord Lyons*, vol. ii. p. 251 (1913), writes : "The real instigator of the Tunis expedition was not Lord Salisbury, but Bismarck. The latter . . . could have stopped French action at any moment he pleased, but instead of doing so, he naturally encouraged an enterprise which was certain to lead eventually to difficulties between France, Italy, and England."

he calculated that, by involving her in Africa, he would distract her attention from Alsace-Lorraine and the Rhine. Italian writers go still further and maintain that in order to embroil France and Italy, he offered Tunis first to the one and then to the other. But it is remarkable that the French statesmen of the time, and many French historians, deny the truth of this " legend." Jules Ferry in 1889 wrote an article in a paper called *L'Estafette*, in which he " established . . . the fact that Germany did not offer, and could not have offered, Tunis to any one." On the other hand, the French Government and French writers were unanimous in affirming that it was Lord Salisbury who invited France to exercise " a free hand " in the Regency.

Perhaps we shall never know exactly what happened when Lord Salisbury took M. Waddington aside into a corner of the Berlin Congress. All that we can say with certainty is that the French Minister was left with the impression that he took the train from Berlin for Paris with Tunis in his pocket, and that the man who had put it in his pocket was Lord Salisbury. " Carthage," the English diplomatist had diplomatically said to him, " Carthage ought not to remain in the hands of the barbarians (*Carthage ne doit pas rester aux barbares*)," [1] and the Frenchman had interpreted this diplomatic oracle as meaning in plain language that since Britain had got her pickings out of the Congress by the seizure of Cyprus, so France would be allowed to take hers [2] by obtaining a " free hand " in Tunis. Lord Newton, writing as late as 1913, speaks of the French occupation of Tunis as " bare-faced aggression " and an " act of flagrant immorality," and he protests that "to make Lord Salisbury responsible" for it "is unjustifiable." But even the French have never attempted " to make Lord Salisbury responsible " for the expedition to Tunis. All that the French have maintained is that Disraeli and Lord Salisbury, having seized upon Cyprus for the British Empire, intimated to France that if she had any idea of doing the same by another Turkish possession, Tunis, Britain would (as Lord Newton himself phrases it) look on with indifference. In proof of this the French Government proposed to publish the confidential despatches and papers which passed between the two Governments in 1878, and Lord Salisbury himself considered this to be so important that, although out of office at the time, he took the extraordinary and irregular course of writing personally and directly to our Ambassador in Paris protesting against the French proposal.[3] Lastly, it must be remembered that

---

[1] See D'E. de Constant, *op. cit.* p. 86.

[2] Austria, of course, obtained hers, also on the proposal of the British representatives, in the shape of Bosnia-Herzegovina. Bismarck alone contented himself with the position of cynical and honest broker.

[3] See Lord Newton, *Lord Lyons*, vol. ii. p. 242.

the Egyptian question intervened between the Berlin Congress and the Tunis expedition. The French statesmen, people, and historians have always regarded the British occupation of Egypt in exactly the same light as Lord Newton regards the French occupation of Tunis. To them it appeared, and appears, to be "bare-faced aggression," and an " act of flagrant immorality," and when Lord Newton says of the French and Tunis "they went there, under distinctly false professions, announcing that the expedition was intended solely to punish refractory tribes, and that the occupation was merely temporary," it must not be forgotten that two generations of Frenchmen have unanimously said precisely the same thing about ourselves in Egypt. It is not without significance that the two acts of flagrant immorality were contemporaneous, for, even internationally and among States, evil communications sometimes corrupt good manners. It seems certain that our new position in Egypt had something to do with our giving France the " free hand " in Tunis, and also something to do with the idea, adopted by both Conservative and Liberal British statesmen, that Carthage ought not to remain in the hands of the barbarians.[1]

At any rate, whatever the causes, it is clear that between 1878 and 1881 the objections of Britain to the French State penetrating into Tunis, in the same way as it had penetrated into Algeria, weakened, and that the French Government were made aware of this weakening. But the struggle for concessions and the motives of economic imperialism continued to operate with even greater violence, and the curious incident which preceded and, as we shall show, caused the French expedition deserves to be told in detail. Italy, as a State, did not by any means regard with approval the weakening of her ally's opposition to French " aggression." She was one of the few Powers who picked up nothing at the Congress of Berlin. She was flushed with the new wine of nationalism, and her affairs were falling into the hands of a number of politicians, traders, and financiers, eager exponents of a policy of imperialist and economic expansion outside Europe. Their policy was pursued first in Tunis and later, as we shall see, on the north-east coast of Africa, in both places by the same men, in curiously similar circumstances, and with the same unfortunate results. Both in Tunis

---

[1] M. Darcy, *Cent Années de rivalité coloniale*, p. 213, maintains that even some English writers admit that Britain agreed at the Congress of Berlin to the occupation of Tunis by France in exchange for France agreeing to the British occupation of Egypt. He refers to articles in the *Times* of January 15 and February 1, 1895, and to an article by Admiral Maxse in the *National Review*. Apart from the difficulty in dates which this view obviously involves, the statement of M. Darcy is a curious example of national bias producing historical inaccuracy. The articles in the *Times* of January 15 and February 1, 1895, are not articles at all, but letters in a controversy between Mr. St. Loe Strachey and a Frenchman. In those letters, Mr. Strachey, the Englishman, maintains the view that the French had no right to occupy Tunis, but that the English had every right to occupy Egypt.

and in Eritrea "expansion" was aimed at by a combination of the political party, led by Crispi, and of the financiers of the Rubattino Company; and in both places their policy was supported to a considerable extent by Britain and strenuously opposed by France and the French exponents of the *politique coloniale*.

In Tunis the Italian expansionists, as we have seen, had been active for many years before 1878. Their tactics had been principally confined to "pressure" upon the Bey, to using the power of the Italian State through the Italian consul for the purpose of exacting economic privileges and monopolies and concessions for Italian subjects. The policy had often been successful, and had occasionally been successfully opposed by the French. The "interests" thus acquired by Italians were still in 1878 markedly inferior to the similar interests acquired by French subjects and companies; but these Italian "interests" were the pretext used by the Italian press and politicians for opposing French intervention, and, sometimes, for proposing Italian intervention.

History seems to show that there is often a curious telepathic sympathy between diplomatists, foreign offices, newspapers, and money markets. Neither Lord Salisbury nor M. Waddington immediately published to the world the "very satisfactory" conversation (as Lord Salisbury called it) which they had about Tunis at Berlin. Yet an intimation that something unpleasant was shortly going to happen in Africa, a kind of diplomatic-financial intuition, seems to have stolen into the minds of Italian statesmen, journalists, and financiers. There developed in the press an enormous interest in the future of Tunis, and violent attacks upon France and French policy. Activity spread to the money market in Rome and to the Italian consul in Tunis. This activity manifested itself first, according to the French historians, in 1879 in an attempt by the new Italian consul, Signor Maccio, to rob the French of their monopoly of the telegraph in Tunis. After a year's negotiation the attempt was defeated, and the French were confirmed in their monopoly.

But the real struggle came in 1880. It will be remembered that in 1857 Mr. Wood, the English consul, had obtained from the Bey a concession for an English company to construct a railway from Tunis to Goleta, and again in 1871 an extension of the concession. Financially the undertaking had not proved very successful, and, shortly after Lord Salisbury's satisfactory conversation with M. Waddington, the English company seems to have decided that the time had come to stop building railways for the inhabitants of Tunis at a loss to the British shareholders. It was decided to sell their line and their rights, and negotiations began with a natural purchaser, the French Bône-Guelma Company, which already owned important French interests in Tunis. Then suddenly, in 1880, the Italian Rubattino Company appeared upon the scene, and offered first 1,200,000 francs, and then 2,500,000 francs for the railway—not a bad price when it is remembered that the French estimated its total value at a million francs. However, the French company saw the danger and promptly offered 2,605,000 francs, and the Goleta line was sold to it on April 14. A terrific outcry arose in Italy, and the Italian company gave notice that it would contest the validity of the sale. This it did in the London Courts, and on June 16 judgment was given in its favour setting aside the sale as invalid.

The question of the sale and purchase of this railway had now become an international question between France and Italy, a test case of whether Tunis was to fall to the French State or to the Italians. This is shown by the fact that after the Court's judgment of June 16 " it was agreed between the two Cabinets of Rome and Paris," we are told by no less an authority than the French Prime Minister, " that (the new sale) should proceed without any intervention from either Government." [1] It is also shown by the fact that Jules Ferry " attributed clearly the origin of our expedition to Tunis to the purchase of the railway by the Italians, an acquisition made by the Italian Government under cover of the Rubattino Company and in defiance of their formal promise." [2] For, on July 7, it was announced that the fortunate English company had sold its railway and its rights to the Rubattino Company for the enormous sum of 4,125,000 francs, and the Italian Government, placing a curious and narrow interpretation upon their agreement with the French, immediately obtained from the Italian Chamber an annual Government subvention of 600,000 francs for the Rubattino Company.

The Italian " victory " was, however, short-lived. The first result of it was significant, and must be given in the words of a French historian : " M. Roustan (the French consul) went to the Bey and requested him to show openly that he was well-disposed towards us by granting to our Bône-Guelma Company advantages which would be a compensation for the defeat. The Bey was intimidated and granted a concession for railways from Tunis to Bizerta, and from Tunis to Susa, and in addition the railway of the port of Tunis. These promises, which were realized after a long time and at great cost, it is true, made indifferent amends for the prejudice which the London judgment had caused us." [3] Thus the fact that an English railway company in Tunis had sold its rolling-stock and permanent way to an Italian rather than a French

[1] Jules Ferry, *Tonkin et la mère patrie*, 1890, p. 30.
[2] D'Estournelles de Constant, *op. cit.* p. 94.
[3] D'Estournelles de Constant, *op. cit.* p. 96.

company was regarded as a "defeat" for France, and, in order to retrieve that "defeat," the power of the French State was immediately set in motion, not against Italy or Britain, but against the Bey in order to extort compensation in the form of other economic privileges for Frenchmen. It is not often that the motives and methods of economic imperialism are displayed so openly or stated so ingenuously by those who approve of them.

But the forward policy of the Italian imperialists, by its vigour and "victory" in this affair of the railways, showed the French imperialists that, unless the power of the French State were employed promptly and directly, the logic of events would place, not the French, but the Italian State, in possession of Tunis. Fortunately, a good pretext for intervention was not wanting. The taxation necessary for meeting the interest due to the European creditors ensured that some of the subjects of the Bey were always in a state of anarchy and rebellion. Among these subjects were a peculiarly anarchic tribe called the Kroumirs. For the sixteen years preceding 1881 they had lived in their mountains in a condition of chronic rebellion against the government of the Bey. The Kroumirs and their mountains lay upon the borders of the French colony of Algeria. Naturally the disorders among the Kroumirs were a subject of "vital interest" to France and a menace to their peaceful rule of kindred tribes in Algeria. But for sixteen years the rebellion of the Kroumirs had pursued its uneventful course without calling for French intervention in Tunis. On July 16, 1880, the Italian company took possession of the Tunis-Goleta Railway. On August 2, 1880, the French consul in Tunis reported to M. de Freycinet, the French Minister for Foreign Affairs, that there were "secret agitations among the natives and a recrudescence of purchases of arms and gunpowder." Shortly afterwards the Governor of Algeria, in a despatch to the home government, "deplored the absolute independence of the tribes of the Tunisian frontier." Their absolute independence was not to last very long. Opportunely in this crisis a change of ministry in France placed in power Jules Ferry and Barthélemy Saint-Hilaire, the leaders of the party of the *politique coloniale*. In February, 1881, an incursion into Algeria of a band of Kroumirs was reported, and the Governor-General of Algeria mobilized forces upon the frontier. Six weeks passed; then, within twenty-four hours, four telegrams, one after the other, arrived in Paris from the Governor of Algeria. The Kroumirs had risen and were invading Algeria in force; the other tribes were threatening; the French railway and the lives of Frenchmen were in danger. The Prime Minister, Jules Ferry, and the War Minister, General Farre, came down to the Chamber and informed the Deputies that the frontier of Algeria was being threatened. A vote of credit of over $5\frac{1}{2}$ million francs was carried almost unanimously in the Chamber and the Senate, and one month later—less than ten months after the Italian company had taken possession of the Tunis-Goleta Railway—a French army had entered Tunis and captured Bizerta, and in the "treaty of peace between France and Tunis," signed at Casr-Said,[1] the Bey had agreed that his kingdom should become a protectorate of France and that "the French military authorities should occupy the points which they may deem necessary to ensure the re-establishment of order and security of the frontiers and the coast."

Such in brief is the complicated story of Tunis and the French State, of the Beys and the khaznadar, the financiers and the diplomatists, the patriots, the press, and, finally, the armed men. Through the manifold complications it is sufficiently clear that the logic of certain desires and beliefs, not of events, ensured finally that "the French military authorities should occupy the points which they may deem necessary." Those desires and beliefs had their roots in the markets of Paris, London, and Rome. There was, it is true, an "inevitable" chain of cause and effect between the speculation of French speculators, the loan of the Paris bankers, the disorder in Tunis, and the armed occupation of 1881. In this sense we may agree with the French historians that French intervention in Tunis was inevitable. But it was inevitable only because certain Frenchmen—and Italians and Englishmen—had certain economic beliefs and desires, and because the power of the French State was placed at the disposal of the men who had these beliefs and desires. We are concerned here, not with metaphysics, but with history. The metaphysician may dispute whether man's will is free, and discuss the question whether or not the Tunisian speculator and the Paris banker are free to grant or refuse a loan to a Bey. But the historian has to assume that man is a rational animal, with some choice between good and evil, truth and falsehood. For, if a French banker has no power of controlling his desire to make money out of a Tunisian Bey, and the French statesman no power of choosing between the support of the Tunisian debtor or the Parisian creditor, then history is merely the useless record of blind and random forces.

By the treaty of Casr-Said, Tunis, its Bey, and its people passed under the domination of the French State. Before leaving the subject, it is necessary to deal with certain questions which arose out of the final expedition and the events immediately connected with it. There is, first of all, the question of the intentions and international obligations of France in 1881. These were not unimportant, because disputes regarding them for many years embittered the international relations of France and Britain, and still more of France and Italy. There is no doubt that the French

[1] Often called the Treaty of Bardo.

Government gave the most explicit assurances to the world in 1880 and 1881 that their occupation of Tunis was to be purely temporary, that they had no idea at all of conquest or annexation. The military expedition was a " sacrifice " on the part of France, and all that she was asking in return was a "guarantee for her safety." We who can look back at these events, with the knowledge of what has happened in the intervening forty years, may have some difficulty in seeing exactly what the sacrifice of the French State was, or how the safety of a Great Power like France could be threatened by Sidi-Saddok. But that does not alter facts. And the fact that the French Government gave to the world these assurances of its objects and intentions can be proved by quoting a single passage from a speech of the French Prime Minister. This is what Jules Ferry said in the Chamber just before the expedition in 1881 :

> The sacrifices which France is imposing upon herself at this moment . . . would not be sufficiently compensated for by an apparent or precarious submission, or by promises quickly forgotten. Our security requires durable guarantees. It is from the Bey of Tunis that we demand them. We do not desire either his territory or his throne. In beginning this expedition the French Republic has solemnly repudiated any project of annexation, all idea of conquest ; at this moment, when the solution is approaching (le dénoument est proche), she once more makes the same declarations (elle renouvelle les mêmes déclarations).[1]

Nothing could well be more explicit than these " declarations " ; on the other hand, nothing can be more certain than that within a few months the assurances and promises were broken. France was " temporarily " occupying Tunis, and the Regency had become a French protectorate, but everyone realized that the temporary occupation would become—as it has become—permanent, and that the protectorate would develop—as it has developed—into possession.

On May 14, 1881, Lord Lyons officially protested on behalf of the British Government to M. Barthélemy Saint-Hilaire against the form of the French treaty with Tunis, on the ground that it did not conform with the declarations of Jules Ferry, who had several times publicly repudiated all idea of conquest or annexation. A quotation from a French historian, a keen supporter of the Tunisian expedition and of economic imperialism, will show most clearly the result of the protest, and will supply most admirably the necessary comment :

> M. Barthélemy Saint-Hilaire, being very far from wishing to raise a discussion on these delicate points, gave a sufficiently evasive reply.

[1] Rambaud, *Jules Ferry*, p. 293.

He glided lightly over the character of our occupation, for he knew well that on this point the opposition of England was purely formal. In colonial affairs, the words military occupation, conquest, annexation, protectorate have fundamentally the same meaning, and, if at the beginning of an expedition statesmen willingly employ euphemisms, these are simply oratorical precautions destined to reassure the parliament which votes the credits and the foreign chanceries which show signs of uneasiness.[1]

It is hardly possible, in view of these historical facts, to maintain that France in this matter internationally kept her faith with Europe. Whether we go so far as to say with Lord Lyons—and with Mr. St. Loe Strachey and the majority of English and Italian writers—that France thus committed an " act of flagrant immorality," or whether we agree with M. Jules Ferry, M. D'Estournelles de Constant, M. Darcy, and nearly all writers in France, that the action of the French Government was entirely praiseworthy and brought to France nothing but profit and glory, will depend upon whether we were born north or south of the English Channel or the Alps. But for English students of international affairs two facts connected with this side of the question are noteworthy. The French always maintained that their action with regard to Tunis was on all fours with, and more justifiable than, our action in Egypt. If the French Government had promised the world that their occupation of Tunis was to be temporary, Britain had promised the world that her occupation of Egypt would be temporary.[2] But it is more important to recognize that these two contemporaneous acts, and the mutual recriminations which arose out of them, for years maintained a state of international hostility and unrest between the two countries. An English reader notes with amazement the bitterness among French writers [3] at what they consider

[1] Darcy, *Cent Années*, p. 209.

[2] In the *Times* of January and February, 1895, there took place a most illuminating and entertaining controversy between Mr. St. Loe Strachey, editor of the *Spectator*, and an anonymous Frenchman who signed himself " A Frenchman Twenty Years Resident in London." Mr. Strachey, the Englishman, was still after fourteen years morally indignant with France at her breach of international good faith with regard to Tunis. The Frenchman replied that if France had broken her word with regard to Tunis, Britain had broken hers far more shamefully with regard to Egypt, and, if France in 1895 had no right to be in occupation of Tunis, Britain had far less right to be in Egypt. Mr. Strachey maintained that the two cases were entirely different. The Frenchman retorted (Feb. 1, 1895) in a long letter by quoting documentary evidence to support his assertions. Mr. Strachey's answer to this was to assure the Frenchman that he (Mr. Strachey) had just read through the Blue Books on Tunis, and that he (the Frenchman) was undoubtedly wrong. There the correspondence, we believe, ended.

[3] See Darcy and D'Estournelles de Constant, *op. cit.* ; see also Lémonon, *L'Europe et la politique britannique* (1912), p. 122. M. Lémonon remarks that the French Yellow Book of 1897 is very instructive as regards British policy in Tunis, for " all the Powers of Europe had renounced their capitulations, and England alone refused to allow hers to be abrogated. It was only on September

the persistent hostility of Britain to France in Tunis after 1881, a hostility which manifested itself principally in the obstinacy with which we refused for sixteen years to agree to any abrogation of our rights under the old " capitulations." The " colonial rivalry " and the international hostility which the Tunis affair engendered and fostered between Britain and France had a most pernicious effect upon the whole of the European international relations of the last twenty years of the nineteenth century. The anger and jealousy which it aroused in commercial and political circles in Italy was even more disastrous. We shall see in the following section a curious example of how Italian disappointment and hostility to France in northern Africa continued to smoulder after 1881 and to produce a chronic condition of acrid bad feeling between the two Governments. But this particular outburst of economic imperialism produced something even more definite and disastrous than bad feeling. There is no historical phenomenon more strange, and at first sight more inexplicable, than the fact that Italy, for the thirty years preceding the war of 1914, stood out in the armed peace an ally of Austria and a member of a hostile alliance against France. In Europe the traditions and aspirations of Italian policy brought her in direct opposition to Austria, and to Austria alone among European States, while within the circle of European politics and economics everything ought naturally to have tended to produce a close understanding and alliance between the two Latin nations. It was the hostility of economic imperialism, starting up and persisting in northern Africa and spreading thence to the Somali coast and Abyssinia, which cemented that unnatural union of Italy with the Germanic Powers against France. The effect which the consolidation of the great continental Powers in the two hostile alliances had upon the history of Europe was made clear to the world on the battlefields of the war. It was the desires and beliefs of economic imperialism which caused Italy to take her stand on the Austrian side in this system of armed alliances.

18, 1897, that she agreed to follow the example of the other States and sign an " arrangement " with us. Even then she took care to impose conditions which we accepted, and which the other Powers had not demanded of us : we agreed that, up to January 1, 1912, her cotton goods should not be subjected to duty in the Regency higher than 5 per cent." It is interesting to note that M. Lémonon, writing in 1912, goes on to assert that, despite this concession, Britain continually complained of French exactions in Tunis, forgetful of the fact that in no British colony could France trade freely, " having to pay duties varying according to the country and the goods imported, but rising sometimes as high as 50 per cent ad valorem." Britain also forgot the discrimination in the Canadian tariff. " In these circumstances was it not bad grace on the part of the English in 1897 to reproach us with doing in Tunis what they were doing in Canada—and what, moreover, they were hoping to do everywhere else ? " Finally, with regard to the economic question, M. Lémonon claims that our own Board of Trade statistics prove that British trade, and especially textiles, have increased since the French occupation of the Regency.

There. is one other point connected with the occupation of Tunis by France which cannot be entirely omitted. The beliefs, desires, and ideals which combine, like chemical elements, to precipitate national policies are so many and so complicated that the philosophical historian will never commit himself to the rash selection of any one series of beliefs and desires as the *only* cause of any large historical event. What I deduce from the facts given in the preceding pages is that the French occupation was not due to the logic of events nor to a desire for national security, but *mainly* to the fact that certain Frenchmen, Italians, and Englishmen had certain definite economic beliefs and desires with regard to Tunis, and that they and their Governments acted upon those beliefs and desires. We must, however, consider, as we did in the case of Algeria, the possible objection that we have taken too narrow a view of the forces which direct nations along a given line of policy. These machinations and operations of financiers, it may be argued, so minutely investigated, did, indeed, determine to some extent national action and policy ; but the particular beliefs and desires of particular classes of men are only part of larger movements of opinion, which are the real forces determining the destiny of empires. It is these larger and great natural movements and forces which may rightly be regarded as producing the logic of events. It was not an individual railway company or a handful of Paris bankers and speculators, or even the imperialist Government of Jules Ferry which sent the French State into Tunis, but the imperious demand, the almost unconscious force, of popular opinion.

In the first place, even at the risk of repetition, we must observe that the objector cannot hope in this way entirely to escape from the compulsion of the facts given in the preceding pages. Assuming for a moment that the final impulse towards the occupation of Tunis came from an irresistible movement of popular opinion, a blind instinct on the part of Frenchmen and the French nation towards expansion, yet it still remains true that this final position was caused by the economic beliefs and desires of a small class of financiers and traders, and by the fact that the Governments of France, Italy, and Britain placed the power of the European State at the disposal of this class to be used in furthering its aims.

But the objection makes it necessary to consider at some length the state of public opinion in France at the time of the expedition, the motives for intervention given by those in control of the French State, and the relation of the French Government to the French people. A little investigation into the political history of the expedition reveals a very curious situation, which is not explicable by the theory that the French Government yielded willingly or reluctantly to popular opinion. The expedition and the acquisition of Tunis by France was the work of the Government of Jules Ferry, and it has been admitted both by contemporaries and by subsequent historians that the credit or discredit attaching to the achievement belongs very largely to Jules Ferry himself. That statesman has, in his speeches and books, told us what, in his opinion, were the causes of the French seizure of Tunis. His account is not, as we shall see, always consistent, but there is one cause which he himself never assigns to his action, and that is popular opinion. We have already seen how, in giving his considered view of the event, nine years after it happened, he attributed " the origin of our expedition in Tunis to the purchase of the railway by the Italians," in other words, to the pure policy of economic imperialism. But we have also pointed out that the older, strategic, Mediterranean policy of " equilibrium " and " Balance of Power " occasionally occurred to his mind as a motive for action. The clearest explanation of this policy is given by Ferry in a speech in the Chamber of Deputies, where, six months after the expedition, he was attempting to justify his action to a rather hostile audience. " The question of Tunis," he said, " is as old as the Algerian question. It is contemporary. Can a good Frenchman contemplate the thought of leaving to any but a Power which is weak, friendly, or under our influence, the possession of territory which is, in every sense of the word, the key of our house ? "

So much for the motives assigned to the policy by those who carried it through : the history of the political events which immediately succeeded the expedition is even more illuminating. The expedition began in April, 1881. On April 4 the Government asked for the vote of credit to which reference has already been made, and Ferry himself explained the situation to the Chamber. Now, it is a most significant fact that the Government was admittedly not frank with the representatives of the French nation. The vote asked for was a small one, and insufficient for anything but a small punitive expedition. In fact, a small punitive expedition was all that the Government professed to have in view, an expedition to chastise the Kroumirs and to enforce order upon the Algerian frontier. And yet the Government itself was well aware at this time that it was undertaking, not a trumpery colonial expedition, but a great imperialist adventure, the occupation of a neighbouring country about the size of England. It knew that the vote asked for was quite inadequate for the objects which it had in view. Even the most whole-hearted supporters of the French Prime Minister admit that Ferry deceived the Chamber at the very outset of the expedition. " To-day," writes M. de Constant in 1891, " it appears clear that the Government, so firm and prudent in the conduct of the expedition which was to result in the treaty of May 12, thought that it should not or could not explain itself entirely to the Chamber, and allowed deception, more or less sincere, to be produced which became in time a formidable weapon against it in the hands of the opposition." M. de Constant admits that in April the Government knew already that "the enterprise was threatening not only the Kroumirs, but the Bey and the opponents of our legitimate influence in the Regency." The French historian's view is that these "deceptions" on the part of the Government were an error of judgment, because they played into the hands of its political opponents; but, whether we adopt this kindly view or not, we cannot avoid the conclusion that a Government which has decided upon a policy of permanent annexation, and then considers it politic to represent its initial military measures as those of a temporary and unimportant colonial expedition, can hardly be said to have been driven into a policy of imperialism, annexation, and expansion by the "imperious demand of public opinion."

The vote of credit of April 7 was passed without opposition, but within a week it became apparent that there was a large part of public opinion definitely hostile to the real policy of the Government, the policy of economic imperialism. The nature and the growth of this opposition, which eventually led to the break-up of M. Ferry's Government, provide one of the most curious stories in the history of modern imperialism in Europe. On April 11, deputies belonging to the extreme Right in the Chamber proposed an Order of the Day definitely instructing the Government to limit their action in Tunis to an expedition against the Kroumirs. The Government succeeded in defeating this motion, although M. Clemenceau, who had supported the Government on April 7, together with his party of the extreme Left, abstained. The vote and the ominous abstention were a presage of the strange combination against the Government which was finally to be fatal to it.

The early successes of the military expedition and the treaty of May 12 provoked no enthusiasm. In Parliament M. Clemenceau once more ominously abstained from supporting the Government on a vote approving the treaty. In a large part of the Paris press the whole policy of the adventure began to be attacked with the bitterest ridicule. But, as soon as the inhabitants of Tunis showed that they preferred the rule of their Bey to that of the French State, and, when it became clear that in order to subject these "Arabs" and their country to France a second and serious military campaign would have to be undertaken, the real nature and force of opposition became apparent. The Government found itself attacked from three different sides, from the anti-Republicans of the extreme Right, from the Republicans of the extreme Left, and from the small group which in France answered to the humanitarians and Little Englanders of this country. The man who placed himself at the head of this opposition was M. Clemenceau, to-day (1918)

Prime Minister in France. Now, no one can suspect M. Clemenceau of any sympathy with or leanings towards sentimental humanitarianism in national or international politics. He is not by nature or by political convention a "Little Frenchman": he is not an anti-militarist or an anti-imperialist: in fact, many of his opponents and some of his friends would say that he is in some respects a typical jingo. In his outlook upon foreign and colonial affairs he differs as widely from a man like M. Yves Guyot as, among us, Lord Curzon differs from Lord Morley. Both the motives and the grounds of his savage attack upon the Tunisian policy of Jules Ferry are, therefore, of importance.

The motives of M. Clemenceau and many of the opponents of the Government were clear. M. Clemenceau has always taken a not unnatural pleasure, and has displayed an extraordinary ability, in turning other politicians out of office. But the main motive which he and his friends had in opposing the imperialism of M. Ferry was, that they considered that colonial adventures distracted the attention and dissipated the forces of France, both of which should be concentrated upon European politics and, above all, upon the lost provinces and Germany. It is in the ground taken by M. Clemenceau for his attack upon Jules Ferry that we find the fullest revelation of the causes of the Tunisian policy and its relation to popular opinion. The full attack was not opened until November, 1881, when M. Clemenceau finally showed his hand by demanding an enquiry into the origins of the expedition. He based his demand upon the statement that the whole expedition was nothing but a *coup de Bourse*, and was due to the militancy of the French consul in Tunis, M. Roustan, and to the support given to certain commercial and financial enterprises, *e.g.* the Bône-Guelma Company, the Société marseillaise, and the Credit foncier. "In all these enterprises of which I have spoken," he said, "I see only persons who are in Paris, who wish to do business and make money on the Stock Exchange. . . . It is not for such affairs that one should have engaged in a struggle with the Bey and caused the crisis which led to the expedition. . . . In short, it is to satisfy such 'interests' that you have made war, violated the Constitution, and have placed Parliament face to face with an accomplished fact. . . . Those are the grave accusations which I make against the Ministry: you have deceived the Chamber, deceived the country." [1] Ferry's reply to these accusations is remarkable for a courage and candour not common in political contests and crises. Clemenceau had attacked the Government, alleging that it had governed its policy by the principles and objects of what in this book I have defined as economic imperialism.

[1] D'Estournelles de Constant, *op. cit.* p. 277, and Rambaud, *Jules Ferry,* p. 303.

Instead of denying the charge, Ferry admitted it, and then went on to counter-attack his opponents by defending economic imperialism and its aims in the following instructive passage :

One of two things : you must blame and reject as unworthy of occupying the attention of the Chamber and the country that which is called the economic conquest . . . or you must admit that the capitalists and companies which undertake the establishment out there of railways, banks, mortgages, and similar undertakings, are collaborators in the economic conquest, and not cut-purses who deserve the anger and contempt of Parliament. . ǫ . Among the " plutocrats," the Bône-Guelma Company has particularly attracted to itself the animosity and censure of M. Clemenceau. . . . Here at the door of Algeria, which has cost us so dear to conquer and conserve, here is a line of railway which is established running from Tunis to the Algerian frontier. . . . And it is a bad thing, a thing which is no concern of France, a stroke on the Stock Exchange (*un coup de Bourse*). I say that it is a patriotic thing ; that it is an honest thing and useful thing, and that it was a stroke of fortune for France (*coup de fortune*). . . . And I ask, in truth, if the Governor-General of Algeria, if the present Government, had let slip such an opportunity, what just reproaches would have been addressed to us, what maledictions, what accusations of want of foresight, of contempt for French interests, of weakness and bureaucratic red-tape ? I can hear the eloquent philippic of the honourable M. Clemenceau.[1]

It will be seen that, although at other times Ferry defended his seizure of Tunis on the strategic ground that it was the key to the French house in the Mediterranean, here he defends it on the grounds of imperialist economics. There are three facts which go to prove that, so far from acting thus under popular pressure, his views and policy were actually in opposition to French parliamentary and popular opinion. Ferry made this speech on November 7, 1881, and it resulted in a parliamentary crisis from which only the personal intervention of Gambetta temporarily saved the Ministry. The very next day Ferry resigned, and Gambetta himself was compelled to form a Ministry from which Ferry, Barthélemy Saint-Hilaire, and the War Minister, Farre, the three men primarily responsible for the acquisition of Tunis, were excluded.

But the current of popular opinion may be gauged from other sources. The French as a race are gifted with a peculiar sense of humour which, unlike some other nations, they allow to play even upon politics and patriotism. The solemn allegations of Ferry's Ministry before the event, that the real object of the Tunisian expedition was the chastisement of a people with the fantastic name of Kroumirs, seems to have tickled the fancy of

---

[1] Quoted in Rambaud, *op. cit.* pp. 303-304.

Paris. When the press revealed the fact that behind the turbulent Kroumirs there was concealed a struggle of financial and commercial interests, the papers, Parliament, and the public greeted every move and official statement of the Government with open and cynical derision. In Parliament it became impossible for Ministers to mention the Kroumirs at all. On October 28, 1881, a curious scene took place in the Chamber, a scene which no Englishman can picture as happening under similar circumstances in the House of Commons. The inhabitants of Tunis were at the moment " in revolt " against their new masters : the French army was struggling in a difficult campaign to add this great stretch of territory to the French Empire. The Ministry received a telegram announcing an important victory in this work of " pacification." The important position of Kairouan had been captured by the French. The Prime Minister rose in his place in the House and read out the telegram. It was greeted with roars of laughter. " The Prime Minister looked astonished ; the laughter rose louder. Some one called out : ' The joke has failed.' They laughed louder still. Kairouan took the place of the Kroumirs in being able to make Paris laugh, and the hilarity lasted several days." Again, " on November 5, when M. Ferry had the imprudence to announce that ' we have put down the insurrection at Sfax,' the Chamber roared with laughter : it laughed when he spoke of the victories of Ali-Bey, when he announced that the Tunisian army was joining battle with ours." But the joke reached its climax for Paris on November 7, when the unfortunate General Farre, Minister of War, rose to defend the Government policy. The General was a soldier rather than an orator, and the tremendous burst of laughter which greeted his first words : " Gentlemen, the war in Tunis " so disconcerted him that he became speechless and trembling. The Chamber, in fact, laughed poor General Farre into a retirement from which he did not again emerge, and in a sense it is true to say that it laughed the whole Ministry of Ferry out of office. This happened because the people of Paris and France were, on the whole, laughing with the Chamber against the Ministry. The significant point to notice, however, is that the spectacle of a Ministry talking about Kroumirs, Kairouan, Sfax, glory, and war, when they might more truthfully have talked about stocks and shares and the money market, was too much for the political and cynical humour of the population of Paris.

It is the duty of the historian to be perpetually on guard against himself, to pull himself up whenever he comes to a point where he seems to himself to have proved any fact or principle with peculiar cogency, and to say to himself : " But is it not possible that I am allowing a thesis to select the facts rather than facts to prove a thesis ? " We have reached such a point in our investigation of economic imperialism. The facts which have just been related about the

Tunisian expedition, and the state of feeling in the French Parliament and people, seem to me to be too good or too cogent to be true. I should feel happier if they were less remarkable, for nothing fills me with more mistrust than the perfect proof of any political generalization. Unfortunately, there is no doubt that these facts are facts, and, therefore, all that is possible is to follow my natural instinct, and tone down rather than exaggerate their import. In one respect it is possible, and indeed necessary, honestly to do this. It is possible to guard against any tendency to exaggerate the meaning and importance of the opposition to the policy of Ferry in Tunis. All political actions, manœuvres, and agitations are to a very large extent factitious. No one who has been within a hundred miles of a House or Member of Parliament believes that the motives behind any political campaign are simply those which appear upon its surface. The complications of parties and persons, of personal and party ends, of popular ignorance and indifference are always so great that it is never safe to draw any positive conclusion from the fact of popular opinion supporting successfully a parliamentary campaign. So, too, in this case no positive conclusion can be drawn from the fact that popular opinion supported the politicians who successfully attacked the Tunisian policy of Jules Ferry. We cannot assume that even M. Clemenceau's opposition was based mainly upon objection to the beliefs and desires of economic imperialism. With some politicians opposition, when they are out of office, becomes a habit, and with M. Clemenceau any stick is good enough with which to beat to death a dying Ministry. In the case of Tunis, there can be no doubt he objected to Germany and the Germans rather than to the French Stock Exchange and French financiers, and that the motives of his action are to be looked for in Alsace-Lorraine rather than in the ethics of finance and imperialism. And the further one goes from the centre of the parliamentary opposition, the more fluctuating and vague become the motives which determine opinion. We cannot argue from the facts given above that there was any clear appreciation among the French people in 1881 of the principles involved in the Tunisian affair, or any clear and reasoned opposition to the policy of economic imperialism.

This does not mean that our negative conclusion does not stand. The facts do prove quite conclusively that the policy of Ferry was not determined by popular opinion, that there was nothing in the nature of some great, blind, "natural," psychological force sweeping statesmen and people into a particular path of national development. The subjection of Tunis by the French State was planned and carried out by a small number of men—statesmen, soldiers, traders, and financiers ; and, in so far as there was a popular opinion, that opinion was hostile to them. This view is confirmed by the history of an incident with which the curtain may fittingly be rung down upon Tunis and its Bey.

In the Paris press the leader of the attack upon Ferry's Tunisian policy was M. Rochefort in *L'Intransigeant*. From the outset M. Rochefort had declared the expedition to be a *coup de Bourse*, " a speculation organized by some sharpers." Later on he published a series of articles containing " revelations " of the secret history of the intervention. He alleged definitely that M. Roustan, the French consul at Tunis, was associated with the ring of speculators who were operating there. The occupation of the Regency, he wrote, has put a hundred million francs into their pockets, and " there you have the reason why 50,000 of our soldiers are dying out there of sunstroke and misery." The statements against M. Roustan were so detailed and definite, and the attack was so damaging, that the Government was forced to invite the consul to take legal steps against *L'Intransigeant* for libel. In December, 1881, the case was tried, and, despite the fact that M. Barthélemy Saint-Hilaire and M. Waddington gave evidence on behalf of M. Roustan, the jury found in favour of M. Rochefort. French historians point out with some justice that little importance can be attached to the result of a political trial in Paris. Two things are, however, clear : the verdict of a jury in such a case is a very good indication of the state of popular opinion, and the jury which acquitted M. Rochefort indicated pretty clearly their opinion of the actions of the French financiers and representatives in Tunis. Secondly, although all M. Rochefort's allegations were not proved, the evidence clearly showed that the French representative was closely connected in Tunis with as disreputable a set of adventurers as ever gathered about an oriental court. What really secured M. Rochefort's acquittal was M. Roustan's intimacy with " General " Massali and the wife of " General " Massali. Massali appears to have been an ex-domestic in the service of the Bey, but he was dismissed for dishonesty or " unmentionable deeds," and fell on very evil days. He and his wife then became the intimates of the French consul. Massali's fortunes immediately began to mend, until at length he became Minister of Foreign Affairs, while at the same time Volpera, described as a " fishy stockbroker," who had once been condemned for coining, was appropriately appointed Master of the Tunisian Mint. Both these appointments were said to be due to the influence of Roustan, who also obtained for his protégé the ribbon of the Legion of Honour. The evidence for the defence was a mere welter of assertion and gossip, but out of it one fact seemed to emerge fairly clearly, namely, that the Massalis were the channels of the shadiest financial speculations and of bribery and corruption. M. Roustan's witnesses could not deny his intimacy with these people, and M. Waddington offered the feeble excuse that " General

Massali was the only official from whom the French consul could get information, and the latter had to overcome oriental and rival opposition by making use of his surroundings."

Perhaps the best comment upon this case and upon the whole story of Tunis is to be found in a contemporary judgment. *The Times*, it is perhaps unnecessary to point out, was in 1881 hostile to the French occupation of Tunis. Immediately after the Roustan-Rochefort verdict, it published on December 16 and 19 two leading articles dealing with the whole Tunisian question. It remarked that the verdict was surprising, for the evidence against Roustan would not have been sufficient in an English court to justify the charges originally made by Rochefort. No overt act of corruption had been proved. "We shall probably not be far wrong if we regard the verdict not as a direct condemnation of Roustan on all the charges . . . but . . . as evidence of the growth of a conviction . . . that French officials—even the highest—are not as careful as they should be to hold themselves aloof from questionable associates and discreditable financial transactions." Roustan was most discredited by his relations with the Massalis : his intimacy with them was worse than his use of them as tools. But Roustan's character was not the only question. The present head of the French Government and the whole policy of the late Government were implicated and brought under review. The verdict was a severe criticism on that policy with which Roustan had completely identified himself. M. Saint-Hilaire's evidence was not disinterested. He still believes in the Kroumirs as the cause of war, but his explanations are too contradictory as to the real objects of the war not to excuse the belief of the jury that there may be suppressed causes and objects " which M. Saint-Hilaire either never heard of, or has not found it convenient to explain." One of these causes is very likely to have been clandestine financial transactions, and this view is sustained by Roustan's well-known relations with " a gang of adventurers in Tunis."

Such is the verdict of *The Times* in its first article, but its second article, published three days later, is even more instructive to the student of the psychology of international imperialism. *The Times* has always been an advocate, for this country, of that policy of expansion which Jules Ferry advocated and practised so successfully in France. Its more mature reflections upon the Rochefort trial are, therefore, interesting. The leader-writer notes that a feeling of compassion for Roustan is growing in France. But " M. Roustan represents a policy which has both humiliated and embarrassed the Nation. He has to pay." " Had the Bey yielded to a vigorous display of French military strategy, . . . a jury of Paris tradesmen would have been less tender to Rochefort's venomous pen. M. Roustan and his superiors would not have been

censured for enlarging French influence by very ambiguous means."
What has annoyed the French people is that M. Ferry's policy
has not shown itself to be immediately and fully successful. A
series of diplomatic and military blunders have been committed,
for " bubbles of private French capitalists and schemes of national
ambition were mixed in inextricable confusion. . . . Thursday's
verdict . . . pronounces the condemnation of Ferry, Saint-Hilaire,
and General Farre for not weighing the cost and securing the
reward."

Then *The Times* draws a most curious moral and conclusion.
France, it says, does not see that the real blunder was not this
failure in detail, but the general consent to be encumbered with a
Tunisian protectorate on terms however favourable. It foresees
great difficulties for the French in Tunis, for they can now hardly
abandon the business, since the authority of the Bey has been
destroyed by them. But—and here, we suspect, comes the point
of this leading article—" could French susceptibility endure to
request Europe to apply to Tunis the system which . . . is restoring such prosperity to Egypt, France would be the first to profit."
Not that France need be alarmed, adds *The Times*, that Europe
wishes to share any of her responsibilities in Tunis.

Looking back over what has happened in Tunis and Egypt
since December 19, 1881, we shall hardly be surprised to find that
the French imperialists showed no eagerness to accept this disinterested suggestion of *The Times*.

CHAPTER IV

MEDITERRANEAN AFRICA : TUNIS AND TRIPOLI

I HAVE now examined in detail the history of two places upon the northern coast of Africa, Algeria and Tunis, into which the European State penetrated. The main causes and motives of these two national movements have been shown to have been widely different. A French army conquered Algeria because a few Frenchmen had beliefs and desires of the Higher Policy and Higher Strategy ; a French army conquered Tunis because a comparatively few Frenchmen believed that the power of the French State should be used to promote the economic interests of Frenchmen in Tunis. The preceding chapter has given us some idea of the nature of these economic interests. Once more we must draw the reader's attention to the vast change in the conception and aims of policy which the facts show to have taken place between 1830 and 1880. A fly-whisk and the equilibrium of the Mediterranean were the ruin of the Dey, the Kroumirs and the Paris Stock Exchange of the Bey.

In order to complete the survey of Europe's penetration of Mediterranean Africa, it would really be necessary to examine the policies which have given Egypt to Britain, Tripoli to Italy, and Morocco to France. It is only after some hesitation that I have decided not to pursue this rather heroic course. A complete study of the Mediterranean question, in so far as it is affected by the policies of European Powers on the coast of Africa, might be of very great value. It would have the artistic merit of completeness, and it might, if the investigator had sufficient patience, imagination, and skill, reveal in a wide, and at the same time limited, field the origin and effects of the desires and beliefs which have determined Mediterranean policy. But there are substantial reasons against undertaking the task in this book. Italian action in Tripoli and French action in Morocco took place so recently that only a very rash or biased historian could believe that he had a clear or complete view of facts, causes, and motives. To-day no one who was not behind the scenes of the diplomatic negotiations, or who has not access to the confidential official documents, possesses the information without which it would be impossible to give even an account as full, or a judgment as confident, as those which we have ventured upon with regard to Tunis. The difficulties which confront an investigator of the Egyptian question are of a precisely opposite kind. Even in England, where contemporary history is not written or studied, and where serious and scientific books on policy are neither written nor read, there is quite a considerable literature dealing with the Egyptian question, while in France it has formed the subject of a large library of polemic and research. The ground, therefore, has been well broken up, and in political history a ploughed field makes slow and heavy going. An adequate investigation of the British acquisition of Egypt, from the point of view of beliefs, desires, causes, motives, and effects, would require a volume to itself. The question of Policy and Egypt will not, therefore, be dealt with by me in this book, except in so far as it enters into problems which arose in Abyssinia and the valley of the Nile.

But before passing from the northern coast of Africa to other regions and other problems, there are a few facts, immediately connected with the French occupation of Tunis, which claim attention. It is difficult not to cling to the belief that man is a rational animal, rational in the sense that a burnt child fears the fire. But if this be so, one of the uses of history should be to help man as a political animal to learn by his political experiences. When in some phase of events the full circle has come round, when the passions and the shoutings have died down, and failure or success has crowned the efforts of statesmen, we are justified, if in nations and politics man is really a rational being, in pausing and asking what were the aims and objects of these movements, and how did the past fare at the hands of the future? Did success prove that the beliefs of the victors were founded upon truth, that their desires stretched out to things having stability, permanency, reality? Or did the future show their beliefs to be hallucinations and their desires the flickering of illusion?

This task of periodically testing the rationality of man in masses is one which the historian cannot avoid. It is a distasteful task for any one brought up in the hope that the gregariousness of men is higher than that of sheep and cattle. For sometimes, when the historian looks back from his pinnacle in the present over great men and great events, and sees them reduced by the remorseless action of time to a level where they are displayed below him in all their littleness and greatness, he is brought face to face with the conviction that the great political and national beliefs and desires, for which men have striven and fought and died nobly, and for which they have covered the face of the earth with death and misery, are meaningless delusions.

The reader will remember that, with some idea of thus testing the rationality of our ancestors who lived in 1830, we took a very brief survey of the light which the future threw upon the beliefs and desires of those who fought for and against the policy which gave Algeria to the French State. The survey was not encouraging. We found it difficult to discover that the future attached any meaning or importance to the Balance of Power in the Mediterranean and the equilibrium. Yet de Polignac and Charles X. had been willing to risk a European war in order to upset, and Wellington and Aberdeen in order to maintain, these meaningless delusions. It is now necessary to enquire whether the French, British, and Italian statesmen and people were shown by events in Tunis to have learnt anything from their experiences in Algeria.

The question of how the future dealt with the desires and beliefs of those who struggled over the Regency of Sidi-Saddok is not quite so simple as the similar question which we enquired into with regard to the Dey of Algeria. Jules Ferry, who at any rate ought to have known, gave, as I have shown, at different times a different account of the motives with which the French State seized the Bey's kingdom. Usually the motives are admitted to be economic : it is a movement in that " new form of colonization . . . which is adapted to peoples with a mass of disposable capital, or an excess of manufactures." The French required Tunis as a colony because " colonies are for rich countries one of the most lucrative methods of investing capital," because it was " a question of finding outlets for our industries, exports and capital." We have seen reasons for believing that French dealings with Tunis must, even before its occupation, have proved " one of the most lucrative methods of investing capital " for some Frenchmen. But in this place the economic motives cannot be further investigated, because we propose to reserve for a future chapter the whole question of the economic results of economic imperialism. Here we are concerned rather with the non-economic motives assigned to the French policy. They can scarcely be defined more clearly than in the words of the spokesman of that policy. He said once that France seized Tunis as a " compensation " or a " redemption " of some French failure. The failure of France seems to have been her failure to prevent England acquiring Cyprus. It is the old idea of the Balance of Power and the equilibrium of the Mediterranean. The fact that England extracted Cyprus from the Porte upset in the Mediterranean the delicately poised balance of power, territory, and prestige. As compensation, and in order to restore the equilibrium, France had to extract Tunis from the Bey. " Certainly the acquisition of Cyprus by England influenced our expedition to Tunis." So, with perfect consistency, Ferry could say that " the question of Tunis is as old as the Algerian question," and that Tunis was for France "the key of our house."

What we have to ask ourselves is, how the years which followed 1880 dealt with this desire for a balance and equilibrium in the Mediterranean. In the case of Algeria we found some difficulty in attaching any very clear or definite meaning to the beliefs implied in this desire for equilibrium. The same difficulty presents itself with regard to Tunis. It is not easy to see the kind of scales in which to weigh Tunis against Cyprus. We may say, perhaps, that France received "compensation," because any time during the last thirty-seven years, any Frenchman might comfort and compensate himself with the reflection that, if Englishmen ruled over Famagusta, Frenchmen ruled in Bizerta. But that clearly is not all that was embraced in the national desire interpreted by Jules Ferry. The desire was not wholly, though it was partially, for a psychological equilibrium in the national pride which Frenchmen and Englishmen could feel at possessing territory in Africa and Asia. In considering national psychology, the historian must allow for the fact that at certain times territory is still desired for its own sake by a large number of persons, who obtain a vicarious satisfaction from the knowledge that those who govern them in Paris or London are also governing millions of brown and black men in Asia and Africa. But the possession of territory is more often and more persistently sought after as a means to other things, and those things, when they are not wealth and commerce, are nearly always vaguely associated with strategy. A definite economic motive and a vague strategic motive are, in fact, continually combined in the policy of modern imperialists, and Jules Ferry was able at different times to assign economic and strategical reasons for the Tunisian expedition. The image of Tunis as the key to the house of the French people shows his conception of the strategical object. When he takes this point of view, the acquisition of Tunis by France becomes a necessity, not in order to provide compensation for Cyprus or outlets for industry and capital, but as ensuring national and military security.

The last thirty-seven years have dealt in a curious way with these strategic motives of Jules Ferry's policy. The idea that Tunis had for France a vast military importance has not died so quickly or so completely as the similar theory which once prevailed with regard to Algeria. Thus a distinguished French statesman, who has held the highest offices in France, M. Hanotaux, writing in 1892, disregarding all economic motives, lays the whole stress upon the strategic value of Tunis in the following remarkable words: "Bizerta has the Mediterranean by the throat. At this decisive point Nature herself has dug a lake which offers an area of 15,000 hectares, 1300 of which are sufficiently deep to float the largest vessels. Thus one of the finest ports in the world is situated at one of the world's most important points. It was necessary that we should have that point and that port. Such is the undertaking to which France has devoted herself for twenty years, an undertaking which she has carried through with a tenacity of purpose . . ." This remarkable statement by a man who has held the offices of Prime Minister and Foreign Minister in France deserves some attention, if only because it shows the beliefs and desires of one who was responsible for guiding the policy of a Great Power. M. Hanotaux believes that it was right for Frenchmen to " have the Mediterranean by the throat," that Tunis, through Bizerta, gives to its owner this strategic hold upon the Mediterranean, that its possession was, therefore, a necessity for the French State, and that French statesmen were, therefore, right to work tenaciously for twenty years for the acquisition of Tunis.

In the first place, it is extremely doubtful whether the " fact," upon which the whole of this policy is based, rests on any sure foundation. France has been in possession of Bizerta for thirty-seven years, and she has converted it into a great military and naval port. There is absolutely no evidence that it has given her any strategic hold upon the throat of the Mediterranean. Take the case of her strategic and international position with regard to one other Great Power—Britain. Throughout those thirty-seven years her relations with us were usually precarious, except during the last decade, and twice at least she was faced with the choice between a national " humiliation " at our hands or a resort to war. Until the present century the two States built and disposed their fleets on the assumption that the primary consideration was a naval war between them. Britain is pre-eminently the land of naval experts, and every man, woman, or child, whether expert or inexpert, has an unshakable conviction that a complete command of the sea is vital to the existence of the British Empire, that Egypt is the spinal cord of the Empire, and that for any Power to be in a position to cut our communications with India means the extinction of the Empire. But these postulates of British policy are not peculiar to Britons ; they have been held universally by the strategists, statesmen, and historians of America, Germany, and France. Admiral Mahan agrees with Bernhardi, and Bernhardi with M. Hanotaux himself, that you would only have to destroy the British command of the sea, or cut our communications with Egypt and India, and you would have destroyed the British Empire.

One would naturally expect that, if man be a rational animal, the postulates of national policy would influence a nation's policy. Euclides would not have lived as a model of rationality if, after laboriously stating the postulates of geometry, he had worked out his geometrical problems and theorems without ever again referring to or paying attention to his postulates. Yet that is precisely what, in the realm of policy, the statesmen and people of France and Britain have done, if M. Hanotaux's view of Tunis and Bizerta is the true one. France has held and fortified Bizerta, and if, thereby, she had the Mediterranean by the throat, she also has had the British Empire by the throat. Nobody in England or France seems to have been aware of this tremendous fact. No British statesman or admiral ever told the British people between 1881 and 1904 that our communications with Egypt and India were absolutely in the hands of France, or that M. Hanotaux in 1898 had us by the throat in the Mediterranean. The policy of every British Government was always based on the assumption that Cyprus, Malta, and Gibraltar were still valuable strategic possessions, and ensured our communications with Egypt and command of the sea between the Atlantic and the Suez Canal. Even in 1904, in our negotiations and secret treaty with France, our policy was controlled by the postulate that Gibraltar gave us command of the Mediterranean, that the northern coast of Morocco from the River Sebu to Melilla was of great strategic importance, and that we could not allow any Great Power to fortify it. But what was the good of worrying about the River Sebu, or Ceuta, or Melilla, about Gibraltar or Malta, if M. Delcassé really had us by the throat at Bizerta? But this blindness to a fact of paramount strategic and international importance was not confined to British statesmen: neither M. Delcassé, nor M. Hanotaux, nor any other French statesman ever acted on the assumption that they held the Mediterranean by the throat, or that the policy of Jules Ferry had given them a strategic position which allowed them to dominate our communications with Egypt. In 1898, when we issued an ultimatum to France over the Fashoda affair, it is reasonable to suppose that, if the French Cabinet had believed that they could sever the spinal cord of the British Empire, acquire Egypt from us, and cut us off from India, it would not have acquiesced in the national " humiliation," and bowed before our command of the sea. Clearly, M. Gabriel Hanotaux, Minister for Foreign Affairs at the beginning of the Fashoda incident, did not consider that he could act on the belief of M. Gabriel Hanotaux, the author of *La Paix Latine*, that " Bizerta has the Mediterranean by the throat."

The possession of Bizerta has had no strategic influence upon the national destiny or safety of France or Britain, or any other Power. That would not have been the case if it were true that Bizerta has the Mediterranean by the throat, or even if for France it were the key to her house. The reader may think, perhaps, that I am labouring and over-emphasizing a minor point, but if he has followed and has any sympathy with the purpose of this book, he will, upon reflection, revise that opinion. Here we have a clear case of beliefs and desires which have helped to determine a particular line of national policy, involving great risk of war between Great Powers, inevitably creating international hostility and unrest, and carrying with it the forcible subjection of unwilling subjects and much slaughter of Africans and Frenchmen. And yet, when the policy has succeeded and the desire—in this case for a strategic point—has been attained, we find that the very men and statesmen who held and hold the belief, who proclaimed and proclaim the desire as an adequate and rational motive for the policy, shrink from the inevitable and fatal consequences of acting upon their belief. Men who are frightened to put their beliefs and desires to the test of acting upon them confess their beliefs and desires to be delusions, and although no one who has outlived the hopes and enthusiasms of youth will believe that man can be made more rational by showing him where he has been irrational, yet the chief duty of the historian, as the recorder of man's wisdom and folly, remains to trace how time has dealt with past beliefs and desires.

Tunis and Bizerta have proved of little strategic importance to France. If we are to set down the naked truth, drawn from the history of the last forty years, we may say that Bizerta is a fine harbour for a fleet, and one of a number of strong strategic points in the Mediterranean. Only once in those forty years has the occasion arisen when it was of supreme importance that France should hold the Mediterranean by the throat strategically; but when, in 1914, the *Goeben* and *Breslau*, after bombarding towns on the coast of the French possession of Algeria—which lies, it should be remembered, west of Tunis—steamed eastwards up the whole length of the sea past Bizerta, and through the combined fleets of France and Britain, into the Dardanelles, the hold which Tunis gives to France upon the Mediterranean became apparent. That does not alter the fact that in 1881 M. Hanotaux's delusion was shared by others than Frenchmen, and that in international relations beliefs which are delusory operate no less powerfully than those which are founded in truth and reason. I cannot leave this subject without drawing attention to the effect upon the relations of France and Italy caused by the fact that the statesmen of Italy shared M. Hanotaux's delusion as to the strategic importance of Bizerta.

The previous chapter has shown that in Italy statesmen, traders, and financiers had the same beliefs and aims with regard to Tunis as similar circles in Paris. A rival policy of economic imperialism was pursued in the two countries, and the treaty of Casr-Said was recognized as a victory for Paris and a severe defeat for Rome. I have already referred to the effect of this struggle upon the orientation of Italian policy in Europe. In Africa the loss of Tunis to France turned the attention of the Italian expansionists to Tripoli and Eritrea and Abyssinia as fields for economic and political penetration. But the hostility, engendered in Tunis, continued to permeate the whole policy of the two countries, and its influence can be traced in all their relations, whether in so remote a question as that of a commercial treaty or in their subsequent meetings and collisions in northern Africa.[1]

The Italian imperialists did not acquiesce in their defeat in Tunis. They found an ardent leader in Francesco Crispi, who became Premier for the first time in 1887. The Memoirs of Crispi reveal the curious forces and ideas underlying the hostile imperialism of France and Italy. The strange combination of economic and financial aims, peculiar to modern capitalism, and of the strategic conceptions belonging to an older tradition, which we have noted as so persistent upon the Mediterranean coast of Africa, reappears in the policy of this extraordinary Prime Minister. Crispi himself surpassed most other statesmen in his ability to hold inconsistent political beliefs and ideals, and his genius for inconsistency found considerable scope in the Italian Foreign Office. A revolutionary republican, who promised that " he would free the workman from the slavery of capital," he aspired to do for the Italian capitalist what Jules Ferry had done for the French, Bismarck for the German, and Providence for the British ; and his youthful passion for freeing Italians from the empire of Austria matured as a passion for saving Africans from the empire of France and subjecting them to that of Italy. His policy, founded upon such beliefs and desires, found two different sets of material, one economic and the other strategic, for its hostility to France in the deserts of Africa.

Italy, like all the other Powers of Europe, had recognized the position created by the Treaty of Bardo. France was in possession of Tunis, and, if possession is nine-tenths of municipal law, it is more than ten-tenths of international law. The most sanguine of Italian statesmen knew that after 1881 only force of arms would ever cause the French State to loose its grip upon Tunis and Bizerta, and that, unless the Italians were prepared to fight France, the Italian Empire of their dreams would have to begin somewhere west of ancient Carthage. They were not prepared to fight France, and they therefore, as other men have done before and since, bowed before a *fait accompli*. But it has been remarked that part of the art of statesmanship consists in bowing before the *fait accompli* with mental reservations, and the international position in Africa left ample scope for the practice of the art. France

---

[1] According to Singer, *Geschichte des Dreibundes*, p. 100, when the Triple Alliance was renewed in 1891, Italy bound herself in case of war to send, on Germany's demand, two army corps to invade France.

was still living under the shadow of the Treaty of Frankfort, and Bismarck had more than once brutally reminded her of the fact. The rulers of new Germany and the possessors of the victorious Prussian army, when they wanted an African empire in 1884, could afford to take it with a strong and steady hand and clearly warn off all other European trespassers. The French had to step delicately in a more devious path to imperialism. This explains the readiness of the French Cabinet in 1881 to allow their position in Tunis to remain in part undefined. They were content with the accomplished fact of occupation, and were extremely anxious to avoid any kind of international complication. They therefore practised a cautious imperialism, and showed themselves very accommodating to European rivals and competitors. It was this enforced hesitation on the part of France which afforded a loophole to the mental reservations of Italian policy.

The determination of the French Ministry of 1881 not to allow their new position in Tunis to become an "international question" showed itself in two ways. The French Government, in the first place, immediately after the signature of the Treaty of Bardo, formally agreed that all the Conventions then existing between Tunis and foreign Powers should be maintained and respected.[1] The value of this concession was primarily economic, for it covered those economic privileges which the subjects of the different European States enjoyed in Tunis under the "capitulations," and which Europeans would never claim or expect to enjoy in the territory of any European State. Since France was a European State, these privileges naturally became, as soon as she had conceded them, extremely irksome to her, and, as her position became consolidated in Tunis, she grew more and more determined to escape from the commercial agreements which she had inherited from that victim of economic imperialism, Sidi-Saddok. On page 103 mention has been made of the bitterness which British policy roused in France by refusing for sixteen years to waive any rights to economic privileges : the same policy of clinging to the capitulations was practised for many years, with similar results, by Italy.

This was Italy's first loophole for mental reservation and economic hostility. But Crispi, soon after his accession to power, discovered another. To the east of Tunis lay Tripoli, another Regency nominally under the Porte and ruled by another Bey. Tripoli at first sight is a country which might seem to have few

---

[1] See Hertslet, *The Map of Africa by Treaty*, 1894 (1st edit.), pp. 910 and 548. The agreement was contained in an Exchange of Notes between the Governments, but it only confirmed the fourth article of the Treaty of Bardo itself, which runs : "The Government of the French Republic guarantees the execution of the Treaties at present existing between the Government of the Regency and the different European Powers."

attractions, even for the most imperialist of imperialists : it consists almost entirely of sand and desert, and some notion of its barren poverty may be derived from the fact that, whereas Egypt can support twenty-eight inhabitants per square mile, Tunis thirty-nine, Algeria (even including the vast stretch of desert in the south) five, and Morocco thirty-six, the 900,000 square miles of Tripoli contain a population of 1,100,000, or one inhabitant to the square mile. A country and population of this nature would not appear to offer a very fruitful soil for economic exploitation, and, even strategically, the coast has no attraction to compare with that of Tunis and Bizerta. Somewhere, some day, it may be possible to construct a great harbour upon this barren stretch of coast, but no one has ever been able to delude himself into believing that Tripoli could hold the Mediterranean by the throat, or could ever be a strategic base of importance. But national beliefs and desires, as the reader has probably now realized, are not controlled or determined by facts and statistics, and Crispi and the Italian imperialists made up their minds that if Tunis was lost to them they would find at least some compensation and consolation in Tripoli.

Crispi's policy in Mediterranean Africa consisted, therefore, in earmarking Tripoli for Italy, and the first step which he had to attend to was to keep the French out of it, for the French economic and strategic imperialists were by no means content with having added Tunis to Algeria, and were now turning their attention to the task of adding Tripoli to Tunis. The situation as it developed about the year 1890 gave rise to some curious diplomatic and military incidents, which throw a little light upon the working of economic imperialism.

About the year 1890 the " hinterland " theory, as a principle of policy to be applied among European States to their possessions and objects in Africa, had already become fashionable. The principle was never clearly defined, and led to much controversy and manoeuvring, but, roughly, it was accepted as meaning that a European State in possession of territory upon the coast of Africa acquired some prescriptive right to that territory in the interior lying immediately behind its possessions. Statesmen and strategists and traders found a fruitful source for international disputes in this principle of policy ; for instance, a rich empire might be included in or excluded from the possessions of a European State according as the boundary of the hinterland was taken to be formed by a straight line drawn at right angles to the coast, or by a line drawn merely as an extension of the existing boundary of the coastal territory actually occupied. Again, the fact that coastal territory was everywhere occupied by a number of different States meant that, somewhere in the interior of Africa, there must be a number of points where the different hinterlands would meet, and no principle was laid down for determining these points. The French imperialists were among the first to see the possibilities in this theory of hinterlands. By 1890 France was in possession of a solid block of coastal territory on the Mediterranean and of five distinct blocks of territory on the Atlantic coast in Senegal, Guinea, the Ivory Coast, the Slave Coast, and Gabun. Her imperialists saw that, by prolonging the hinterlands of all these possessions until they met at a point in the Sahara, an immense and continuous empire, uniting the Congo with the Upper Niger and both with the Mediterranean, would be won for France. The pivot of this scheme was Lake Chad, for, unless access for the French was obtained from the Congo and Ubanghi to, at any rate, the northern shore of Lake Chad, their southern possessions on the Congo would be cut off from their northern possessions on the Mediterranean.

Lake Chad and the Congo may seem at first sight to the reader very remotely connected with Italian aspirations in Tripoli, and, unless he reads what follows with the hinterland theory in his mind and a map of Africa open before his eyes, I shall fail to make the connection plain to him. Crispi and his followers, with an optimism characteristic of economic imperialism, soon found an economic value in the sands of Tripoli. The great economic importance of Tripoli, they said, lies in the fact that it contains the caravan route for trade between Lake Chad and the Mediterranean. This route starts from Tripoli and runs thence to the oases of Ghadames and Ghat; from Ghat it divides into two, one running to Agades and northern Nigeria, the other through Bilma to Lake Chad (see map, p. 52). Anyone who considered only a map of Africa and the statistics of world commerce might be astonished to find that the caravan trade between Lake Chad and Tripoli should appear to have importance in the eyes of Italian statesmen and traders. The total foreign trade of Italy at the end of the nineteenth century was over £100,000,000 per annum, that of Tripoli was under £800,000. And while the whole foreign trade of Tripoli in 1899, for instance, amounted only to £795,000, 37 per cent of it fell to Great Britain, 18 per cent to France, and less than 6 per cent to Italy.[1] These figures show the kind of claim which Italian industry and commerce had upon Tripoli; the economic importance of this African territory to

---

[1] The fact that British trade with Tripoli so enormously exceeded Italian was all the more remarkable when it is remembered that the carrying trade between this part of Africa and Europe had, owing to Government subsidies, fallen to a very large extent into the hands of Italian shipping lines. At one time British shipping in the port of Tripoli surpassed that of all other nationalities put together, but by 1898 about 50 per cent of the shipping cleared in that port was Italian, and only about 18 per cent British. See *Diplomatic and Consular Reports*, Annual Series, No. 2453. Trade of Tripoli for the Year 1899.

Italy can be seen even more clearly in the following figures for the year 1898:

Total Italian exports	. . . .	£48,142,770
Italian exports to Tripoli	. . .	25,000
Total Italian imports	. . . .	56,533,412
Italian imports from Tripoli	. . .	8,000

And these figures, it should be noted, refer to the *total* trade of Tripoli; what proportion of it was derived from the Saharan and Sudan caravan trade can only be a subject of conjecture. Taking, however, 1898 and 1899 as typical years, we can say with certainty that the caravan trade with the Nigerian district, Bornu, and Lake Chad contributed nothing to the total foreign or internal trade of Tripoli, for, according to the British consul, it had ceased, and "no hopes are entertained here of its (Bornu) being reopened to trade." [1] This is, perhaps, not very surprising to anyone who examines a map of Africa, for he will see that, whereas Bornu and Lake Chad are separated from the Gulf of Guinea by only about 700 miles, and that trade passing in that direction can make use of the Rivers Benue and Niger, they are separated from Tripoli by about 1300 miles of the Desert of Sahara, which is the home of nomad tribes who "are aggressively hostile, and attack caravans which may be moving along without a sufficiently large and well-armed escort to defend them." [1]

But Italian and French statesmen, generals, and traders looked with longing eyes upon the Desert of Sahara and the exiguous caravans which occasionally and painfully struggled across 1300 miles of sand in order to increase Italian exports and imports by the total sum of about £30,000 a year. Crispi, the Italian Foreign Office, and Italian financial and commercial circles alleged that, as soon as France had obtained possession of Tunis, her Government set in motion a carefully thought out scheme for cutting off Tripoli from its hinterland, for annexing that hinterland to Tunis and the French African Empire, and thus obtaining control of the commerce between Tripoli and the interior, and ultimately becoming masters of Tripoli itself. According to the Italians, in this scheme, so typical of economic imperialism, the French Government pursued those methods of which rival empires always accuse one another in uncivilized regions. After 1881, it was said, the French continually fomented disturbances among the tribes on the south-eastern frontier of Tunis, and then, by interfering to put down the disturbances which they had themselves fomented, gradually pushed back the frontier of Tripoli to the east and worked round the southern frontier of Tripoli in order to get possession of its hinterland. The immediate goal of the French was the occupation of

[1] *Diplomatic and Consular Report*, No. 2453, p. 4.

Ghadames and Ghat, for, once they held these two places, they would have the whole caravan trade in their power and could divert it, whenever they chose, from Tripoli to Tunis.

The reader who desires to study the details of the Italian allegations as to French encroachment upon Tripoli between 1881 and 1890 will find them in the *Memoirs of Francesco Crispi.*[1] The official documents published in those *Memoirs* also enable us to obtain a clear view of the beliefs and desires of eminent Frenchmen with regard to Tunis and Tripoli. On August 5, 1890, the French and British Governments signed two important declarations with regard to their possessions and spheres of influence in Africa.[2] This was the year of African bargains among the Great Powers of Europe, and the Anglo-French agreement consisted mainly in a bargain whereby France recognized our Protectorate over Zanzibar in exchange for our recognition of her Protectorate over Madagascar. But the French statesmen induced Lord Salisbury, in addition to recognizing the French Protectorate over Madagascar, to throw in a somewhat vague French sphere of influence in Central Africa. The second clause of the second declaration provided that "the Government of Her Britannic Majesty recognizes the sphere of influence of France to the south of her Mediterranean possessions, up to a line from Saye on the Niger to Barruwa on Lake Chad. . . ." Reference to the map will show that this clause gave to France a sphere of influence of enormous extent but of the vaguest outline. The southern boundary is clearly defined by the line drawn from the Niger at Saye to Lake Chad at Barruwa, and was of great importance, because it ensured for France access to the shores of Lake Chad, the pivot, as I have pointed out, of her imperialist policy in this part of Africa. But the northern boundary is defined merely as " her Mediterranean Possessions," so that the eastern and western boundaries of this gigantic sphere of influence, about ten times the size of the United Kingdom, would depend upon what, in fact, were taken to be the eastern and western boundaries of the French Mediterranean Possessions. Whether Ghadames and Ghat and the caravan trade between Lake Chad and Tripoli were included in the French sphere of influence depended upon whether Tunis was included in " her Mediterranean Possessions," and also upon an agreement as to the boundary line between Tunis and Tripoli. In fact, however, the question of French possession of Tunis was left doubtful, and the position of the Tunisian-Tripolitan frontier was a matter of vehement dispute. According to the Italians, part of the consideration for French recognition of our

[1] *The Memoirs of Francesco Crispi*, compiled by Thomas Palamenghi-Crispi, translated by Mary Prichard-Agnetti, 1914, vol. iii. pp. 20-31.
[2] The agreement was contained in two declarations, the first being a recognition by France of the British Protectorate over Zanzibar, and the second the recognition by Britain of the French Protectorate over Madagascar.

Protectorate over Zanzibar was to have been a recognition by Lord Salisbury of French claims in Tunis, and this concession was not included in the agreement only because Crispi, "supported by the Chanceries of Berlin and Vienna, despatched an earnest remonstrance to London."

A very little study of international treaties will reveal a curious characteristic of statesmen and diplomacy. It seems to be recognized that, if two Governments ask a third to make two different and contradictory promises or contracts, it is safe for the latter to compromise by making a promise in such vague terms that it can be interpreted in either way according to the desire of the interpreter. In this case France desired Britain to promise— and Italy desired her not to promise—certain concessions and recognitions in Tunis. Lord Salisbury, yielding to the earnest remonstrance of Crispi, then made a promise, enshrined in the agreement of 1890, in terms so vague that it was extremely doubtful whether he had or had not conceded what France desired with regard to Tunis. French statesmen naturally acted on the assumption that what they had asked for had been granted, and Crispi and the Italian statesmen were soon complaining that, despite their "earnest remonstrance," all material concessions had been made to France.

In 1890 Crispi directed General Luchino Dal Verme to draw up a memorial on the Tripolitan question, and the document, which was printed in Crispi's *Memoirs*, is most enlightening. The General begins by stating that France is pursuing a policy of determined and persistent encroachment upon the western and south-western frontier of Tripoli. "The Anglo-French agreement of August 5, 1890," he proceeds, "while appearing to respect the Tripolitan *Hinterland*, in reality leaves France free to act as she may see fit in the regions of the east, and this to the serious detriment of the power which rules in Tripolitania." The Anglo-French agreement is "a menace to the oasis of Gadames," and now France has "at the expense of Tripoli, arbitrarily moved the frontier of the Tunisian Regency farther eastwards for the purpose of drawing nearer to the capital, surrounding the defences on the plateau to the south-west, and cutting off Gadames." The General then explains the objects of this French policy and its menace to Italian policy, and in this explanation the reader will see again appear precisely that combination of economic and strategic beliefs and desires which dominated the policy of Frenchmen and Italians with regard to events in Tunis before 1881. "This work of gradual destruction," he writes, "was begun by the French as soon as they set foot in Tunisia, and is still going on. To-day their aim is Gadames. Up to the present the region has merely been drawn within the circle of French commerce, but it will of necessity fall into the hands of France at last, and with it will go the oases of Derji and Sinaun, and the distant region of Rhat. But how about the balance of power in the Mediterranean when France shall have become arbiter of the entire *Hinterland* of Tripoli, mistress of the great caravan ways from Tsad to Tripoli, and, consequently, of all the commerce of that vast African basin ? Turkish domination, reduced to the coast region, will become, little by little, but a semblance of rule in Tripoli itself, so that, on the first favourable occasion, that country will become the easy prey of the Power which already presses her on the west and south, and will end by dominating her entirely. Thus the uninterrupted dominion of France will stretch from the Atlantic and the Mediterranean to Lake Tsad, across a vast territory amounting in area to nearly one-third of the whole continent of Africa. Mistress of the coast from Morocco to Egypt, she will have upset the balance of power in the Mediterranean ; once mistress of the vast country between the two seas and the central basin of the Tsad she will eventually reach Uadai, Darfur, and the Nile Valley." [1]

The General's beliefs and desires and fears are, it will be noted, partly economic and partly strategic : they were all adopted and endorsed, as we shall show, by Crispi and the Italian Government. In the first place he represents the aim of French policy as being " the great caravan ways from Tsad to Tripoli," and " all the commerce of that vast African basin." The General, presumably, had not studied the economic statistics of Tripoli, or he would have learned that all the commerce of these great caravan ways left Tripoli with a foreign trade of only a few hundred thousand pounds. Presumably, too, he had not studied the map of Africa, otherwise he could hardly have imagined that the sole outlet for " all the commerce of that vast African basin " of the Chad was the caravan route across the Desert of Sahara to Tripoli. A General may be excused for holding hazy ideas of economics and commerce, and perhaps geography, for it has been recorded of more than one general that they were unable to understand maps ; but, when a general writes about strategy, his opinion has to be treated with some respect. Yet the layman will find some difficulty in following General Dal Verme's strategical nightmare of French domination. Like Wellington in 1830 and Ferry in 1880, he is dreaming dreams and seeing visions of the Balance of Power and the equilibrium in the Mediterranean. The more one learns of this Balance of Power, the more extraordinary a phenomenon it seems to be. To the horror of Wellington and other statesmen who were not Frenchmen, it was upset and destroyed by the French in 1830. Nothing happened, and, despite its destruction in 1830, it still existed to be destroyed and upset again by the French in 1881. And yet,

[1] *Crispi's Memoirs*, vol. iii. p. 43.

less than ten years later, it is still found to be existing in the nightmare of the Italian General, who is horrified by the consequences which will follow if the French—who destroyed the Balance of Power in the Mediterranean in 1830 by seizing Algeria, and in 1881 by occupying Tunis—are allowed once more to destroy the indestructible by seizing Tripoli in 1890.

But such considerations are nothing in the metaphysics of true belief. The Italian Government, adopting the outlook and theories of General Dal Verme, began to work hard in London, Constantinople, and Paris to preserve the Balance of Power in the Mediterranean, and prevent the commerce of the Desert of Sahara falling into the hands of France. In Constantinople their efforts were so far successful that the Porte drew the attention of the French and British Governments to " His Imperial Majesty the Sultan's rights to the south of the provinces forming his Tripolitan possessions." But the Turks have learned by bitter experience that the integrity of the Ottoman Empire is endangered even more by a European State which is over-zealous to protect it than by one which openly attacks it. Crispi's solicitude for Tripoli began to excite suspicion at Constantinople that Italy was defending Tripoli against the French for the sake, not of Turkey, but of Italy ; and towards the end of 1890 the Sultan was directing his ambassadors at Rome and Berlin to ascertain whether there was any truth in the report that " Italy is preparing a military expedition " against His Imperial Majesty the Sultan's Tripolitan possessions. The French press and agents of the French Government did their best to fan Turkish suspicions, and an acute situation began to develop between the two Latin Powers. Tension increased when the German Government was induced to support Italy, rather cautiously in Paris and rather mysteriously in London. The German-Italian manœuvres in Downing Street are mysterious, partly because it is only by piecing together little bits of information that we can get a glimpse of what Crispi was trying to get out of Lord Salisbury. Apparently the British Cabinet, which had only just succeeded in concluding an agreement with France which settled various African questions, was not anxious to embroil itself with Paris over the wilderness of the Sahara or even over Tripoli. Crispi was endeavouring to get Lord Salisbury to support his protests against French action on the Tripolitan frontier. In November, 1890, the Italian Premier met Caprivi, the German Chancellor, at Milan, and the question of the renewal of the Triple Alliance—which was to expire early in 1892—was discussed between them. The French press asserted that the two statesmen had also come to an agreement for " the occupation of Tripoli by Italy." Baron Marschall von Bieberstein gave an official denial of this rumour to the Turkish representative at Berlin, assuring him that " the Chancellor derived the best of impressions from his interview with Signor Crispi," and that "the Sublime Porte need attach no importance to lying rumours concerning Tripoli, as the name of that province of the Ottoman Empire was not once mentioned during the interview." However that may be, we know from Crispi's diary that he and Caprivi did discuss Bizerta and "conditions in the Mediterranean," and that the German Chancellor was in favour of deferring a formal protest against French action with regard to Bizerta, at any rate until "April, when the army rifles are to be changed."[1] A discussion of Bizerta and conditions in the Mediterranean must have come perilously near to a discussion of Tripoli and the Balance of Power in the Mediterranean, and it is not altogether surprising to find that in January, 1891, Count Hatzfeld, the German Ambassador in London, had "received instructions to discuss the matter with Lord Salisbury, who is watching the action of the Republic in these regions (Tripoli) with the keenest attention, but who does not feel that the time has arrived to assume a more determined attitude."[2]

That the pressure exerted upon Lord Salisbury from Rome and Berlin was not directed merely to a vague request for a vague diplomatic support may be inferred from two isolated sources. A despatch from General Menabrea, the Italian Ambassador in Paris, reveals to us the immediate action which the Italians were urging upon the British Cabinet. He discusses a "proposed Turkish occupation" of Ghadames and Ghat, on the assumption that "it is absolutely essential that the two oases, and especially Ghadames, be preserved from falling into the hands of the French."[3] The Sultan is to send troops to protect these regions, and "a small garrison would be sufficient," for "the sight of the Ottoman flag would suffice to check those vain aspirations which are attributed to France. The Turkish troops, however, should be sufficiently numerous to resist possible attacks by followers of the Mahdi." The General then goes on to reveal the part which Italy is to ask Britain to play in Ghadames : the British Government is to subsidize the Turkish troops who are to oppose the French imperialist aspirations in Tripoli and the Sudan. "The all-important interests," he explains, "which she has at stake make it even more necessary for England than for Italy to prevent Sudanese trade from being monopolized by a Power which already holds a large share of the African coast on the Mediterranean. I am, therefore, of opinion that England more especially, and with her Italy, should

---

[1] *Crispi's Memoirs*, vol. iii. p. 49.
[2] *Ibid.* p. 10.
[3] Despatch of the Italian Ambassador in Berlin, January 21, 1891. See *Crispi's Memoirs*, vol. iii. p. 63.

in some way further the proposed Turkish occupation, if necessary, by furnishing a subsidy for its maintenance." [1]

It is not, perhaps, surprising that Lord Salisbury hesitated to lend himself to this Italian proposal. The following fact, however, seems to show that Crispi had succeeded in getting his German ally to support the proposal in London. On March 26, 1918, Sir Valentine Chirol wrote a letter to *The Times*, the object of which was to expose the devious methods of German diplomacy. He relates a personal experience of the Berlin Foreign Office in the following words, and, although he gives no precise dates or details, internal evidence makes it extremely probable, as the reader will see, that the negotiations to which he refers were those of 1890 and 1891 regarding the Tripolitan frontier and the caravan trade of the Sudan. "I gained," he writes, "an insight into the complex machinery of German diplomacy when I went to Berlin as correspondent of *The Times* in the early years of the present Emperor's reign, through Baron Holstein. . . . It was in connection with Anglo-French relations that I had my first difference with Baron Holstein, who pressed me to support an appeal to Downing Street for closer co-operation with the Italians in the Soudan, though, in the form then contemplated by Germany, it was chiefly calculated and doubtless intended to irritate French susceptibilities. To such a course I saw no reason to lend my support, and, as I happened to know that Count Hatzfeld fully understood and appreciated the reluctance of our Foreign Office to aggravate French opposition to our occupation of the Nile Valley, I told Baron Holstein frankly that I could not reconcile his suggestions with the views held by his Ambassador in London." [2]

These schemes and machinations did not help to relieve the tension between France and Italy. In the last days of 1890 the Italian Ambassador in Paris had an interview with Monsieur Ribot, the Minister of Foreign Affairs, which he described to his Government as "a heated, not to say violent, one!" Monsieur Ribot made some "heated remarks" about Crispi's attitude and

---

[1] Despatch of the Italian Ambassador at Paris to the Prime Minister, dated January 13, 1891. See *Crispi's Memoirs*, p. 59.

[2] Baron Holstein was, as Sir Valentine Chirol remarks, "known as the *Éminence Grise* of the German Foreign Office from the commanding influence he wielded without the slightest ostentation of power." The reader will probably be interested to know Baron Holstein's reply to Sir Valentine Chirol, though it is hardly relevant to my purpose in quoting the letter : "Baron Holstein countered me by proceeding, without the slightest hesitation, to read me portions of a letter from Count Metternich (German Councillor of Embassy in London), written on very different lines from the Ambassador's, and with little concealment of his contempt for his chief." The most interesting revelation in Sir Valentine Chirol's letter is perhaps one of which he himself appears to be unconscious : it is the extraordinary influence upon " Downing Street" which both he and Baron Holstein assume as a matter of course to lie in the hands of a newspaper correspondent in Berlin.

accusations, and General Menabrea, who had " listened with calm attention," formally informed the French Minister that " any Power . . . attempting to appropriate Tripolitania must be prepared to encounter serious opposition on the part of other Powers which have interests to protect." At the same time the Italian representative informed his own Government that, in his opinion, Italy should " prepare to oppose the establishment of French domination in Tripolitania by every means at our disposal, which establishment might possibly mean *Finis Italiae*, at least as a maritime power of the first class."

The tension was, however, suddenly relieved, for in the latter half of January, 1891, Crispi, owing to a ministerial crisis, went out of office, and under his successors for three years the Italian Government appeared to have forgotten Tripoli. But in 1894 Crispi returned to power, and the oases of Ghadames and Ghat again began to acquire an international importance. Although he now " found England indifferent and Germany and Austria unenthusiastic," he at once began to renew his protests against French action. He still hoped to save the oases and the caravan trade, and with this end in view he had two memoranda prepared by the Colonial Department of the Ministry of Foreign Affairs. These official documents are of some interest. In the first we read that " the oases of Ghadames and Ghat are situated on the caravan way which, starting from Tripoli, divides into two branches, one leading past Agades to Sokoto, the other past Bilma to Lake Tsad. As Tripoli's prosperity depends entirely upon trade, deprived of her caravan ways which lead into Sokoto, Bornu, Baghirmi, and Wadai, Tripoli might well be compared to an empty jewel-case." It will be seen that the Italian Foreign Office in 1894 shared General Dal Verme's extraordinary delusions as to the economic value of Tripolitan trade. The jewel-case of Tripoli, even when it was full, contained the minutest of economic jewels, and Italy's share in this minute jewel was £30,000 worth of trade, which was equal to about ·002 of the total foreign trade of Italy.

The second memorandum deals with a point of some interest to the student of economic imperialism. A whole chapter in the history of economic imperialism could be written on the subject of maps. It is a frequent custom among those inhabitants of a European State who covet the territory or kingdoms of uncivilized peoples to prepare and distribute a map, in which the coveted kingdoms are coloured in such a way as to indicate that they are already under the dominion of the European State. Whether these maps are intended to lay the foundations of a legal claim to dominion, or whether they serve to whet and encourage the imperial appetites of European populations, is doubtful, but their manufacture and distribution have been a frequent subject of mutual recrimination among European nations. The second memorandum of the Italian Foreign Office is devoted entirely to protesting against a map of this kind. A map had recently been published, it was alleged by order of the French Colonial Office, for distribution among members of the French Chamber of Deputies. It was called "Carte générale des possessions françaises en Afrique au premier janvier, 1895," and it indicated, by two different shades of pink, (1) French possessions under direct protectorate and (2) the French zone of political influence. The impression given from this map to French members of Parliament would have been that the predominant tint of Africa was pink, and therefore French, and the Italian Foreign Office devoted many pages to its iniquities. But what infuriated the Italians more than anything else was that the French Colonial Office had made "waves of delicate pink . . . wash around the oases of Ghadames and Ghat."

Crispi was determined that the oases of Ghadames and Ghat should remain white, or whatever other colour signified Turkish dominion, until perhaps the time came when they might be coloured green by Italy. The tension between France and Italy which had characterized his previous period of office grew again in 1895, and matters did not improve when, in August of that year, France, in the name of the Bey, denounced the commercial treaty which had been concluded twenty-seven years before between Italy and Tunis, and which ensured to Italians the economic privileges of the capitulations. He seems to have entertained the idea of bartering these privileges for the independence of the Tripolitan Hinterland and the oases ; but once more at the critical moment his ministry fell, and his successors abandoned to France both Italian rights in Tunis and Turkish rights in Ghadames.

Thus ended the first act in a curious incident of imperialism. It invites reflection. If the reader will turn to a map of Africa, he will see that the enormous French empire of the Sahara and Sudan stretches right across the hinterland of Tripoli. In the north the Tripolitan frontier on the west reaches as far as longitude 8° east of Greenwich, and on the east longitude 25°; but already at Ghadames the French make a great bite into the hinterland, enclosing in their empire Ghat, which is at longitude 10° east of Greenwich, and then again, farther south, making another great bite almost up to longitude 25° and embracing Tibesti, Borku, and Wadai. It must, therefore, be admitted that the allegations of Crispi and the Italians as to French designs have been justified. France has paid no respect to the doctrine of the hinterland in the Sahara and Sudan. And there is ample proof that the Italians were correct when, between 1889 and 1895, they complained that the French State was carrying through with great method and deliberation this policy of imperialist encroachment from economic and strategic motives. The French themselves now admit the fact. We need only refer here for proof to two authors of the highest authority. Monsieur Gabriel Hanotaux, the statesman, writing in 1896 of French exploration, particularly in the territory now forming this Saharan and Sudanese empire, says : [1] " In the last years it has acquired a character of method and practical activity, due in great measure—there is no use concealing the fact— to the intervention of the State. In these matters the institution of ' scientific missions ' has played an important part." He then goes on to relate how, about the year 1889, the " gigantic plan " of Savorgnan de Brazza—the " idea of uniting our colony of equatorial Africa with those of the Mediterranean and west coasts "— was consciously adopted as a practical policy by certain classes in France. The French commercial classes, the recently created *Comité de l'Afrique française*, the Colonial Administration under the vigorous direction of M. Etienne, " the flower of our young men, particularly our military young men," who " offered themselves with a smile on their lips," all these united in " a great effort which had as its aim the definite joining up of all our colonies by a system of simultaneous exploration." And then he briefly relates the amazing story of that series of " scientific missions," led out into the African wildernesses and deserts by " the military young men with a smile on their lips," from Senegal and Dahomey and the Congo and the Mediterranean, to cross and recross from every direction the most pitiless regions of Africa—those " scientific missions " of Binger and Monteil, of the great de Brazza himself, and of Mizon, who died with a smile on his lips in Baghirmi, of Maistre, Dybowski, Decazes, Ballay, Liotard, d'Uzès, Julien, Bonnier, Decœur, Toutée, Brosselard-Faidherbe, Ballot, Hourst, Beau and Marchand, missions which scientifically consolidated a French empire in Africa greater in extent of territory than the whole continent of Europe.

M. Hanotaux's evidence is valuable as being that of a practical statesman. It is confirmed by so high an academic authority on the history of diplomacy and policy as M. Edouard Driault. In his great work, *La Question d'Orient*, he states that " in 1892 France denounced the commercial treaties which under the Second Empire she had signed with the majority of European nations, and organized her customs upon the lines of the most rigorous protectionism : a great number of markets was thus closed to her products, and it became necessary to secure other outlets (*d'autres débouchés*) " ; consequently " colonial expansion became for her an economic and social necessity of the first importance." " That is why," Monsieur Driault continues, " she has made since, in western Africa, a tremendous effort, according to a very concise plan,

[1] *Fachoda*, by G. Hanotaux, 1909, p. 60.

applied with a persistency which is very remarkable and of indisputable grandeur. She has clearly aimed at the empire of northern Africa." And then, like M. Hanotaux, M. Driault runs through the long and heroic list of " scientific missions." [1]

This is the same determined *politique coloniale* of which, on page 25, we quoted Monsieur Fallot's judgment that " it is impossible not to recognize in it the execution of a political plan carefully studied, applied methodically in the face of innumerable difficulties, and finally realized with complete success." It gave to France an imperial Mittel-Afrika which to-day is the dream of German imperialists, a French Mittel-Afrika which, between 1890 and 1900, roused in many Englishmen and Italians exactly those feelings of exasperation and fear which in 1918 the German Mittel-Afrika inspires in Italians, Englishmen, and Frenchmen. It gave her, among other things, command of the oases of Ghadames and Ghat and of the caravan ways, and of "all the commerce of that vast African basin." The jewel-case of Tripoli was empty, but, empty or full, it was still desired by Italy. Consequently, when the direction of French policy came into the hands of M. Delcassé, who saw that his country had more to gain from African expansion west of Algiers than east of Tunis, a way was opened to an arrangement and compromise between the imperialist aspirations of France and Italy. The diplomatic conversations of 1900–1902 led to the Franco-Italian agreement by which Italy was given a free hand in Tripoli and Cyrenaica, and France a free hand in Morocco. Both countries exercised their licence of conquest. On September 27, 1911, Italy declared war on the Ottoman Empire and began her conquest of the Arabs of Tripoli, an event which, as the Turkish Grand Vizier is said to have prophesied, led directly, through a chain of violence and war in Eastern Europe, to the war of 1914.[2]

It is noteworthy that, when Italy had acquired Tripoli and France Morocco, the imperialists of neither country were satisfied. Signor Palamenghi-Crispi, writing in 1914 of the Franco-Italian agreement, remarks that " the surrender of Morocco to the influence of France alone was a severe blow to Italian interests, and the future of our Mediterranean policy was seriously compromised by it. France, over-powerful upon the sea which surrounds us, is a permanent menace to us." The policy of his father, he says, had been based upon the idea that Italy should acquire Tripoli " in compensation for the expansion France had already achieved by her occupation of Tunisia." The result of the agreement of 1902

---

[1] *La Question d'Orient*, by E. Driault, 7th edit., 1917, p. 372.

[2] See Gibbons, *The New Map of Europe*, p. 247, where the Grand Vizier is represented as having said in conversation : "If she (Italy) does attack us, all Europe will be eventually drawn into the bloodiest struggle of history—a struggle that has always been certain to follow the destruction of the integrity of the Ottoman Empire."

was that M. Delcassé gained for France the rich land of Morocco in exchange for Tripoli, where she had no rights at all, and of which the "commercial value had been much impaired by the encroachments on their hinterlands of the French themselves." If France in Morocco, Algeria, and Tunis appeared in 1914 to this school of Italian policy to be a permanent menace to Italy, the presence of Italy in Tripoli was no less a menace to France in the eyes of French imperialists. Writing just before the Italian declaration of war on Turkey, M. R. Pinon asserted that "the *status quo* in Tripolitania is the best guarantee for the continuance of friendly relations between France and Italy in the Mediterranean. Should Italy take possession of Tripoli, friendly relations would become impossible."[1] And when Italians, Turks, and Arabs were already fighting for the possession of Tripoli, M. Gabriel Hanotaux, forgetting the bargain of 1902, declared that Italy's occupation of Tripolitania "marks the beginning of a great struggle between Italy and France."[2]

"A great struggle between Italy and France"! The words were written two years before the outbreak of the great war, not by an irresponsible fire-eater, but by an ex-Minister of Foreign Affairs. They are an apotheosis of the Mediterranean policy of rival imperialisms. Another and a greater struggle, having perhaps its roots in similar beliefs and desires, the creature of a similar policy, has intervened to avert or to postpone this struggle of the Italian and French States for the barren coast of Africa. But if M. Hanotaux's "great struggle" had or shall come, the reader now knows the beliefs and desires which would have been or will be the cause of it. They are the same beliefs and desires which caused Italians, Turks, and Arabs to shed their blood on the barren coast in 1912,—the ancient policy of the Balance of Power in the Mediterranean, an alternation of fear and hope of strategic aggression, visions of "*Finis Italiae* as a maritime power of the first class," and dreams of gripping the Mediterranean by the throat. And mingling with these strategic and political nightmares of generals and statesmen are the phantoms of the most modern *auri sacra fames*,—the jewels of the trade of Tripoli, the caravan ways of the desert, and all the commerce of the uninhabited Sahara.

Chance has thrown in our way the means of estimating the value of that country and commerce for which General Menabrea and Crispi and M. Hanotaux and M. Pinon were prepared to enter the great struggle. In 1910 an agreement was signed between Turkey and France regulating the boundary between Tripoli and the French possessions, and a Commission was appointed in 1911

---

[1] R. Pinon, *L'Empire de la Méditerranée.*

[2] In the *Figaro*: "Le Danger punique," quoted in *Crispi's Memoirs*, vol. iii. p. 83.

to trace the frontier line upon the ground. A geologist, M. Léon Pervinquière, was attached by the French Government to the Mission, and he has given us his impressions of the hinterland of Tripoli. M. Pervinquière went to Ghadames, that place to which Italian and French statesmen, strategists, and traders attached so much importance because it controlled the caravan trade routes. "I must say at once," writes M. Parvinquière of the country, "that the first and the lasting impression is one of profound poverty. There are not ten rich families in Ghadames, and the others perform prodigies of economy in order not to die of hunger." [1] As to the caravan trade, "the importance of the trans-Saharan commerce has been singularly exaggerated. A caravan arrived from Ghat during our stay: it ought to have carried gorgeous merchandise; in fact it counted twenty camels and carried only some 'filali' and cotton-cloth. . . . According to Lieutenant Bouvet, the profits of all the traders of Ghadames amount to some 300,000 francs in the aggregate. That officer estimates the profits at 40 per cent, which would make the total value of the trade a little more than a million francs. . . . Let us accept this figure of a million. It is a mere trifle! In 1875 Largeau estimated twelve millions as the minimum. It is possible that the commerce has declined, but that traveller was certainly the victim of the mirage of the Sahara which has so often attacked and which still attacks certain people." [1]

May we not also say that Crispi and General Menabrea, M. Ribot and M. Hanotaux, were victims of a mirage of politics and economics which has so often attacked and which still attacks many people, even with regard to a country like Tripoli, of which the first and the permanent impression is one of profound poverty?

---

[1] L. Pervinquière, *La Tripolitaine interdite*, 1912, pp. 183-185.

CHAPTER V

In the dominions of the Emperor of Abyssinia, as Dr. Johnson pointed out many years ago, " the father of waters begins his course ; whose bounty pours down the streams of plenty and scatters over the world the harvests of Egypt." Any one who wishes to understand the mysterious and complicated history of the relations of European policy to Abyssinia must never forget that fact. If the reader will examine the map on the opposite page he will see that Eritrea, British Somaliland, French Somaliland, Italian Somaliland, and Abyssinia together form a great ear or flap on the east coast of Africa. The whole of this territory possesses two geographical features of primary importance, which have necessarily affected the light in which it has been regarded by the European State. The first is its relationship to " the father of waters." The White Nile, it is true, nowhere touches Abyssinian territory, for, gathering its head-waters from the Bahr-el-Ghazal and Uganda, it flows northward through the Sudan parallel with the frontier of Abyssinia to unite with the Blue Nile at Khartum and the Atbara, or Black Nile, at Atbara. But the Blue Nile and the Atbara, which the Arabs call the Cream of the Nile, both have their sources in the highlands of Gojam and Amhara and Shoa, the northern districts of Abyssinia. Thus this eastern ear of Africa has an obvious *strategic* importance : it commands directly a considerable part of the head-waters of the Nile, and it commands indirectly and provides from the east the most direct route of access to the Nile Valley. As soon as Egypt, the Nile, and the Nile Valley came within the orbit of the European State's policy, its strategic position was bound to direct the eyes of military men, and therefore of statesmen, towards Ethiopia, and after 1880 what we may call the Nile Valley-Abyssinia strategic theme continually recurs to complicate the harmonies and discords of European policy in Africa. But its geographical position gives to this block of African territory another importance in the eyes of the strategist. Its sea-board " commands "

ETHIOPIAN AND EAST AFRICA

EGYPT

RED SEA

ARABIA

R.NILE

BERBERA

SUAKIM
TOKAR

KASSALA
R.ATBARA

ERITREA

MASSOWAH

KHARTUM

ADOWA
TIGRE

SUDAN

BLUE NILE

KORDOFAN

DARFUR

FRENCH
SOMALI-
LAND

OBOCK
DJIBUTI
ZEILA

C.GUARDAFUI

PASHODA

BRITISH SOMALI-
LAND

BAHR
EL
GHAZAL

SHOA

HARRAR

ABYSSINIA

OGADEN

ITALIAN SOMALILAND

MIJJERTAINS

*ADDIS ABBABA

OPFIA

L.RUDOLPH

L.ALBERT
KAVALLI'S

UN-ORO

UGANDA

*MENGO

L.EDWARD

BRITISH

EAST AFRICA

BENADIR COAST

MOGADISHU
MEURKA
BRAWA

R.JUBA

L.VICTORIA

NAIVASHA

NAKURU

KIKUYU

WITU

PATTA
MANDA
LAMU
KIPINI

L.KIVU

NYANZA

UGANDA RAILWAY

MOMBASA

*KILIMANJARO

L.TANGANYIKA

GERMAN

EAST AFRICA

PANGAHI

WANGA

OPEMBA

USEGUBA

USAGARA

OZANZIBAR

DAR·ES·SALAAM

the whole of one side of the Gulf of Aden, of the Bab el Mandeb, that narrow strait between the Red Sea and the Indian Ocean, and of the southern quarter of the Red Sea itself. As soon as the Suez Canal was constructed, Egypt became for strategists the "throat of the British Empire," as Herr Rohrbach calls it. But the throat of our Empire is in fact a very long one; it extends, as the map will show, from Port Said to the Strait of Bab el Mandeb, if not to Socotra. Consequently, the cutting of the Canal not only changed the strategic position of Egypt in the world by placing it upon the lines of communication with India; it also did precisely the same thing with the whole coast which lies about the mountains of Abyssinia.

The Suez Canal was opened on November 17, 1869: in 1875 Disraeli bought for £4,000,000, and on behalf of the British State, the Khedive's shares in the Suez Canal Company; in 1876 was instituted the Dual Control of France and England in Egypt; in 1877 Major Baring (later Lord Cromer) went out to that country as British Commissioner to the Public Debt; in 1879 England, Germany, and France deposed the Khedive Ismail; in 1881 came the mutiny of Arabi; in 1882 the bombardment of Alexandria and the landing of a British army in Egypt. In this chain of events there is a connection which we may perhaps call the logic of facts. We can scarcely be surprised to find that for French historians the salient fact in this chain and logic is that, within about a decade of the opening of the Canal, Egypt was under the military occupation of that European State which ruled India. For us it is also significant that the change of sovereignty in this part of Africa occurred at a moment when the doctrines of economic imperialism had just begun to cause the partition of Africa.

Between 1880 and 1890, the spring-tide of economic imperialism in Africa, Egypt and the Nile entered the orbit of European policy. We shall find that between those two dates Abyssinia and the Eritrean and Somali Coasts also entered that orbit. The link between the two events is strategic, and it must never be overlooked; it runs, a chain of strategic beliefs and desires, through the whole history of European policy in Ethiopian Africa, just as we found that a chain of strategic beliefs and desires ran through the whole history of economic imperialism in Mediterranean Africa.

The story of European relations with Ethiopian Africa [1] strictly begins for us in the decade between 1880 and 1890; but, sixteen years before that decade, Abyssinia was for a moment brought into intimate contact with a European State. The curious and

[1] In the following pages I propose to call the whole block of territory which includes Abyssinia, Eritrea, and the three Somalilands, Ethiopian Africa. They are all closely linked together in the history of the African policy of European States, and it is convenient to have a single name by which to refer to them.

still mysterious incident of the British expedition to Magdala may at first sight have no connection with the later manifestations of policy and economic imperialism ; but a nearer and more philosophic view of the history of policy will show that the incident has a considerable bearing upon later events and upon the object of my enquiry ; and, if the reader is to understand the later events, a brief account of the earlier ones is necessary.

The position of Abyssinia in Africa is peculiar. To-day it is the only native State which has retained even the semblance of independence. It is the only African State whose inhabitants belong by religion to Christianity, for the Abyssinians were converted by Frumentius, the envoy of the great Athanasius, 1600 years ago, and the Abyssinian Church is one of the oldest Churches of Christendom. The population is by blood predominantly Semitic, though there has been a considerable admixture, particularly in some districts, of negro blood. All these factors combine to give to the Abyssinian people and their rulers a peculiar position in Africa, of which they themselves are not unconscious. They possess a civilization which may differ from the Anglo-Saxon, the German, or the French civilizations, but it is nevertheless a real civilization, because it is built up around an ancient religion and ancient traditions, and because those who possess it are prepared to defend it against aggression with all the tenacity which belongs to a very proud and warlike race. If the reader will also remember that Abyssinia is one of those rare regions in Africa where climate and temperature would make European settlement and colonization possible, he will now be in possession of the general facts without which he cannot hope to understand the story which follows.

The country has for centuries been subject to the government of a single emperor or Negus. But it was divided into several great districts, each of which was administered by an hereditary chief or Ras. The history of Abyssinia has been a continual fluctuation between a strong central government under an energetic and warlike emperor, and anarchy and rebellion, in which the districts under turbulent chiefs asserted and maintained what was practically independence. About 1850, during a period when the central government of the Emperor Johannes was extraordinarily weak and the provincial chiefs had become almost independent, there suddenly rose into prominence an extraordinary man, Lij Kasa, by birth a nephew of the Chief of Kuara. Kasa belonged to that type of human being which, in other environments, have produced an Alexander and a Napoleon. In Abyssinia it converted Kasa from a poor man and an outlaw into the Emperor Theodore, the Chosen by God, King of Kings of Ethiopia. The process by which, in a few years, Theodore conquered the whole of Abyssinia does not here concern us, but in 1855, after completely defeating the last unconquered chief, the powerful Governor of Tigre, he was crowned King of Kings by the head of the Abyssinian Church, and a German botanist called Schimper, it is recorded, "superintended the floral decorations of the church at Derezgye," in which the ceremony took place.[1]

The collocation of Herr Schimper and Theodore's coronation as King of Kings will help the reader to understand the history of the next ten years. This was a period when the policy of economic imperialism had not been formulated, when the idea that the power of the European State should be consciously directed to further European interests in Africa had not been born. The African knew Europe only in the persons of individual Europeans, scientists, traders, missionaries, and adventurers, who appeared suddenly, and often as suddenly disappeared, in its mountains, deserts, and forests. The behaviour of these irresponsible representatives of European civilization was often unintelligible to the African, and led to serious complications, and this is what now happened in the kingdom of the Emperor Theodore.

Theodore was a very proud man, deeply imbued with the traditions of his religion and his race. His whole history proves him to have been one of those generous and quick-tempered men who are capable of the most appalling cruelty and ferocity in moments of passion, but who, like all great leaders, possess the power of calling out in others great personal affection and fidelity. Between 1855 and 1865 there wandered in and out of the kingdom of this African Napoleon a large number of Europeans of various countries and classes. There were scientists, like Herr Schimper; there were a number of missionaries of the London Society for the Conversion of the Jews, who are referred to in some books as English, but whose names—Stern, Rosenthal, Flad, Steiger, Brandeis, etc.— would seem to indicate a different origin; there was a German painter called Zander, a Pole who had served in the Russian army called Hall, a French gunsmith called Bourgaud, a discharged Alsatian soldier called Mackerer, another ex-soldier of France called Bardel, and two huntsmen of the Duke of Saxe-Coburg, called Schiller and Essler.[2] Then there were two Englishmen, Bell and Plowden, the latter of whom became English Consul, and a French Consul, Lejean. These were the more regular visitants and settlers in Abyssinia. Occasionally, however, the country was brought into contact with still stranger visitors from Europe : for instance,[3] early in the 'sixties there suddenly appeared upon the northern frontier of Abyssinia a French " general," calling himself Count du

---

[1] See Clements F. Markham, *A History of the Abyssinian Expedition*, 1869, p. 64.

[2] See Hormuzd Rassam, *Narrative of the British Mission to Theodore*, 1869, vol. ii. p. 29 ; and Markham, *op. cit.* p. 103.

[3] See Rassam, *Narrative*, vol. i. p. 45.

Bisson, at the head of a small army, of which part consisted of forty Europeans whom the Count had " picked up in Egypt." The general and his army announced that they had come to form a colony in the province of Hamasen. The inhabitants of Hamasen, not perhaps unnaturally, opposed the foundation of the colony by force, and the general disappeared whence he had come, leaving his destitute followers to the mercy of God and the Abyssinians.

In the early days of his reign Theodore was very well disposed towards Europeans, and particularly Englishmen. This was due to the great influence exercised over him by Plowden and Bell, whose conduct he was in later times never tired of contrasting with that of the missionaries and British Consul languishing in his prisons. Plowden was virtually Counsellor of State to the Emperor, and Bell, who married an Abyssinian, actually fought and died in Theodore's service. Both of them were killed fighting against rebellious Abyssinian chiefs in the year 1860. Almost immediately afterwards trouble began. It arose from two facts : first, that the Europeans who were wandering in and out of Abyssinia did not take the trouble to understand the point of view of the King of Kings, and, secondly, because the King of Kings could not understand the aims and objects of Europeans and European civilization. The trouble, in fact, came from a clash between two different civilizations, and such a clash always raises one of the most difficult and dangerous of problems. A single example will show the elements of the problem, as it appeared to Theodore himself in 1866.

One day the Emperor said to Mr. Rassam : " How can I trust any European now after the ill behaviour of those whom I have treated like brothers ? " He then gave a long list of grievances against different persons, and at length came to the case of Lejean, the French Consul. He said : " A man came to me riding on a donkey" (this appears to be a grave breach of etiquette in Abyssinia) " and said that he was a servant of the Emperor of the French, and that he had come to my country for the sole purpose of establishing friendship between me and his sovereign. I said : ' I do not object to making friends with great Christian kings ; you are welcome.' The next day he said he wished to see me on business, and I assented ; but to my astonishment he came to me with a bundle of rags. I asked him what those were. He replied that the French had a large town in their country where they made silks, and that the merchants of that place had commissioned him to bring them to me for the sake of barter. I said to myself, ' What have I done that these people insult me thus by treating me like a shopkeeper ? ' I bore the insult then and said nothing. Another day, while I was out on a war expedition, this Frenchman sent to say that he wished to see me. I told the messenger that I was very busy and could not see him. On receiving my message he rushed out of his tent, dressed in his uniform, and said that, as he was wearing his king's robes, he could not disgrace them by taking them off before he had had an interview, and that I must see him. On hearing this I said, ' Who is his father ? Seize him ! ' and I put him in chains in the very dress of his king. After a shor'; time I had pity on him, as I thought the man was not in his right senses, so I ordered him to be unfettered and sent out of the country. All the time he was with me I treated him kindly and hospitably ; and when he reached Massowah he rewarded my kindness by sending me an insulting letter, in which he abused me most grossly."

The king's account is illuminating. M. Lejean would never have lost his temper if, after dressing in uniform for a levee, he had been refused an immediate audience by the Emperor of Austria ; and he could not understand that an African Emperor, who had conquered and ruled an empire nearly three times the size of Austria, expected to be treated with imperial respect. Theodore, on his side, could not understand the economic beliefs and desires of Europeans, and a whole chapter in the tragic clashing of European with non-European civilizations is contained in that cry, wrung from him by a book of silk patterns : " What have I done that these people insult me thus by treating me like a shopkeeper ? "

This incident will show the difficulties raised by the problem of the penetration of Abyssinia by individuals from European countries. We may add that the dangers were not lessened by the bitter quarrelling among the European adventurers themselves. The centre of these quarrels was M. Bardel. This gentleman had been a sergeant-major in the French army and later a commercial traveller for a firm of Bordeaux wine merchants. Whether he travelled in wine as far as Abyssinia is not recorded, but at any rate he arrived in the country accompanied by M. Bourgaud (or Bourgon), a French mechanic, Mme. Bourgaud, and a child of six years. He appears to have represented himself as a person of some importance in France, and the ex-commercial traveller was appointed by Theodore to be his minister, to educate his children, and later to organize his army. Bourgaud was set to the more appropriate task of manufacturing the Abyssinian ordnance. In 1863 Bardel induced the King of Kings to send him to France with a letter to the French Emperor, but the Government of Napoleon refused to have anything to do with the envoy, who returned " with loud complaints of the way he, as the bearer of Theodore's letter, had been treated." The incident served to increase the Emperor's growing exasperation against Europeans and their Governments.

A further difficulty arose with the missionaries. Protestant missionary effort in Abyssinia dates from 1855, when Bishop Gobat of Jerusalem arranged to send six lay missionaries into the country.

The six lay preachers were in fact German artisans, and it has been remarked that Theodore appears to have preferred their work to their preaching: at any rate, he employed them to make his ordnance and military roads. For some years this curious experiment in the combination of religion and armament manufacture seems to have been successful. There were also in the country four regular missionaries belonging to the London Society for the Conversion of the Jews. French writers almost invariably represent British missionaries as political agents of the British Government, and Messrs. Stern, Rosenthal, Brandeis, and Steiger, who were labouring to convert the Jews in Abyssinia in 1860, have not escaped this suspicion. An otherwise negligible book, *Abyssinie et Angleterre*, by C. Bussidon, published in 1888 by the "Librairie Africaine et Coloniale," furnishes an admirable example of this French obsession, which lasted until the early years of the twentieth century. According to M. Bussidon, the British statesmen, even in 1860, had resolved to establish a protectorate over Abyssinia, " but in order to accomplish this act of spoliation, this international outrage, they still required a pretext. They then had recourse to that contemptible and hypocritical body which is composed of the legions of methodists, quakers, parsons, and pious laymen." " All these missionaries were spies, agents provocateurs, well paid, without faith or law." " They poisoned Ethiopia with their fantastic Bibles, outraging the beliefs of the inhabitants," and " dragging in the mire of their unclean publications Her who had been venerated for fourteen centuries as Queen and Mother of the country, the Virgin Mary." By secret societies, by encouraging rebellious chiefs—to whom " the government at Aden supplied arms "—these missionaries worked to supply " a pretext for intervention " and " the proclamation of a protectorate." They actually supplied the pretext by being arrested for " their criminal manœuvres," and immediately Sir Robert Napier marched with an English army upon Magdala.[1]

Such charges are the commonplaces of pioneers of European civilization in savage countries. We may disregard them, just as we may disregard M. Bussidon's insinuation that the English missionaries instigated the murders of French and Italian sailors, traders, and explorers by Somalis and Hovas. Nevertheless it remains true that, about 1860, Theodore's attitude towards the

[1] Charles Bussidon, *Abyssinie et Angleterre*, Perfidies et Intrigues anglaises dévoilées, 1888, p. xii. This, as I said, is a negligible book, but it is a very good example of a certain type of imperialist book produced in all countries. It was written at the very height of the hostility engendered in Africa by the economic imperialism of the 'eighties, and its object appears to have been to bring pressure to bear on the French Government and incite it to occupy Cape Sheik-Said, opposite Perim, and thus give to France the command of the exit from the Red Sea against England. The book itself is clearly immediately inspired by the hostilities which had just taken place between the British and French representatives at Djibouti and Zeila, to which we shall have to refer below.

European missionary changed. It is uncertain whether his sudden displeasure was in any way connected with religious dogma and the Virgin Mary. A passage in a book, *Theodore II.*, written in 1865 by the French Consul, M. Lejean, who offended Theodore over the book of silk patterns, seems to show that Theodore had become aware that European missionaries were sometimes used in Africa as the thin edge of the wedge of European imperialism. M. Lejean relates how, while he was in Abyssinia as the representative of France, the French Government in an official communication asked Theodore to grant religious tolerance to Roman Catholic missionaries. The Emperor refused, and the reasons he gave for his refusal were these : " I know the tactics of European Governments when they desire to acquire an Eastern State. First they send out missionaries, then consuls to support the missionaries, then battalions to support the consuls. I am not a rajah of Hindustan to be made a mock of in that way : I prefer to have to deal with the battalions straight away." Theodore's animosity against the missionaries was thus in its origin political rather than religious ; in 1862 an unfortunate incident added to it a flavour of personal bitterness, which was certainly exploited by the enemy of the missionaries, M. Bardel. For one of the missionaries—Mr. Stern—delivered himself into the hand of his enemy by writing a book, *Wanderings among the Falashes*, in which he spoke slightingly of Theodore and, what was worse, of Theodore's mother. The offending passage was very soon brought to the notice of the King of Kings, who had the missionary flogged, and then, having put him and Mr. Rosenthal in chains, sentenced them to an indefinite term of imprisonment.

Almost immediately afterwards another incident occurred to fill the cup of the Emperor's displeasure with Europeans. The successor of Plowden as British Consul was a Captain Cameron, who arrived at Theodore's court with a letter from Earl Russell, Secretary of State for Foreign Affairs. The Emperor took the letter to be a personal message from Queen Victoria, and this, in his own words, is what he understood the message to mean : " In the letter the Queen said that she wishes to be my friend and relation, and that she heard that I loved and befriended her on account of what I had done for Plowden and his party against the people of my country ; that formerly England and Abyssinia had an interest ; and now she wished that her Consul should remain with me, and that sportsmen and merchants should be allowed to pursue their avocations. He (the Consul) said to me that a consul from me should go to England, and my sportsmen and merchants also, and that, by the power of God, we would protect them. I was glad at hearing this, and said, ' Very well.' "

When Cameron left the Court, he was given a letter addressed to Queen Victoria, in which Theodore proposed sending an embassy to England, and asked the Queen to arrange for its safe passage. To understand what followed, it is necessary to remember that Theodore was at this time in considerable difficulties. His own people were seriously disaffected in many parts of Abyssinia, and in the south he had on his hands a chronic war against the negro tribes. From the north came even a worse danger, for he was perpetually threatened by the aggressions of the Turks and Egyptians. There is no doubt that he already suspected England of favouring the Turkish designs against Abyssinia. Mr. (later Sir) Clements Markham, writing in 1869 of Earl Russell's policy in this matter, said: "Instead of protecting Abyssina from the Turks, it seemed a preferable course to withdraw as much as possible from Abyssinian alliances. His policy was founded entirely on the desire to promote trade, and he trusted that interference on behalf of a Christian country, as such, would never be the policy of the British Government."[1] At any rate the Foreign Office, on receiving Theodore's letter, put it on one side and left it unanswered. Meanwhile Cameron, on his way to the coast, had heard that some Christians in northern Abyssinia were being raided by the tribes under Egyptian rule, and he proceeded into Egyptian territory at Kassala and Matamma to see what he could do for his co-religionists. This visit of the British Consul to the Turks increased Theodore's suspicions. When Cameron returned to his Court, his first request was for the Queen's answer to his letter. There was no answer, and Theodore's anger against Europe was now uncontrollable. He seized the British Consul and every other European upon whom he could lay hands and flung them into prison.

The sequel was a tragedy. The first act of the British Government was to send Mr. Hormuzd Rassam, a Syrian and Assistant to the Political Resident at Aden, on an embassy to Theodore. Mr. Rassam carried with him the belated reply of Queen Victoria and a request that all the European prisoners should be released. It took him two years to obtain an interview with the Emperor, and at first it looked as if the embassy would succeed. But suddenly Theodore's disgust with Europe and Europeans returned upon him: he arrested the British Ambassador and sent him to join the other captives in prison at Magdala. The British Government then considered sterner measures necessary, and in 1867 decided to send General Sir Robert Napier, Commander-in-Chief at Bombay, with an army of 12,000 men to invade Abyssinia. The expedition arrived at an inopportune moment for Theodore, for in 1867 practically the whole of the country was in rebellion against him, and

---

[1] Markham, *A History of the Abyssinian Expedition*, p. 78. Note that in 1869 it is assumed that trade will be promoted by *non-intervention* in Africa. This is significant of the beliefs of Europeans prior to 1880.

the rebel chiefs gave comfort and aid to Sir Robert Napier's army. Theodore withdrew with a few thousand loyal troops to Magdala and waited until he was invested there. He was in considerable doubt as to whether he should resist or yield, but at length determined upon resistance. The Abyssinian army of about 3000 men, armed with matchlocks and percussion guns, attacked 2000 British and Indian troops armed with Snider rifles. The result was a massacre. The Abyssinians had over 2000 killed and wounded, the British twenty wounded. The King now decided to capitulate : he sent to the British General two of the prisoners with proposals of peace. The reply of General Napier was as follows : "Your Majesty has fought like a brave man, and has been overcome by the superior force of the British army. It is my desire that no more blood may be shed. If, therefore, your Majesty will submit to the Queen of England, and bring all the Europeans now in your Majesty's hands, and deliver them safely this day in the British camp, I guarantee honourable treatment for yourself and all the members of your Majesty's family." [1]

Theodore, perhaps naturally, did not understand from this reply that he was to deliver up his person and his throne. But, as a matter of fact, such was the intention of Sir Robert Napier : he had received the aid of the rebel chiefs " on the tacit but clearly implied understanding that Theodore's power should be destroyed and the dreaded tyrant dethroned." The King sent into the English camp all the prisoners and their baggage, and also 1000 cows and 500 sheep, " being all the live stock in his possession," as a gift to the English General and army. "Never," says Sir Clements Markham, " was a surrender, when once resolved upon, so freely and unreservedly made. Not a hostage, not a child, not a box was kept back. It was the act of a king, an act without cunning or treachery, how slight soever, to mar its fulness." [2] Now, according to Eastern custom, if the present of the cattle and sheep were accepted, it meant that peace had been re-established. Napier gave Mr. Rassam to understand that the present was accepted, and Mr. Rassam instructed a messenger to inform the King accordingly, and it was after the news had reached Theodore of the acceptance that he sent down the remaining prisoners. However, it should be noted that Napier on his return to England publicly said that he " authorized nothing that could have led Theodore to believe that he would accept one jot less than the terms of his first demand."

Here there was a misunderstanding. At any rate, when the last prisoner was safely in the British camp, the cows and sheep were returned to the King. Theodore understood what this meant. Next day the English artillery opened fire upon Magdala, which was now occupied by the King, a few faithful followers, and about

[1] Markham, op. cit. p. 327.   [2] Markham, op. cit. p. 341.

3000 women, children, and prisoners. The small band of loyal fighting men were caught like animals in a trap : they and their King fought bravely to the end. Some of them were pounded to death by the artillery ; a few survived to be shot dead by the British storming-parties. Theodore himself remained untouched whether by shell or by shot until the British troops had scaled the outer wall and were almost upon him. He then drew his pistol, saying : " Sooner than surrender into the hands of the Franks I will shoot myself." He put the muzzle into his mouth and fired : he was dead when the storming party reached him. The body was brought to Sir Charles Staveley, second in command of the British forces, and identified by the prisoners. " Sir Charles walked on, and a crowd came round the body, gave three cheers over it, as if it had been that of a dead fox, and then began to cut and tear the clothes to pieces until it was nearly naked. The days of chivalry are gone ! " [1]

Mr. Rassam, in the book in which he relates his experiences and the history of the expedition, considers the question whether there is any truth in the rumour that King Theodore, just before his death, cursed Mr. Rassam for having deceived him into believing that his terms of peace had been accepted. He is careful to explain that " even if the story were true, Theodore's malediction, being wholly undeserved, would cause me no compunction." He comes to the conclusion that the story is false. Upon the whole, we may agree with the British Ambassador that there is no conclusive evidence that he was cursed by the dying King.[2]

The object of the expedition had been attained. Sir Robert Napier marched his troops down to the coast and re-embarked them for England and India. He took with him out of Abyssinia all the Europeans who had been in service or captivity there—all except Herr Schimper, the German botanist who had arranged the floral decorations of the church at the coronation of the King of Kings. " Herr Schimper preferred to remain in the land of his adoption."

Sir Robert Napier received as his reward a peerage, a Grand Cross of the Bath, and a substantial pension. Two K.C.B.'s, twenty-seven C.B.'s, fifteen colonelcies, eighteen lieutenant-colonelcies, and thirty majorities were given as rewards to officers of the expedition. " Never," wrote one who participated as official geographer in the expedition, " never were services so fully and handsomely recompensed." History and posterity will not, we think, disagree with that verdict.

I have given the history of Theodore and Lord Napier's expedition at some length for more reasons than one. In the first place,

---

[1] Markham, op. cit. p. 353.   [2] Rassam, op. cit. vol. ii. p. 337.

it shows very clearly one side of the problem of the relations between European civilization and non-European peoples which no impartial student can afford to ignore. In 1860 the Governments and peoples of Europe were not imperially minded in the modern sense of the word : particularly is there no trace in these events of the doctrines or policy of economic imperialism. The idea of using the power of the British State directly in Abyssinia to further the economic interests of Englishmen never crossed the minds of Earl Russell and those who directed or influenced British policy. The British Empire was prepared to spend several millions upon sending an army to Africa in order to rescue a British consul and some Teutonic missionaries, but, having killed the king and some thousands of Abyssinians and rescued all the Europeans, the expedition withdrew and left Abyssinia to the Abyssinians. It is inconceivable that after 1880 an incident of this kind should have ended in this way. But in 1868 the sequence of events seemed right and proper to almost every one. Trade and commerce flourished best where political interference was least; and this applied to Abyssinia no less than to Manchester. Consequently, the less intervention of the British Government in Abyssinia, the better for British trade and, therefore, for civilization. Only a very few persons, who, like Sir Clements Markham, were ahead of their age, protested against these postulates of policy. Sir Clements, writing immediately after his return from the expedition, was most strongly against our immediate withdrawal. In his opinion we should have taken the " opportunity of unlocking and throwing wide open the gates of Abyssinia." We ought to have removed the curse of the Egyptian occupation of the coast, converted Mulkutto (in Annesley Bay, south of Massowah) into a " free port like Aden," appointed resident consuls, and entrusted the sovereignty to " an Abyssinian Beharne-gash." " The anxious desire to avoid political complications has prevented our conferring this great blessing on the people whose country we invaded." [1]

Sir Clements Markham, as a political thinker, was some ten or twelve years ahead of his time. Abyssinia was left to the Abyssinians, or rather—temporarily—to the Turks and Egyptians. The important point, however, for us to notice is that the absence of a policy of imperialism, or economic imperialism, did not solve the problem of Europe and Africa. The trouble in Abyssinia arose from the unofficial efforts of individual European adventurers to spread their civilization and promote their economic interests in Theodore's country. The effect upon policy of the actions of such irresponsible pioneers must be carefully studied by any one who proposes or pretends to discover any solution of the problem of Europe and Africa. To this part of the problem I shall have to

[1] Markham, *op. cit.* pp. 390 and 391.

return again in a later chapter; meanwhile, I would point out that nowhere are its elements more clearly displayed than in the story of Theodore of Abyssinia. Only the most grotesque prejudices of patriotic history could have induced French writers [1] to assert or believe that the Government of Earl Russell was seeking a pretext for intervention and was aiming at a protectorate. The policy of 1865 was the exact opposite of this. Yet intervention of a most drastic order followed, and it is important to understand the cause. The economic, religious, and other aims of irresponsible European adventurers in Africa were bound to lead to trouble between them and the native rulers and peoples. Once more it is not "facts" but beliefs and desires which make history, produce "incidents," guide the use of power, and mould policies. The actions of European Governments with regard to incidents and trouble, arising from the contact of their subjects with Africans, were in 1860 guided by two postulates of policy which necessarily led in Abyssinia and other places to intervention and armed expeditions. The first postulate was that the European State had nothing to do with the actions of its individual citizens in Africa. Whether a British or a French subject rode into the presence of the King of Kings upon a donkey or a mule, whether he spoke ill of the Virgin Mary, or treated an emperor like a commercial traveller, or proceeded to "colonize" part of an African State—all this was no concern of the European State. The Briton was a free man, only subject to the law of the land; the King's writ did not run in the mountains of Abyssinia, and, even if it did, the English law does not distinguish between donkeys and mules. Thus, in effect, the European State washed its hands of all responsibility for its subjects' actions in Africa. But the second postulate of policy is curiously different. It has never been more clearly stated than it was on June 25, 1850, in Palmerston's famous speech on the Don Pacifico question : " I therefore challenge the verdict which this House . . is to give on the question now brought before it—whether the principles on which the foreign policy of Her Majesty's Government has been conducted and the sense of duty which has led us to think ourselves bound to afford protection to our fellow-subjects abroad are proper and fitting guides for those who are charged with the Government of England ; and whether, as the Roman in days of old held himself free from indignity when he could say *civis Romanus sum*, so also a British subject, in whatever land he may be, shall feel confident that the watchful eye and the strong arm of England will protect him against injustice and wrong." This principle of policy was extended by Britain and other European States to apply to non-European

---

[1] This patriotic hallucination is not confined to such negligible writers as M. Bussidon. It reappears, for instance, in M. Morié's *Histoire de l'Éthiopie*, 1904, vol. ii. p. 385.

countries where ideas of " injustice and wrong "—just as the ideas with regard to mules and donkeys—were very different from those of Europe. The results were curious and often unfortunate; the European State refused to control the actions of its subjects in Africa, and yet made itself responsible for protecting those subjects with the full power of the State against the consequences of their actions.

When Lord Napier sailed away from Annesley Bay, having won a peerage and a pension, Abyssinia was left to the Abyssinians. That, as we have seen, was the result of beliefs and desires which determined European policy in 1868. Within twenty years Abyssinia again entered the orbit of European policy : that short interval marked the transition stage in the political psychology of Europe, the stage in which beliefs and desires were forming themselves into the policy of economic imperialism. Nowhere are the effects of this change upon State action brought out with more startling clearness than in Ethiopian Africa, in the differences between the British policy of 1868 and the British, French, and Italian policies between 1880 and 1890.

In order to understand the later history, it is necessary that the reader should have some knowledge of what happened to the Abyssinians in the interval. The defeat and death of Theodore were followed by anarchy. The chiefs of Amhara, Shoa, and Tigre were all independent, and the two first each proclaimed himself Emperor. In the south-east the important district of Harrar also became independent. While anarchy weakened the country from within, a worse danger, the Egyptians, threatened it from without. For years the Egyptian Government had been steadily encroaching from the north, and, by occupying the whole sea-board and threatening the south, it seemed upon the point of absorbing the whole of Ethiopian Africa.

The years 1868 to 1872 were occupied in internecine warfare between the three chiefs. In 1872 victory went to the ruler of Tigre, who proclaimed himself Emperor with the title Johannes VI., although Menelik of Shoa maintained his independence for another six years. The rise to power of Johannes established some measure of internal equilibrium and made a stand against the external danger possible. This change came none too early. By 1872 the Egyptians were pressing on from the north-east and occupied Keren. In 1875 the whole district of Harrar passed into their possession. Munziger Pasha, a Swiss who had been French Consul at the time of the expedition to Magdala and was now Governor of Massowah in the service of the Khedive, attempted to invade Abyssinia from Zeila and the Danakil coast, but his force was defeated by Johannes and he himself was killed. At the same time another Egyptian army under Arendrup Bey, a Danish officer, and Count Zichy, an Austrian officer, armed with Remington rifles and Krupp guns, advanced from Keren and the north ; but this army too was annihilated and the European officers killed in a great battle at Gundet, near Adowa. This defeat enraged the Khedive, who was determined to avenge it. Another large Egyptian army was collected, and the invasion of Abyssinia again attempted from Massowah and the north. But the attempt ended in an even more disastrous failure, and the Egyptians were defeated and almost annihilated at Gura in 1876.[1]

In 1880, then, the position in Abyssinia was as follows : Johannes, by his victories over the Egyptians and his defeat of Menelik of Shoa in 1878, had consolidated the government of the country and definitely checked the Egyptian aggression. The Government of the Khedive was, however, still in possession of Kassala, Keren, Massowah, the coast, and Harrar. Hitherto the European State had left Ethiopian Africa to itself. But suddenly that outburst of economic imperialism had come upon Africa. Beginning upon the Congo, it had spread to Tunis and Egypt. Immediately Ethiopian Africa became another centre of interest for statesmen and strategists and traders. Several facts made this inevitable. In Egypt itself France and England were being brought into close touch with the Egyptian Government, and the position of that Government in Ethiopian Africa necessarily became of importance. Strategy and trade combined to turn the thoughts of Frenchmen and Englishmen to the Nile, the Nile Valley, and the Red Sea route to the East ; and that meant that their thoughts had to take in Abyssinia, Harrar, and the Somali Coast. At the same time Italian expansionists were looking about for some place in Africa where they might satisfy the aspirations which the French had defeated in Tunis, and they suddenly decided that they might gain in Annesley Bay and Ethiopia what had escaped them in Bizerta.

The first effect of the new orientation of European policy was a somewhat indiscriminate scramble for territory on the Red Sea and Gulf of Aden coasts between France, Italy, and Britain. France, in 1881, suddenly remembered that about twenty years before she had purchased Obock, at the mouth of the Gulf of Tajura, from the local Sultan. Until the era of economic imperialism the French Government had not realized that there was any value in Obock, and it had been untouched and unoccupied. The new policy revealed that it had a twofold value. It " was chosen," as a French writer explains,[2] " as a stepping-stone on the route to the Far East ;

[1] See Augustus B. Wylde, *Modern Abyssinia*, 1901, pp. 23-28 ; and L. J. Morié, *Histoire de l'Ethiopie*, 1904, vol. ii. pp. 388-390.
[2] C. de la Jonquière, *Les Italiens en Erythrée*, p. 42.

from that point of view its position at the exit of the Strait of Bab-el-Mandeb gave it a real strategic importance. At the same time it was possible to hope that it would become a centre of commerce with the Harrar and Shoa, that is to say, with the south of Abyssinia." In 1881, then, the French State suddenly occupied Obock. But the French did not stop at Obock; like other European nations, they discovered that the native chiefs and sultans of Africa suffered from a strange and generous passion for giving away their kingdoms and their territories. The Sultan of Tajura, Ahmed-ebn-Muhammad, was unable to resist the desire to free himself from the cares and duties of sovereignty, and he had in a few years transferred the whole of his dominions, including the important Bay of Tajura, to France or to Frenchmen. But the appearance of the French State in 1881 at Obock was very disturbing to the Italian statesmen and financiers who had had their imperialist dreams so recently shattered in Tunis. They were determined not to suffer the same loss of trade and territory upon the Red Sea which had come to them upon the Mediterranean. Luckily, they too suddenly remembered that, if the Sultan of Tajura had sold Obock in 1862 to Frenchmen, in 1869, within a stone's throw of Tajura, another Sultan in another bay had sold another port—to Italians. It was an extraordinarily lucky coincidence. Immediately north of Tajura is another bay, smaller, but still a bay, opening upon the Red Sea where it narrows to the Bab-el-Mandeb and the route to India. In 1869 an Italian explorer, Joseph Sapeto, had found himself in this Bay of Assab, and at Assab he discovered a Sultan who wished to divest himself of his kingdom and his sovereignty. Sapeto, with uncommon prescience, bought Assab from the weary Sultan, and he bought it on behalf of that Rubattino Company which, the reader will remember, bought the Tunis-Goletta Railway from the English Railway Company and so very nearly snatched Tunis from the French imperialists. But in the 'sixties, as we have so often had to observe, the flag refused to follow trade, and, just as the British State neglected to take advantage of the victory at Magdala, and the French State neglected to take advantage of the generosity of the Sultan of Tajura, so the Italian State considered that it was not concerned with the generosity of the Sultan of Assab and the purchase of the Rubattino Company.[1] For over ten years the Company left its purchase untouched, but by 1880 the relation between the State and Empire and commercial companies had changed, and when the French remembered that they had bought Obock, the Italians remembered that they had bought Assab. The Rubattino Company acted promptly, and—a

[1] The Porte, supported by Britain, is said to have opposed this purchase: in 1881 Britain withdrew her formal protest. See La Jonquière, *Les Italiens en Erythrée*, p. 21.

significant fact—the Italian State acted with it. Joseph Sapeto, accompanied by a steamer of the Company and two *warships*, sailed from Genoa to take possession of the territory which he had bought so many years ago. Within a year Assab was under the sovereignty of the Italian State and subject to official administration.

This sudden appearance of the French and Italian States upon the Somali Coast immediately opposite Perim and Aden could not but interest Englishmen. Already in European policy upon this coast three strands of beliefs and desires, closely interwoven, can be distinguished. Two of them are clearly stated in the quotation from M. de la Jonquière given above, in which he describes the motives for the French choice of Obock as a valuable possession. The coast was a stepping-stone on the route to the East and India. That was one strand of policy. But men had already begun to think of Harrar and Shoa as "centres of commerce," and for the first time the importance of the Somali Coast, as giving access to Harrar and thence to the highlands of Abyssinia, began to play its part in determining policy. This second, "commercial," strand of policy became, as we shall see, more and more prominent, but both it and the strategical position of Somaliland could not but engage the attention of the British Empire. British policy was, between 1880 and 1885, in a peculiar and a difficult position in Ethiopian Africa. In the year 1882, when the French State was absorbing Obock and the kingdom of the Sultan Ahmed-ebn-Muhammad of Tajura, and the Italian State Assab and the kingdom of the Sultan Berehan, the British fleet was bombarding Alexandria and the British State was proceeding to a military occupation of Egypt. The British Foreign Office and the Government of Mr. Gladstone were involved by these events in complications from which they eventually delivered themselves only by that patient statesmanship which remembers that time and inaction must in the end unravel all difficulties. The difficulties were sufficiently complicated and extended. If the British Government militarily occupied Egypt, the Egyptian Government militarily occupied the Red Sea and Somali Coast, the Harrar, the north of Abyssinia, and the Sudan. In all these territories the relation of the British to the Egyptian, and still more to the Turkish, State was ill defined. The French State, to the astonishment and indignation of many of its subjects, had, by an inexplicable turn of the wheel of policy, found itself quite suddenly barred out of Egypt by the British occupation. To all enquiries as to the meaning and intention of their acts of sovereignty upon the Nile, the British Government replied with one assurance, namely, that their occupation of Egypt was temporary.

Now, whether an occupation of Egypt be temporary or permanent, the occupying Power cannot long overlook or neglect

Ethiopian Africa. Egypt is the Nile, and Ethiopian Africa contains or commands the head-waters of the Nile and the Nile Valley. It has frequently been pointed out that by artificially manipulating the head-waters of that river, it is easy to modify the whole course. "It would only be necessary," says a French historian,[1] "for a rival Power to make a breach in the barriers of rock (on the Upper Nile), and this beneficent river, which has created Egypt, would be transformed into a destructive flood." As long as the uncivilized Africans were left to themselves in uncivilized Africa, the idea of blowing out rocks in the highlands of Abyssinia in order to allow the Nile to rush down and spread destruction and death over the plains of Egypt did not occur to the rulers of Egypt and Abyssinia. But, when civilized and Christian nations like France and Britain appeared in these regions as "rival Powers," this ingenious device had to be reckoned with as a practical possibility of strategy and policy. "If I were the Mahdi," said a distinguished British officer (quoted by Sir E. Ashmead-Bartlett in the House of Commons on March 28, 1895), "if I were the Mahdi, I would make Egypt pay for every quart of water that runs down the Nile." And Sir Colin Scott-Moncrieff made even more clear the difference between the ideals and the methods of civilization and uncivilization in savage Africa. "As for diverting the Nile in the Soudan and depriving Egypt of its water, though there might be no danger from the Mahdi, what the Mahdi could not do, a civilized people could do. It is very evident that the civilized possessor of the Upper Nile Valley holds Egypt in his grasp. . . . A civilized nation on the Upper Nile would surely build regulating sluices across the outlet of the Victoria Nyanza and control that great sea as Manchester controls Thirlmere. This would be an easy operation. Once done, the Nile supply would be in their hands, and if poor little Egypt had the bad luck to be at war with this people in the upper waters, they might flood Egypt or cut off the water supply at their pleasure."

By 1885 British statesmen and strategists were satisfied that they had made it effectually impossible for French statesmen and strategists to obtain a footing in Egypt from the north, but they were immediately haunted by the fear—the years 1890 to 1898 showed that it was not an idle fear—that French strategical statesmanship would seek to penetrate into the Nile Valley, and therefore

[1] J. Darcy, *Cent Années de Rivalité Coloniale*, p. 349. The same idea is contained in an official report of a chief engineer in the Egyptian service, a Frenchman, M. Prompt, who says that the very existence of Egypt lies in the hands of those who hold the Upper Nile. See, too, a speech by Sir R. Webster in the House of Commons, March 28, 1895. The control of the upper waters of the Nile remained and remains a most prominent object of British African policy. As a proof, we may refer to the stipulations in the treaties which settled the Abyssinian question between France and Britain, and which formed part of the Anglo-French entente of 1906.

Egypt, from the south and the south-east. Even a State in "temporary occupation" did not wish to see France sitting astride the Upper Nile, and threatening to blow out a few rocks and sweep the army of occupation, together with the Egyptians and the Turks, into the Mediterranean Sea. The ownership of the territory whence the White and Blue Niles and the Atbara took their rise, Uganda, and the Bahr-el-Ghazal, and lastly Ethiopia, became of intense interest to British policy. And no one could be certain that the appearance of the French State as owner of Obock, and of the Italian as owner of Assab, might not lead rapidly to a change in the ownership of Abyssinia.

But the position of British statesmen was not easy. An unkind fate had just loaded the Liberal and anti-imperialist Government of Mr. Gladstone with an embarrassment of imperial spoils and triumphs. The Prime Minister already had all and more than he wanted in Egypt and the Sudan, where wise men knew that the path of empire would be particularly dark and difficult. He certainly wanted nothing in Somaliland and Abyssinia. And even those Englishmen who thought of trade and strategy, and who, therefore, did want something in Ethiopian Africa with which to offset and check the encroachments of France and Italy, found themselves in a curious position. If territory was to be seized and occupied, the natural place in which first to raise the Union Jack was some port on the coast : but the coast was occupied or claimed by the Egyptian Government. Now, the Egyptian Government was either part of the British Government or under its protection ; and, therefore, for Britain to follow the example of France and Italy and seize a piece of the coast meant that she was either robbing herself or robbing her protectorate. On the other hand, the claims of Egypt had not been able to save either Assab or Tajura Bay from France and Italy, and this made it desirable to take some definite step to prevent the rest of the coast passing into the hands of "rival Powers."

In 1884 the considerations of economic imperialism triumphed over all the others in British policy, and the Union Jack was raised over that piece of the coast which is now British Somaliland. The map will explain the significance of this move. When Italy seized Assab, she set a narrow limit to the possibility of French expansion northwards from Tajura : the British, by seizing the coast from Zeila to Bender Siyada, set a narrow limit to the possibility of French expansion southwards. The moment the British flag was raised in Zeila, and the three rival Powers—France, Italy, and Britain—found themselves sitting cheek by jowl on the outskirts of Ethiopian Africa, a position arose which gave rise to one of the most complicated stories of policy in the history of African imperialism. To unravel the different strands in the complicated situation and policies will necessitate making some demands upon the patience of the reader, but it is only in the details of history that the meaning and the causes and effects of men's beliefs and desires become apparent; and, if the reader's patience will carry him through and over the dull details which follow, he may at the end be rewarded with a strange vision of what the beliefs and desires of Frenchmen, Italians, and Englishmen produced between 1882 and 1906 in Ethiopia.

We have compared the policy of European States in Ethiopia to a rope of action twisted out of three main strands of beliefs and desires. As these three psychological strands are twisted round one another they issue from the hands of statesmen in the form of national action. To unravel this rope we must seize upon a particular strand, follow it for a time through the complication of policy, and then drop it to follow in the same way the windings of the other strands, until finally there fall apart in our hands, distinct and intelligible, the different strands, so shadowy and impalpable, which when woven together appear as the tough chain of national and imperial policy.

The "commercial strand," to which we have already referred, is the first which we must follow. France went to Obock because it might become a door to the centre of commerce in Abyssinia and the Harrar. As soon as Britain went to Zeila, there began a struggle between the two countries, an economic struggle for the Ethiopian market, which lasted for at least twenty-two years. The struggle centred in the district of Harrar. The natural entrance and outlet for the trade of Abyssinia is eastwards from and to the coast, and the natural terminus of the trade routes on the coast is the Bay of Tajura. Inland, Harrar is the centre of all the commerce of the south of Ethiopian Africa, and the problem of the economic exploitation of the whole region presented itself to Europeans as a problem of the control of the trade routes between the coast at Tajura and Harrar, and through Harrar to Abyssinia. The position created by the British occupation of Zeila in 1884 was, therefore, that France was in possession of Obock and the northern shore of the Gulf of Tajura, while Britain was in possession of Zeila, immediately south of the Gulf. A struggle immediately began through the desire of the French to connect the trade routes to Harrar and the interior with their possessions, and so to control them, and the desire of the English to deflect the trade to and control it from Zeila. Now, in 1884 those who had this desire believed that the best method of attaining it was to use the power of the European State directly upon Ethiopian or Somali territory. The first act in the struggle was a curious one, and shows the difficulty of the British position in the complicated policies of Ethiopia and Egypt. In 1885 the French Consul at Zeila was a

M. Henry and the British representative Captain King. M. Henry desired to bring the trade from Harrar through Darmi into French hands at Tajura ; Captain King desired to deflect it into British hands at Zeila. At Zeila itself there was an Emir, Muhammad Abu Bakr, who had been created a Pasha by the Khedive Ismail. It might have been expected that the position of Britain in Egypt would have ensured the co-operation of the Egyptian Pasha at Zeila, but, as a matter of fact, Muhammad Abu Bakr worked unceasingly with the French against the British representative. M. Henry and Captain King agreed only on one point, and that was in their belief that the control of the trade routes depended upon the possession of a place called Dongarita, which was to be on the coast the terminus of the caravans from Darmi and Harrar. M. Henry claimed Dongarita as a possession of the French Republic, Captain King claimed it as part of the British Empire ; and, as often as the French representative raised the French flag there, the English representative pulled it down and flew above Dongarita the Union Jack. The struggle went on until 1886, when it led to bloodshed and the loss of the lives of seven seamen and of the captain of a French vessel. This incident seems to have caused the Governments of the two Powers to reflect upon the question whether, after all, Dongarita was the key to the commerce of Ethiopia, and, even if it were, whether it was worth fighting for. At any rate, in January, 1887, both M. Henry and Captain King were recalled, and five months later France and Britain signed a treaty delimiting their spheres of influence upon the Somali coast.[1] The French flag finally ceased to wave over Dongarita.

One reason which may have helped British and French statesmanship to this decision was that the importance of the control of Dongarita for the trade of Harrar and Abyssinia had become academic, for in the meanwhile trade with those regions, so far as Europeans and European States were concerned, had simply ceased to exist. This did not mean that policy ceased to be influenced by the desire for the non-existent commerce of Harrar and Ethiopia : it only meant that the desire and the policy were complicated by the logic of other unpleasant facts and the emerging of other desires. Between 1881 and 1885 there was rising to power in the Sudan, just west of Ethiopian Africa, the terrible Mahdi. By 1883 the Mahdi and his Dervishes were masters of Kordofan and Darfur, and towards the end of that year the Anglo-Egyptian Army under Hicks was defeated and annihilated. Next year the Mahdi occupied the Bahr-el-Ghazal, and then, moving eastward, took Tokar and Suakim on the Red Sea, just north of Ethiopian Africa. In 1885, the year of the fall of Khartum and the death of Gordon, Kassala,

---

[1] For these facts see Dr. Philipp Paulitschke, *Harar, Forschungsreise nach den Somâl- und Galla-Ländern Ostafrikas*, 1888, pp. 394-396.

on the borders of Abyssinia, fell to Osman-Digna, the Mahdi's general. These events had in four years profoundly changed the situation in Ethiopian Africa for the three rival European Powers, but particularly for Britain. With the fall of Khartum the whole of the Sudan was lost to Egypt, and the policy of, at least temporarily, acquiescing in that loss was adopted by the British Government. But the withdrawal from the Sudan made it difficult to hold the Harrar, which had been in Egyptian occupation since 1875. Consequently, the withdrawal of the Egyptian garrisons in Harrar was decided upon in 1885 and carried out in 1886. When, therefore, France and Britain settled their quarrel over Dongarita, not only Abyssinia and Harrar, but Dongarita itself and the French, British, and Italian possessions on the coast seemed to be in imminent danger of being overwhelmed by the Mahdi and his Dervishes.

Then began a strange chapter in European imperialist policy, a chapter of which no candid historian will claim to have fathomed all mysteries. The beginning dates from the occupation of the important port of Massowah by Italy in 1885. Massowah had been for many years in the possession and occupation of Egypt. It passed into the hands of Italy with the approval—perhaps at the instigation—of Britain. The beliefs and desires behind this first move are represented differently in the histories of the different nations. To French historians the agreement between Britain and Italy as to Massowah marks the first step in a sinister policy by which the covetous Italian expansionists were easily induced to become the dupes of the no less covetous British imperialists. According to this vision of history, the Italians, after their seizure of Assab, had determined to find in Ethiopian Africa the empire which they had failed to snatch from France in Tunis. They had to reckon with two rivals, the French and the British. Now the British imperialists—who had also earmarked Ethiopia for themselves—had more to fear from France than from Italy; but the rise of the Mahdi and the difficulties in Egypt did not for the moment admit of their having free hands to use against their French competitors in the Harrar, in Abyssinia, and on the Somali Coast. They conceived the idea of taking the Italians as their allies, and of using Italian ambitions as a bulwark against both the Dervishes of the Sudan and the traders and financiers of Paris. Italy was invited to seize Massowah; she was encouraged to found her colony of Eritrea and to send " scientific " and " commercial " expeditions into the Harrar; she was secretly told that Britain was willing for her to seek a great Italian empire in the rich and temperate land of Abyssinia. By this Machiavellian policy the British were killing three rival birds with one stone. By putting Italy into Massowah and luring her on into the interior towards Kassala, Britain, during a period of temporary embarrassment, provided, at her ally's expense, a much-needed resistance to the threatening advance of the Dervishes from the north, while, by converting the whole of Ethiopian Africa into an Italian sphere of influence, France would be effectually prevented from taking advantage of England's difficulties in the Sudan to " expand " into Harrar and Abyssinia, and so to turn the British position in Egypt from the east and south. At the same time, " Albion perfide," with her *flair* for profiting by other people's misfortunes and her genius for imperial robbery, comfortably reflected that she had little to fear from the incompetent cupidity of her Italian ally, who would be useful as a temporary dam against the Dervish, but would certainly meet with disaster when she turned against the Abyssinians. And when the inevitable Italian disaster came, " Albion perfide " would step into Ethiopia over the corpse of the Dervish slain by the Italian, the corpse of the Italian slain by the Abyssinian, and the corpse of the Abyssinian slain by the Dervish and the Italian.[1]

We have before had to remark that Continental writers, and particularly the French, attribute to British policy a deep Machia-vellian quality which every Englishman recognizes as singularly un-English. We may safely assume that here again we have a case of the bias of French nationalism and patriotism. We may dismiss the idea that English gentlemen, although statesmen and financiers, between 1885 and 1896 consciously entertained the beliefs, desires, and hopes attributed to them by French historians and Ministers. Yet it would be unwise to dismiss entirely the picture of British policy as it appears or is represented to the eyes of foreigners. It must be admitted that many facts fit with a strange neatness into the French picture. The facts, therefore, cannot be dismissed : they must be investigated.

The first of these facts is the Italian occupation of Massowah. The Italians had no shadow of a claim to that port. They could not have entered it without the approval of Britain, and we may even accept the statement of M. Etienne and other Frenchmen that they entered it at the invitation of Britain. We may go still further : we may accept the view that the object of British policy was to provide in the Italian occupation a strong defence against any further encroachment of the Mahdi's power, a view which is

---

[1] The above is not an exaggerated summary of French opinion of British Ethiopian policy. The reader will discover that it is mild compared to the view taken by an historian like M. Darcy, *Cent Années de Rivalité Coloniale*, chap. ix. sect. iii. But the same view, stated less violently, is taken by such authoritative writers as Lémonon, *L'Europe et la Politique Britannique*, p. 129 ; and Debidour, *Histoire Diplomatique*, La Paix Armée, p. 196. But, more remarkable still, materially the same account of British motives and policy was given on June 7, 1894, to the French Chamber by M. Etienne, who, as Under-Secretary of State for the Colonies between 1887 and 1892, must rank with, or even above, Ferry as the creator of France's colonial empire.

confirmed by the secret clause in the Anglo-Italian Treaty of 1894, by which it was agreed that Italy should be allowed temporarily to occupy Kassala, then in the hands of the Dervishes. Italy was, in fact, allowed by Britain to obtain a footing on this important piece of coast in return for the service which she could render to British policy in the Nile Valley by helping to keep the Mahdi in check.

But as soon as Italy acquired Massowah, a most complicated and interesting situation arose. The Italian expansionists had no intention of remaining a mere bulwark against Mahdism. The object of an expansionist is to expand, and the desire of an imperialist is for empire. The ideas and hopes of Signor Crispi and his fellow-imperialists were not bounded by the sands and sun of Massowah; they looked for expansion and empire towards Abyssinia and Harrar. Let us follow them first to Harrar and then to Abyssinia.

When the Egyptian garrisons were withdrawn from the Harrar in 1885 and 1886, the British officers who carried out the evacuation established the Emir Abdulla, a fanatical Muhammadan, as ruler of the country. In the time of the Egyptian occupation trade in Harrar had flourished, although even then very few Europeans or European firms participated in it. But the Emir Abdulla took his religion and its edict against usury so seriously that he included under usury all " wholesale trade." Since wholesale trade was a sin, he hated, with the hatred of a good Muhammadan, all Europeans who in his eyes were inseparably connected with wholesale trade. He forbade absolutely all wholesale buying and selling in his kingdom, thereby destroying at a blow all openings for European commerce.[1] But although the Emir could close his frontiers to European traders, he could not destroy the desire of Europeans for the trade of Harrar. That desire seemed to increase and to play an increasing part in the policy of the rival States in proportion to the decrease and destruction of the trade itself. We have the authority of the French Under-Secretary of State for the Colonies for the fact that French policy was directed after 1884 towards creating through Harrar " commercial relations with that immense empire of Abyssinia which has been one of the preoccupations of England for fifteen years " (i.e. from 1880 to 1894). As soon as Italy acquired Massowah, Italians began to share with Frenchmen and Englishmen this desire for commercial relations with a country in which the ruler had just made all commercial relations illegal and impossible. In 1886 a movement was started in the " colonial " circles of Italy with the

---

[1] It is interesting to observe that the Emir Abdulla made one exception to his condemnation of Europeans and European trade : the only product of European civilization which he allowed to be imported wholesale into his dominions was firearms. When Dr. Paulitschke, an Austrian scientist, came to Harrar on a scientific expedition, the Emir asked him to be so good as to import on Abdulla's account 1000 of the most up-to-date European rifles.

object of capturing the trade of Harrar for Italy. The idea seems to have originated with a trader called Sacconi, an Italian Jew, who did business between Harrar and the coast and had brought down upon himself the anger of the Emir by defying his and Muhammad's law and dealing wholesale in coffee. Sacconi got into communication with influential imperialists, particularly Umberto Romagnoli and Count Porro, who seem to have conceived the idea that, in the existing disordered and unstable conditions of Ethiopian Africa, it would be easy to win, not only the trade, but also the territory of Harrar for Italy. They therefore founded in Italy an association with the discreet but significant title " Society for the Commercial Exploration of Africa." The Society immediately fitted out an expedition of which the object was to establish " commercial enterprises " in the Harrar, but, when it landed at Zeila under the command of Count Porro, it had the outward appearance of a military rather than a commercial enterprise. Count Porro and his seven Italians and other followers were in fact too well armed to pass with the fierce Emir as peaceful travellers, and insufficiently armed to play the part of conquerors. When they appeared on the frontier of Harrar, the Emir sent messengers to tell them to return to the coast. They replied that they were peaceful travellers who wished to bring presents to the Emir. But the Emir wanted none of their presents, and warned them not to enter his kingdom. The Italians insisted upon bringing their gifts to Abdulla, but, as soon as they crossed the frontier, they were surrounded by Abdulla's warriors and all the Europeans were massacred. The casualties among the Emir's forces were confined to seven Somalis who, in their ignorance, appear to have indulged too indiscriminately in the contents of their victims' medicine chest.[1]

This disaster checked for the moment any forward movement of Italy in Harrar and the south. We must now turn for a moment to Massowah, the north, and the internal history of Abyssinia. It will be remembered (see p. 152) that in 1880 the Emperor of Abyssinia was Johannes VI., who had consolidated his rule by defeating his rival chiefs and the invading Egyptians. When Britain appeared in Africa *in loco parentis* of the Egyptian Government, and, almost immediately afterwards, found that she had to protect her child from the ferocious Mahdi, the British Government approached Johannes with a view to obtaining his alliance and assistance. In 1884 Admiral Hewett, on behalf of England, signed a treaty with Johannes by which it was agreed (1) that there should be free transit " through Massowah to and from Abyssinia for all goods, including arms and ammunition, under British protection," and (2) that the " country called Bogos " should be restored by Egypt to Abyssinia and that Johannes should help the evacuation

---

[1] See Paulitschke, *Harar*, pp. 399-404.

of the Egyptian garrisons from Kassala, Amedeb, Keren, Metemmeh, etc. King Johannes performed his part of this contract, and afforded very considerable assistance to Britain at a moment of great difficulty. Ras Aloula, the King's General, successfully relieved the garrisons of Amedeb, Algeden, Keren, Ghirra, and Metemmeh. "These five stations were the only ones throughout the length and breadth of the Egyptian Soudan that did not fall into the hands of the Mahdi; Ras Aloula accomplishing what England, with all her resources, was unfortunately unable to perform with Singat and Tokar, only a few miles off Suakim."[1]

The position in 1885, then, was that Britain was in alliance with King Johannes and had already received valuable services under the alliance. It may be argued that the British invitation to Italy to occupy Massowah was not formally a breach of Admiral Hewett's treaty. In effect, it was a breach of faith on England's part. Massowah was claimed by Johannes as Abyssinian territory, and he protested ineffectually against the Italian acquisition. Moreover, that acquisition led inevitably to a serious breach of the first clause of the Hewett treaty: England had bound herself to see that there was free transit for goods and arms between Massowah and the territory of Johannes, whereas, a few years after the Italian occupation, the only transit consisted of arms which were being supplied by the Italians to Johannes's enemy, King Menelik of Shoa.

The action of the British and Italian Governments in Massowah came as an unpleasant surprise to the Abyssinian King, but things more surprising and more unpleasant were to follow. He was soon to become acquainted with that axiom upon which the European State seems, unfortunately, compelled to direct its policy: Necessity knows no law. Necessity very soon required that Britain should sacrifice either her Italian or her Abyssinian ally, for the aspirations of the Italians for empire in Ethiopia could only be satisfied at the expense and by the extinction of Johannes. Italy lost no time in starting to "expand" from Massowah towards and into Abyssinia. In 1886 she occupied several places on the coast and began to advance inland, sometimes with armed forces and sometimes with "scientific-commercial" expeditions. In 1887 Count Salembeni, the leader of one of these scientific-commercial expeditions, was taken prisoner on Abyssinian territory some fifty miles from Massowah by Ras Aloula, who then sent a demand to the Italian Governor that the Italian occupation should be confined to Massowah. The demand was refused, and war between the two allies of Britain immediately began. The war for the conquest of Abyssinia opened disastrously for Italy: an Italian force advancing into Ras Aloula's territory was surrounded and annihilated at

[1] Wylde, *Modern Abyssinia*, p. 35.

Dogali on January 26. The Governor of Massowah then withdrew to that town and sent to Rome a request for reinforcements.

But, though Johannes had checked the Italian advance for the moment, his position was precarious : the Dervishes were threatening Abyssinia from the west ; in the south Menelik, in quasi-alliance with the Italians and receiving arms from Massowah, was waiting for a favourable opportunity to seize for himself the crown of the King of Kings ; in the east the tribes were being stirred up by the Italians to rebellion; and in the north the Italians themselves were only waiting for more troops in order to recommence their advance. His only ally was Britain. As to the value of the British alliance and the ethics of British policy in 1886, we cannot do better than quote the opinion of a British Vice-Consul for the Red Sea, who was in Ethiopian Africa at the time and is not unfavourable to the policies of imperialism and economic imperialism. Mr. A. B. Wylde remarks that at this time

from the north he (King Johannes) ought to have been safe if our treaty with him went for anything. Look at our behaviour to King Johannes from any point of view and it will not show one ray of honesty, and, to my mind, it is one of our worst bits of business out of the many we have been guilty of in Africa, and no wonder our position diplomatically is such a bad one with the rulers of the country at present. England made use of King Johannes as long as he was of any service, and then threw him over to the tender mercies of Italy, who went to Massowah under our auspices with the intention of taking territory that belonged to our ally, and allowed them to destroy and break all the promises England had solemnly made to King Johannes after he had faithfully carried out his part of the agreement. The fact is not known to the British public, and I wish it was not true for our credit's sake; but unfortunately it is, and it reads like one of the vilest bits of treachery that has been perpetrated in Africa or in India in the eighteenth century.[1]

The British public were, as Mr. Wylde points out, not informed of British and Italian policy towards the King of Kings in 1886, but they were fully informed as to the barbarous objection which this King of Kings, Johannes VI. of Abyssinia, had to the smoking of tobacco and the taking of snuff, and how he punished those who indulged in snuff by cutting off their noses and those who indulged in tobacco by cutting off their lips. That the information was untrue [2] is perhaps not of any great importance, for the history of the dealings of all European States with African kings is one

[1] A. B. Wylde, *Modern Abyssinia*, 1901, p. 39.

[2] Mr. Wylde, pp. 44 and 45, says that, after careful enquiry, he found no truth in these accusations. It is true that King Johannes objected very strongly to the smell of tobacco and the taking of snuff, and prohibited them within the precincts of his palace. The basis of the invention of the mutilation stories seems to have been the fact that on four or five occasions men caught smoking in or near the palace " had their lips and nose slightly scarified, so as, until the slight wound healed, they could not use tobacco."

of almost unredeemed treachery and breach of faith. At the same time, all that the ordinary European is allowed to hear about African rulers, from Theodore to Mwanga, and from Johannes to Samory, are stories of their barbarous habits and uncivilized cruelty. The comfortable inference is easy that a treacherous savage cannot expect to be treated even according to the ordinary code of morality of civilized States, and breach of faith and treaties becomes in this way an almost holy weapon for the noble crusaders who are spreading European civilization through the "Dark Continent." The barbarous notions of Theodore with regard to asses, consuls, and missionaries justify the misunderstanding and the massacre of Magdala, just as the imaginary mutilation of smokers by Johannes must be taken as absolving Britain from "one of the vilest bits of treachery that has been perpetrated in Africa."

Johannes was spared a full experience of the methods of European policy and of the value of European treaties. Death saved him from further civilization, and the experience, with that ironical and divine justice which flickers so unexpectedly and variably over history, was reserved for his enemy and the ally of his enemies, Menelik of Shoa. When the Italians recoiled after Dogali and Menelik made no open move against him, Johannes, seeing himself surrounded by a world of enemies, decided to strike quickly at the one who was most pressing, the Dervishes, hoping in this way to be able to encounter his foes one by one rather than in combination. In 1887 Menelik had occupied the Harrar; in 1888 the Italians had concluded a treaty with him which appears to have recognized him as King of Abyssinia on condition that he would join Italy in a campaign against Johannes. In accordance with this treaty Menelik received from Massowah money and arms. Johannes was certainly not ignorant of these negotiations: it became essential for him to free his hands on the west and north in order to be able to meet the combined forces of Menelik and the Italians on the south and east. In 1888, therefore, he mobilized his army against the Dervishes who had successfully invaded Abyssinia the year before. This time the Mahdi's hordes were defeated, and Johannes made great preparations for a decisive campaign against them in 1889. Time was pressing, for in May, 1889, the Italians signed with Menelik the famous Treaty of Uccialli, to which we shall have to refer again. Accordingly the King put himself at the head of his army, and in 1889 marched north against the Dervishes. He met them at Gallabat[1] and totally defeated

---

[1] According to most writers (e.g. Wylde, p. 41), the battle of Gallabat was fought on March 9, and the King died on March 10, 1889. L. J. Morié, *Histoire de l'Éthiopie*, says that this is incorrect, and that the events really took place on November 4, 1889. I have adopted M. Morié's date (although he does not give his authority): if he is wrong, and the ordinary account is correct, then, of course, the death of Johannes preceded the Treaty of Uccialli.

them, but in the moment of victory was himself mortally wounded. He died twenty-four hours after receiving his wound.

After the death of Johannes, Menelik succeeded to his throne, but for some time his position was not secure. What the precise terms of his agreement with the Italians were is not known, but it seems probable that, according to the agreement, Italy was " to help him to the throne," and the price to be paid by him was " the provinces of Bogos, Hamasen, and Oculu-cussei, with the Mareb, Belessa, and Mai Muna rivers for the frontier." [1] At any rate, towards the end of 1889, the Italians under General Baldissera occupied this country, and early in 1890 they advanced still farther across the Mareb and took Adowa. By entering Adowa they showed clearly their intention to expand at the expense of Abyssinia, and Mr. Wylde is probably right in dating all their troubles from the crossing of the Mareb. It made it inevitable that their ally Menelik, now King of Kings and " Conquering Lion of the Tribe of Judah," would become their enemy, for even an ally does not like to be deprived of his territory. But for the moment Menelik was occupied in subduing parts of his newly-won kingdom, and he remained openly friendly with the Italians, who supplied him with the arms required by him for subduing his subjects.

A curious international position began to develop, and the first symptom of it is to be discovered once more in the Harrar. Both France and Britain continued to be interested in the trade of Abyssinia, and therefore in the Harrar. So long as the Emir Abdulla ruled in that district and refused to allow any trade at all, both sides appear to have been satisfied. But it was known both that Italy had " aspirations " with regard to Abyssinia and the Harrar, and that Britain had come to some understanding with Italy which gave her considerable latitude in which to aspire. The Italians were allies of Menelik and were supplying him with arms, and with those arms the King of Shoa was subduing the Harrar and its Emir. France began to be nervous about the future of this district and its commerce, and French interest in its future was increased by the inclusion of the port of Djibuti in French Somaliland in 1888. In Paris, Djibuti was regarded by commercial-colonial circles as the ideal point of departure for the economic penetration of the Harrar and Abyssinia, as indeed it proved to be. But the value of Djibuti depended upon the condition of its hinterland : according to the doctrines of economic imperialism, that value would sink to nothing if some other European State— say Italy or Britain—or even an African king like Menelik under the domination of Italy, were to be in occupation of the Harrar. The French therefore approached the British Government and

---

[1] Wylde, *Modern Abyssinia*, p. 50. See also Morié, *Histoire de l'Éthiopie*, vol. ii. p. 402.

proposed that the two countries should agree in the first place not to occupy or annex Harrar, and in the second place to oppose its annexation, occupation, or "protection" by Italy.[1] Lord Salisbury's Government was placed in a somewhat difficult position by this proposal. They wanted very much to keep the French out of Harrar, and they were not at all anxious to see the Italians enter it : but their engagements with Italy made it impossible to bind themselves to oppose an Italian occupation or protectorate. Lord Salisbury found a way out of this dilemma which is frequently adopted in such circumstances by those who direct the policies of nations. He signed an agreement which could be, and in fact was, interpreted to mean two different things by the two parties to the contract. He refused to bind himself to oppose an Italian protectorate, but he agreed to sign the following clause of a secret agreement :

The two Governments engage not to endeavour to annex Harrar, nor to place it under their Protectorate. In taking this engagement, the two Governments do not renounce the right of opposing attempts on the part of any other Power to acquire or assert any rights over Harrar.

The wording of this fourth clause of the Anglo-French Agreement of the 2nd–9th February, 1888, is sufficiently remarkable. By promising not himself to acquire the Harrar, Lord Salisbury obtained a similar engagement from the French. He refused to promise to oppose its acquisition by the Italians, because, we may presume, he knew of the Italian desire to acquire it and because he had some understanding with Italy regarding her future in Ethiopian Africa. If he had stopped there, that is, at the end of the first sentence of the clause, his actions and his words would have been unambiguous. But he went on to add that second sentence of which the meaning may at first sight appear to be obvious and straightforward, but of which the intention and object are obscure. For if the words merely mean what they say, what was the sense of including them in a solemn international agreement ? Two nations declare that they will not annex or place under their protectorate a piece of territory belonging to an "uncivilized" Power. Would any sane man imagine that such a declaration could possibly imply that either of these nations was thereby renouncing its right to oppose an attempt on the part of a third nation to acquire rights over the territory ? Such an implication would occur to no one, but, if it did not exist, what was the sense of this second sentence ? The French, as we shall see, maintained that these words had a very

---

[1] The statement that the initiative came from the French is taken from an important article, "France et Angleterre," by the well-known publicist, E. Lavisse, in *La Revue de Paris* of February 1, 1899. The article is addressed to Sir Charles Dilke who, according to M. Lavisse, confirmed this statement.

different implication, which at least gave sense to them. Britain, out of regard for her friend and ally at Rome, was not willing formally to acquiesce in the French proposal to guarantee the independence of the Harrar against third parties, but in these words she recognized the justification of the French request.[1] In other words, the British Government did not bind itself formally to oppose an Italian protectorate, but did morally bind itself not to promote one.

The French view of this curious clause is confirmed to some extent by the fact that the whole of the agreement of 1888 was kept secret until, in 1894, it led to an international incident between France and England. Now, the only conceivable reason for not publishing the agreement must have been the unwillingness of one of the parties to allow this clause with regard to the Harrar to be made public, for all the other important clauses refer only to the delimitation of the frontier between French and British Somalilands. It seems, therefore, to be almost certain that the clause was kept secret because the British Government did not wish their Italian allies to learn of its existence.

The treaty of 1888 was soon to lead to trouble between France and England. In order to understand how this happened, it is necessary to return to the treaty signed at Uccialli between Menelik and Italy on May 2, 1889, and to trace the steps by which Italian action, based upon that treaty, aimed at acquiring not only Harrar, but the whole of Abyssinia. The Treaty of Uccialli consists of twenty clauses, which define the boundaries between the territories of the two Powers, and contain various other stipulations relating to commerce, extradition, etc. The crucial clause is the seventeenth, which deals with the foreign relations of Ethiopia. Two texts of the treaty were made, one in Italian and the other in Amharic, and the version of Clause XVII. differed materially in the two texts. Menelik maintained later that the clause which he had consented to sign, and which in fact he had signed in the Amharic text, ran as follows :

Article XVII.—His Majesty the King of Kings of Ethiopia shall be at liberty to avail himself of the Italian Government for any negotiations which he may enter into with the other Powers or Governments.

But in the Italian text the words " shall be at liberty " appear as " shall be obliged " or " consents." The difference was vital for the future of Abyssinia and Menelik. The Amharic version

---

[1] This is the explanation given by M. Lavisse in the article already referred to. The article of M. Lavisse forms the basis of the accounts of these Abyssinian negotiations and policies given by practically all the French historians, Debidour, Lémonon, Darcy, etc. M. Lavisse's explanation on this point is adopted by these historians, but with the most extraordinary inaccuracies and exaggerations which make out British policy to be blacker than it was. For an analysis of these authorities see the note at the end of this chapter.

meant that Menelik was given the right to use, when he so desired, the services of Italy as an intermediary between himself and other governments: the Italian version meant that Menelik bound himself never to enter into relations with foreign Powers except through the Italian Government as intermediary—in other words, that the King of Kings had agreed to convert Abyssinia into an Italian Protectorate.

This seventeenth clause in the Italian-Ethiopian treaty produced one of the most curious incidents in the history of international relations. It was another case of misunderstanding between a civilized and an uncivilized Power. The Amharic version, which appears to have been the only one actually signed, is said to have remained in possession of Menelik; Count Antonelli, who signed in the name of the King of Italy, went off with the Italian translation in his pocket. French historians do not hesitate to say that Antonelli and Crispi between them, by a " clever forgery " (une habile falsification),[1] deliberately tried to convert a treaty of friendship and commerce into a treaty of submission. But no European nation has the right to use rude words, or even to call spades spades, in describing the policy and actions of other European States in Africa. If the Englishman says that Lord Napier of Magdala had a misunderstanding with the Emperor Theodore, the Italian may be permitted to say that Count Antonelli and Signor Crispi had a misunderstanding with the Emperor Menelik. It must, however, be admitted that the Italian misunderstanding fitted in most admirably with the scheme of Italian aspirations, and that Signor Crispi hastened to take advantage of it.

The Treaty of Uccialli was signed on May 2, 1889. On October 1, 1889, an additional convention was signed between Italy and Ethiopia containing provisions which indicate the nature of the Italian objects. By Article V.[2] it was agreed that a loan of 4,000,000 lire should be contracted by Menelik with an Italian bank, under guarantee of the Italian Government, on security of the Harrar Custom House, and Article VI. gave Italy the right to take over administration of the Harrar Custom House in event of non-payment of the loan regularly. Eleven days after the signature of this treaty, Crispi sent a circular letter to the Great Powers notifying them, under Article 34 of the General Act of the Congo Conference of 1885, that under Article XVII. of the Treaty of Uccialli " His Majesty the King of Ethiopia consents to avail himself of the Government of His Majesty the King of Italy for the conduct of all matters which he may have with other Powers and Governments." This notification shows the interpretation which Crispi put upon the Treaty of Uccialli, namely, that it constituted Ethiopia an Italian Protectorate, for Article 34 of the General Act of the

[1] Morié, op. cit. vol. ii. p. 425.   [2] Hertslet, Map of Africa by Treaty.

Congo Conference requires the notification only of "Acquisitions and Protectorates" in Africa. Having declared to the world the new international status of Abyssinia, Crispi immediately afterwards published the Treaty of Uccialli (in the Italian version) together with the additional Convention, and then proclaimed that in future the Italian possessions on the coast of Ethiopian Africa should be known as "the Colony of Eritrea."

But there had been somewhere a grave misunderstanding. Everything which we know of Menelik and his subsequent history makes it certain that even on May 2, 1889, he would never have consented to place himself and his territories under the "protection" of Italy. As soon as the Italian Green Book containing the Italian version of the treaty was published in 1890, the French, through M. François Deloncle, hastened to bring to the notice of the Emperor the interpretation which was being placed upon Article XVII. at Rome.[1] Menelik at once refused to ratify the treaty and later, in 1893, he denounced it : at the same time he in turn sent a circular letter to the Great Powers informing them that he had never consented to his territories becoming an Italian protectorate.

The Italian Government was determined, even if Menelik abided by the Amharic version, themselves to abide by the Italian. In fact, Italian statesmen seem to have considered that it was of less importance to obtain the consent of the Emperor of Ethiopia to their acquisition of his territories than the acquiescence of Great Britain. On March 24 and April 15, 1891, two Protocols were signed at Rome between Italy and England, and on May 5, 1894, an additional Agreement was signed between the two Powers. There are facts connected with the history of these agreements which are both curious and mysterious, and I propose to deal with them in a note at the end of this chapter. But there is no doubt or dispute as to what these treaties actually effected or as to the policy which lay behind them. They recognized as an Italian "sphere of influence" an enormous block of territory comprising the whole of Eritrea, Abyssinia, the Harrar and Ogaden, and Italian Somaliland. In other words, England agreed to hand over to the Italians the whole of Ethiopian Africa except French and British Somaliland. At the same time, as the French were quick to perceive and to point out, the boundaries were so drawn as to keep the Italians well away from the Nile Valley. If the agreements stood, Britain would therefore maintain her claim to the Nile Valley and would have erected in this Italian empire an insuperable obstacle to any attempt of the French to reach the Valley of the Nile from the east.

The two maps annexed will show the partition of Ethiopian

[1] Morié, *op. cit.* vol. ii. p. 493.

ETHIOPIAN AFRICA

1894
ACCORDING TO ANGLO-ITALIAN AGREEMENTS

1900

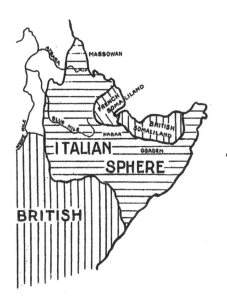

Italian
British
French
Independent

Africa which these Anglo-Italian treaties of 1891 and 1894 contemplated and attempted, and the modifications which the logic of facts had introduced by 1900. We have already had to remark that an intelligent anticipation in map-making has often been a useful weapon in the carving of empire out of other people's dominions. It is interesting, therefore, to note that in the map of Africa at the beginning of the first edition of Sir Edward Hertslet's *The Map of Africa by Treaty*, which was published in 1894 with the sanction of the Secretary of State for Foreign Affairs, the whole of the " Italian Sphere " is coloured green, signifying that it is Italian, and is called " Italian Abyssinia." To what extent the Anglo-Italian agreements were kept secret is dealt with fully at the end of this chapter in a note. In 1894 they came to the knowledge of the French Government. It is hardly surprising that they called forth a vigorous protest from Paris. The French complained that, in the first place, Britain was giving to Italy an immense stretch of territory which she had no right to give, because it belonged to other people, and they added that " England in the public protocol is giving the whole cake to Italy, but in the confidential declaration Italy is handing back under the table that piece which England promised France that she would never touch." [1] This last sentence refers to a secret declaration which the French alleged was attached to the Treaty of May 5, 1894, and which stipulated that " Italy would allow Great Britain to exercise a temporary intervention in the Harrar up to the time when she should be herself in a position to establish an effective protectorate there." I shall give reasons in the note at the end of the chapter for believing that there never was such a secret declaration, but that does not alter the fact that almost all French writers and publicists believed and believe in its existence. At any rate, the official protest of the French Government in 1894 was confined to the question of Harrar, and the line which they took was that Britain by her agreements with Italy had broken the Anglo-French Treaty of 1888. The grounds upon which M. Hanotaux based his protest and the reply of the British Government are given as follows by M. Lémonon : [2] " On June 18, 1894, we learned of the treaties of 1891 and of the public protocol of May 5, 1894 ; M. Hanotaux lodged a protest with the Foreign Office, invoking the Franco-British Treaty of 1888 which had . . . affirmed the independence of Abyssinia (Harrar ?). The English Cabinet gave us evasive replies : one of them, however, given on August 11, was in fact an acknowledgment of faults committed, and an undertaking—but of what value ?—to make reparation. 'Any action of England,'

---

[1] See the article in the *Revue de Paris*, February 1, 1899, by Ernest Lavisse, referred to *supra*.

[2] Lémonon, *L'Europe et la Politique Britannique*, 2nd edit. 1912, p. 129.

it was said in a Note handed by the English Ambassador at Paris to M. Hanotaux, ' based upon the Agreement of the 5th May will be carefully *limited* to such communications and measures as will be compatible with the arrangement between France and England, and will in no way affect the political situation in the Harrar, in which the Government of Her Majesty has no intention of meddling.' "

It must be admitted that the position adopted by the British Government was curious. It had just signed three agreements which permitted its Foreign Office to issue a map in which the whole Harrar was shown to be Italian and was coloured green, agreements which undoubtedly gave Italy a protectorate over not only the Harrar, but Ogaden and Abyssinia. There is no doubt at all that in 1888, and up to 1891, Britain had recognized the independence of the Harrar. It must be left to the diplomatists to explain how the action of England, in changing the independence of the Harrar into an Italian protectorate, was compatible with the assurance that it " will in no way affect the political situation in the Harrar."

For the moment the French had to be satisfied with these assurances. But the curious mistranslation of the Treaty of Uccialli and the revelation of Italy's intentions in the Anglo-Italian treaties of 1891 and 1894 had completely changed the diplomatic situation in Abyssinia, and the French were quick to take advantage of it. Crispi had been mistaken in thinking that Menelik was one of those African monarchs with a passion for abdicating in favour of a European State. The Italian Premier might have been saved from his error if he had studied a photograph of the monarch, for, if ever a man showed in his face the determination and the capacity to rule, it was Menelik. He had entered into an alliance with Italy for a definite purpose, namely, to win the Empire of Abyssinia, and he had paid the price for that alliance in territory on the north and east. As soon as he discovered that his possessions were being treated by his ally as if they were or must become Italian, he made it clear that Italy would never win an empire by mistranslating Amharic. In 1893 he denounced the Treaty of Uccialli, and the following year placed himself at the head of his armies, after issuing a proclamation that " Ethiopia had need of no one : she stretches out her hand to no one but God."

The proclamation was only formally and officially accurate. It is true that after 1893 Abyssinia's only official ally was the Deity, but, as soon as it became clear that Italy would, if she were still determined to seize Abyssinia, have to fight for it, France, unofficially at least, stretched out a hand towards Menelik. Unofficially, too, Menelik stretched out his hand towards France. The process consisted in the hand of France placing in the hand of Menelik arms and munitions of war produced by French armament firms. Menelik had very early in his career learned the value of guns and explosives produced by European civilization, and, though he prohibited the import from Europe of missionaries, he encouraged that of munitions. The value of the Italian alliance had, for him, consisted in the fact that the Italians supplied him with arms from Massowah with which he might rebel against King Johannes. Now that he had to look for an immediate Italian attack from Massowah upon his own kingdom, the value of his unofficial understanding with France lay in the fact that the French supplied him with arms from Djibuti to use against the Italians. " There is no doubt," says Mr. Wylde, " that had it not been for the French supplying Abyssinia through the port of Djibuti with unlimited quantities of arms and ammunition, both as presents and by purchase from their merchants, that Menelik would never have been able to have gained the crushing victory of Adowa." [1]

The attempt of the Italians to substantiate their claim to Abyssinia by force of arms took place in 1895 and 1896. I am not concerned with the details of that incompetent and disastrous adventure of imperialism. Early in 1896, when the campaign had dragged on many months, Crispi wrote to Baratieri, the commander of the Italian troops : " This is military tuberculosis, not a war— we are squandering heroism to no purpose—I see that the campaign is conducted without any plan, and I would wish that one were established. We are ready for every sacrifice required to save the honour of the monarchy and the prestige of the monarchy." Thus admonished, the Italian Commander-in-Chief, against his own judgment, took the offensive. It resulted in Menelik's crushing victory at Adowa on March 1, 1896.

At Adowa the Italian hopes of an Empire of Ethiopia were definitely and dramatically destroyed by Menelik, the French Government, and French munition makers. Italy was compelled to recognize the revocation of the Treaty of Uccialli and the independence of Abyssinia ; her possessions shrank on her maps, and on those of the English Foreign Office, to the small colony of Eritrea and that stretch of the Somali Coast between Cape Guardafui and British East Africa which she had acquired between 1889 and 1892. Italy and her economic imperialists therefore, after 1896, drop out of the story of Europe's efforts to " absorb " Ethiopia. But before passing on to the last chapter in that story, it is necessary to say a few words about Italian Somaliland, for its history has points of interest for the student of economic imperialism. The possession of the coast between Guardafui and British East Africa was vital to the Italian scheme of an Ethiopian Empire. It is a curious fact that an empire, unless it is in solid blocks, is for the imperialist

[1] Wylde, *Modern Abyssinia*, p. 52.

not strictly empire. The dream of the German is of a Mittel-Afrika stretching in a solid block from the Atlantic to the Indian Ocean. Nothing would satisfy M. Etienne and his supporters but a solid block of French territory stretching from the Mediterranean to the Gulf of Guinea, and another solid block stretching from the Gulf of Guinea to the Gulf of Aden. The imperial destinies of Portugal required a solid block of Portuguese territory from Angola to Mozambique, while Rhodes and his followers, with that originality which is characteristic of the Englishman, decided that the destinies of Britain required a solid block from the Cape to Cairo, running from south to north and therefore, necessarily, making all the other nations' solid blocks—which ran from west to east—impossible. The " solid block " of Italian dreams was comparatively modest ; it was to stretch only from the Red Sea to the Indian Ocean, but, if it was to be obtained, the Somali Coast south of Guardafui was a " vital interest " to Italy. It was, therefore, an extremely fortunate coincidence that in the very month of May, 1889, in which Count Antonelli signed the Treaty of Uccialli with Menelik, and in which Crispi imagined that the whole of Abyssinia had become an Italian protectorate, the Italian Consul at Zanzibar, a Signor Filonardi, discovered that this vital strip of Somali coast was ruled over by the Sultan of all the Mijjertayns and the Sultan of Oppia, two African sovereigns who were eager to hand over the sovereignty of their territories to Italy. Signor Filonardi immediately complied with the request of the Sultan of all the Mijjertayns and the Sultan of Oppia, and the Italian Government formally notified Lord Salisbury that an Italian protectorate had been established over the Sultanate of Oppia. Six months later Crispi was fortunate enough to be able to inform Lord Salisbury that Italy had been able to assume the protectorate of the territory south of the Sultanate of Oppia between Kismayu (the most northerly point of what is now British East Africa) and the southern boundary of Oppia.[1]   Thus in six months the Italian Prime Minister had obtained, as he thought, a protectorate not only over the whole of Abyssinia, but also over the whole coast between British East Africa and Cape Guardafui.

The southern portion of this piece of coast is called the Benadir Coast. At the time when it was taken over as an Italian protectorate it belonged by right to the Sultan of Zanzibar.[2]   The position of this Sultan was an unfortunate one. His territories had been, ever since 1885, a subject of dispute between Germany and Britain, and there had been much controversy among Germans and English-

---

[1] See Hertslet, *The Map of Africa by Treaty*, 1st edit. 1894, vol. ii. pp. 772-6.

[2] It is recognized as such in the Agreement between Germany and Britain of October 29 to November 1, 1886, Article I., and in the Italian Notification to the British Government of November 19, 1889.

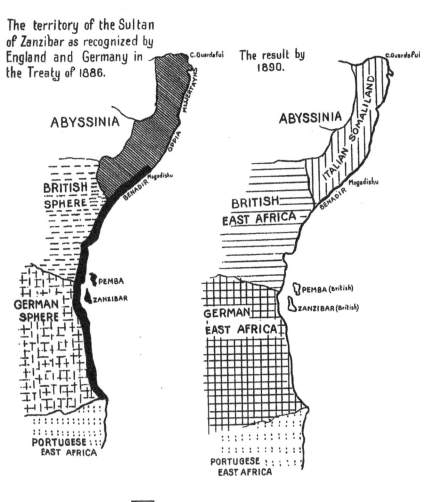

The territory of the Sultan of Zanzibar as recognized by England and Germany in the Treaty of 1886.

ABYSSINIA

C.Guardafui

MIJJERTAYNS

OPPIA

BENADIR Mogadishu

BRITISH SPHERE

GERMAN SPHERE

PEMBA

ZANZIBAR

PORTUGESE EAST AFRICA

The result by 1890.

C.Guardafui

ABYSSINIA

ITALIAN SOMALILAND

BRITISH EAST AFRICA

BENADIR Mogadishu

GERMAN EAST AFRICA

PEMBA (British)

ZANZIBAR (British)

PORTUGESE EAST AFRICA

British Sphere

German Sphere

Portugese

Territory of Zanzibar

Other Independent Sultans

British Possessions

German Possessions

Italian Possessions

men as to whether the Sultan was an African ruler who wished to get rid of his possessions, and if so, whether he desired to abdicate in favour of Englishmen or of Germans. I shall have to deal with this question fully in the next chapter : here it is sufficient to remark that in 1886 Germany and Britain temporarily settled the matter by an agreement (October 29 to November 1, 1886), in which they recognized the sovereignty of the Sultan over the whole coast line between Portuguese East Africa and the Sultanate of Oppia, including the Benadir Coast. The result of this solemn international agreement between the two Great Powers, Germany and Britain, recognizing the sovereignty of the Sultan of Zanzibar over certain territories, was that those territories immediately passed from the sovereignty of the Sultan into the hands and under the sovereignty of Britain and Germany (see map opposite). This remarkable consummation was brought about in five years, and was finally and officially recognized in the Agreement between the two Powers signed at Berlin on July 1, 1890. Under that agreement Germany took from the Sultan of Zanzibar all his territory on the coast of German East Africa, while Britain took Zanzibar, Pemba, and the territories on the coast of British East Africa. This, however, still left the Benadir Coast theoretically under the sovereignty of the Sultan. Part of the " arrangement " of 1890 had consisted in an understanding that the Benadir Coast should go to Italy, and accordingly on August 12, 1892, Sir Gerald Portal, the British Consul-General, signed, in the name of the Sultan of Zanzibar, a treaty with Italy by which the Benadir Coast was to be handed over by Zanzibar to Italy and by Italy to an Italian company.[1]

The end of the nineteenth century was a period in which the colonial policy of all European States looked to chartered companies and concessionary companies as the cheapest and most effective means of acquiring and consolidating an economic empire. In Britain, Germany, France, and Portugal the State was, at the instance of the imperialists, handing over to privileged commercial companies the administration and exploitation of newly-acquired African territory. Thus Britain and Germany on the east coast made over the territory which they took from the Sultan of Zanzibar to the *British East Africa Company*, which received its charter in 1888, and to the *Gesellschaft für Deutsche Kolonisation*, which received its charter in 1885, and the *Deutsch-Ostafrikanische Gesell-schaft*, which was its offspring. It was not unnatural that Italy should also think of handing over the territory which she had

[1] The agreement calls the transaction a " concession " of territory, and Italy agreed to pay to Zanzibar a premium of 40,000 rupees, and an annual sum of 160,000 rupees. The concession is for twenty-five years, renewable for another twenty-five years. These stipulations cannot be taken very seriously ; after 1892 the Benadir Coast became in fact an Italian possession.

acquired from the Sultan of Zanzibar to a commercial company. What is, however, interesting is that the company to which the Italian Government proceeded to entrust the administration and exploitation of the Benadir Coast was promoted and controlled by that Italian Consul, Signor Filonardi, who had discovered that the Sultan of all the Mijjertayns and the other rulers of the Somali Coast were determined to submit their territories to the control of Italy. Thus, the man who was immediately responsible for bringing these territories politically under the domination of Italy himself obtained from the Italian Government the right to administer them politically and exploit them commercially. He not only obtained this right, but he also obtained an annual subsidy for his company from the Italian Government of 300,000 lire, the company undertaking to pay the annual sum due to the Sultan of Zanzibar.[1]

Filonardi's company was not successful either administratively or commercially, but it continued in existence until 1896. In that year the defeat of Adowa caused, as we have seen, a revision of the aspirations of Italians in Ethiopia. This revision extended to the Somali Coast, which now became a separate and not very eligible colony instead of the sea-board to an immense and lucrative empire. In June, 1896, the concession to the Filonardi Company was revoked, and the Italian Government handed over the territory to a new company with a capital of 1,000,000 lire called the " Benadir Company." Unfortunately, either the passion of the sultans of this district for Italian rule had cooled, or perhaps the sultans' subjects had never shared their rulers' eagerness for losing their independence : at any rate, when in November the Italian Consul-General, Cecchi, attempted to wind up the affairs of the Filonardi Company and establish the Benadir Company in possession, he and his military escort were attacked by the inhabitants near Mogadishu. Cecchi himself, the newly-appointed collector of customs, and twelve other officers were killed, and the Italians had to send a military expedition from Massowah, which, by hard fighting, eventually succeeded in re-establishing among the sultans and inhabitants their desire for Italian government. These events, which took some time, and the effects of the defeat at Adowa upon the whole position of Italy in Ethiopia, made it desirable to introduce modifications into the conditions upon which the company had acquired the concession. In 1898, therefore, the Government signed a new agreement with the company, which now took the name " Societa anonima commerciale italiana del Benadir." The

---

[1] See Hauptmann a.D. K. von Bruchhausen, "Die Italiener im Benadir-Gebiet," in *Beiträge zur Kolonialpolitik u. Kolonialwirtschaft* for the year 1899–1900, vol. i. p. 572, from which the facts in this and the following paragraphs are taken. See also Angus Hamilton, *Somaliland*, 1911, pp. 194-200.

new agreement, which was most severely criticized in the Italian press as being far too favourable to the company, handed over to it the territory of the Benadir Coast until 1946. All mining rights and sovereign rights over the soil were vested in the company, but a condition was introduced whereby the company had to obtain the sanction of the Government before sub-letting these rights to any persons other than native-born Italians. The Government bound itself to pay the company an annual subsidy of 400,000 lire, while the company in return was responsible for the annual sum, about 200,000 lire, due to the Sultan of Zanzibar. The company also acquired the right to levy taxes and customs dues.

I have given these facts with regard to Italian Somaliland because they show very clearly, on a small scale, the working of economic imperialism. We can see on the Benadir Coast exactly what the Italian expansionists hoped to gain from Abyssinia if their plans succeeded. Their hopes centred in economic privilege and economic exploitation. The initial stages of expansion in Abyssinia and Somaliland were the same; they were political and imperial. The Emperor Menelik in Abyssinia, and the Sultan of all the Mijjertayns in Somaliland, were suddenly found to be bitten by a desire for accepting the political overlordship of the Italian Government. A protectorate was then proclaimed over both countries. But there the resemblance ends. The Emperor Menelik protested that he never desired anything but independence, and proved strong enough to defend his independence by force of arms; the protests of the little sultans of the Somali Coast were unheard, and they were unable to defend their possessions except by sporadic attacks upon Italian officers, attacks which were easily punished by two companies of native troops sent from Massowah. Thus the political power of the Italian State was beaten off by Menelik from his kingdom, but it settled effectively upon the Somali Coast, and therefore the second stage of economic imperialism was confined to Somaliland. That second stage consisted in economic exploitation. The territory (of which the total exports and imports amounted in value for the year 1896–97 to a paltry £100,000) was handed over for economic exploitation to a company formed by the Italian official who was responsible for bringing the territory under the Italian flag. The kind of exploitation contemplated is shown by the terms on which the Government handed over the country to the " Societa anonima commerciale italiana del Benadir." This subsidized company received sovereign rights over the mineral wealth and soil of Benadir, and no provision was made for protecting the rights of ownership or the interests of the native inhabitants.[1] At the same time, the power to levy taxes and customs was given

---

[1] The same objection applies to the concessions granted by the German Government to privileged companies in the Cameroon in 1899. No protection is accorded

to this private company. The whole country is, therefore, reserved
for the economic exploitation of a small group of shareholders in
Italy, and the only result of such exploitation, if it be successful, is
to increase the dividends of a handful of Italians.[1] No better
example could be found than this of the use of the power of a European State in Africa for the purpose of promoting the economic
interests of its citizens in Europe.

The defeat at Adowa was not only a defeat for the Italian army,
it was a defeat, a temporary annihilation, of Italian imperialism.
Crispi and the expansionists were "hurled from power amid the
execrations of the people," and although "King and army demanded
an avenging campaign to wipe out the shame of defeat," popular
discontent and disgust with their rulers and their imperialist ad-
ventures were too strong, and a "Peace Ministry" was formed.
The result was a treaty of peace, signed at Addis Abbaba on
October 26, 1896, between Menelik and Italy, which revoked the
Treaty of Uccialli and recognized the independence of Abyssinia.
For the moment at any rate Italy dropped out of the game of
European policy in Ethiopia, and Britain and France were left
alone to face one another in the struggle for domination of the Nile
Valley and Abyssinia.

The struggle between France and Britain lasted for eight years
—from 1896 to 1904. It falls into two parts, the first of which
was a short, sharp, dangerous political-military struggle which
ended at Fashoda in 1898, and the second an obscure, economic-
political struggle which was finally settled at the time of the Anglo-
French Entente.

The strategic-political struggle of 1896 to 1898 must be dealt
with first. It is, unfortunately, extremely complicated, for it is
connected by many strands of policy with regions and aspirations
far distant from Ethiopian Africa. And it is necessary to insist
upon the fact that, although it was, on the surface, a strategic-
political struggle, yet the beliefs and desires which produced it
were fundamentally those of economic imperialism. This will
immediately become apparent if we examine the general position

---

to the natives under the charters given to the Gesellschaft Süd-Kamerun and the
Gesellschaft Nord-Kamerun, which received powers under the charters "to conclude agreements with the owners or other interested persons with a view to the
cession of lands." On the other hand, in the concessions granted to privileged
companies by the French Government in French Congo in 1897, a somewhat
vague provision is included prescribing that the companies shall scrupulously
respect the customs, habits, religion, and organization of the native populations.
See on this point, with regard to the German and French companies, Pierre Decharme,
Compagnies et Sociétés coloniales allemandes, 1903, pp. 196-8.

[1] The company in 1910 paid about 11 per cent on its paid-up capital, which
amounted to £12,000. Its revenue, including the subsidy of £1600, was £226,116,
and the expenditure £224,736. See Angus Hamilton, *Somaliland*, 1911, p. 106.

of France and Britain in Africa in 1896 and the broad principles of policy which were pursued by each at the time, and which caused the events of 1896 to 1898.

In 1896 Britain was firmly established in Egypt, while the Nile Valley was still in the hands of the Dervish power. It was an era of "imperialism." Empire and expansion were being preached as the noblest and the most profitable duties of Englishmen. The spokesmen of this imperialism were Mr. Chamberlain and Mr. Rhodes. The latter was himself an empire-builder in the south of Africa, but his vision was large and he began in the 'nineties to look far beyond his own sphere in South Africa. A financier and a millionaire, he took, naturally, the same view as Mr. Chamberlain with regard to empire and commerce, and his beliefs and desires were those of the purest economic imperialism. Their economic colour was deepened owing to the fact that in South Africa Rhodes had built his empire upon a commercial company and had built the commercial company into the framework of the Empire. The Chartered Company and its shareholders very often seemed to be for him and his followers indistinguishable from the Empire and its citizens : [1] and this was not unnatural, because every day they had before their eyes and under their hands a living and concrete proof of Mr. Chamberlain's statement that "Empire is commerce." In the Chartered Company empire actually *was* commerce and commerce *was* empire.

But although the imperialism of Rhodes, like that of Chamberlain, was fundamentally economic, there was a personal difference in the two men which produced a marked difference in their doctrines and influence. Chamberlain's mind, like his face, was singularly hard, precise, and clear-cut. He was a popular orator, but it is remarkable that he hardly ever appealed to the vague and hazy emotions which are the happy hunting-grounds of oratory. An analysis of his speeches will show that his appeal is almost always to the reason of his audience, and his aim is to convince them that the path of his logic ends in their material interests. This is not to say that he was without idealism, but his idealism was of the kind in which a practical business man can move without feeling out of place or uncomfortable. The substance of his ideals was

---

[1] There is a curious example of this in Sir Lewis Michell's *Life of the Rt. Hon. Cecil John Rhodes* (1910), vol. i. p. 330. Sir Lewis remarks that Rhodes gave to the Chartered Company dominions nearly equal in area to the combined areas of Great Britain, France, Prussia, Austria, and Spain, and then quotes Rhodes's own defence of this action in his letter to Mr. Stead : "I desire to act for the benefit of those who, I think, are the greatest people the world has ever seen, but whose fault is that they do not know their strength and their greatness and their destiny." Sir Lewis adds : "A curious commentary on this remark is that the shareholders are scattered literally all over Europe. In other words, the province added by Rhodes to the Empire was built up and developed, in part, with foreign money, our greatest trade rivals thus unconsciously aiding us to enlarge our Dominions."

not imagination or beauty or morality or any kind of vision, but simply expediency, and this helped to keep their edges hard and clear-cut. These characteristics gave a peculiar quality to the imperialism preached by him. It appealed to practical men and to business men as something very big which might be owned and made to pay. The citizen of this kind of empire would feel all the emotions of pride and affection towards it which the owner feels towards a very large business built up by himself. The imperialism of Chamberlain, therefore, had in it a real and effective idealism and was capable of rousing in many people an emotional warmth, but it always suffered from its concreteness and the sharpness and hardness of its edges. It could never quite conceal the fact that it was a product of modern industry, machine made.

Rhodes, too, as his career shows, was an eminently practical business man. But he had a quality which Chamberlain lacked. Around the very practical and business-like and material ideas in his mind there used to gather other very large, vague, and hazy ideas which some people regard as a sign of genius, others as a sign of sentimentality. He was a romantic financier, millionaire, and empire-builder, and the romance of his own career and ideas supplied the necessary touch of romance to the imperialism of the 'nineties. Without this Rhodesian romance it is doubtful whether the imperialism of Chamberlain would ever have succeeded in making a wide popular appeal to the British public. The best example of this quality of Rhodes's mind appears in his will. It is impossible to conceive of Mr. Chamberlain directing in his will that he should be buried in a particular spot because it had a grand view and was lonely. Yet every one can feel the appeal of that quality, which is genius or sentimentality, or the genius of sentimentality, in Rhodes's words: " I admire the grandeur and loneliness of the Matoppos in Rhodesia, and therefore I desire to be buried in the Matoppos on the hill which I used to visit and which I called the 'View of the World,' in a square to be cut in the rock on the top of the hill, covered with a plain brass plate with these words thereon: 'Here lie the remains of Cecil John Rhodes.' "

Rhodes and his followers did not believe in dominion which did not produce dividends, or patriotism which did not produce a profit.[1] But the largeness and haze of Rhodes's ideas made his economic imperialism romantic. This applies particularly to the

---

[1] A curious instance of this has recently become public in the case before the Judicial Committee of the Privy Council, which has arisen from a claim of the Chartered Company to the ownership by conquest of the whole of the unalienated land of Southern Rhodesia. The claim is based on the conquest which followed the invasion of Matabeleland by officers of the Company in 1893. When the invasion was only in contemplation, and Dr. Jameson was engaged in recruiting a force adequate for the conquest, he wrote the following letter laying down the conditions of service :—

conception with which he was peculiarly associated and which was the central point in his African policy during the 'nineties, the "Cape to Cairo railway." Rhodes worked unceasingly for the realization of this idea,[1] and there is no doubt that the vision of an all-British railway running from north to south through the whole continent of Africa had a great and romantic attraction to many ordinary Englishmen. To such ordinary men the appeal was both romantic and hazy, and unconnected with the beliefs and desires of economic imperialism. But in the economic imperialism of Rhodes himself imperialism and romance were always secondary to economics,[2] and the primary object of this railway was for him commercial and

---

"To CAPTAIN ALLAN WILSON, Victoria.

Sir—The following are the conditions of service for members of the Victoria force for Matabeleland:

"(1) That each member shall have protection for all claims in Mashonaland until six months after date of cessation of hostilities.

"(2) That each member will be entitled to mark out a farm of 3000 morgen in any part of Matabeleland. . . .

"(6) That any member of the Victoria force is entitled to 15 claims on reef and five alluvial claims. . . .

"(7) The 'loot' shall be divided one-half to the British South Africa Company and the remainder to the officers and men in equal shares. . . .

"(10) From the date on which the force crosses the border the rights of any member of the force dying, invalided, or killed on service will be protected and secured to his estate.—Yours etc., L. S. JAMESON, for the B.S.A. Coy."

After the invasion and conquest, Mr. Rhodes made a speech to the volunteers when they were being disbanded; the following is an interesting extract:

"You have been able, with the co-operation of the Bechuanaland Mounted Police, to conquer Matabeleland. . . . Now the time has come for you to disperse and select your ground. . . . There will probably be reserves for the natives and the remainder will be what I might call public land, so that you will be the first entitled to select land, and you will deal with it after provision has been made for the natives. . . . It is your right, for you have conquered the country."

See The Times of April 23 and April 26, 1918.

[1] In 1892 Rhodes wrote to Schnadhorst with regard to his contribution to the funds of the Liberal Party and his fear that Gladstone might evacuate Egypt: "The matter that is troubling me is your policy as to Egypt. I was horrified when I returned from Mashonaland to read a speech of Mr. Gladstone's evidently foreshadowing a scuttle if he came in. . . . However, if your respected leader remains obdurate when he comes into power, and adopts this policy of scuttle, I shall certainly call upon you to devote my subscription to some public charity in terms of my letter to you. . . . As you are aware, the question of Egypt was the only condition I made, and it seems rather extraordinary to me that the first public speech your leader should make, which sketches generally his views upon the near approach of office, should declare a policy of abandonment. I asked you at the time I wrote to see him and tell him of my action, and I suppose you must have mentioned the Egyptian question, which was really all I cared about. We are now one-third of the way with a telegraph through the Continent from the south, only to hear of your policy of scuttle from the north " (Michell, op. cit. vol. ii. p. 49). The passage is instructive as indicating the possible relation of imperialist policy and the party funds.

[2] This explains Rhodes's willingness to come to agreement with the German Emperor for the railway to be built partly over German territory. See Michell, op. cit. p. 250.

financial. "As to the commercial aspect," he wrote in 1900, "every one supposes that the railway is being built with the only object that a human being may be able to get in at Cairo and get out at Cape Town. This is, of course, ridiculous. The object is to cut Africa through the centre, and the railway will pick up trade all along the route. The junctions to the east and west coasts, which will occur in the future, will be outlets for the traffic obtained along the route of the line as it passes through the centre of Africa. At any rate up to Bulawayo, where I am now, it has been a payable undertaking, and I still think it will continue to be so as we advance into the far interior. We propose now to go on and across the Zambesi just below the Victoria Falls. I should like to have the spray of the water over the carriages." [1]

The Cape–Cairo scheme was in many respects the pivot of British imperialist policy in Africa during the last decade of the century. Rhodes, even in 1892, as his letter to Schnadhorst shows, was pushing up from the south, and was horrified at the idea of a " scuttle from the north " and Egypt, because that would make a British Mittel-Afrika running from north to south for ever impossible. But the completion of this British Mittel-Afrika, which was to centre round a railway and a telegraph line, implied in 1890 a very ambitious programme. The reader must try to see the problem as it would present itself to a man looking, as Rhodes did in those days, northwards from the hill in the Matoppos which he liked to call the "View of the World." The world which he saw immediately stretching out before him was what we now call Southern and Northern Rhodesia. This territory, nearly 500,000 square miles in extent, equal in area to the combined territories of Great Britain, France, and Prussia, had to be incorporated in the British Empire. They were so incorporated in a very few years by means of the Chartered Company. The first step from the south was comparatively easy; the territory was in the hands of African kings or chiefs, capable of being conquered; and conquest is still the shortest and safest road to empire. But just north of Southern Rhodesia, on the Zambesi River, in the Shire highlands, and the land to the west of Lake Nyasa and to the south of Lake Tanganyika, was the first real difficulty, the first complication of rival imperialisms. This piece of territory is the hinterland of Portuguese East Africa and also the hinterland of Portuguese West Africa. Portugal, by laying claim to it, aimed at a Mittel-Afrika which would cut right across the Cape–Cairo scheme and would stop Rhodes and the British Empire before they were "one-third of the way through the continent from the south." Rhodes and his followers early saw this danger: by subsidizing the African Lakes Company, which operated in Nyasaland, they obtained a footing in that

[1] Introduction, dated September 7, 1900, to *The Cape to Cairo*, by E. S. Grogan.

country which was the key to the position, and were thus successful in preventing its abandonment by the British Government to Portugal. There followed a sharp struggle between the Chartered Company and the Portuguese Government, an ultimatum from Great Britain to Portugal, a withdrawal of the Portuguese claim to the hinterland of their African possessions, and in due course a band of red appeared upon the maps between Lakes Nyasa and Tanganyika, proclaiming to the world that all this was now British territory.

The British Mittel-Afrika was now an accomplished fact from the Cape of Good Hope to Lake Tanganyika. But it was north of this point that the real problem of imperial policy began. The problem was to obtain another band of red upon the map which would join Egypt to Tanganyika. In the north the path of policy was obvious, though difficult; the Sudan and Nile Valley and Uganda would have to be incorporated in the British Empire. The incorporation of Uganda was successfully accomplished in 1894, thanks to the efforts of Captain Lugard and the British East Africa Company, whose history we shall have to examine in the following chapter. The determination to incorporate the Sudan and the Nile Valley led to the struggle between Britain and France in Ethiopian Africa with which we are immediately concerned. But, even if Egypt, the Sudan and Nile Valley, and Uganda were coloured red, there would still be a gap in the Cape–Cairo railway and the British Mittel-Afrika, because there was an awkward strip of territory between Tanganyika and the southern boundary of Uganda. In this gap, which lies, roughly, between the south of Lake Albert Edward and the north of Lake Tanganyika, German East Africa from the east meets the Belgian Congo from the west.

The reader who has now these geographical facts in his mind must also try to reconstruct in his mind the problem of policy, as it appeared at the beginning of 1894 both to British and to French imperialists. The Briton wanted to acquire a solid block or strip of British empire running from Egypt to the Cape. From the north he had reached the Sudan; from the south he had reached the southern shore of Tanganyika. He still had, therefore, to acquire, somehow or other, the Sudan, the Nile Valley, the sources of the Nile, Uganda, and a strip of territory between Lakes Albert Edward and Tanganyika. The pivot of this problem and policy was the Nile and Ethiopian Africa, because it was practically certain that Abyssinia itself would be involved in British aspirations. British desires embodied themselves in Rhodes's railway, and that railway, owing to the swampy nature of the ground in the regions of the Upper Nile, would, in fact, for a certain distance have to be built over Abyssinian territory. This was the British side of the imperial picture. The French side, as is usually the case with such pictures, was the exact opposite. It is a postulate of imperial policy that if a State A desires to obtain a solid block of empire running from a point X in the north to a point Y in the south, any State B will oppose that desire, and it is an axiom of imperial policy that the easiest method of opposition is for the State B to endeavour to obtain a solid block of empire running from a point T in the west to a point U in the east and intersecting a straight line drawn from the point X to the point Y. Acting upon this postulate and axiom, the French imperialists saw at once that the problem for them centred in the Nile and Ethiopian Africa, and that they must obtain a solid block of empire running from west to east and cutting the line of the Cape–Cairo railway somewhere between the Sudan and Tanganyika.[1] In 1894 any of three spots was for them crucial, namely, the Nile Valley and Abyssinia, Uganda, and the "gap" between Lakes Albert Edward and Tanganyika. The negative side of their policy must be to keep the British Empire out of all or any of these three regions; the positive side must be to acquire one or more of them, as part of a solid block of French territory running from the west to the east coast of Africa. The line which this French Mittel-Afrika would have to follow was obvious. The French State had acquired on the west coast of Africa an immense piece of territory, the French Congo, on the north of the Belgian Congo. The boundary between the French Congo and the Belgian Congo had been fixed by a Protocol of April 29, 1887, as the River Ubanghi, but the boundary on the west was undefined. Before 1894 the French had already pushed out northwards towards Lake Chad (in order to join up their territory with their Sahara Empire), and westwards towards the Bahr-el-Ghazal and the Nile; and it had become clear to the French imperialists that, if a French empire was to be thrown across the Cape–Cairo British scheme, it could only be accomplished by penetrating into the Bahr-el-Ghazal, the Nile Valley, and Abyssinia from French Congo, and by linking up these territories with French Somaliland by a solid band of French possessions or spheres of influence.

Here then, in 1894, were two incompatible schemes of empire in the minds of certain Frenchmen and Englishmen. The year 1894 was a turning-point in the rival policies. We have already seen how, in May of that year, the British Government signed an agreement with Italy which was intended to reserve the Valley of the Nile for British occupation, and Abyssinia for an Italian

[1] M. André Lebon, who was Minister for the Colonies at the time of the Marchand expedition, writes in his book, *La Politique de la France en Afrique*, 1901, p. 5, with regard to the policy behind that expedition : "This conception was its own defence. The idea of covering Africa from west to east, while Mr. Cecil Rhodes flaunted his ambition to cross it from south to north, had prevailed in France for several years. People were unwilling that England, *de facto* mistress of Egypt and mistress of the Cape both *de jure* and *de facto*, should seize the whole of the Nile Valley."

empire. Seven days after the signature of the Anglo-Italian Treaty, the same British Government signed a remarkable agreement with Leopold II. as sovereign of the Belgian Congo. The British Government granted to Leopold what amounted to a perpetual lease of a large block of territory, including the Bahr-el-Ghazal, while Leopold granted to Great Britain a similar lease of a corridor of land between Lakes Albert Edward and Tanganyika. The effects of this arrangement were that Article II., which leased the Bahr-el-Ghazal to the Belgian Congo, when read in conjunction with the Anglo-Italian Treaty, completely shut off the French from any possible entrance into the Nile Valley, while Article III. filled up with a band of red the " gap " in the Cape–Cairo railway between the two lakes. Exactly a month after the signing of this agreement the British Government proclaimed a protectorate over Uganda, so that on June 18, 1894, the French imperialists suddenly found themselves confronted by a *fait accompli*; the three crucial spots, the Nile Valley, Uganda, and the " gap," had dropped into the capacious lap of the British Empire, and, on paper at any rate, a solid block of red ran from the Cape to Cairo.

But the French were not to yield without a struggle, and there began immediately a bitter conflict between the French and British imperialists and imperialisms, which culminated at Fashoda in 1898. The Anglo-Italian and the Anglo-Belgian treaties were met by an outburst of indignation in Paris. M. Etienne in the French Chamber led the attack. " To-day," he said,[1] " we are submitting to affronts and encroachments of the Congo Free State ; but, above all, we have been too long exposed to the opposition, the continual hostility, of the British Government. . . . We have built up, and we intend to preserve and develop, a colonial empire in order to assure the future of our country in the new continents, in order to reserve there an outlet for our products (*un débouché à nos marchandises*) and to find there raw materials for our industries. But if, after the effort we have made, after the expenditure already made by us in men and treasure, we are to see all our efforts wasted one day, no, gentlemen, it would be better to renounce at once all colonial empire." The Government adopted the view of the imperialists. Speaking to M. Etienne's interpellation on the same day (June 7), M. Hanotaux, Minister of Foreign Affairs, said : " This treaty places the Free State in a position of rupture, I hope peaceful, but certainly a position of rupture with the Powers who gave their signatures to its creation : it is in formal contradiction with the public law of Africa." He ended his speech by asking for a Vote of Credit of 1,800,000 francs in order " to take the necessary steps on the Ubanghi and in the French Congo." The Chamber

[1] See Eugène Etienne, *Son Œuvre Coloniale, Algérienne et Politique*, Discours et Ecrits réunis et édités par la " Dépêche Coloniale," 1907, vol. i. p. 235.

voted the money unanimously, and a few days later Commandant Monteil was despatched to take charge of the French forces which were being concentrated on the Ubanghi.[1]

The action of the French Government amounted to a threat of war, a war between France and England for the control of the Upper Nile. It would have been a war, as M. Etienne, the leader in this aggressive policy, showed in his speech, with its echoes of the words of Jules Ferry and the economic imperialists of 1881, for commercial outlets and the raw materials of industry. War was averted because the British Government gave way. M. Hanotaux followed up his bellicose speech in the Chamber by a formal protest in London and Brussels, and he was joined in this protest by the German Government. Lord Rosebery and King Leopold yielded immediately : on June 22, 1894, a Declaration was signed between Great Britain and the Congo Free State withdrawing Article III. of the Agreement of May 12, which had given to Britain the lease of the strip of territory between the lakes ; and, on August 14, an Agreement was signed between France and the Congo Free State by which King Leopold bound himself " to renounce all occupation, and to exercise in the future no political influence " in the Bahr-el-Ghazal and on the Upper Nile.

This result was hailed with enthusiasm by French imperialists as a defeat of British imperialism and as opening to France a road to the Nile and immense vistas of empire. " We have opened for ourselves," said M. Deloncle in the Chamber on February 28, 1895, " access to the Upper Nile, not indeed to establish ourselves there, for those regions belong to the Ottoman Empire and are dependencies of Egypt, but in order to place ourselves in a good position, to turn from the rear certain positions of our rivals. . . . We have taken forfeits : that is our right colonial policy. To-day the English dream of possessing the whole Upper Nile has been, I believe, for ever upset." [2] For a public declaration this was sufficiently menacing ; the actual steps taken by the French Government showed that an even more forward imperialist policy was contemplated. In September, 1894, M. Delcassé, Colonial Minister, sent M. Liotard as Government Commissioner to the Upper Ubanghi, instructing him to extend his French sphere as far as the Nile. At the same time Lieutenant Mizon was despatched to Abyssinia with instructions to make a " voyage de reconnaissance " to the Nile, while yet a third French mission, under Captain Clochette, was sent from Djibuti through Abyssinia into the Nile Valley.

The ideas and policy behind these movements are not obscure, and they are admitted by most French historians. Liotard and Monteil from the French Congo were to move eastward into the

---

[1] See Darcy, *Cent Années de Rivalité Coloniale*, pp. 384-6.
[2] Darcy, *op. cit.* p. 388.

Nile Valley, there to be joined by Mizon and Clochette, who were to start from French Somaliland and travel westward through the territory of Menelik. It was precisely the same expansionist policy of converging expeditions, half military and half scientific, which had borne such rich imperial fruit for France in the Sahara and the regions of Lake Chad. The policy, which was the immediate answer of France to the Anglo-Italian and Anglo-Belgian treaties of May, 1894, seemed to have every prospect of success. Menelik saw from the agreement between Italy and Britain that his independence was threatened by those two Powers, and he immediately turned for help and comfort to France. The help and comfort consisted largely of French munitions, and, as is usual in such cases, this kind of help and comfort was not given for nothing. In 1894 Menelik granted to a M. Ilg and a French company a concession for the construction of a railway from Djibuti to the Harrar, and thence through Addis Abbaba to the White Nile. The training of the Abyssinian army was largely entrusted to French officers. These are well-known symptoms of the beginning of " peaceful " imperialist penetration, and with a strategic railway from French Somaliland through Abyssinia to the Nile in French hands, with the Abyssinian army armed and officered by France, with French expeditions moving hither and thither across Abyssinian territory, it was not unnatural to consider as a practicable possibility the incorporation of Abyssinia in a solid block of French empire stretching from Somaliland to the Congo Coast.

For a moment it looked as if the trial of strength between the British and French States would come immediately. The London Chamber of Commerce called upon the British Government " to take adequate measures with a view to assuring the control of England over the whole valley of the Nile from Uganda to Fashoda."[1] Rumours flew about London with regard to the French expeditions which were to converge from east and west, from Abyssinia and the Congo, upon the Nile Valley. In the House of Commons, on March 28, 1895, Sir Edward Grey, Under Secretary of State for Foreign Affairs, gave the clearest of warnings to France that Britain claimed the whole of the Nile Valley, and would consider as an " unfriendly " act any attempt to dispute this claim by the sending of French expeditions into that territory. He said :

I stated the other day that in consequence of these claims of ours, and in consequence of the claims of Egypt in the Nile Valley, the British and Egyptian spheres of influence covered the whole of the Nile waterway. . . . I am asked whether or not it is the case that a French expedition is coming from the West of Africa with the intention of entering the Nile Valley, and occupying up to the Nile . . . ; and I

---

[1] April 10, 1895.

will go further and say that, after all I have explained about the claims we consider we have under past Agreements, and the claims which we consider Egypt may have in the Nile Valley, and adding to that fact that our claims and the view of the Government with regard to them are fully and clearly known to the French Government, I cannot think it is possible that these rumours deserve credence, because the advance of a French expedition, under secret instructions, right from the other side of Africa, into a territory over which our claims have been known for so long, would be not merely an inconsistent and unexpected act, but it must be perfectly well known to the French Government that it would be an unfriendly act, and would be so viewed by England.

Whether this explicit warning of the British Government caused the French to hesitate is not certain, but suddenly the aggressive policy was abandoned in Paris. The orders to Commandant Monteil to proceed to the Ubanghi were cancelled, and he and the vote of 1,800,000 francs were diverted to the purposes of imperialism in other parts of Africa. The expedition of Lieutenant Mizon to Abyssinia was countermanded, and Captain Clochette was left to spend eighteen months in Addis Abbaba "without resources and without instructions."[1] French colonial circles at the time, and French writers who have the advantage and misfortune of being able to look back over the whole course of policy which culminated in Fashoda, are very severe in criticizing the pusillanimity and apathy of French policy between 1894 and 1896. They point out with some force that, if the policy of setting up a French claim to the Nile Valley by means of converging expeditions was to be adopted with any chance of success, the steps necessary for pushing it through should have been taken at once in the years 1894 to 1896, when Italy was involved in hostilities with Menelik and the English were still shut off from the Nile Valley by the Mahdi. It was useless to open "access to the Upper Nile" in 1894, and to take the first steps in the only line of action which could allow France to make full use of that access, if at the first sign of opposition the French Government withdrew and relapsed into apathy. French policy, in fact, vacillated between timid inaction, when bold action might have borne fruit in an empire on the Nile, and feverish action, when the opportunity had passed and the fruit was in process of being picked by Lord Kitchener and a British army.

Such vacillations are not unknown among the imperialists and in the imperial policy of all countries. Statesmen and governments have continually charged boldly up to an imperialist fence, but as soon as they have seen another country raise the notice "ultimatum" or "unfriendly act" upon the top of it, they have swerved aside and refused the final and dangerous leap into imperialism. Lord Rosebery, we have seen, shied at the protest of France

[1] Darcy, op. cit. p. 411.

and Germany over the Anglo-Belgian treaty; the explanation of French policy between 1894 and 1896 is probably that M. Ribot shied in much the same way at Sir Edward Grey's sudden raising of the notice " Unfriendly Act " upon the last fence dividing France from an empire on the Nile.

At any rate " cette néfaste période 1894-96," [1] as the French historian calls it, passed in inaction. Suddenly, on March 1, 1896, the defeat of the Italians at Adowa reopened in its acutest form the whole problem of the rival imperialist policies of France and Britain upon the Nile and in Ethiopian Africa. The course of events shows clearly the close connection upon which I have had so often to insist between the position of Abyssinia and imperialist aspirations in the Nile Valley.

The Italian army was defeated at Adowa, in the north-east of Abyssinia, on March 1; the detailed news reached Europe about March 5; on March 12 the British Government telegraphed to Lord Cromer in Egypt that it had been decided to reoccupy Dongola in the Sudan. Lord Cromer in *Modern Egypt* comments upon the extraordinary suddenness of this decision, which in effect meant that the British Government had decided to reconquer the Sudan. Exactly four months previously he had received instructions from London which meant that the British Government had decided to " postpone *sine die* the question of reoccupying the Sudan," and he had been told that " the financial arrangements of the Egyptian Government could be made without reference to the cost " of a Sudan expedition, because " there was not any prospect of the Government consenting to the despatch of a military expedition into the Sudan." Lord Cromer explains that this sudden and complete reversal of policy " in the twinkling of an eye " was " in some degree the outcome of the rapid growth of the imperialist spirit, which about this time took place in England " : he admits, however, that the immediate cause was the battle of Adowa. It is difficult to believe that the imperialist spirit could have grown quite so rapidly as to cause the British people to realize in the short space of four months that the national honour could no longer be baulked of the salve for which it yearned—the words are Lord Cromer's—the salve being the slaughter of Dervishes at Omdurman in 1898 and the wound the murder of General Gordon in 1885. National psychology must completely baffle a rational interpretation of history if it could determine that in November 1895 the recapture of Khartoum was not required as a salve for the nation's honour, and in March 1896 that it was. [2]

In this instance it seems more reasonable to accept the interpretation of French historians, who find the cause of the reoccupation

---

[1] M. Daroy.
[2] See Lord Cromer, *Modern Egypt*, vol. ii. pp. 81-110.

of Dongola and Lord Kitchener's reconquest of the Sudan in the
Italian defeat on March 1. As soon as the magnitude of that
defeat became known in Europe, it was clear that the situation in
Ethiopian Africa and in the Nile Valley, so carefully built up by
the Anglo-Italian treaties of 1891 and 1894, had been destroyed.
It was no " sharp squall " of the imperialist spirit blowing through
the people of England which caused that telegram to be sent on
March 12 to Lord Cromer, but a calculation on the part
of Lord Salisbury's Government that the defeat of their Italian
allies had uncovered the eastern flank of the Nile Valley, and that
it was, therefore, time to comply with the demand of the London
Chamber of Commerce and " take adequate measures with a view
to assuring the control of England over the whole Valley of the
Nile from Uganda to Fashoda."

The events of 1896 to 1898, which are too well known to need
detailed narration, confirm this view. Kitchener's forward movement into the Sudan was begun at once with the occupation of
Akasha on March 20. The French immediately began, rather
feverishly, to put into operation the plan of converging expeditions
which they had hesitated to push through in 1894. Captain
Marchand was despatched to the French Congo on April 25,[1] with
instructions to march his expedition from the west into the Bahr-
el-Ghazal, and so to the White Nile. But it was an integral part
of the French plan, just as it had been in 1894, that another expedition should converge through Abyssinia and Ethiopian Africa
and join hands with Marchand in the Nile Valley. Accordingly
M. Lebon, Minister for the Colonies, sent confidential instructions
to M. Lagarde, the Governor of Djibuti and French Somaliland.
M. Lagarde was immediately to order Captain Clochette, who had
been waiting without instructions for eighteen months at Addis
Abbaba, to proceed to the right bank of the Nile ; meanwhile
another expedition, under M. Bonvalot, was being fitted out in Paris
and would also proceed through Abyssinia to join hands with Captain
Clochette in the Nile Valley.[2] Captain Clochette left Djibuti in
January, 1897 ; M. Bonvalot reached Addis Abbaba in April.
From that moment the history of the expeditions is involved in a
mysterious obscurity and confusion. M. Bonvalot was ordered
by M. Lagarde to return to France, and this expedition was handed
over to the second in command, M. Bonchamps. The policy with
which the Governor of Djibuti and the two leaders had been entrusted is clearly indicated in the confidential instructions issued
by M. Lagarde to M. Bonchamps. "It will be necessary," he

---

[1] The expedition was actually despatched in three parts on April 25, May 10
and 25. Marchand himself left France at the beginning of June and arrived at
Loanga in the French Congo in July.

[2] Lebon, *Politique de la France en Afrique*, 1901, p. 30.

wrote, " to establish on the right bank of the Nile an Ethiopian fortress, which part of the Clochette expedition might garrison, while you will construct a French fortress on the left bank, ensuring communication between the two by boats big or small, whichever you can obtain, and upon which you will fly our flag. . . . If, as we hope, MM. Liotard and Marchand reach the left bank of the Nile during this favourable time, you will get into touch with them . . . but, in any case, it would be necessary to have two solid fortresses from which hereafter an extension of Franco-Ethiopian influence may be made."

The plan which M. Lagarde had to carry out was simple. Marchand from the west, and Clochette and Bonchamps from the east, were to converge upon the Nile ; when Marchand arrived at Fashoda he was already to find two permanent fortifications upon the river banks flying the Abyssinian and the French flag respectively. These fortifications and the converging expeditions would form the basis of an Abyssinian claim to the right bank, and a French claim to the Bahr-el-Ghazal and left bank. Kitchener and the British army, when they arrived from the north, would find three strong French expeditions, supported by their allies the Abyssinians, strongly entrenched in " solid fortresses " right across the path of Mr. Rhodes's railway and Mittel-Afrika. The French " solid block " of empire from the Congo to Somaliland would already be in existence, and M. Deloncle's policy of " taking forfeits " and turning the British position in Egypt from the rear would have succeeded.

The plan failed. French historians lay the blame for its failure upon M. Lagarde, and certainly the inability of the Abyssinian expeditions of Clochette and Bonchamps to join hands with Marchand is remarkable. The Governor of Djibuti appears to have provided neither camels nor boats, two essentials for any expedition proceeding from Addis Abbaba to the Nile by the route selected. The consequence was that the expeditions, after struggling through a maze of swamps about the Rivers Baro and Sobat, eventually found themselves confronted by a stretch of water which they had no means of crossing, and they were compelled to retrace their steps to Addis Abbaba. When Marchand reached Fashoda with a handful of men he found no fortresses and no converging expedition of French and Abyssinians to support him, and, therefore, when after the battle of Omdurman in September, 1898, Lord Kitchener proceeded south to " take adequate measures with a view to assuring the control of England over the whole Valley of the Nile from Uganda to Fashoda," he found that his position had been turned from the rear only by Captain Marchand and a small body of Sengalese soldiers.

The negotiations and crisis which followed show very clearly the dangers to the peace and amity of nations inherent in economic imperialism. The sympathies of the world, including England, were with Captain Marchand, who, with a tenacity, courage, and skill worthy only of the highest aims and ideals, had struggled through the terrible swamps and forests of Africa to face with his handful of men Kitchener and the British army upon the banks of the Nile. But the aims and ideals of Marchand, as of Kitchener, were ultimately simply the acquisition of territory for France or for England. The Frenchman claimed the Valley of the Nile for France, the Englishman claimed it for the British Empire, and the national psychology of imperialism is such that even to-day, when the bitterness of this covetous rivalry has died down, French writers almost unanimously represent the rights as being with France, and English writers represent them as being with England.

It is interesting to examine these national " rights " for which, as the Prime Minister (Lord Salisbury) admitted, it seemed one moment as if a European war would have to be fought between France and England.[1] The British claims—"stamped with so much bad faith," M. Lémonon can still write of them in 1912![2]— rested (1) upon the fact that Sir Edward Grey had, three years before, warned France that an attempt on her part to acquire the Nile Valley would be " an unfriendly act," and that in 1897 the British Ambassador had made an even clearer representation in Paris to the French Government, and (2) that Fashoda and the Nile Valley belonged to Egypt. The French claims rested upon possession, the prior possession of Fashoda by Marchand and his Senegalese soldiers. And to the British claim that the whole Nile was British because the whole Nile belonged to Egypt, the French replied : " It is natural that if you speak to us to-day in the name of Egypt, we ask you in virtue of what mandate you do so, and in what respect your title is better than ours." " To return to the arguments derived from the rights of Egypt," wrote the French Ambassador in London to M. Delcassé, " I asked Lord Salisbury how it happened that we were opposed, not by an Egyptian minister nor by a representative of the sovereignty of the Sultan, but by the Prime Minister of England discussing the matter with the Ambassador of France."

" Our cause was so just, our rights so incontestable," laments M. Lémonon fourteen years later and eight years after the *Entente Cordiale*. The newspapers of Paris and London [3] between Sep-

---

[1] Speech on November 9, 1898 : " We have had quite recently to consider the question of European war, not, I will say, from a very near distance, but at all events with anxiety and consideration. The result has turned out happily. At one moment it seemed possible that it would be otherwise. . . ."

[2] Lémonon, *op. cit.* p. 134.

[3] The tone of a leading article in *The Times* on October 19, 1898, is character-istic : " Eight or nine fortuitous Frenchmen in the Khartum province are of no

tember, 1898, and January, 1899, which lashed themselves and their readers into a frenzy of bellicose patriotism, are full of their "just cause" and their "incontestable rights"; in the Yellow Books and the Blue Books, Ministers and Ambassadors can still be heard insisting upon French rights and British rights; French historians are as convinced of the bad faith of England and the incontestable rights of France as English historians are of the bad faith of France and the incontestable rights of Britain. The simple truth is that there were no just cause and no rights involved in the Fashoda incident. Neither France nor the British Empire had the slightest right to the possession either of Egypt or the Sudan or the Nile Valley. The claims of each State, when they are stripped of the fig-leaves of diplomacy and patriotic journalism, are based upon economic imperialism and nothing else, and the claims of economic imperialism are founded not in right but in might. Marchand was recalled from Fashoda and France suffered that "sharp wound," as M. Hanotaux calls her submission to the demands of England, not because there was any principle of right involved, but because a victorious British army of many thousands faced Marchand's handful of men in the Nile Valley, and because M. Delcassé knew that the French fleet was not in a condition to enter into a European war against the British fleet, which had already been sent by the British Government to cruise before Bizerta. The philosophic student of history who wishes to learn the beliefs and desires, the claims and the principles which lay behind the policy of the Fashoda incident, must turn to a speech delivered on November 15, 1898, by Mr. Chamberlain, who within the British Government was the leader and spokesman of imperialism :

"I am sure," he told his audience at Manchester, "it is the hope of every friend of peace that the decision of the French Government to withdraw Major Marchand from Fashoda is to be taken as only an indication that they accept the principle for which we have been contending. Fashoda is only a symbol. The great issue is the control of the whole valley of the Nile. . . . We claim on behalf of Egypt—which is occupied and protected by our troops—Egypt that we have redeemed from ruin and anarchy; Egypt that, at great sacrifice on our part, we have restored to a position of prosperity such as she has never known in these later centuries—we claim on her behalf the full control of all the territories which formerly were in her possession, or which fell under the rule of the Mahdi or his successor, the Khalifa. It is not a point of honour we are pressing, it is not a sentimental con-

consequence one way or the other, and do not so much as afford a subject for negotiation. . . . We are in effective occupation. We are going to remain in effective occupation without discussing the fact. That is all for the present, and that is all there will be unless the French should unfortunately take some ill-judged action, in which case we should, of course, have to defend ourselves."

sideration that we are putting forward. This claim is for Egypt a
matter of life and death, and all these sacrifices that we have made
have been in vain if we are to suppose that the sources of the Nile—
that great waterway upon which the life of Egypt depends—should be
in hands which are hostile, and which in any circumstances would be
unfriendly hands. . . . French politicians should once for all abandon
the tactics which they have been pursuing for so many years, and which
have as their object to hamper and embarrass British policy in every
part of the globe. . . ."

The argument in this passage is remarkable, and the logical
sequence of thought is not at first sight so lucid as it usually was
in Mr. Chamberlain's speeches. The " principle " for which the
British Government was contending, even at the risk of a European
war, was " the control of the whole valley of the Nile." It was
the principle, therefore, which the London Chamber of Commerce
had three years before enunciated when it called upon the British
Government to " take adequate measures with a view to assuring
the control of England over the whole valley of the Nile from
Uganda to Fashoda." The control was to be, and in fact has been,
the control not of Egypt but of England. And at first, from Mr.
Chamberlain's words, the reader might be led to believe that this
control by England was to be her reward for the " sacrifices " which
we had made in order to occupy Egypt by our troops and restore
her from ruin and anarchy to prosperity. What exactly these
great sacrifices were, Mr. Chamberlain does not tell his Manchester
audience, although the history of Algeria, Tunis, Tripoli, and
Abyssinia, which we have examined in the preceding chapters,
makes it probable that the Governments, the financiers, and the
imperialists of other European countries would have been only
too willing to make the same sacrifices in order to occupy Egypt
with their troops and restore her from ruin and anarchy to commercial prosperity. Four years before, on January 22, 1894, Mr.
Chamberlain had told a Birmingham audience that the reasons
why " I approve of the continued occupation of Egypt " was in
order that " new markets shall be created and that old markets
shall be effectually developed." It is legitimate to suppose that
when, on November 15, 1898, Mr. Chamberlain began the passage,
quoted by me, about the sacrifices which we had made in Egypt,
he still had at the back of his mind the argument for empire which
had appealed to him on January 22, 1894. The creation of new
and the development of old markets in Egypt and the Nile Valley
were to be regarded legitimately as part payment, as an inadequate
reward, for the sacrifices entailed in the policy of imperialism. It
probably escaped Mr. Chamberlain's notice that in France the
imperialists and their leader were using precisely the same argument
to justify their resistance to " the continual hostility of the British

Government" and their claim to control the Bahr-el-Ghazal and Nile Valley. If Mr. Chamberlain had inserted the sentences which we have quoted from the speech of M. Etienne into his speech at Birmingham or Manchester, no one in his audiences would have found them inconsistent with his argument or his policy : " We have built up and we intend to preserve and develop a colonial empire in order to assure the future of our country in the new continents, in order to reserve there an outlet for our products and to find there raw materials for our industries. But if, after the effort we have made, after the sacrifice already made by us in men and treasure, we are to see all our efforts wasted one day, no, gentlemen, it would be better to renounce at once all colonial empire."

It is noticeable, however, that in his speech at Manchester Mr. Chamberlain does not pursue the argument of economic rewards for imperial sacrifices. The principle which he is concerned with is the right of Egypt to the control of the Nile Valley. This right England was determined to uphold—otherwise all England's sacrifices would have been in vain. That the right was upheld by giving the control, not to Egypt, but to England, does not appear to have disturbed Mr. Chamberlain's sense of logic or humour. He was too occupied with explaining to his audience that Egypt would be doomed, and all England's sacrifices would be in vain, if the sources of the Nile, which England left for twelve years in the barbarous hands of the Mahdi, fell into the hostile, and in any circumstances unfriendly, hands of civilized France.

By recalling Major Marchand, said Mr. Chamberlain, the French Government recognized the principle for which England had been contending. The French Government had always recognized that principle, the principle that the territory of Africa should belong to the European State which was strong enough to seize and to hold it. " Fashoda is a symbol," said Mr. Chamberlain. He was right ; it was a symbol that the economic imperialism of Britain had triumphed in the valley of the Nile over the economic imperialism of France.

.   .   .   .

The real symbol of the triumph of British imperialism in the Nile Valley was, however, not Fashoda, but the Anglo-French Declaration of March 21, 1899. By this declaration the frontier between the British Sudan and the French Equatorial Africa was defined in such a way that the whole of the Bahr-el-Ghazal, the Nile Valley, and Darfur became British territory. France thus abandoned all claim to a foothold in the Egyptian Sudan or on the banks of the Nile : the dream of a solid block of French empire from Somaliland to the Congo was destroyed, and Rhodes's Mittel-Afrika—with the exception of the " gap " between Lakes Albert Edward and Tanganyika—became an accomplished fact.

There remained Abyssinia and Menelik. The position of the King of Kings was now a curious one. We have seen that an integral part of the French plan of countering British imperialism in the Nile Valley was co-operation with Abyssinia. Menelik had always claimed that his dominions on the west extended to the banks of the White Nile, and the object of the converging expeditions of Clochette and Bonchamps in 1897 was to work in co-operation with Abyssinian expeditions which were to establish themselves on the right bank of the river. That is why, in the confidential instructions to M. Bonchamps, quoted above, he was directed to see that "an Ethiopian fort" should be constructed on the right bank and a "French fort" on the left. French policy aimed at buying Menelik's co-operation by recognizing his claim to the right bank of the Nile: the expeditions of Marchand, Clochette, and Bonchamps were to establish a French claim only to the Bahr-el-Ghazal and the left bank of the White Nile.

Up to 1896 there had been no formal alliance between Menelik and France. Owing to the hostilities between the King and the Italians, France was unable to enter openly into such an alliance unless she were prepared for an open breach with Italy. This she was not willing to risk, and French aid to Abyssinia was strictly "informal" and confined to the supply of arms.[1] But the defeat of Italy at Adowa changed the situation. It left the French and British face to face in the struggle, now clearly imminent, for the possession of the Nile Valley, and it seemed to the statesmen of both countries that the issue of that struggle must very largely depend upon whether Menelik inclined to the one side or the other. Accordingly, while Kitchener moved south upon Khartum, and from east and west the French expeditions converged upon the Nile to cut across the path of the British army, ambassadors of England and France hurried to Addis Abbaba upon diplomatic missions to the ruler of Abyssinia.

We do not know accurately the history of the missions of Sir Rennell Rodd and M. Lagarde to Menelik in 1897, for official documents relating to diplomatic negotiations withhold more information than they impart : but the general objects and course of the negotiations can be inferred. It is probably correct, as the French maintained, that the British mission was not unconnected with the Dongola expedition, and that Sir Rennell Rodd, according to his instructions, attempted to come to an agreement with Menelik as to the western boundary of Abyssinia, which would both secure the left wing of Kitchener's army and leave intact the British claim to the Nile Valley. It is not surprising that the mission

---

[1] See Lebon, op. cit. pp. 24-26. The question of the traffic in arms between Djibuti and Addis Abbaba was the occasion of innumerable "incidents" between the French and Italian Governments.

failed in these objects. The European State which had signed away in the Anglo-Italian treaties the independence of the whole of Abyssinia was necessarily suspect to the Emperor of Abyssinia. His victory at Adowa did not help to make Menelik more tractable to European diplomacy, particularly when it was the diplomacy of the ally of his victim. Moreover, the aspirations of Britain in the Nile Valley were incompatible with the aspirations of Menelik himself. The only result of the mission was the signing of an agreement on May 14, which fixed the eastern boundary between Abyssinia and British Somaliland, and under which Menelik agreed to stop the traffic in arms between his territory and the Dervishes, whom he was good enough to declare to be "the enemies of his empire." The question of the western boundary, the crucial question at the moment, was, as Mr. Curzon informed the House of Commons, "reserved for a future arrangement."

M. Lagarde was more successful. He had the advantage of representing a European State which, instead of signing away Menelik's kingdom to another European State, had supplied him with European munitions wherewith to defend it. And, what was perhaps more important in diplomacy, he was able to base his negotiations not upon past favours but a future *quid pro quo.* In return for Abyssinian co-operation he was prepared to offer French recognition of Abyssinian sovereignty up to the right bank of the Nile. There seems to be little doubt that an agreement upon this basis was arrived at between Menelik and M. Lagarde. On March 20, 1897, an Abyssinian-French treaty was signed which was declared to be a treaty of commerce and delimitation of boundaries : but its exact terms were not published, and this alone would point to the fact that it was not unconnected with the international situation in Ethiopian Africa and on the banks of the Nile. The events which immediately followed confirm this hypothesis.

During the twelve months which followed, Addis Abbaba and the court of Menelik were the centre of a network of international intriguers. There were not only M. Lagarde and the French mission, and Mr. Rodd and the English mission: there were Swiss, Greek, Russian, and even Austrian envoys, official and unofficial, prosecuting the most extraordinary economic, political, scientific, and military schemes. A glance at their activities, in so far as they can be seen through the mist which invariably covers the career of the international adventurer, will reveal the trend of policy and commerce during these critical months in Abyssinia. There was first a M. Alfred Ilg, a Swiss engineer, who was "Minister and Imperial Councillor of State" to Menelik, and enjoyed the Abyssinian title which answers to that of "His Excellency." Though a Swiss by nationality, M. Ilg placed his services and his influence at the disposal of French policy, commerce, and finance.

It was to him that Menelik had granted, in 1894, the concession for the railway which was to be built from Djibuti to the White Nile. At the time of the battle of Adowa the construction of the railway had not been begun, but a few months later, in November 1896, the construction of the first section was sanctioned by Menelik on somewhat modified terms. The concession was now made to M. Ilg and M. Chefneux, on behalf of a French company, the Compagnie Impériale des Chemins de Fer Éthiopiens. M. Chefneux, a French engineer, was not only chairman of this French company, he was also adviser to Menelik for "Railways, Roads, and Communications," and "Consul-General for Ethiopia in Europe." In March, 1897, M. Chefneux on behalf of his company entered into an agreement with the French Government with regard to the immediate construction of the railway. Work was at once begun and was pushed forward with the greatest energy—a significant fact when one remembers that nothing was done to exploit the concession between 1894 and 1897, and in view of the strategic importance which such a railway would acquire in the event of a struggle between Britain on one side and France and Abyssinia on the other for the control of the Nile Valley.

The activities of M. Ilg and M. Chefneux were thus directed to the strategic and commercial communications between French Somaliland, Abyssinia, and the White Nile. But there was a whole swarm of Europeans in Abyssinia at this time who were concerned with the use rather than with the construction of communications. They were all bent upon expeditions, the objects of which were extremely mysterious. The most mysterious of all was the expedition of two Russians, Leontieff and Babicheff. Leontieff was a Russian count: he appeared in Abyssinia shortly after Adowa at the head of a heavily-armed force. He was in intimate alliance with the French, and his expedition is referred to by French writers as "la mission franco-russe." In 1897 Menelik, at the time of the signature of the treaty with France, took the significant step of creating M. Lagarde "Duke of Entoto," and Count Leontieff "Governor-General of the Equatorial Provinces of Ethiopia." The step was the more significant because nobody knew what the Equatorial Provinces of Ethiopia were. They presumably lay somewhere towards the south and the west, just where the frontier between Abyssinia and the Nile Valley and Uganda was in dispute. If Leontieff during 1897 had been able to instal himself at the head of a Franco-Russian military expedition as Governor-General of the Abyssinian King in these disputed regions, he might have created a situation in the rear of Fashoda very favourable to French and very unfavourable to British policy. It should be remarked, too, that the Russian count combined economic imperialism with strategic and political imperialism.

He obtained from Menelik not only the Governor-Generalship of the Equatorial Provinces, but very wide commercial concessions in the form of mining rights in his new dominions, and one of the objects of his expedition was to hunt elephants for ivory. Armed with these powers, the expedition disappeared into the interior. Exactly what happened to it and to its leader is even to-day not clear : but, both imperially and economically, it was a failure. It began disastrously with a serious casualty among the Europeans at the unskilled hands of the African troops who were being instructed in the use of European fire-arms ; and, though Leontieff himself [1] remained some time in Abyssinia, he never succeeded in making the Equatorial Provinces, either for himself or for Menelik, anything more than an imperial name.[2]

The south-west corner of Abyssinia and Lake Rudolph were a subject of interest to others besides Count Leontieff. In June, 1897, M. L. Darragon, a French explorer, at the head of 15,000 men marched across the Boran district to the north of Lake Rudolph with the express intention of cutting across the path of an English expedition under Mr. Cavendish which was said to be making for the Nile. M. Darragon, on his return to Addis Abbaba, seems to have instigated Menelik to establish a military occupation of the territory through which he had just travelled. The military occupation was accomplished in a curious way. A Russian officer, Lieutenant Boulatowitch, who was attached to the Russian Legation at Addis Abbaba, early in 1898 disappeared alone into the interior of Abyssinia. It was subsequently discovered that he had joined one of Menelik's generals, the Governor of Kaffa, who,

---

[1] Count Leontieff had as co-leader of the expedition Prince Henry of Orleans. The accident referred to happened to Leontieff; he was instructing some Abyssinians in the use of a Maxim gun, and, while he was standing in front of his pupils, some one fired it and shot him in the legs. According to Mr. Wylde, *Modern Abyssinia*, pp. 74-75, after this accident Leontieff and Prince Henry returned to Europe and the expedition never even started from Harrar. This is not improbably the true account of this adventure, in which case the officers and men who had been got together for the count's expedition were not used by him at all, but were subsequently employed in the expeditions which will be described in the following paragraphs. On the other hand a small book, *Chez Ménélick*, was published in French, which purports to record the actual experiences of the Leontieff expedition.

[2] It is an interesting fact that Leontieff, whose expedition was originally directed against the English, eventually appears to have sublet his mining rights to an English company. It is said that Menelik regarded this as a breach of faith, and that he therefore, in 1900, revoked all the concessions which he had granted to the Russian. European diplomacy and policy in Abyssinia during 1897 was combined with intense activity among Europeans in obtaining mining concessions from Menelik, particularly for gold but also for silver and aluminium. M. Ilg, who had obtained the concession for the Djibuti railway, also obtained all mining rights in Wallega and the Baro region for fifty years, and to exploit this concession a company was formed in Antwerp largely financed by Italian capital. See Major a.D. Karl von Bruchhausen, " Abessinien als Goldland," in *Beiträge zur Kolonialpolitik und Kolonialwirtschaft*, vol. iii., 1901–1902.

at the head of an army of 30,000 men, was setting out towards Lake Rudolph and the frontiers of Uganda and British East Africa. The Governor of Kaffa also had at his disposal, besides the Russian lieutenant, several French officers and a few Cossacks. Lieutenant Boulatowitch on his return reported that in the extreme south this expedition had come upon the tracks of another armed expedition of about 500 men under the command of four Englishmen who "were secretly proceeding north-west in order to reach the right bank of the Nile." The 30,000 gave chase to the 500, and the latter had to fly so precipitately that the whole of their baggage fell into the hands of the Abyssinian army. Boulatowitch satisfied himself that this small expedition "was composed of English troops and was making for the White Nile, which it would have reached in a few days' march, five or six stages at most. For a second time the plans of England had failed."

The plans of Boulatowitch and his French friends for the moment seemed to have succeeded. The army of 30,000 men, which included French native soldiers from Senegal, occupied the whole of the district between the sources of the Omo River and Lake Rudolph, and established a number of military stations in these regions "in order to prevent a possible return of the English." [1]

The meaning of this Russo-Franco-Abyssinian expedition of Bulatowitch in conjunction with the Franco-Russian scheme of Leontieff is obvious. The two schemes were subsidiary to the policy of the converging expeditions of Marchand and Bonchamps. They were designed to establish, with French and Russian help, an Abyssinian occupation of all the territory to the north-west, north, and north-east of Lake Rudolph. If successful, they would have placed Menelik in possession of a block of territory running right across the north of British East Africa and Uganda, and touching the Bahr-el-Ghazal on the west and the White Nile on the north-west. The Marchand-Bonchamps expeditions would thus have been protected against any English attempt to reach the White Nile from the south or east. The Leontieff scheme failed, and the sign of its failure is that to-day the territory north-west of Lake Rudolph is British ; the Boulatowitch expedition so far succeeded that to-day the regions of the Omo River are Abyssinian, and the frontier between Abyssinia and Uganda and British East Africa touches Lake Rudolph.

Menelik's main movement in co-operation with the French policy of converging expeditions took place elsewhere. In April, 1898, the king's cousin, Tesama, started direct for the River Sobat and the White Nile with a force said to number 5000 men. Attached to this expedition were a French naval artillery officer,

---

[1] For the facts in this and the preceding paragraph, see Morié, *Histoire de l'Éthiopie*, vol. ii. pp. 450-53.

M. Faivre, who was a member of the Bonchamps expedition, and a Russian, Colonel Artamonov. M. Morié states that "this expedition formed part of a Franco-Abyssinian plan in which the Marchand expedition was to play the chief rôle ": in other words, the intention was that the force under Tesama should occupy the right bank of the White Nile between the Sobat and Fashoda, while Marchand and the French expeditions occupied the left bank. The Abyssinians are said to have reached the White Nile at its confluence with the Sobat and to have raised the Abyssinian flag on the right bank, while M. Faivre swam to an island in mid-river and flew the French flag there as a sign of French sovereignty over the left bank. But the main object, namely, to effect a junction with Marchand, was not attained. The Abyssinian army was decimated by fever, and the mortality was so high that Tesama had to retrace his steps into Abyssinia before Marchand arrived at Fashoda.[1]

. . . .

The political pretensions of France to sovereignty in the Nile Valley were destroyed by Kitchener and the Agreement of 1899 : but the rival claims of Menelik and Britain still remained uncomposed. The situation in 1899 was both curious and dangerous. The French, even after the failure of their policy, maintained a complete ascendancy in Abyssinia, and the British were naturally even more suspect than they had been before. To many people it seemed certain that the French, working behind Menelik, would succeed in stirring up trouble, and that Britain would still not be allowed to make good her claim to the possession of the Nile Valley without a struggle.[2]

Within three years these forebodings were proved to be groundless, and the British Empire obtained peacefully all that it wanted from the Emperor of Abyssinia. The exact steps which led to this desirable conclusion are somewhat obscure, for the darkness which surrounds diplomatic negotiations becomes thicker when

[1] See Morié, op. cit. vol. ii. pp. 454-55 ; also Wylde, Modern Abyssinia, pp. 64 and 73.

[2] See Wylde, op. cit. p. 64, where the author, writing in 1901, says : " England is still in the dark as to where Menelik's territorial influence to the west extends, and how much he has compromised himself with France will perhaps never be known until some dispute arises between them. It is known that he has given French subjects, including Monsieur Lagarde, the French Minister, grants of land. . . . Supposing no dispute arose with the present king, diplomatic questions might arise over these grants of land and concessions with his successor, and the French Government might take the part of their subjects and make a cause of interference in the affairs of Abyssinia, the same as they have done in Siam and Madagascar. . . . The mode that France employs in her annexations and claims on territory is so well known that it is not likely that her new coaling station at Djibuti is only to be used for purely commercial purposes and to supply fuel to the Messagerie Maritime Company and her men-of-war." See, too, p. 75, the passage beginning : " The present position is fraught with danger and perhaps many unseen possibilities of a disagreeable nature."

the negotiators spin their webs in a place like Addis Abbaba. Two facts, however, certainly contributed to the success of British and the failure of French policy between 1899 and 1902. In 1898 there went to the court of Menelik as Agent of the British Government a Colonel Harrington, who proved himself a most skilful diplomatist, and who did a great deal to dispel Menelik's suspicions of British, and leanings towards French, imperialism. He was greatly helped in these efforts by the French themselves who, as we shall see, by action very typical of economic imperialism, succeeded in alienating at a stroke the sympathies of Menelik and in destroying the "influence" which they had so carefully built up in Ethiopian Africa.

The sound diplomacy of her own agents and the mistakes of her rivals resulted for Britain, in 1902, in a treaty signed on May 15 between herself and Menelik. This agreement marks definitely the end of the political and strategic struggle between European States for the Nile Valley. It placed the coping-stone, so far as northern Africa was concerned, upon the work of Rhodes and Chamberlain, for it gave to Britain all that the most imperialist of imperialists could desire between the Second Cataract of the Nile and Uganda. Its first clauses delimit the frontiers of the Egyptian Sudan and Abyssinia in such a way that, although the sources of the Atbara and Blue Nile are included within Abyssinian territory, the whole of the White Nile is recognized as British. Thus in these articles British political control of the Nile Valley, which had been recognized by Italy in 1894 and had been wrung from France in 1899, is finally recognized by Menelik in 1902. Article III. is directed at giving to Britain, as the owner of Egypt, that strategic security against any tampering with the sources of the Nile which, as we have seen, the ethics and ingenuity of European civilization have made important. By this article Menelik bound himself not to construct any works upon the Blue Nile, Lake Tsana, or the River Sobat which could interfere with the flow of the Nile, unless he obtained the assent of the British Government. Article V. ensured the completion of that section of Rhodes's Mittel-Afrika which lies between the Sudan and Abyssinia. As I have pointed out above (p. 183), the swampy nature of the ground upon both sides of the White Nile, as it approaches its sources in Uganda, made it impossible to construct the Cape–Cairo Railway upon the territory of the Nile Valley which had been won for Britain and lost to France at Fashoda. At this point it is necessary that the trace of the railway should follow the high ground which falls within the dominions of Menelik. Article V. gives to the British Government "the right to construct across Abyssinian territory a railway joining the Sudan to Uganda." Finally, in Article IV., the economics of imperialism are provided for:

Menelik agreed in this article to lease to the British Government a piece of territory at Itang, on the River Baro, to be used as a " commercial station."

Itang, upon the River Baro, is the " first point of penetration " into the Abyssinian highlands from the Nile Valley. In 1902 French imperialists were not slow to emphasize this fact. They saw in the Anglo-Abyssinian treaty the beginning of the end of the political and economic independence of Abyssinia. Certainly this convention is a remarkable example of the way in which the angels of imperialism seem to watch over the growth and the interests of the British Empire. Between 1880 and 1902 three European States—Italy, France, and Britain—transmuted political, strategic, and economic beliefs and desires into imperialist policy of a serious nature in Ethiopian Africa. In the case of France and of Italy we can lay our finger upon a definite and conscious plan or policy through which an attempt was made to use the power of the State in order to obtain control of African territory. Great and sustained efforts—political, military, and economic—were put forth to pluck the fruit of empire in Abyssinia. The effort of Italy ended in Adowa, and that of France in Fashoda. In the case of Britain no such sustained and conscious policy is visible. French writers are, it is true, vehement and eloquent in their assertions of the persistence, the subtlety, and the treachery with which British Governments worked successfully at the undermining of the political and economic independence of Abyssinia. The assertions may be true : but, while it is easy to unravel the actual strands of French and Italian policy, those of the British are singularly impalpable. There is no fact in the history of British policy which can compare in definiteness with the deliberate attempt of Crispi to conquer Abyssinia, or with the instructions issued by the French Colonial Office to M. Lagarde with reference to the " converging expeditions " of 1898. A few treaties with Italy ; a telegram from the British Government to Lord Cromer ; the march of a British army to Fashoda ; the demonstration of a British fleet before Bizerta ; some plain speaking by Mr. Chamberlain, *The Times*, and the *Daily Mail*; and, lastly, the appearance of a diplomatic British colonel in Addis Abbaba : these are the only outward manifestations of a plan which, according to the French historian, was pursued with " a consummate art." And yet in the end, almost as though by an act of God, the fruit of empire which had defied the efforts of France and Italy dropped gently into the hands of General Kitchener and Colonel Harrington, and thence as gently into the lap of the British Empire.

. . . .

I have now traced the history of European policy in Ethiopian Africa from the time of Theodore to its final stage. It has been, upon its surface, mainly political and strategic, but beneath and behind it we have seen continually the motives and symptoms of economic imperialism. There was no conceivable political or strategic reason why Italy should covet Eritrea or the territories of Abyssinia, and in her " commercial expeditions," her attempt to " penetrate " into Harrar, her efforts to exploit the telegraph system of Abyssinia, and in the presence of the Rubattino Company and the Benadir Company behind her political and military actions, we see clearly the economic background of Italian imperialism. The same symptoms are evident in the early struggle between the French and British for the commercial control of the Harrar either from Obock or Zeila, in the commercial exploitation of Abyssinia by the French which accompanied their policy after 1896, in the struggle for mining concessions, and in the declarations both in France and England that the Nile Valley was a question of the control of trade and markets.

But when Menelik seemed, by his victory over Italy, to have succeeded where all other African States and kings had failed, and to have secured his independence against the hungry imperialism of Italy, France, and Britain, and when the political and strategic struggle in the Nile Valley had been finally settled at Fashoda, there came a strange final stage in which the economic desires and beliefs of Europe, now stripped of their political and strategic ornaments and disguises, produced one more struggle for the control of Abyssinia. The struggle was between England and France, and it is curious to observe how the same beliefs and motives followed the same channels and created the same situation in this last imperialist manifestation as they had followed and created in the very first meeting between Frenchmen and Englishmen in Ethiopian Africa.

The reader will remember how, when the French seized Obock in 1882 with a view to its becoming a centre of commerce with Harrar and Abyssinia, the English immediately answered the move by seizing Zeila. There followed a political-economic struggle between France and Britain over Dongarita and the trade routes to Harrar. France tried to deflect the caravan trade to her possessions on Tajura Bay, and England tried to deflect them to hers at Zeila. The struggle was interrupted by the closing of Harrar to European trade by the Emir Abdulla and by the complications which accompanied the Italian attempt to conquer Abyssinia, but it immediately broke out again as soon as the situation had been simplified by the elimination of Italy at Adowa. The result of that battle was to leave France and Britain not only politically and strategically, but also economically, face to face alone in Ethiopian Africa. The situation was now the same as in 1884, except that the French had made Djibuti instead of Obock their centre of penetration upon Tajura Bay. In 1894 M. Ilg obtained from Menelik the concession for a French company of a railway from Djibuti through the Harrar to Addis Abbaba and the Nile. We have seen how, in 1896, the French Government attempted to hurry on the construction of this railway line when it appeared that it might be used to forward the strategic designs of imperialism. But the railway was from the first connected with economic as well as strategic purposes. A railway connection between Djibuti and the interior would work far more effectually than any "deflection of caravan routes" for French commercial penetration and the shutting off of Zeila and the British from trade with Harrar and Abyssinia. A struggle, therefore, immediately arose over the railway concession and railway termini which exactly reproduced the struggle of 1884 over caravan routes and their termini. Its history is interesting because it shows so clearly the forces behind, and the methods pursued by, modern economic imperialism.

Fashoda and its sequel destroyed, at least for the moment, any strategic utility that the Djibuti railway might have for France. It became a purely commercial enterprise. It was in the hands of a French joint-stock company, with its offices in Paris, La Compagnie Impériale des Chemins de Fer Éthiopiens. The company, like most similar enterprises of economic imperialism, worked in close connection with and almost under the supervision of the French Government. This connection began with the agreement [1] of March 12, 1897, between the company and the French Government, under which, "in order to facilitate the construction and exploitation of the railway," the French Colonial Office authorized the construction of the section in French Somaliland and gave the company the right of levying a rate of 10 per cent on the value of all merchandise carried by the railway. The capital was subscribed by "a group of French financial houses," and the construction was begun in 1897.

As soon as the work of construction had begun, great interest began to be taken in the enterprise by French colonial circles and interests. "It was pointed out that a railway was the most invaluable instrument of penetration into a new country, that Abyssinia was a country of vast undeveloped resources, both mineral and agricultural, and that, with a monopoly of the railway communications of the country in French hands, an immense field would be opened for the profitable employment of French capital, while the commercial predominance which France would thus establish would necessarily bring with it a certain amount of political control." [2] But it is an axiom of economic imperialism that what

---

[1] The text of this agreement will be found in *Abyssinia : The Ethiopian Railway and the Powers*, by T. Lennox Gilmour, 1906, p. 68.

[2] T. Lennox Gilmour, *op. cit.* p. 16.

is one nation's gain must be every other nation's loss, and therefore this projected railway and the concession, which roused enthusiasm among the financiers and imperialists of Paris, roused in similar circles in London nothing but anger and alarm. This anger and alarm was not immediately expressed; they were concealed under some rather intricate financial operations.

The financial circles of London peculiarly interested in the economic exploitation of Ethiopian Africa were, in 1897, grouped in the New African Company, and later in two other closely associated companies, the New Egyptian Company and Oceana Consolidated Company. They belonged to a well-known type of capitalist concern, floated with a kind of roving commission to lend money and acquire " concessions," to practise the profitable business of financial knight-errantry and exploitation, in the undeveloped regions of the world. A quotation from the " Objects " of the New African Company, which are repeated almost word for word in the articles of incorporation of its sister companies, will show how wide a financial net they sought to throw over Africa. The objects are " To negotiate for and acquire concessions, privileges and rights, absolute or conditional, from any Sovereign Powers, Rulers, Governments or States, or person or persons, or from any corporate or other body, and to enter into any arrangement with any Government, Ruler or Authority, municipal or otherwise, for any purpose or to any effect, and from time to time to alter and vary the same accordingly. To negotiate loans of all descriptions, either alone or jointly with any other Company or person, to any State, country, or corporate or other body, or any person or persons. To advance money for, or otherwise assist in making exploration and surveys of every kind, and in promoting exploration and surveys of every kind; and in promoting immigration into any country, Colony or State."

These three companies were very closely interlocked. Oceana Consolidated held a large block of shares in the New African Company and the New African Company held a large block of shares in Oceana Consolidated. The New African Company, again, was a large shareholder in the New Egyptian Company. The three together had, by about 1900, acquired very wide financial interests in Africa. They had mining rights in the Transvaal and South Africa, an interest through Oceana Consolidated in the Mozambique Railway and the Congo, important interests through the New Egyptian Company (and a Soudan Development and Exploration Company) in Egypt and the Sudan. The membership of the boards of directors is interesting, for through the boards finance was kept in close touch both with the aristocracy and what may be called the Governmental and administrative side of imperialism. The aristocracy was represented upon the New Egyptian Company by the Marquis of Lothian and (in 1900) on the New African Company by Lord Chesterfield. In 1898 Sir Charles Euan-Smith was appointed a director of the New African Company, and after that year he is found regularly presiding at the annual meetings. Colonel Sir Charles Euan-Smith had already had considerable experience of economic imperialism upon the East Coast of Africa. In 1890 he had been the representative of the British Government in Zanzibar, and while in that post he had materially helped the British East Africa Company to acquire Uganda. Sir Charles must have been a valuable acquisition for the shareholders in the New African Company : the shareholders in the New Egyptian Company had made acquisitions of a similar kind almost as valuable. Their manager was, in 1899, Lieutenant-Colonel Sir John Rogers, who had only just vacated a high post under the Egyptian Government, and the gentleman who presided over their annual meeting was Sir Gerald Fitzgerald, K.C.M.G., who in a long and distinguished career had held such varied posts as Deputy-Controller-General of Military Expenditure, Assistant-Comptroller-General of India, Accountant-General and Director, Bank of Madras, Director-General of Egyptian Accounts, and Accountant-General of the Navy. Finally another and a not unimportant stratum of society is represented upon the board of directors by such names as Baron Louis de Steiger and Baron Albert de Dietrich, and yet another— in the New Egyptian Company—by Prince Hussein and Borghos Pacha Nubar.

The reader will remember that it was in 1897 that the French company first began to make use of the concession granted by Menelik and to construct the railway from Djibuti to the Harrar. The interest of the British financial groups in Abyssinia does not appear to have been aroused until this happened. But at the annual meeting of the New African Company in 1898 the chairman informed the shareholders that " certain interests had been secured in Abyssinian business where they would do what they could to harmonize English and French interests." At the next annual meeting of the company Sir Charles Euan-Smith vaguely informed the shareholders that the directors had selected two new enterprises which they had now taken up " in conjunction with a French banking group connected with their Company in Paris." In 1900 Sir Charles was a little more explicit : he told the shareholders that the directors hoped to " participate, through their Paris connections, in the construction of the Jibuti Railway in Abyssinia in fair co-operation with the French capitalists." A shareholder would have had to be a very acute and a very well-informed man to have understood from these reticent announcements the policy which his directors were pursuing in Ethiopian Africa. Next year, in 1901, considerably more information was given to him. It was suddenly announced that the New African Company, the New Egyptian Company, and Oceana Consolidated had syndicated and vested their interests in the Djibuti Railway in a trust company, the International Ethiopian Trust and Construction Company, of which the chairman was Lord Chesterfield. The chairman's speech at the annual meeting of this new company on October 31, 1901, for the first time gave the public and the shareholders an opportunity of understanding what these financial groups were doing and pursuing in Abyssinia.

In 1897 " some Paris friends," as Lord Chesterfield put it, " took up " some of the bonds issued to the concessionaires of the Djibuti Railway. These bonds appear to have become the property of the New African Company, and are those " certain interests " which the chairman in 1898 referred to as having been secured " in Abyssinian business." Thus the British New African Company, through its " Paris friends," had very early acquired an interest in the French Compagnie Impériale des Chemins de Fer Éthiopiens. The French company, as it proceeded with the work of construction, found that the expenditure had been under-estimated and that an increase of capital was required if the railway was to be completed. The French directors found difficulty in obtaining the new capital in France, and it was then that the British financial groups in the three British companies came forward and offered to furnish the money in exchange for shares in the French company. The French, after another unsuccessful attempt to find the funds in France, reluctantly accepted the offer, and their reluctance was embodied in a clause of the agreement whereby they were allowed to break the agreement at any time on forfeiture of 625,000 francs. It was in order to vest these new interests in a special company that the three British companies syndicated in the International Ethiopian Trust and Construction Company.

It will be observed that these rather complicated transactions provide a very typical example of that financial " peaceful penetration " which is practised by all the great imperialist nations. The British financiers and ex-imperial administrators had peacefully penetrated into a French economic enterprise which had political and imperial as well as economic objects and importance. By 1901 the British had obtained almost a controlling interest in the French company, they had two British directors on the board, and they had obtained the monopoly for building the future extensions in Abyssinia, and important interests in the shape of various contracts for the further finance and construction of the line.

When French colonial circles found that British financial-colonial groups had quietly, by peaceful penetration, secured a controlling interest in this railway there was both anger and alarm.

The reason was that behind the financial transactions there lay an imperialistic struggle half economic, half political. Lord Chesterfield, in his address to the annual meeting of the Trust Company in 1901, dealt with this struggle in carefully-chosen words. He explained that "while the construction of the line . . . was going ahead, the political importance of the railway with respect to English and French interests in Abyssinia became daily more and more apparent, and . . . on both sides of the Channel no small interest . . . is being taken in the development of the railway, and its effect on the future of British and French commerce and policy in Abyssinia is being carefully watched." He then explained the English "policy." From Djibuti, the French port, 270 kilometres had already been constructed, of which 170 were in French Somaliland and 90 in Abyssinia. By 1902 it was expected that the line would have been carried as far as " the foot of the hills upon which the important centre of Harrar is situated." The railway would then be extended south by a branch line to Harrar, and afterwards west to Addis Abbaba, the capital of Abyssinia. The line would form the trunk line from the Red Sea to Abyssinia and would be of vast importance to Ethopia. Then he came to the real point : he called attention "to the belief that the traffic. . . and its prospects generally would be greatly enhanced by securing its connection with one of the ports of British Somaliland, and the hope was expressed that arrangements might be arrived at for the connection of the British port of Zeilah . . . with the trunk line . . . as the French port of Djibouti was already connected. . . . Such a policy would give to both French and English an equal chance of commercial influence in Abyssinia, and thus help in assisting good relations between the two countries, whilst furthering the interests of the railway itself and the prosperity of Abyssinia. The intention was expressed of doing everything . . . to further this aim and to assist generally in the development of Abyssinia. . . . I can only confirm our intention to pursue this policy ; . . . we have been able to increase our influence in the undertaking, and shall continue to do so."

If these words of Lord Chesterfield be read as carefully as they were carefully chosen, it will be seen that they contain a threat and almost a declaration of war. They were so understood by the French. The British policy was to nullify the advantages, economic and political, which the French had obtained from the concession of this railway with its terminus at the French port of Djibuti, by forcing upon the scheme the construction of a branch line to the British port of Zeila. It was the old imperialist struggle over Dongarita and the caravan routes translated into the modern terms of railway lines, concessions, and trust companies. The policy which Lord Chesterfield represented as giving " to French and English an equal chance of commercial influence in Abyssinia " was represented by the French as an attempt to acquire by peaceful penetration a valuable French concession and to ruin Djibuti for the benefit of Zeila.[1] When Lord Chesterfield announced that he could "only confirm our intention to pursue this policy," and when he used the threat that " we have been able to increase our influence in the undertaking, and we shall continue to do so," the French understood him to mean that the English financiers proposed to use uncompromisingly the power which they had obtained over " the undertaking " by means of peaceful penetration.

The result was a tremendous campaign in French colonial circles. The campaign took the form of appealing to the patriotism of the French public to find sufficient capital for buying out the English capitalists and freeing the railway from " foreign control." The appeal to patriotism failed in so far as the obtaining of capital from the public was concerned, but it succeeded in another object, which was to bring pressure to bear upon the Government. It was represented that, if patriotism was insufficient to induce Frenchmen to put their money into Abyssinian railways, it was at least the duty of the French Government to come to the help of French capitalists and prevent them being outwitted and expropriated by the financial imperialists of England. French imperialists have no little influence in the Paris press, and a tremendous clamour arose in the newspapers calling for Government action. At the moment a General Election was approaching, and at those times a Government is peculiarly sensitive to well-organized pressure. The Government of M. Waldeck-Rousseau was no exception ; it yielded to " popular opinion," in other words, to the Paris journalists who shouted, like human megaphones, the wishes of the colonial capitalists of the Compagnie Impériale des Chemins de Fer Éthiopens. It was announced that the French Government would come to the rescue of this patriotic company and save it from peaceful penetration and " foreign control."

In the hurry of the press campaign and the impending election, the capitalists of the Compagnie Impériale and M. Waldeck-Rousseau's Government overreached themselves. The help which the Government gave to the Company was of a very singular kind. It took the form of an Agreement. In this Agreement the Government undertook to grant to the Company an annual subvention of 500,000 francs for fifty years. This part of the arrangement was natural and simple. The subvention would provide the Company with the capital which they required for continuing the construction of the railway and which they had failed to get out of the patriotism of the thrifty French people. This would make

---

[1] See Darcy, *Cent Années*, pp. 261-62.

recourse to British capital for the new construction unnecessary, and would allow the Company to invoke that clause which gave them the power to determine their agreement with the British capitalists. It is true that the British would still hold a large part of the capital of the Company in the form of the original bonds which they had acquired in the process of peaceful penetration, but the French would at least have obtained the revocation of the agreement, and of the contracts for further construction, which were far more dangerous instruments of peaceful penetration than the bonds. For, provided that the construction remained in French hands, the railway would still continue in all essential points to be a French enterprise. Moreover, it was also contemplated that a sufficient sum might be raised in France, on the security of the subvention, for buying out eventually the whole of the interest of the foreign capitalists.

But the Agreement also imposed upon the Company certain significant obligations. The Company was bound to remain a French company, with its registered offices in Paris; all the members of the board of directors were to be French; no modification in its articles or in the trace of the railway, as approved, could be made without the consent of the Minister for the Colonies. Other powers of control were given to the Minister of Foreign Affairs, the Minister for the Colonies, and the Minister of Finance. Certain powers to fix railway rates were given to the French Administration in French Somaliland, and a special reduction of rates was to be made in the case of transport of Government officials and goods. It was further stipulated that after the expiration of ninety-nine years the French Protectorate of Somaliland should succeed to all the rights of the Company over the section of the line between Djibuti and Harrar, that after 1920 the Protectorate should have the option of purchasing part of the line, and that in certain cases the Minister for the Colonies should have the power to annul the Agreement and confiscate the section of the line between Djibuti and the River Hawash.

The effect which this remarkable arrangement had upon the influence of the French State in Abyssina and upon the relations between France and Menelik was not foreseen by the Government and the imperialists. The original concession had been made to a Swiss and a Frenchman, and to a private French company: the agreement in effect substituted for the company the French State. It made it almost certain that in time the French State would acquire rights over the railway not only within its own Somaliland territory, but also within Abyssinia. In the arrangements which effected this vital substitution Menelik, the independent ruler who had granted the original concession, was not consulted either by the concessionaires or by the French Government. Now

Menelik was no more anxious to lose his independence to France than he had been to lose it to Italy or to Great Britain : he had cultivated the friendship of France, and had allowed Frenchmen to monopolize the commercial exploitation of Abyssinia, precisely because with French aid he hoped to preserve his independence against the other two European Powers. Just as M. Deloncle had opened his eyes in the early 'nineties to the designs of the imperialists of Rome against his kingdom, so now in 1902 Sir John Harrington, the British representative at Addis Abbaba, helped to open his eyes to the designs of the economic imperialists of Paris, which were ill concealed behind the agreement with the Compagnie Impériale.

French writers lay the whole blame for the failure of French policy in Abyssinia after 1901 upon the underhand machinations of Sir John Harrington. Such a view is certainly coloured by the bias of patriotism.[1] Sir John was no doubt too good a diplomatist to neglect the opportunity to advance the interests of his country and of his country's financiers presented to him by the action of the French Government. As Mr Gilmour puts it : " Nothing is to be gained by denying that the British Minister has used his best endeavours to oppose the designs of France to make Abyssinia a French preserve. In doing this Sir John Harrington was merely discharging his duty to the Government he represented and the country he served." That in opposing the interests of France he was also opposing the interests of the French capitalists of the Compagnie Impériale, and that in furthering the interests of Britain he was furthering the interests of the financiers of the Ethiopian Railway Trust Company, was one of those accidents which must always occur so long as the beliefs and desires of economic imperialism direct the policy of European States. Sir John was only playing the game when he grasped the weapon presented to him by the French statesmen and financiers, and used it very effectively against the economic imperialism of France. The result of the agreement between the French Government and the Compagnie Impériale was to place the control of the only means of communication between the sea and Abyssinia in the hands not of a private company but of the French State. Such " peaceful penetration " was not what Menelik had bargained for when he first gave the concession to M. Ilg. It was only necessary to bring the agreement to the notice of Menelik, and immediately—" French influence at Addis Abeba fell below zero." [2]

The agreement between the Compagnie Impériale and the

---

[1] The best statement of the facts connected with the Ethiopian Railway is contained in T. Lennox Gilmour, *Abyssinia : The Ethiopian Railway and the Powers*, 1906. The French view is to be found in Darcy, *Cent Années*, pp. 461-62, and in Lémonon, *L'Europe et la Politique Britannique*, pp. 137 and 353-55.

[2] Gilmour, *op. cit.* p. 31.

French Government was signed on February 6, 1902. Its immediate effect upon Menelik is shown by the fact that upon May 15, 1902, he signed the treaty with Great Britain referred to above, which gave to British imperialists all that they desired with regard to the Nile Valley and the Cape–Cairo railway. On the same day he signed another treaty with Britain and Italy delimiting the boundaries of Ethiopia and Eritrea. So completely is international friendship at the mercy of the fitful winds of economic imperialism that a financial agreement in Paris was sufficient in the twinkling of an eye to convert the two signatories of the treaties of 1891 and 1894 into close friends of Menelik, and to place France, the close friend of Abyssinia, in Italy's place as the imperialistic wolf in sheep's clothing.

Menelik did not confine himself to reversing the international policy of Abyssinia. He protested to the French Minister against the agreement, and "declared that he regarded those clauses of the Convention which contemplated the ultimate acquisition of the railway up to the Hawash Valley by the French Government as a direct infringement of his rights as an independent sovereign." He showed his displeasure by refusing to be present at the official opening of the line on Abyssinian territory. Very soon it became apparent that he could, and would, make his displeasure felt in ways which would very materially affect the financial future of the French company. He refused, for instance, to sanction a scheme proposed to him for allowing the collection of a duty of 10 per cent on merchandise carried over the railway between Djibuti and Harrar, "on the ground that he had granted the privilege to a commercial company, and not to a company which was practically owned and controlled by a foreign government." [1] He gave the same reason for refusing to issue a decree without which the extension of the railway beyond the Harrar was impossible. These refusals had a serious effect both upon the earning power of the railway and upon the credit of the company. The question of credit became important, for the company required more capital for the further extension of the line. It is difficult to discover exactly what happened in the private and governmental transactions which, in these circumstances, followed. Apparently the French company failed once more to raise the capital which they required in France, and, when they again asked for Government assistance, they were refused. The British financiers and imperialists had still maintained some hold over the French company by means of the shares which they retained and which were vested in the Ethiopian Railway Trust Company. French writers assert that the British company continued after 1901 to use the power, which they obtained through holding these shares, to exercise a controlling

[1] Gilmour, *op. cit.* p. 35.

interest in favour of British policy and British finance over the French enterprise. They add that Sir John Harrington in Addis Abbaba and at the court of Menelik supported the efforts of the financial group in London. Such accusations are the common-places of economic imperialism. They can be neither proved nor disproved until the foreign offices, the chancelleries, and the legations give up their dead documents to the historian. At any rate, between 1902 and 1904, by a typical turn of the wheel of international finance, the British group once more came to the rescue of the French enterprise and advanced a considerable sum of money to the Compagnie Impériale.

Financial companies do not, however, advance money to the financiers of other countries in any spirit of financial or national altruism. Lord Chesterfield and his co-directors of the Ethiopian Railway Trust Company showed in 1904 that they expected a *quid pro quo*, an imperialist *quid* for a financial *quo*, and that they were not disposed to acquiesce in the French agreement of 1902 as a final solution of the Abyssinian railways question. They came forward with a new and very interesting proposal. At the annual meeting of the British company in 1904 Lord Chesterfield pointed out to the shareholders that there were alternative ways in which the whole question could be settled. The scheme which he and his board of directors favoured was the internationalization of the railway over its entire length and the establishment of its terminus, Djibuti, as a free port. The alternative was the plan which the directors had long advocated, namely, that the railway should remain a French enterprise and that " the English port of Berbera " should be given " the same connection to Abyssinia as the French port of Jiboutil." He added the significant statement that " pour-parlers are now being conducted with a view to putting into effect the (latter) policy which we have so long advocated."

It will be seen that Lord Chesterfield's words were a courteously worded ultimatum to the French imperialists. What he in effect said to them was this : " We have always denied the right of French capital and the French Government to establish an exclusive control of the Abyssinian railway system for French economic and political purposes. Our claim hitherto has been that the railway must be connected with a British port on the same terms and in the same way as it is connected with the French port of Djibuti. But we are prepared not to insist upon this solution. We propose that the principle that both Britain and France are interested in this railway shall be recognized by internationalizing the line. The company must cease to be a purely French enterprise. The board and management of the railway will become international and the port of Djibuti a free port. On those terms we are prepared not to ask for a connection with an English port. But if you refuse this offer then we shall insist upon the connection with the British port of Berbera—and I may tell you that we have already taken steps to give practical effect to our threat."

This proposal to internationalize the railway produced a very complicated financial and diplomatic situation. It came at the moment when in the region of high politics France and Britain were drawing close together in the *Entente Cordiale*. There was a powerful impulse towards a friendly settlement of all the rivalries and competitions of economic imperialism. The proposal had much to recommend it even from the point of view of French economic and political interests. It provided a means whereby the French Government might extricate itself without humiliation from a most difficult diplomatic position in Abyssinia, created by a bad political mistake ; at the same time it allowed the French financiers to extricate themselves from the financial noose which was still in the hands of Lord Chesterfield and the British Trust Company. It was, in fact, for these reasons promptly accepted and supported by many of the interests concerned, by the French financial interests of the Compagnie Impériale, by many of the important chambers of commerce, and by other important commercial bodies. But it met with strong opposition in some imperialist circles, particularly the Comité de l'Afrique française, which was against any abandonment of the exclusive control of the line by the French Government.

Menelik himself seems to have accepted the internationalization scheme as a guarantee against the peaceful penetration of France. On April 11, 1905, he summoned the French, British, Italian, and Russian Ministers to an audience, the report of which appeared in "La Dépêche Coloniale" of May 18, 1905.[1] According to this report, the Emperor addressed to the Ministers a kind of ultimatum in the following words : " I should have been glad to see the construction of the railway assured with the least possible delay by an agreement among the different Powers, giving to each of them the necessary guarantees. Up to the present I have received no proposal from you. If I receive no proposal from your Governments, no proposal reconciling your international interests, and so putting an end to this conflict, I shall find myself, in order to ensure the construction of the railway, under the necessity of undertaking its construction myself, without asking or accepting assistance from any one." To this the British Minister, Sir John Harrington, replied : " A railway constructed with the money of a single nation, and under the control of a single foreign government, would place Ethiopia in a situation incompatible with its independence or the integrity of its territory. My personal opinion is that the railway ought to remain on a commercial basis, and ought not to be a political instrument. The best means of giving to the various interests

---

[1] Quoted by Gilmour, *op. cit.* Appendix X., p. 88.

the necessary guarantees would be to permit the capital of all the nations to participate in the construction of the railway. I do not see any inconvenience in entrusting the direction of this enterprise to the French Company provided that the character of the enterprise remains international. . . . It is impossible for me to understand how the maintenance of the independence of Ethiopia can be reconciled with the idea of the construction of a French railway from the coast to the capital, under the sole control of the French Government. I regret to be obliged to say that I do not understand this French policy, the less so as the proposals which have been made to me by my colleague, the French Minister, were incompatible with the very principle of the independence of Ethiopia. . . ." The Italian Minister went even further than the British, and informed Menelik that his Government had instructed him that " it desired to see the railway internationalized " and that " all its efforts in Europe aim at attaining this end." But the French Minister refused to express any opinion, and only made the statement that " when my Government shall have come to some decision I shall have the honour to submit its decision to your Majesty."

Although this report is not official, its accuracy has not been denied. It reveals a curious diplomatic situation. The internationalization project was being officially supported by Menelik, and by the Italian as well as the British representative. Here we see one of the first symptoms of the renewal of Italian claims in Abyssinia. In the negotiations with regard to the railway Italy had once more acted in co-operation with Britain, and in the proposal for internationalization, which the French were asked to accept, the railway would be placed under an administration in which France, Britain, and Italy would participate equally.[1] It is perhaps not surprising that, despite the *Entente Cordiale*, the French Government did not welcome this coalition, and yielded to the demand of the Comité de l'Afrique française that the French control and character of the whole enterprise should not be abandoned. On April 1, 1905, M. Delcassé made a statement[2] in the Senate definitely rejecting the proposal for internationalizing the line, and, as Mr.

[1] This appears from a resolution of the Rouen Chamber of Commerce, quoted by Gilmour, p. 40, which runs : " The Chamber resolve that the French Government should continue the negotiations with the British and Italian Governments, with the object of assuring the neutrality of Ethiopia, and the neutralization of the Ethiopian Railways, under the administration of a purely commercial company, in which France, Great Britain, and Italy would equally participate, and of guaranteeing to our countrymen equality of treatment. . . ."

[2] The important passage in M. Delcassé's statement, quoted by Gilmour (p. 46) is as follows : " M. d'Aunay asks what reception the Government intend to give to a proposal which would tend to transform the character of the enterprise, that is to say, to internationalize the line. I reply very plainly that the Government cannot favour any such proposal. . . . The best thing henceforth is that the

Gilmour suggests, it is probable that this statement was cabled to Addis Abbaba, and was the immediate cause of Menelik's ultimatum to the four Ministers ten days later.

Finance and policy thus combined in 1905 to produce an imperialist deadlock. There is no doubt that the Governments in France and Britain were as anxious to come to an agreement with regard to Abyssinia as they had been to compose their differences in other parts of the world. But the financiers of the British Company still refused to let go the financial noose which they had placed round the neck of the French imperialists, and the French imperialists still refused to let go the economic noose which they imagined that they had placed round the neck of Abyssinia in the shape of a French railway. The deadlock lasted until July 1906, and we have no detailed or accurate information as to the negotiations which led up to its solution. According to the French historians the British financiers, through Sir John Harrington, induced Menelik in the middle of 1905 to refuse to the French the right to extend the railway to Addis Abbaba, and they then insisted that either this extension should be constructed out of funds supplied by the Bank of Abyssinia (*i.e.* out of British funds) or that the French should agree to the internationalization of the line. M. Lémonon maintains that the French, " strong in the good will of the Government in London," succeeded eventually in upsetting the calculations of " M. Harrington and his group," and in obtaining by the Agreement of July 6, 1906, a solution favourable to France. Mr. Gilmour's book suggests one reason which may possibly have weighed with the British and French Governments in insisting upon an agreement which should finally settle this long quarrel between their imperialists. Mr. Gilmour wrote in 1905, when the deadlock still persisted. He was strongly in favour of a compromise, and he pointed out that if the French and British imperialists do not settle their differences Germany and her imperialists may intervene in Abyssinia. He asserted that Dr. Rosen, who had been sént on a special mission to Abyssinia in 1904 to conclude a commercial treaty, had informed Menelik that Germany would be ready to discuss the question of the railway with him " should an occasion arise." Germany had hitherto taken no part in the politics of Ethiopian Africa or in the imperialist struggles in that region. But Dr. Rosen had " been followed to Addis Abeba by a German Consul-General, and a German Consulate is now permanently installed at the

---

enterprise be continued precisely on the conditions in which it was undertaken, with its French character, and that the company complete its work, on the one hand continuing to respect scrupulously the sovereign rights of Menelik on that portion of Abyssinian territory traversed by the railway, and on the other hand giving facilities as much as possible for the use of the line by international commerce as by French commerce, to the great benefit of the port of Jibutil, which will thus receive new and precious elements of prosperity."

Abyssinian capital." These are signs that the Emperor William might at any moment claim in Abyssinia, as he did in Morocco, that he is going to take a hand in the great game in which Italy, France, and Britain had been playing for the stakes of dividends and empire. "Germany," says Mr. Gilmour, "is strictly within her rights in seeking to increase her interests and extend her influence in Abyssinia. It is childish to gird at Germany for doing what it is the business of every country to do—look after its own interests. Great Britain and France must do the same for their interests. Is it to the interest of either country that the Emperor Menelik should be drawn into the arms of Germany ? "

The first serious round in the imperialist struggle for Morocco took place between March 1905 and January 1906, when the International Conference met at Algeciras. The position and intentions of Germany which were revealed in those negotiations may well have convinced the financiers of Paris and London—as well as the Governments—that it was high time to compose their differences in Abyssinia. At any rate, three months after the Conference of Algeciras had finished its labours, the Governments of France, Great Britain, and Italy signed the Agreement of July 6, 1906, which ended the struggle, so far as those three Powers were concerned, for the political and economic domination of Ethiopian Africa. The agreement was a compromise weighted on the economic side in favour of France. The three States began by binding themselves to respect the integrity of Abyssinia and to maintain the political *status quo*. Great Britain obtained an assurance that nothing should be done to interfere with the upper waters of the Nile. Italy was given the right to extend the railway and telegraphic system from her colony of Eritrea. Finally, France was confirmed in her right to construct and exploit the Djibuti–Addis Abbaba railway with the proviso that the board of administration for the railway should include an Abyssinian, an Englishman, and an Italian.

. . . .

The agreement of July 6, 1906, to which the Government of Abyssinia was induced to give its adhesion on December 13 following, may be said to have ended the struggle of economic imperialisms in Ethiopian Africa, so far as the European States were concerned. Two incidents of a later date deserve, however, some mention in order to complete the story. In June 1907 the French Compagnie Impériale, which had formed the centre of the economic battle, succumbed to the financial difficulties which had surrounded it from its birth. It went into liquidation, and, pending the formation of a new company, the Governor of French Somaliland and the French Consular Agent in Abyssinia took possession of the line. On January 30, 1908, Menelik, at the request of the French Minister, granted to Dr. Vitalien, physician to the court of Abyssinia, a concession for all lines of railway constructed or to be constructed on Abyssinian territory. It is significant that, according to M. Lémonon, Germany protested, unsuccessfully, against this concession. Thus the joint-stock company of the court physician, Dr. Vitalien, stepped into the shoes of the defunct joint-stock company of the Minister and Imperial Councillor of State, M. Ilg. M. Ilg and his financial friends of the Compagnie Impériale were not, however, allowed by the French Government to suffer for their patriotism. Although their company had gone into liquidation, the terms of the law of April 3, 1909, which recognized the new company of Dr. Vitalien, laid it down that the new company should pay to the old and bankrupt company for ninety-nine years an annuity of over 600,000 francs, and that this sum should be guaranteed by the French State.[1] The obligations of the French tax-payer were thus raised by 600,000 francs for the next ninety-nine years, and the great principle was established that under economic imperialism even bankruptcy pays the patriotic financier.

Finally, there remains the question of the present political position of Abyssinia and its ruler. In Europe the liberty and independence of States, even of small States, are considered to be among the highest interests and the most sacred of trusts for those who inhabit them. The world gives a very high and honourable place to the patriotism of the ruler and people who show themselves prepared to make great sacrifices in order to defend the integrity and independence of their country against the aggression of more powerful neighbours. There seems to be considerable doubt whether the European believes that his standards of good and evil, of nobility and dishonour, are applicable once one crosses the Mediterranean into Africa. If those standards which we apply to the Poles, the Magyars, the Italians, and the Belgians *were* applicable to the African, then we should be compelled to do honour to the noble patriotism with which the ruler and people of Abyssinia, for over twenty years, in the face of enormous odds, defended the independence of their country. In 1906, by an agreement, which in its wording recalls the famous Belgian treaty of 1839, the three Great Powers guaranteed the integrity and independence of Abyssinia. That this kingdom was the only one in Africa to retain a real independence at this date was due primarily to what in Europe would have been considered the tenacious patriotism, the passion for liberty, in its Emperor and its people. Twenty years before, one of the Great Powers which signed the agreement, in collusion with another, had made an attempt by force of arms to conquer and subdue this small nation. The Abyssinians defended their independence at Adowa in the same way as the Greeks defended

[1] See Lémonon, *L'Europe et la Politique Britannique*, p. 355.

theirs at Thermopylae and Marathon, and the Belgians theirs at Liége. The battle proved to the European States that the statesmanship of Menelik and the warlike courage of his subjects made a direct attack by force upon their independence a hazardous operation. For the next ten years, if we are to believe the French, the English, and if we are to believe the English, the French attempted to overthrow that independence by the subtler financial and diplomatic methods of economic imperialism. These attempts were also frustrated by the astuteness of Menelik and by the rivalries and competitions of the European States and their financiers. At last, in 1906, the three Great Powers composed their quarrels and united to guarantee the independence of Abyssinia. It might seem reasonable to assume that with this guarantee the gallant struggle of this small nation had been crowned with success. But the history of nations, and of Africa in particular, shows that the independence of small States is often better guaranteed by the disagreement than it is by the agreement—even in a solemn treaty—of the great ones. French munitions, as we have seen, certainly helped Menelik to save his independence from Italy and Britain; and British diplomacy helped him in later years to save it from France. But, nine years after the three Great Powers signed the agreement which composed their differences and guaranteed the independence of Abyssinia, they signed another and a secret agreement[1] in the middle of a great war, a war which was being fought by them in defence of the independence of small nations. One of the clauses of this secret treaty reads as follows : " Should France and Great Britain extend their colonial possessions in Africa at the expense of Germany they will admit in principle Italy's right to demand certain compensation by way of an extension of her possessions in Eritrea, Somaliland, and Libya. . . ." The meaning of this clause is not entirely clear, but Eritrea and Somaliland adjoin Abyssinia, and the only extension which in the past Italy has aimed at would have been at the expense of the independence of Abyssinia. Any one who recalls the history of the European State in Africa will feel some doubt as to whether Italy's compensation may not be found within Abyssinian territory. For the Emperor Menelik is dead, and the beliefs and desires of economic imperialism still live in Africa.

[1] This is the " Secret Treaty " signed by Britain, France, Russia, and Italy at London on April 26, 1915.

APPENDIX

THE ANGLO-ITALIAN TREATIES OF 1891 AND 1894

THE rather complicated facts concerning the documents of these treaties afford interesting material for the philosophic student of history. He will observe how truth, transmuted by the bias of patriotism, passes into history so disfigured, perverted, and distorted as to be little better than a lie. The actual documents with which we are concerned are four (the reader will find the last three printed at the end of this appendix) :

(1) Article 4 of an Agreement between Britain and France concluded by an Exchange of Notes on February 2-9, 1888.

(2) A Protocol between Britain and Italy signed on March 24, 1891.

(3) A Protocol between Britain and Italy signed on April 15, 1891.

(4) An Agreement between Britain and Italy signed on May 5, 1894.

The relevant facts with regard to the publication and contents of these documents are as follows. The Agreement between France and Britain of 1888 was kept secret. As explained above, the reason for this secrecy was almost certainly Britain's unwillingness that the fourth clause should come to the knowledge of Italy. This important fourth clause ran as follows :

4. The two Governments engage not to endeavour to annex Harrar nor to place it under their Protectorate. In taking this engagement the two Governments do not renounce the right of opposing attempts on the part of any other Power to acquire or assert any rights over Harrar.

The British Government were unwilling that this clause should become known to the Italian Government, because, presumably, they knew that Italy, with whom they were co-operating in Ethiopian Africa, desired and intended to acquire the Harrar.

The Protocols of March 24 and April 15, 1891, were published in the usual way by being presented to both Houses of Parliament by command of Her Majesty in May, 1891.

The Agreement between Britain and Italy of May 5, 1894, although not immediately published, seems to have become known in Paris in some form towards the end of May. M. Deloncle, a leading member of the " Colonial Group," put down an interpellation with regard to it and to the Anglo-French Agreement of 1888 for May 31, and on May 29, in connection with this interpellation, the Minister of Foreign Affairs distributed to members of the French Chamber copies of the Anglo-French and Anglo-Italian Agreements (see The Times of May 30, 1894). Mr. Lowther and Mr. Labouchere immediately put down questions in the House of Commons for June 1. Mr. Labouchere asked on that date

Whether the Anglo-French Convention entered into on February 8, 1888, which appears in The Times of May 30, has ever been presented to the House ;

and, if not, whether it will be presented; whether this Convention conflicts
in any way with the Anglo-Italian Harrar Treaty; whether a new Convention
was signed with Italy on May 5, 1894; whether this country has been a party
to any other Conventions which have not been presented to this House; . . ."

To this question Sir Edward Grey replied that

The second of these Agreements (*i.e.* the Anglo-Italian Agreement of
May 5, 1894) was presented yesterday, and the former one (*i.e.* the Anglo-
French of 1888), which was recorded in an Exchange of Notes, can be laid
immediately, provided . . . the French Government do not object. . . .
We are not aware of any Conventions to which Great Britain has been a party
in Africa which have not been presented to Parliament except the Anglo-
French arrangement of 1888.

The Anglo-French Agreement of 1888 was then published as " Parliamentary Paper, France, No. 1 (1894)." It should be noted that the
Anglo-Italian Agreement of May 5, 1894, which was said by Sir Edward
Grey to have been published on May 31, 1894, was not published in a
complete form. As presented to Parliament on May 31, it consisted
simply of three clauses. But in fact, as signed, it had contained a
" Note officieuse annexée au Protocole Anglo-Italien du 5 mai, 1894,"
of which the following is a translation :

The delimitation starts from Gildessa because the Somali territories, which
lie to the right of the line Lavadu-Bia-Catuba-Gildessa, up to the frontier of
the Harrar, were in 1888 left by England to France.
The Italian sphere of influence is formed by the Harrar, practically the
whole of Ogaden, and of the Medjertine peninsula of Guardafui.
In the English sphere remain the tribes Issa Gadaboursi, Abr Aoual Abr
Gheragis, Abr Folgela, Al Giableh, Uarsangueli, and Dolbohanta.

This note was first made known by being printed in the first edition of
Sir Edward Hertslet's *The Map of Africa by Treaty*, which was published in December 1894. It is a very curious fact that in the later
edition of Hertslet's book the note is silently omitted.
So much for the bare facts. The account of them which has passed
into French history, into even so authoritative a work, for instance,
as M. Lémonon's *L'Europe et la Politique Britannique*, is extraordinarily
inaccurate. The most serious inaccuracies, which have been copied
by one historian from another, are ultimately traceable to an article
which the well-known historian M. E. Lavisse wrote in *La Revue de
Paris* of February 1, 1899. I propose to examine some of these inaccuracies.
Practically all French writers maintain that the British Government
kept the Anglo-Italian Protocols of 1891 secret because they conflicted
with the Anglo-French Agreement of 1888. Thus M. Lémonon says
(*op. cit.* p. 84) : " The treaties of 1891 were kept secret until 1894," and
(p. 129) " On June 18, 1894, we learnt of the treaties of 1891." M.
Darcy (*Cents Années*, p. 373) writes of the Protocols of 1891 : " These
extraordinary conventions were carefully kept secret for three years," [1]
There seems to be no foundation for this statement. The two Protocols

---

[1] See, too, Debidour, *Histoire Diplomatique*, vol. i. p. 196.

of 1891 were laid before Parliament in the usual way in May, 1891, and if the French Foreign Office and the French public did not make themselves acquainted with their contents, it was not the fault of the British Government. It was the Anglo-French Agreement of 1888, not the Anglo-Italian Agreements of 1891, which was kept secret until 1894. What really appears to have happened is this : in the middle of May, 1894, the French Government and " Colonial Group " learned that Italy and Britain had signed the Agreement of May 5, 1894. The preamble of this Agreement refers expressly to the two Anglo-Italian Protocols of March 24 and April 15, 1891. The French immediately perceived that the three Anglo-Italian Agreements, taken together, seemed to conflict with their reading of the terms of the secret Anglo-French Agreement of 1888. It is, in fact, possible to show how, in the case at least of M. Lémonon, the inaccuracy has arisen. M. Lémonon was writing with M. Lavisse's article open before him, for he actually quotes it in the sentence immediately preceding the words : " Le 18 juin, 1894, nous eûmes connaissance des traités de 1891." Now in M. Lavisse's article there occur the words : " Le protocole été signé le 5 mai. C'est le 18 juin que nous avons connaissance de la déclaration confidentielle " (" The protocol was signed on May 5. On June 18 we learned of the secret declaration "). But M. Lavisse is referring here not to the Anglo-Italian Protocols of 1891, but to a secret declaration which, he asserts, was annexed to the Anglo-Italian Agreement of 1894. It is the secret declaration of 1894, not the agreements of 1891, which he alleges came to the knowledge of the French Government on June 18, 1894. M. Lémonon, ignoring the fact that the agreements of 1891 were actually discussed in the French Chamber on May 29, 1894, misreads M. Lavisse and is thus able to write " On June 18, 1894, we learned of the treaties of 1891."

But M. Lavisse's statement with regard to the secret declaration becoming known to the French Government conceals an even more serious inaccuracy which has been widely adopted by French writers. M. Lavisse's article took the form of an open letter to Sir Charles Dilke, and this is the passage in which he deals with the secret declaration attached to the Anglo-Italian Agreement of May 5, 1894 :

> In May, 1894, you recognized the Protectorate of Italy over all the territories of Menelik, including the Harrar, which, it is true, you did not dare to name in the published protocol, feeling that the affair was somewhat suspicious. But now look at this : to the published protocol you annexed a secret declaration in which it was stipulated that " Italy would allow Great Britain to exercise a temporary intervention in the Harrar until she should be in a position herself effectively to establish her protectorate." In the published protocol you gave all the cake to Italy ; in the secret declaration Italy passed back under the table the piece which you had promised us never to touch. . . . The Protocol was signed on May 5. On June 18 we learned of the secret declaration.

This story of a secret clause annexed to the Agreement of 1894, whereby Italy agreed to a temporary occupation of the Harrar by Britain, is repeated in M. Lémonon's book. There appears to be no foundation for it in fact, but it is easy to see how the misstatement came into being and was accepted as true. The "Secret declaration annexed to the published protocol" to which M. Lavisse refers is obviously the "Note officieuse annexée au Protocole Anglo-Italien du 5 mai" (see above), which was not published when the Agreement itself was laid before Parliament in May, 1894. Now it is quite true, as M. Lavisse says, that the published Agreement never refers to the Harrar by name, and it is more than probable that, in view of their Agreement with France of 1888, the British Government were not willing to state openly that they had handed over the Harrar to Italy. Consequently that statement was reserved for the secret declaration, the "note officieuse." The existence of this secret "note officieuse" presumably came to the knowledge of the French on June 18, and, as is so often the case with secret documents, it did far more harm than if it had been originally published. Its words and its meaning were distorted, and have passed in this distorted form into French history. It declared that the Harrar was Italian, but it did not stipulate for any temporary occupation of the Harrar by Britain. One may conjecture that the original distortion arose by confusing the terms of this "note officieuse" with the second clause of the Anglo-Italian Protocol of April 15, 1891, by which Britain agreed to a temporary occupation of Kassala by Italy until Britain, or rather the "Egyptian Government," should be in a position to reoccupy the Kassala district.

It may, perhaps, be said that these misstatements and inaccuracies are unimportant, and that I have spent an unnecessarily long time in displaying them. But they are a very good example of the process through which historical truth becomes discoloured by patriotism. M. Lavisse, M. Lémonon, and M. Debidour are all very eminent historians. They had only to examine with some care and detachment the documents themselves and they would have discovered the simple truth about them. If they had kept to that simple truth they would have had, as I have shown above in the body of this chapter (see pp. 170-72), a considerable case against British statesmen and British policy. But the bias of patriotism so distorts their vision that, in their eagerness to make a good case better, to show the perfidiousness of Britain and the righteousness of France in the blackest and the brightest of colours, they are unable to see even documentary facts as they are.

I. Protocols between the Governments of Her Britannic Majesty and of His Majesty the King of Italy, for the Demarcation of their respective Spheres of Influence in Eastern Africa.[1]

No. 1.

Protocol signed on the 24th March, 1891.

(Translation.)

THE Undersigned,
The Marquis of Dufferin and Ava, Ambassador of Her Majesty the Queen of the United Kingdom of Great Britain and Ireland, Empress of India; and

---

[1] Parl. Pap., Italy, No. 1 (1891).

The Marquis de Rudini, President of the Council, and Minister for Foreign Affairs of His Majesty the King of Italy;

After careful examination of the respective interests of the two countries in Eastern Africa, have agreed as follows :—

1. The line of demarcation in Eastern Africa between the spheres of influence respectively reserved to Great Britain and Italy shall follow from the sea the mid-channel (thalweg) of the River Juba up to latitude 6° north, Kismayu with its territory on the right bank of the river thus remaining to England. The line shall then follow the 6th parallel of north latitude up to the meridian 35° east of Greenwich, which it will follow up to the Blue Nile.

2. If future explorations should hereafter show occasion, the line following the 6th parallel of north latitude and the 35th degree of longitude east of Greenwich, may, by common agreement, be amended in its details in accordance with the hydrographic and orographic conditions of the country.

3. In the station of Kismayu and its territory, there shall be equality of treatment between the subjects and protected persons of the two countries, in all that relates to their persons, their goods, or to the exercise of any kind of commerce and industry.

Done at Rome in duplicate, the 24th March, 1891.

(L.S.)   DUFFERIN AND AVA.

(L.S.)   RUDINI.

No. 2.

PROTOCOL SIGNED ON THE 15TH APRIL, 1891.

(*Translation.*)

BEING desirous of completing, towards the north as far as the Red Sea, the demarcation of the respective spheres of influence of England and Italy, which the two Parties have already agreed on by the Protocol of the 24th March last, from the mouth of the Juba in the Indian Ocean to the intersection of 35° east longitude Greenwich with the Blue Nile, the Undersigned :

The Marquis of Dufferin and Ava, Ambassador of Her Majesty the Queen of the United Kingdom of Great Britain and Ireland, Empress of India;

The Marquis de Rudini, President of the Council and Minister for Foreign Affairs of His Majesty the King of Italy;

Have agreed as follows :—

I. The sphere of influence reserved to Italy is bounded, on the north and on the west, by a line drawn from Ras Kasar on the Red Sea to the point of intersection of the 17th parallel, north, with the 37th meridian, east, Greenwich. The line, having followed that meridian to 16° 30′ north latitude, is drawn from that point in a straight line to Sabderat, leaving that village to the east. From that village the line is drawn southward to a point on the Gash 20 English miles above Kassala, and rejoins the Atbara at the point indicated as being a ford on the Map of Werner Munzinger " Originalkarte von Nord Abessinien und den Ländern am Mareb, Barca, und Anseba, de 1864 " (Gotha, Justus Perthes), and situated at 14° 52′ north latitude. The line then ascends the Atbara to the confluence of the Kor Kakamot (Hahamot), whence it follows a westerly direction till it meets the Kor Lemsen, which it descends to its confluence with the Rahad. Finally, the line, having followed the Rahad for the short distance between the confluence of the Kor Lemsen and the intersection of 35° east longitude, Greenwich, identifies itself in a southerly direction with that meridian, until it meets the Blue Nile, saving ulterior amendment of details, according to the hydrographic and orographic conditions of the country.

II. The Italian Government shall be at liberty, in case of being obliged to do so by the necessities of the military situation, to occupy Kassala and the adjoining country as far as the Atbara. Such occupation shall in no case extend to the north nor to the north-east of the following line :—

From the right bank of the Atbara, in front of Gos Rejeb, the line is drawn in an easterly direction to the intersection of the 36th meridian, east, Greenwich ; thence, turning to the south-east, it passes 3 miles to the south of the points marked Filik and Metkinab on the above-mentioned Map of Werner Munzinger, and joins the line mentioned in Article I., 25 English miles north of Sabderat, measured along the said line.

It is nevertheless agreed between the two Governments that any temporary military occupation of the additional territory specified in this Article shall not abrogate the rights of the Egyptian Government over the said territory, but that these rights shall only remain in suspense until the Egyptian Government shall be in a position to reoccupy the district in question up to the line indicated in Article I. of this Protocol, and there to maintain order and tranquillity.

III. The Italian Government engages not to construct on the Atbara, in view of irrigation, any work which might sensibly modify its flow into the Nile.

IV. Italy shall have, for her subjects and protected persons, as well as for their goods, free passage without duty on the road between Metemma and Kassala, touching successively El Affareh, Doka, Suk-Abu-Sin (Ghedaref), and the Atbara.

Done at Rome, in duplicate, this 15th of April, 1891.

(L.S.)   DUFFERIN AND AVA.
(L.S.)   RUDINI.

II. AGREEMENT between Great Britain and Italy defining their respective Spheres of Influence in Eastern Africa. (Somali, etc.) Rome, 5th May, 1894.[1]

In order to complete the delimitation of the spheres of influence of Great Britain and Italy in Eastern Africa, which formed the subject of the Protocols signed at Rome on the 24th March and the 15th April, 1891, the Undersigned, authorized by their respective Governments, have agreed as follows :—

(Here follow the names of the Plenipotentiaries.)

Boundary. Spheres of Influence.

1. The boundary of the spheres of influence of Great Britain and of Italy in the regions of the Gulf of Aden shall be constituted by a line which, starting from Gildessa and running towards the 8th degree of north latitude, skirts the north-east frontier of the territories of the Girrhi, Bertiri, and Rer Ali tribes, leaving to the right the villages of Gildessa, Darmi, Gig-giga, and Milmil. On reaching the 8th degree of north latitude the line follows that parallel as far as its intersection with the 48th degree of longitude east of Greenwich. It then runs to the intersection of the 9th degree of north latitude with the 49th degree of longitude east of Greenwich, and follows that meridian of longitude to the sea.

Ogaden Regions. Trade.

2. The two Governments engage to conform, in the regions of the British Protectorate, and in those of the Ogaden, to the stipulations contained in the

---

[1] Hertslet, *The Map of Africa by Treaty*, vol. ii. p. 669, 1st edition, and Parl. Pap., Treaty Series, No. 17 (1894).

General Act of Berlin and in the Declaration of Brussels relative to freedom of trade, in favour as well of British and Italian subjects, and protected persons as of the tribes inhabiting those territories.

Port of Zeyla. Trade, etc.

3. In the Port of Zeyla there shall be equality of treatment between British and Italian subjects and protected persons in all that relates to their persons, their property, and to the exercise of trade and industry.

Rome, 5th May, 1894.

FRANCIS CLARE FORD.
FRANCESCO CRISPI.

NOTE OFFICIEUSE ANNEXÉE AU PROTOCOLE ANGLO-ITALIEN DU 5 MAI, 1894.[1]

La délimitation part de Gildessa parce que les territoires somalis qui se trouvent à droite de la ligne Lavadu-Bia-Catuba-Gildessa, s'arrêtant à la frontière du Harrar, furent, en 1888, laissés par l'Angleterre à la France.

La sphère d'influence italienne reste formée du Harrar, de presque tout l'Ogaden et de la presqù'île Medjertine de Guardafui.

Dans la sphère d'influence anglaise restent les tribus Issa Gadaboursi, Abr Aoual Abr Gheragis, Abr Folgela, Al Giableh, Uarsangueli et Dolbohanta.

---

[1] Not laid before Parliament.

CHAPTER VI

ZANZIBAR AND EAST AFRICA

In 1914 the East Coast of Africa from Cape Guardafui to Cape Delgado was in the possession of three European Powers. Italy possessed the narrow strip of Italian Somaliland, the history of which we have sketched in the preceding pages. Britain owned, besides the islands of Zanzibar and Pemba, an immense solid block of empire of which the coast-line extended from Italian Somaliland and the Juba River to German East Africa and Wanga. The British hinterland stretched right back and united with the Bahr-el-Ghazal and the British empire of the Nile Valley and Sudan. It included the northern half of the great lake, Victoria Nyanza, and Uganda. Germany ruled over a stretch of territory bounded on the north by British East Africa, on the west by the Belgian Congo, and on the south by Rhodesia, Lake Nyasa, and Portuguese East Africa. In 1885 no European State held or owned a square inch of this vast region. The complete destruction of African sovereignty and independence, and the complete absorption of land and population into the imperial system of Europe, took considerably less than ten years. The history is curious. It reveals the same beliefs and desires, the same interaction of power, policy, and commerce, which we have seen at work in Tunis and Tripoli, in Abyssinia and the Nile Valley. But the elements of national and economic psychology, of policy and commerce, were not mixed in quite the same proportions on the East Coast as they were in Ethiopian Africa and on the Mediterranean. In East Africa we must examine another phase of economic imperialism. We shall, indeed, see the same desires and beliefs producing the same effects ; but they will employ different methods and weapons, and will wear new decorations and strange disguises.

The process of absorption began suddenly in 1885, but a word or two are necessary with regard to the previous political history of East Africa. From the middle of the eighteenth century the sovereignty over Zanzibar and the coast from Mogadishu to Cape Delgado was either exercised or claimed by the Imaums of Oman, which lies to the south of the Persian Gulf. In 1804 Seyyid Said became Imaum of Oman and ruler of Muscat. He was a remarkable man, and during the course of his long reign he succeeded in making his power effective over Zanzibar and the whole of his African possessions. During the latter part of his reign, which ended in 1856, he established himself permanently in Zanzibar, leaving one of his sons to govern Muscat. He devoted himself to developing the trade and prosperity of East Africa; and, when he died, he left his African kingdom in a settled and on the whole prosperous condition. In 1861, owing to a series of events which it is unnecessary to relate, the kingdom of Muscat was separated from Zanzibar and the African dependencies; and Seyyid Majid became Sultan and ruler of Zanzibar and East Africa. Seyyid Majid was succeeded in 1870 by Seyyid Barghash, who ruled until 1888.

Between 1820 and 1885 the relations between Europe and East Africa had been peculiar. Great Britain occupied a special position in Zanzibar, for there were two factors which brought her into very close touch with the Sultan and his Government. As ruler over the Indian Empire, she had always been interested in the Persian Gulf, and therefore Oman and Muscat; and as early as 1820 the Government of India despatched an expedition to those regions to co-operate with Seyyid Said in " punishing " piratical Arabs. This link between Muscat and the British Government in India was strengthened rather than weakened through the growing importance of Seyyid Said's African Empire. In Zanzibar and on the East Coast the trade was very largely in the hands of Indian traders, and commercial communication between the two empires was close and constant. Besides the trade in more legitimate commodities there was always a brisk traffic in slaves between the East Coast of Africa and the Persian Gulf. The organized slave trade was not the least among the gifts which the civilization of Europe had bestowed upon Africa. It owed its origin and its perfection to the economic beliefs and desires of Europeans in the seventeenth and eighteenth centuries. The commerce, though extremely profitable to many estimable ladies and gentlemen in Europe and America, had some unfortunate results for the inhabitants of Africa. The simplest way of obtaining slaves was to take them, and this process of " taking " produced a state of anarchy in Africa probably unparalleled in the history of the human race. In order to obtain the human beings who were the staple of the trade, force had to be employed to remove them from their homes and villages. In Africa the idea that war was profitable became under these conditions no illusion. War was not only profitable, but the chief instrument of trade. Village fought against village and district against district in order to acquire, by the right of conquest, the women and children who could be so profitably sold to the Europeans on the coast. Every man's hand was against his neighbour, for, if you did not enslave your neighbour and his wife and children, it was almost certain that he would enslave you and yours. It seemed as if the European had achieved in Africa a state of things which might regretfully have been considered Utopian, Perpetual War. Moreover, the economic desires of Europeans could not be completely satisfied by the " home " industry of African wars and slave raids. The demand called into existence a class of foreign slave raider who led armed expeditions into the interior of Africa, raided villages, and returned with gangs of slaves to the coast. The expansion and success of this method of trade were only made possible by the sale of European firearms to the raiders. The import of arms into Africa assumed enormous dimensions; and Europe profited not only by buying the captured Africans, but also by selling the weapons necessary for killing those who refused to be captured.

In these circumstances the African had not, at the beginning of the nineteenth century, advanced to the same degree of civilization and culture as the European. Africa, as the nineteenth-century explorers, missionaries, imperialists, and financiers repeatedly point out, is " uncivilized," " savage," " the dark continent." The white man, in a sudden spirit of altruism, came to the conclusion that his real mission was to introduce his civilization, in the form of his government, trade, religion, and joint-stock companies, into the " dark continent." He reached this conclusion, as we have already seen, about the year 1880. But before this happened, a curious event occurred in the relations between Africa and Europe. The Briton, as a political animal, has some peculiar characteristics. He belongs to the only European people which, suddenly and at very long intervals, allows its political action to be determined not by self-interest but by morality, by an active sense of what is right and wrong. About once, or possibly twice, in a hundred years a wave of intense, idealistic morality, a passion for purging the earth of some great political or social evil, usually outside the British Isles, sweeps over the British nation, and all political beliefs and desires become suddenly channelled into this current of reform. A wave of this emotional kind swept over the British Isles early in the nineteenth century. In the last decade of the eighteenth century the French people had risen against the despotism of king and aristocracy, had driven out their rulers or beheaded them, had proclaimed the doctrine of " Liberty, Equality, and Fraternity," and established a Republic. Britain and the other Great Powers of Europe promptly declared war upon France in order to uphold the principle that only kings and the upper classes have the right to rule or to execute those who disagree with them politically. The result was that very soon Great Britain, the King of Prussia, and the Tsar of

All the Russias found themselves fighting a war on behalf of liberty and small nationalities against French militarism and autocracy. The British Government and people carried on this war on behalf of freedom and liberty for some twenty years, and in the process of crushing French militarism the British Government contrived so completely to destroy the liberties of the British people that it took them at least another twenty years to recover them. But the more completely the British nation lost its own liberties, the more passionate became its determination to secure the liberty of other peoples. Not content with fighting for the freedom of Germans, Russians, Italians, Austrians, Spaniards, and Portuguese, it suddenly decided towards the end of the Napoleonic Wars that the one thing it was really fighting for was the freedom of the African negro. As the Congress of Vienna approached, the Congress which was finally to bind the hands of French militarism and rebuild the New Europe upon a basis of liberty and public right, a wave of enthusiasm swept over the British Isles, not for Poland or Spain, for the German Confederation or Italy or the Netherlands, or for the retention of the French Colonies, but for the abolition of the slave-trade. Public meetings in favour of the abolition of slavery by international agreement were held up and down the country in every town and village, and popular pressure upon the Government was so great that Castlereagh, in his preliminary instructions to the British representatives at the Congress, informed them that the abolition of the slave-trade must be made one of the principal British war aims or peace terms.

The British statesmen and representatives at Vienna were, in fact, in something of a quandary. They knew that their real task was to re-establish the Balance of Power, the Armed Peace, and the Principle of Legitimacy, and to prevent the principles of Christianity and the Millennium being applied by Alexander to diplomacy and foreign affairs. But the people of England and Scotland suddenly appeared to care for none of these things : they distracted their representatives by calling for nothing but the abolition of slavery. The distracted Castlereagh was at one moment driven by popular pressure at home to offer the surrender of the British colony of Trinidad to France—upon whom he was imposing terms of peace after a crushing military defeat—in payment for the abolition of slavery in the French colonies. Unfortunately a great deal of capital was invested in slavery or the products of slave labour, and it proved to be easier to free Europe from Napoleon than Africa from the capitalist slave dealer and owner. But ordinary men, and particularly ordinary Anglo-Saxon men, as statesmen are well aware, can often be satisfied in their demand for some great political or social revolution, if some noble sentiment be expressed in some official document, and everything else left where it was. The statesmen of Europe, finding it impossible to persuade one another to satisfy the people of England by abolishing slavery, inserted a clause in the Final Act of the Congress in which in principle they accepted the abolition of slavery and said that they would do their best to abolish it.

The export of slaves with which in 1815 the Abolitionists were principally concerned was to America from the West Coast of Africa. It took a very long time to get the Governments of Europe and America to put the principle enshrined in the Vienna treaty into practice. A few obstinate Englishmen persevered, and for the first half of the century Great Britain became the champion of Abolition, adopted it as one of the principles of her foreign policy, and used her fleet as a kind of international police force against the slave-traders. By 1880 all " civilized " countries outside Africa had made slavery illegal, and the trade on the West Coast had largely ceased. On the East Coast, with which we are concerned, matters were somewhat different.

The export of slaves from the East Coast was in two directions, some of them going east to the Persian Gulf, and others west to America. As restrictions were imposed on the trade to America from the West Coast, this trade became driven more and more to the ports on the East. The centres of the traffic were Portuguese East Africa and Zanzibar, and the traders were Frenchmen, Portuguese, Americans, and Arabs. The position of Great Britain as champion of Abolition soon after 1815 brought her into close and constant relations with the ruler of Zanzibar. In 1822 Captain Moresby, on behalf of the British Government, induced Seyyid Said to sign a treaty prohibiting the sale of slaves to Christians in his dominions and the export of slaves to Christian countries. After that date the British fleet regularly policed the waters of the East Coast, and questions continually arose between the British and Zanzibar Governments with regard to the trade. British efforts were not very successful. The trade with the Persian Gulf was still legal, and the Portuguese Government not only refused to make it illegal, but allowed its colony of Portuguese East Africa to derive its chief revenue from an export duty of seven dollars per head on slaves. In 1845 Britain made another attempt to deal with the Zanzibar question, and Seyyid Said was reluctantly induced to sign another treaty prohibiting the export of slaves from the Sultan's African territories and the importation from any part of Africa into his territory on the Persian Gulf. Two British squadrons were then sent to patrol the East Coast, and until the outbreak of the Crimean War something was done to suppress the traffic. After 1854, however, there was a great revival of both the Persian Gulf and Atlantic trade, and French, Spanish, Portuguese, and American ships carried large cargoes of slaves from Zanzibar and Portuguese East Africa.

From 1854 to 1870 the efforts of Great Britain to put down the slave-trade between the East Coast and Arabia were confessedly a failure. According to treaty the trade was "legal within the limits of Kilwa to the south of Zanzibar and Lamu to the north, a distance of 430 miles."[1] There was an export tax on all slaves shipped from the coast and from Zanzibar; and slaves so exported under licence could not be touched by the British cruisers. During the five years 1862–67, an average of nearly 20,000 slaves per year were exported legally from Kilwa, and about the same period it was estimated that some 12,000 illegally exported slaves were carried in dhows which escaped capture. All through the 'sixties the French carried on the trade actively: they "had agents up and down the coast and in Zanzibar," and, while British cruisers were trying to suppress the traffic, "French warships, stationed on the coast, protected the French slavers from molestation." In fact, when the Sultan, "deriving no profit from the traffic, as the French paid no duty on their slaves, endeavoured to stop it (and) remonstrated with the French Consul, that functionary threatened him with the intervention of his Government." Under these circumstances it was not remarkable that the trade in the north, which was in the hands of Arabs, also flourished.

Thus in 1871, fifty-six years after the Congress of Vienna, Great Britain "had been able to accomplish nothing in the direction of putting down the slave trade with Arabia." The remedy next attempted was a Select Committee of the House of Commons, and the result of the Committee's enquiry was the despatch in 1873 of Sir Bartle Frere on a mission to Zanzibar. The mission itself resulted in another treaty between the Sultan of Zanzibar, Seyyid Barghash, who had succeeded to the throne in 1870, and Great Britain. With great reluctance Barghash bound himself to prohibit the export of slaves from the coast of Africa and to close all public slave-markets in his dominions.

There, for the moment, I must leave the question of the slave-trade. I have dealt with it at some length for two reasons. The question continually crops up again in the period of the policy of economic imperialism applied by European States to the East Coast of Africa. The reader may be surprised to find that after all these principles and efforts and treaties, the slave-trade was flourishing in the 'eighties and 'nineties, and that the intervention and acquisition of territory by the European States and European commercial companies were justified on the pretext that the slave-trade should be abolished. But, secondly, it shows the kind of relations which existed between Britain and Zanzibar from 1815 to

---

[1] *Zanzibar in Contemporary Times*, by R. N. Lyne of the Zanzibar Government Service. The facts with regard to the slave-trade and Zanzibar, given above, are derived from this book.

1880. The British and Indian Governments, owing to Britain's attitude towards the slave-trade and her treaties with the Sultans, acquired a very considerable influence at Zanzibar. Her position was still further strengthened by the personal influence of two British subjects. In 1873 Dr. Kirk (afterwards Sir John Kirk, G.C.M.G., K.C.B.), who was medical attendant at the British Agency, was appointed Consul-General and Political Agent at Zanzibar. Sir John Kirk would probably not have objected to the name of " empire-builder " or " imperialist," and in Zanzibar he acquired the position of " the power behind the throne." In later years, when he relinquished his official post, he became a director of the British East Africa Company, with whose operations in the dominions of Zanzibar this chapter will be chiefly concerned. The other British subject was " General " Sir Lloyd Mathews, K.C.M.G. He came out to the East Coast of Africa as lieutenant on the British man-of-war *London*, in 1875. In 1877 Sir John Kirk induced the Sultan Barghash to lay the foundations of a new Zanzibar army by raising a force of 500, arming them with modern rifles, and placing them under the command of a European officer. The officer was, not unnaturally, to be an Englishman, and Lieutenant Mathews was borrowed from the British Navy. In 1881 Lieutenant Mathews resigned from the British Navy, and was appointed Brigadier-General in the army of Zanzibar. This post he retained until his death in 1901.

In the years after 1880, when the British and German States and joint-stock companies were struggling against one another for the territory of Zanzibar, the British capitalists maintained that the earlier rulers of Zanzibar were sultans with a passion for giving away to Europeans, and especially Britons, the sovereignty over their dominions. In 1872 Mr. Mackinnon (later Sir William Mackinnon) started a regular mail steamer service between Zanzibar, Europe, and India, and, so we are told by Sir William and his fellow capitalist imperialists, " Sultan Barghash so intelligently appreciated the benefits conferred on his dominions by this service, and the advantages likely to accrue to his subjects from a closer association with British commercial interests, that in 1877 he offered to Sir William Mackinnon (or to a company to be formed by him) a concession under lease for seventy years of the customs and administration of the whole of the dominions of Zanzibar, *including all rights of sovereignty*,[1] with certain reservations in respect of the islands of Zanzibar and Pemba." [2] I shall have again to refer to this alleged eagerness of the Sultan Barghash to retire from the cares of king-

[1] The italics are mine.

[2] P. L. McDermott, *British East Africa*, 1895, p. 3. This is a most important book for the student of economic imperialism. It was written by the Secretary of the British East Africa Company, and is, for that Company and therefore for British economic imperialism on the East Coast, an *apologia pro vita sua*.

ship in favour of the chairman of the British India Steam Navigation Company; I shall show that there are reasons for believing that either Sir William Mackinnon's memory was at fault or, perhaps owing to difficulties of language, he misconceived the Sultan's desires and intentions. Nevertheless it is probably true, as many Englishmen alleged in the 'eighties and 'nineties, that it would have been quite easy for the British Empire or the chairman of the British India Steam Navigation Company to acquire the dominions of Zanzibar at any time between 1870 and 1880. What with the slave-trade and Sir John Kirk and "Brigadier-General" Mathews, British influence was, to use a conveniently vague phrase, paramount. If in those years, or even earlier, the British Government had chosen to declare a protectorate over the greater part of the East Coast of Africa, it is improbable that any European State would have seriously protested. But there is no evidence at all that the Sultans Seyyid Said, Seyyid Majid, or Seyyid Barghash would have resigned their inheritance to the British Empire or Sir William Mackinnon with any greater willingness than Queen Victoria would have shown in resigning hers to the Sultan of Zanzibar or an Arab slave-trader.

But before 1880, as I have often had to point out, the beliefs and desires of economic imperialism were not accepted as the principles of national policy. Britain neglected the opportunity of acquiring the territories of Seyyid Barghash. A few capitalist economic imperialists, like Herr Woermann of Germany and Sir William Mackinnon of England, were ahead of their times, and their views were not accepted either by the Governments or people of their countries. It is significant that Sir William in 1877 approached the Foreign Office, before accepting the Sultan Barghash's "offer," to see whether the British Government would give him "the support he deemed necessary." The Foreign Office declined to give him the "support," and he therefore declined the "offer." Thus in 1884, when the full tide of economic imperialism began to run in Africa, the Sultan Barghash was still an independent ruler. And though Great Britain, as the chief crusader against slavery, as the ruler of the Indian merchants in Zanzibar, as the mother-country of Sir John Kirk and the Brigadier-General of the Zanzibar army, had, according to the doctrines of economic imperialism, very strong grounds for claiming the dominions of Zanzibar as her own, or at least as the inheritance of a joint-stock company to be created by Sir William Mackinnon, yet in the interval similar claims had accrued to other European countries. Among these countries was the German Empire.

Germany's relations with the East Coast of Africa were commercial, and they began at an early date. In 1840 the firm of U. J. Herz, and in 1850 the firms of O'Swald and Hansing & Co., had established themselves there.[1] They traded in or had branches on the Somali Coast, Zanzibar, Mozambique, and Madagascar. Commerce and exploration went hand in hand in the early days in Africa, and many of the explorers on the East Coast were Germans. According to the doctrines of economic imperialism, the European State which has given birth or nationality to men who trade in or explore African territory thereby acquires a " claim " to that territory. But, if Germany could produce the traders Herz, O'Swald, and Hansing, and such explorers as Rebman and Ernhardt, Britain could produce the Indian traders and such explorers as Burton and Speke, in addition to Sir John Kirk, Sir William Mackinnon, and "Brigadier-General" Sir Lloyd Mathews. Accordingly the impartial historian will probably conclude that in 1884, according to the strict principles of economic imperialism, if the above facts gave to Germany a right to deprive the Sultan of Zanzibar or the King of Uganda of territory, they gave more right to Britain to deprive these rulers of territory, or at least gave her the right to deprive them of more territory than Germany.

At any rate, when in the early 'eighties European States began to seize pieces of territory on the coasts of Africa, many German economic imperialists began to think of the East Coast and the claims which Herz, O'Swald, and Hansing had established there. Among these was Dr. Karl Peters, the explorer. On 28th March 1884, Peters and some other well-known colonialists founded the Gesellschaft für deutsche Kolonisation. For three months this society discussed the question where exactly in Africa it should start Germany upon a career of imperialism. On September 16 it was finally decided to " colonize " the district of Usagara, which lies inland immediately behind Dar-es-Salaam, and that an expedition should start in October and should consist of Peters, Dr. Jühlke, Count Pfeil, and a trader called August Otto. It was realized that there would probably be great opposition from Britain and the British in Zanzibar to any German acquisition on the East Coast, and the most extraordinary precautions were taken by Peters and his companions to prevent their real object becoming known. They travelled to Zanzibar in disguise and under a variety of *aliases* : for instance, Peters became Herr Kirmann in Germany, Mr. Fred Hunter in Austria, Mr. Bowman on the boat between Trieste and Aden, Herr Caumann at Aden, and at Zanzibar Mr. C. F. H. Peters of 81 Portland Road, Notting Hill, W. London. They landed at Zanzibar dressed as poor and ragged emigrants.[2]

The German Government had refused to give any official help or recognition to the expedition in its project of obtaining con-

---

[1] See Zimmermann, *Geschichte d. deutschen Kolonialpolitik*, p. 52.
[2] See P. Decharme, *Compagnies et Sociétés coloniales allemandes*, 1903, pp. 106-110.

cessions on the coast; in fact, the German Consul at Zanzibar is said to have informed Peters, under direct orders from Bismarck, that no protection of any kind would be given to him by Government.[1] It was significant that Peters went to Hansing & Co. and the German traders, and that it was they who fitted out the expedition. On 10th November Peters and his companions landed upon the coast and disappeared into Africa.

The Germans as a race have one rare and valuable characteristic : they have an ingenuous habit of calling spades spades, conquest conquest, and force force. When Peters returned to Europe and wrote an account of his proceedings, he told the truth about them. Being a German he did not call lies, theft, and conquest, civilization. His account therefore throws some light upon some of the more mysterious methods of economic imperialism. We have often in the preceding pages had to refer to the curious phenomenon, which manifested itself in Africa between 1880 and 1900, of native chiefs and rulers with a passion for giving away their dominions to Europeans. The claims of most European States to the territories which they seized in Africa were based ultimately upon " treaties " between the African rulers and European explorers or traders in which the ruler surrendered his territory to the explorer or trader. The Peters expedition found the whole country lying behind the coast from Pangani to Dar-es-Salaam inhabited by such complaisant and retiring rulers, and, after three months in the interior, it returned with a dozen treaties giving to Peters and to Germany sovereignty over Useguha, Usagara, Nguru, and Ukami. Fortunately Peters himself has given us an obviously truthful account of the methods adopted for obtaining the treaties. The procedure was as follows. Before arriving at the village of a chief or ruler, Peters sent ahead a messenger with presents and a request for permission to camp at the village. Having arrived, he then sent an invitation to the chief to dine with him. During dinner the chief was plied with drink and after dinner with more presents. Then Peters asked him whether he would sign a document recording his friendship with the German Empire. The chief could hardly refuse. Dr. Jühlke then read out a document, written in German and therefore unintelligible to the chief. The African signed his name and Germany had acquired a new " Protectorate." Dr. Peters shook his victim heartily by the hand, ran up the German flag, and fired a salute. More drink followed, and sometimes in honour of the occasion Dr. Peters and the Sultan took a bath together. The expedition then hurried off to perform the same ceremony with some other sultan.[2]

[1] See Zimmermann, *op. cit.* p. 113.
[2] Report of the expedition to the Committee of the Gesellschaft für deutsche Kolonisation, quoted by Decharme, *op. cit.* p. 111.

The text of the treaties thus concluded between Dr. Peters and the sultans of East Africa are well worthy of study as international documents. For instance, by a treaty [1] dated 23rd November 1884, Mafungu Biniani, Sultan of Nguru, "cedes to Dr. Peters, representing the 'Gesellschaft für deutsche Kolonisation,' . . . the country of Quaniani Quatunge in Nguru . . ., with all the rights which incontestably belong to him, for eternity and to do with it what he pleases." The "rights which accompany this concession" are then defined : they are "only those rights, orally explained to the Sultan of Nguru, which, according to German law, include the sovereignty of the State as well as private property," they include "the right for Dr. Peters or any other representative of the 'Gesellschaft für deutsche Kolonisation' to establish anywhere they may choose farms, houses, roads, mines, etc. ; the exclusive right to make use of the soil, sub-soil, forests, and rivers as may seem good to them ; the exclusive right to introduce colonists into the country, to introduce an administrative and judicial system, to raise taxes and establish a customs house." The "rights" are sufficiently definite, the consideration is conveniently vague. "In exchange for these concessions" the Gesellschaft and Dr. Peters undertake "to defend the Sultan Mafungu Biniani and his people against the whole world as far as their forces admit ; to respect the domain which has been left to the Sultan as private property, and to pay . . . a rent, payable in cattle and commercial commodities, the amount of which shall be fixed in advance verbally and by agreement." In order to make quite sure of his victim, Dr. Peters induced him on the following day, 24th November, to sign a supplementary treaty in which the Sultan recognizes the company and its representative, "Dr. Karl Peters, his friend and blood-brother, as the sole sovereign of his person and his people" ; "on his side Dr. Peters promises the Sultan of Nguru the aid and friendship of the Society which he represents."

Few explorers or economic imperialists have been as brutally frank as Dr. Karl Peters in explaining to the world the methods by which they obtained the treaties with and "legal" sovereignty over the native rulers of Africa. But it should be remarked that all the imperial States of Europe have used similar treaties as a pretext for robbing Africans of their sovereignty and territory. We have already seen [2] how Italy in 1889 obtained a Protectorate over the coast which is now Italian Somaliland : this Protectorate and acquisition of territory were made on the pretext that the Sultans of Oppia and All the Mijjertayns had signed with the Italian Consul Filonardi "regular treaties" resigning their sovereign

[1] First Journal of the Expedition of Dr. Peters, pp. 40 and 41, quoted by Decharme, pp. 220-222.
[2] See above, p. 174.

rights into the hands of Italy. Great Britain, as we shall see in this chapter, laid claim to and acquired the interior of what is now British East Africa on the pretext that native rulers and sultans had signed similar treaties with Stanley and the agents of a British joint-stock company.[1] In the bitter struggle between France and Britain over the ownership of what is now British Nigeria, each side claimed immense stretches of territory on the ground that the native rulers had, by signing treaties, resigned their kingdoms and sovereignty either to a British joint-stock company or to French military and naval officers. French ownership of the French Congo is based upon " treaties " hurriedly made in 1880 between the famous M. de Brazza and Congo chiefs, like Makoko, with the avowed intention of forestalling Stanley. Lastly, the legal title of Belgium to the 1,000,000 square miles of the Belgian Congo is founded in Stanley's " treaties made with 450 independent African chiefs." Stanley himself tells us that the rights of these rulers " would be conceded by all to have been indisputable, since they held their lands by undisturbed occupation, by long ages of succession, by real divine right "; these rulers by real divine right, " of their own free will, without coercion but for substantial considerations, reserving only a few easy conditions, had transferred their rights of sovereignty and of ownership to the Association." [2] A little investigation of the Belgian treaties shows that they do not differ materially from those of Dr. Peters. One at least of the rulers who, according to Stanley, held his lands " by undisturbed occupation, by long ages of succession, by real divine right " was subsequently proved to have begun life as a slave.

A British consul reported that the princes and chiefs of Palabala who, according to the King of the Belgians and the Association, had signed the usual treaty resigning sovereignty and territory, were themselves extremely surprised when informed of the fact.

---

[1] Parliamentary Paper " Africa No. 4 (1892) " gives a selection of some of the " treaties " made by the British East Africa Company and native chiefs, and on which the company claimed the territory between the coast and Uganda. They are precisely of the same kind as Peters' treaties. I quote the following as an example :

" *Treaty No. 03.*
Done in Arabic and English.

M'Boli, Chief of Ivati, Ukambani, hereby declares that he has placed himself and all his territories, countries, peoples, and subjects under the protection, rule, and government of the Imperial British East Africa Company, and has ceded to the said Company all his sovereign rights and rights of Government over all his territories, countries, peoples, and subjects, in consideration of the said Company granting the protection of the said Company to him, his territories, countries, peoples, and subjects, and extending to them the benefit of the rule and Government of the said Company. And he undertakes to hoist and recognize the flag of the said Company.
As witness his hand at Ivati, this 4th day of August 1880."

[2] Stanley, *The Congo*, vol. ii. p. 379.

"In the Congo," this British consul remarked in 1883, " the native chiefs are made to do exactly as the Europeans require by means of rum and cloth." And the valuable considerations paid by Belgium for the sovereignty and ownership of the territory of Palabala turned out to be " one coat of red cloth with gold facings, one red cap, one white tunic, one piece of white baft, one piece of red points, one 1-dozen box of liqueurs, 4 demijohns of rum, 2 boxes of gin, 128 bottles of gin (Hollands), 20 pieces of red hankerchiefs, 40 singlets, and 40 old cotton caps." [1]

Dr. Peters probably paid similar " valuable considerations " to the sultans of East Africa for their lands and sovereignty. At any rate, within three months he had obtained a considerable number of treaties at the cost of some cloth, drink, and an occasional bath. With the treaties in his pocket he hurried back to Berlin, where he arrived in February 1885. Within a few days of his arrival the Imperial Government granted a charter to the Gesellschaft für deutsche Kolonisation, and on March 6 notified the signatory Powers to the Berlin Act of 1884 that the German company had acquired certain territories and sovereign rights to the west of the kingdom of Zanzibar and that " on their petition to the Emperor, an Imperial Warrant or Charter of Protection had been granted to them." This action by the German Government was equivalent to the declaration of a " protectorate " over Useguha, Usagara, Nguru, and Ukami. The news was received in London and Zanzibar with some dismay. The Sultan of Zanzibar claimed these territories over which Germany was declaring a Protectorate, and on 27th April a telegram was despatched from the Sultan to the German Emperor protesting against their being placed under German sovereignty and rule, and asserting that Zanzibar held military stations there and that the chiefs who professed to cede the sovereign rights had no authority to do so. The German answer was short and simple : Dr. Rohlfs, the German Consul-General, was instructed to inform the Zanzibar Government that the protest and the claims put forward therein were without foundation. On 12th June the Sultan, in a letter to Bismarck, repeated his protest : he laid claim to the whole coast from Warshek in what is now Italian Somaliland to the boundary of Portuguese East Africa, and also to the interior as far as the great lakes. He offered, however, to appoint a commission and leave the question to the arbitration of France and England. The German answer was again simple. They claimed Witu as independent of Zanzibar in the north, and they now produced a further collection of treaties by which the chiefs and sultans of the Kilimanjaro district had ceded their lands

---

[1] Parliamentary Papers, "Africa, No. 4 (1884)," pp. 57-63, and "No. 5 (1884)," pp. 1-5, quoted by H. R. Fox Bourne, *Civilisation in Congoland*, 1903, pp. 44 and 45.

and sovereign rights to Dr. Jühlke and the German East Africa Company which had been founded in Berlin to take over the concessions of the Gesellschaft für deutsche Kolonisation.[1]

The Germans knew that their real danger lay not in Zanzibar, but in London. It was on March 6, 1885, that the German Ambassador officially notified Lord Granville of the protectorate and of the concession to the German Company. The British reply was prompt and its nature significant. On May 25 Lord Granville, with reference to the protest and claim of Zanzibar, informed the German Government that the British Government were satisfied that there was no intention on the part of Germany to do anything against the independence of Zanzibar. There was, however, some doubt as to the extent of the Sultan's possessions on the mainland : the British Government were favourable to the German colonization, but—and this was the significant passage—there was a scheme " of some prominent British capitalists . . . for a British settlement in the country between the coast and the lakes, which are the sources of the White Nile, and for its connection with the coast by a railway." [2] In order to avoid a clash of interests between the German and British capitalists, Lord Granville suggested a delimitation of territory. This suggestion was accepted by Germany on June 30 : she agreed to adhere to the Anglo-French Agreement of 1862 to " respect the independence of Zanzibar," and she agreed to the appointment of an impartial commission to define the territory of the Sultan and incidentally of Germany and Britain.

These negotiations were the beginning of a long and intricate adventure in which policy, commerce, finance, and religion were curiously interwoven. Their significance will not be immediately apparent to the reader. It will be apparent indeed that the German adventure of Dr. Peters was economic imperialism unabashed and unadorned. Peters and his friends were avowed adherents of the ideas of Fabri. To them, as to Mr. Chamberlain, Empire was commerce, and, like Ferry and M. Etienne in France, they determined to obtain colonies for Germany simply as reservoirs of raw material and outlets for German industrial products. They therefore went to East Africa and took African territory. Having obtained the land for colonization, they immediately handed it over to a German commercial joint-stock company, the Deutsch-Ostafrikanische Gesellschaft, and the Imperial Government showed its approval of their methods and policy by granting them a Charter.

The British reply to Germany was to adopt the same methods and the same policy of economic imperialism. The official reply of Lord Granville immediately mentioned the scheme of " some prominent British capitalists " whose interests and intentions

[1] Hertslet, *The Map of Africa by Treaty*, 1894, vol. i. pp. 305-307.
[2] Parliamentary Paper, " Africa, No. 1 (1886)."

might conflict with those of Germany. These prominent British capitalists were the British East African Association, which had been immediately formed in London when the news of the operations of the Gesellschaft für deutsche Kolonisation and the Deutsch-Ostafrikanische Gesellschaft became known to British imperialist and financial circles. Just as the German "Association," the Gesellschaft für deutsche Kolonisation, became the joint-stock purely commercial company, the Deutsch-Ostafrikanische Gesellschaft, so the British East African Association, as we shall see, became shortly the Imperial British East Africa Company ; and just as the German Government granted a Charter to the German capitalists and handed the East African territories over to them for administration and exploitation, so the British Government granted a Charter to the British Company and handed over the East African territories to them.

I propose to trace the history of these capitalist companies, and the effect of their operations upon policy and upon Africa. To the student of history the German Company is comparatively unimportant and uninteresting. It never pretended to be anything other than it was, an instrument of economic imperialism. Openly supported by the Imperial Government, it proceeded, with the thoroughness which is characteristic of the German, to undertake the duty of exploitation for which it had been fashioned. It obtained for Germany the vast territories of German East Africa, but in everything else it was singularly unsuccessful, and it ended a brief and troubled life as a Chartered Company on November 30, 1890.

The history of the group of British capitalists and their company is far more interesting. Though working through a Chartered joint-stock Company, they professed motives other than those of economic imperialism, and they claimed the privileges which might justly be given to patriotism, philanthropy, and religion, but would hardly be accorded to those whose object is merely to buy in the cheapest and sell in the dearest market. These traders and financiers admittedly acquired for the British Empire an immense stretch of some of the most " valuable " territory in Africa : the price of this acquisition was some financial loss to themselves and a considerable amount of bloodshed to the Africans. No study of economic imperialism in Africa can therefore ignore the process by which the promoters of the British East Africa Company added British East Africa and Uganda to the Empire. It is necessary to examine with some care and minuteness the beliefs and desires of these men, their connection with and influence upon the Government of the British State, and the effects of their beliefs, desires, and actions upon the Governments and peoples of Britain and Africa.

As in the case of the Ethiopian Railway Trust, it is important that the reader should have some idea of the composition of the group of men who controlled the joint-stock company. We have seen that the immediate answer to the operations of the Gesellschaft für deutsche Kolonisation was the formation in London by "some prominent British capitalists" of the British East African Association. The most prominent of these British capitalists was Sir William Mackinnon, Chairman of the British India Steam Navigation Company.[1] The Association was formed in 1885 : on April 18, 1888, the Association turned itself into the Imperial British East Africa Company, which received a Royal Charter in September of the same year. Sir William Mackinnon became Chairman of the new Company, and from 1885 until his death, in 1893, it was he who was primarily responsible for the policy of this group of capitalists in Africa. He had as co-directors of the company many men of considerable influence in Government circles. As in the case of the companies which struggled with France over the Abyssinian railways, so in East Africa the aristocracy was well represented. In the Abyssinian companies we found the Marquis of Lothian and Lord Chesterfield ; on the directorate of the British East Africa Company sat the Marquis of Lorne, K.T., G.C.M.G., and Lord Brassey, K.C.B. But the resemblance between the personality of the directorates does not end with the aristocracy. The Abyssinian companies had the assistance of men who had recently held high administrative or military offices under the British Government in Asia or Africa : so too did the British East Africa Company. If in 1898 the New African Company obtained the services of Sir Charles Euan-Smith, who had but recently vacated the post of Consul-General and Political Agent at Zanzibar, in 1888 the British East Africa Company was fortunate in securing the services of Sir Charles's powerful predecessor, Sir John Kirk, G.C.M.G., K.C.B. Among the other directors were one Field-Marshal and three Generals, and the letters after their names indicate that they were not without influence in Imperial affairs : Field-Marshal Sir Donald M. Stewart, Bart., G.C.B., G.C.S.I., C.I.E., General Sir Arnold B. Kemball, K.C.B., K.C.S.I., General Sir Lewis Pelly, M.P., K.C.B., K.C.S.I., and Major-General Sir Francis W. de Winton, G.C.M.G., C.B. Lastly, it should be mentioned that the directorate included Sir Thomas Fowell Buxton, whose interest in colonial affairs was well known and who was a Vice-President and Treasurer of the Church Missionary Society.

Such was the composition, apart from certain obscurer merchants

[1] Sir William Mackinnon might be said to be an international African financier and capitalist. On July 31, 1889, he had joined with the financiers of Brussels and some German bankers to find the 15,000,000 francs capital necessary for floating the Compagnie du Chemin de Fer in the Belgian Congo. In 1891 he and Sir John Kirk, a co-director of the British East Africa Company, became directors of another company destined to exploit the Congo territories of King Leopold, the Compagnie du Katanga.

and financiers, of the group of prominent capitalists. Before proceeding to examine their operations in East Africa, it is necessary to warn the reader that those operations became the subject of severe public criticism and acute political controversy. Luckily for the historian the Imperial British East Africa Company published an official *apologia pro vita sua.* In 1893 Mr. P. L. McDermott, the Secretary of the Company, wrote a volume of some 600 pages called "British East Africa or Ibea: a History of the Formation and Work of the Imperial British East Africa Company, compiled with the authority of the Directors from Official Documents and the Records of the Company." [1] This is a most valuable and interesting book, not only because it gives the facts with regard to the company's policy and operations in Africa, but because it reveals, sometimes consciously and sometimes unconsciously, the beliefs and desires of those who were responsible for the policy. In the account which I now propose to give of the events in East Africa and Zanzibar, I shall rely almost entirely upon this official *apologia* of the company, checking it where necessary by reference to public documents and the works of Captain F. D. Lugard, who represented the company in some of its most critical and criticized undertakings in Africa.

The first steps in the absorption of East Africa by the German and British Companies and their Governments require a careful scrutiny. Let us recapitulate briefly the position in the middle of 1885. Germany had suddenly announced to the world that a group of prominent German capitalists, associated in a joint-stock company, had acquired certain territories and sovereignty in East Africa, and that the German Government had declared a protectorate over the territory and granted a Charter to the Company. The Government of Zanzibar, as was well known, claimed this territory, and a formal protest to Germany and the other European Great Powers was immediately made by the Sultan. Within one month of this action by Germany a group of prominent British capitalists had formed an Association, and the British Government, which stood in a peculiar relationship to Zanzibar and its Sultan, officially recognized the designs—whatever they might be—of this group by informing Germany that it had interests in an undefined stretch of territory to the north of Germany's new protectorate. The nature of the British interests and the extent of territory claimed were left vague, but since that territory was "between the coast and the lakes" it must clearly lie within limits claimed by the Sultan of Zanzibar. The British Government also proposed to the German Government a Delimitation Commission which should define the territory of the Sultan of Zanzibar. Such

---

[1] All references to this work which occur in the following pages are to the *second* edition which was published in 1895.

a Commission could in effect have, and did have, only one object and result, a partition of East Africa between the two European Powers.

The German Government accepted Lord Salisbury's proposal, and the remainder of 1885 was spent by the German capitalists and Government on the one side, and the British capitalists and Government on the other, in hurriedly putting forward claims, based on treaties with the African chiefs,[1] to various stretches of territory.

On October 17, 1885, the Governments of France, Germany, and Britain appointed Commissioners for the purpose of delimiting the possessions of the Sultan of Zanzibar. The Commissioners reported in a Procès-Verbal, dated June 9, 1886. They unanimously found that the Sultan had sovereign rights over the islands of Zanzibar and Pemba and also upon the mainland over territory extending inland to a maximum depth of ten miles between the northern boundary of Portuguese East Africa on the south and Mogadishu on the north. By an Exchange of Notes, dated October 29–November 1, 1886, the British and German Governments agreed to recognize the sovereignty of Zanzibar over the islands of Zanzibar and Pemba, over the coast-line between Portuguese East Africa and Kipini, and over Kismayu, Brawa, Meurka and Mogadishu. The Sultan's territory on the mainland was defined as having an internal depth of ten sea miles measured from the coast direct into the interior. The two Powers then divided the territory on the mainland into two " spheres of influence," the southern, which is now German East Africa, being assigned to Germany, and the northern, now British East Africa, to Britain. Further, Great Britain engaged " to support negotiations of Germany with the Sultan for the leasing to the German African Company of the customs duties at the ports of Dar-es-Salaam and Pangani, in return for an annual payment to the Sultan by the Company." On December 3 the British Government communicated this agreement to the Sultan, with the request that " your Highness will recognize the friendly spirit in which this Agreement has been arrived at, and that by a ready adhesion to its terms, your Highness will assist in bringing about the satisfactory solution of questions which cannot otherwise fail to jeopardize the interests of the Sultanate." The " friendly spirit " in the first part of the sentence combined with the threat in the last had the desired effect : in twenty-four hours the Sultan signified his adhesion to all the requirements of the two Great Powers. Some of the words in which the Sultan communicated his adhesion may be quoted as going to show that a certain confusion of mind came over him when he contemplated the friendly spirit in which the two European States were

[1] I have already referred to the German additional claims based on the treaties of Dr. Jühlke. On February 17, 1886, Lord Rosebery informed the German Government that the British Company claimed the district of Taveta on treaties obtained by Mr. H. H. Johnston from the chiefs.

taking his territory from him. "With regard to our accepting," he wrote, "that this part of our kingdom should be taken from us and given to Germany, we hope the two Governments will do what is just according to this Agreement, namely, to protect our kingdom from being divided among them by other nations, and then, in consequence of the friendly way in which the two Governments of Great Britain and Germany have asked us to adhere to their Agreement, we are ready to give our adhesion. . . ."

These Governmental Agreements dealt with the question of the Sultan's sovereignty. Until that question was out of the way, the schemes of the "prominent capitalists," whether of Germany or of Britain, could not be proceeded with, for they were acquiring by their treaties the sovereignty over territory claimed by Zanzibar. The Agreements settled the sovereignty question, but, as the clause with regard to the German Company shows, it was an integral part of the Governmental Agreement that certain "concessions" should be given by Zanzibar to the two groups of capitalists. These concessions were duly granted by the Sultan, one to the British East Africa Association on May 24, 1887, and the other to the German East African Company on April 28, 1888. They are almost word for word the same. The Sultan made over for a period of fifty years "all the power which he possesses on the mainland" and "in all his territories and dependencies" within the German "sphere of influence" to the German Company, and within the British "sphere" to the British Company. The two Companies were in fact given the right to partition among themselves the sovereignty which the Governmental agreements had recognized as belonging to the Sultan over the coast-line to a depth of ten miles inland. A monopoly of the right to purchase public lands, of regulating trade, navigation, and fisheries, of making roads, railways, and canals; the right to levy taxes on the inhabitants, to establish customs-houses, to levy dues; an exclusive privilege to work mines and to issue notes—all these were included in the Sultan's concession. The Sultan also leased to each Company the customs of all the ports within the territories to which the concessions applied; and for this portion of the concession the Companies agreed to pay over to the Sultan the amount of the customs levied in their respective territories.[1] For all the concessions taken together the Companies each agreed to allot to the Sultan one Founder's Share in the Company (or its equivalent in the case of the German Company) which entitled him to 10 per cent of the net profits of the Company *after* payment of a dividend upon the Ordinary Shares at the rate of 8 per cent. As the ordinary shares of both Companies never paid

---

[1] The clauses dealing with the payment for the customs leases differed slightly in the German and British concessions. They led to interminable disputes, and were subsequently varied by supplementary or additional Agreements.

8 per cent, the Sultan never received a farthing or a pfennig from the British and German capitalists for any of these valuable concessions other than the customs lease.

The true nature of these negotiations and transactions is not immediately apparent in the treaties and documents themselves or in the ordinary German and British histories. The action of Dr. Peters, the German Government, and the German Company was, as British historians have seen and pointed out, robbery : the German capitalists, supported by their Government, simply walked into Africa and took territory to which they had no claim, but to which the Sultan of Zanzibar had a claim. The British and German Governments then appointed a Delimitation Commission which found that the sovereignty of the coast of the mainland in question belonged to Zanzibar. The Sultan's occupation of this coast-line, as the Procès-Verbal of the Commissioners shows, was more effective than that of Italy in Erythrea, of Britain in British Somaliland, or of Britain and France in many places on the West Coast of Africa at the time when these European States claimed these territories on the ground of effective occupation. But facts which give a " just claim " to a Queen of England, a German Emperor, or a King of Italy, give no claim to a Sultan of Zanzibar. The States of Germany and Britain proceeded to require the adhesion of Zanzibar to a treaty which defined the sovereignty of the Sultan as existing only over a narrow strip of territory ten miles broad, along the whole coast, and which partitioned the hinterland of this strip between the two Great Powers. Now over and over again, on the north, on the west, and on the east coasts of Africa, the European States, including Germany and Britain, have applied the " hinterland theory " to themselves and their own claims. According to this principle of international law and relations, effective occupation and sovereignty upon the coast of Africa gives to the occupying and sovereign State a right to the sovereignty over the hinterland. If this principle had been applied to the claims of the Sultan of Zanzibar, the hinterland of his strip of coast, including the whole of what is now German and British East Africa, would have rightly belonged to him. Instead of this, the two Great Powers partitioned the Sultan's hinterland among themselves, calling it euphemistically for the moment German and British spheres of influence. The German Government had no shadow of a just claim to Usagara and the other districts which they seized in this way : their action was flagrant international robbery. And the right of the British Government to Kikuyu and the other districts which they seized was precisely the same, no worse and no better, than that of Germany to Usagara.

But Germany and Britain were not satisfied with robbing the Sultan of his hinterland. Behind the action of their Governments stood the groups of prominent capitalists. This is proved by the fact that both Governments, through the solemn instrument of Royal Charters, simultaneously and immediately handed over the hinterlands for exploitation and administration to the groups of capitalists. The reader must remember that in all this territory there was nowhere any occupation by Britain or Germany : for any system of government and order it had to look to its own tribal system of native chiefs and sultans. Without troubling to take any steps towards occupation or towards setting up any system of good government, the two Powers handed over these territories and their inhabitants into the arbitrary control of two impersonal, commercial, joint-stock companies, to two " groups of prominent capitalists." But even this did not appease the hunger of capitalist imperialism. The Commissioners of the Great Powers had admitted the sovereignty of the Sultan over the coast, and the Great Powers in their treaty, forced upon the Sultan, had ostensibly left those sovereign rights of Zanzibar upon the coast unimpaired. But the position of the two companies and of the spheres of influence, if they had really been left as the public treaties pretended to leave them, would have been grotesque and impossible ; and there was no intention either of the Governments or the groups of capitalists to accept it. Imagine the position of an administration in the hands of a company, the initial duty of which was to pay a dividend to its shareholders, responsible for " developing " and exploiting an immense stretch of territory, roadless and railwayless, enclosed upon one side by the unknown and impassable forests of Central Africa, and on the other by a ten-mile strip of territory in the hands of another administration and State and shutting it off completely from the sea. If the ten-mile strip of coast land had been left in the hands of the Sultan of Zanzibar, the simple imposition by him of a tariff or high transit rates would have made all the acquisitions of Germany and Britain in the hinterland valueless. Consequently though the Anglo-German Treaty recognized the sovereign rights of Zanzibar over the ten-mile strip of coast, it was an integral part of the bargain and arrangement that the Sultan should be deprived, in favour of the German and British Companies, of his sovereignty not only over the hinterland, but also over the strip of coast land.

Hence the concessions to the German and British Companies. By those concessions the Sultan made over to the groups of British and German capitalists the whole of his sovereign rights upon the coast. There have been few more simple, effective, and characteristic operations of economic imperialism in the history of Africa. When the Sultan of Zanzibar had signed the two " Agreements " handing over the different rights and monopolies to the Companies, he had been effectively stripped of every sovereign right and every inch of territory upon the mainland of Africa. In twenty-four hours the kingdom of the proud Seyyid Said had shrunk and dwindled to the islands of Zanzibar and Pemba, and the beauty of the operation, from the point of view of economic imperialism, lay in the fact that it had been performed by the Sultan himself, Seyyid Barghash-Bin-Said, the son of the proud Seyyid Said. For was not the signature of Seyyid Barghash-Bin-Said attached to the Anglo-German Agreement and to the two Concessions ?

No British historian pretends that the Sultan Barghash voluntarily resigned his claims or voluntarily granted the concession to Germany and the German Company. It is rightly realized that only strong pressure from the two European States would have induced him to deprive himself of half his kingdom and hand it over to Germany and the Deutsch-Ostafrikanische Gesellschaft. Most British historians, however, genuinely believe, not only that the Sultan voluntarily gave up his territory to Englishmen, but that for years he and his predecessors had been longing to do so. In this view they presumably rely upon the authority of Sir William Mackinnon and Mr. McDermott's official history of the British Company. In that history Mr. McDermott writes : " On the 25th May 1887, all questions respecting the extent of his sovereignty having now been settled, the Sultan of Zanzibar was able to carry out his long-cherished wish to defend from further encroachment the remainder of his rights by granting the concession to the British East African Association (as the company was then styled). This concession was not sought by Sir W. Mackinnon, but was offered to him voluntarily through the British Consul-General at Zanzibar. . . ." The phenomenon of rulers with " long-cherished wishes " to give away their territories is so remarkable that a short investigation of this contention of Sir W. Mackinnon and Mr. McDermott is desirable. *A priori* one might imagine that to give away his territories, even to Englishmen, is a curious method for a Sultan to adopt in order " to defend them from further encroachment." And there is in fact evidence in Mr. McDermott's book that both he and Sir W. Mackinnon attached an unusual meaning to the adverb " voluntarily."

According to Mr. McDermott—who, the reader must remember, is speaking officially on behalf of the British East Africa Company and its Chairman, Sir William Mackinnon—the passion of the Sultan Barghash for giving his territory and sovereignty to Sir William Mackinnon and a British joint-stock company dated from 1877, when he pressed Sir William to take a concession for seventy years of the *whole* of the dominions of Zanzibar, including *all* rights of sovereignty (with certain reservations in respect of the islands of Zanzibar and Pemba). Sir William Mackinnon declined this valuable offer " on finding that he could not obtain from the Foreign Office the support he deemed necessary." When, therefore, in 1887

the Sultan induced the Chairman of the British India Steam Navigation Company and his brother capitalists to accept the gift of half
his kingdom, he was only renewing his offer of 1877 and fulfilling
a "long-cherished wish." And Sir William in this case did not
decline the offer because this time "he felt assured of the support
of Her Majesty's Government, of which the Royal Charter was
regarded as a pledge."

The whole question of the "voluntary" nature of such concessions as this of 1887 is of some interest. It so happens that
this "long-cherished wish" of the Sultans of Zanzibar formed the
subject of judicial investigation, and the decision shows that the
economic imperialist has a curious idea of voluntariness in an
African Sultan. In 1889 there was a dispute between the British
and German capitalists as to whether a certain island, Lamu, had
or had not been included in the concession to the British Company.
It had clearly not been included in the concession of 1887, but the
British Company maintained that "the Sultan of Zanzibar had,
since 1877, constantly held at the disposal of Sir William Mackinnon
and his friends a concession of territories including the aforesaid
'islands of Manda Bay,' that this offer had never been withdrawn. . . ." The dispute was submitted to the arbitration of a
Belgian Minister, Baron Lambermont. When the case was tried,
Mr. McDermott informs us, the contention of the British Company
that "the Sultan of Zanzibar had, since 1877, constantly held at
the disposal of Sir William Mackinnon and his friends a concession"
of the territories in question, and that "this offer had never been
withdrawn," was "supported by the sworn evidence of General
Mathews, who was the Sultan's representative in the negotiations,
and of Mr. E. N. Mackenzie, who acted at Zanzibar for the concessionaires, and by the telegrams exchanged between the Sultan
(through Mr. Mackenzie and General Mathews) and Sir William
Mackinnon." The reader will in passing note the interesting fact
that negotiations for the cession of territory and sovereignty by
the Sultan to English capitalists are conducted on both sides by
Englishmen, and that telegrams confirming the Sultan's offer are
sent by his representative, the "General" of his army, who happened
also to be an Englishman.

Baron Lambermont gave his decision in August 1889. With
regard to his award, Mr. McDermott remarks that "as regards the
claim put forward by the Imperial British East Africa Company,
Baron Lambermont" was "satisfied that no doubt could exist as to
the intention and desire of the successive Sultans to grant the
concession of Lamu to this Company." The reader from these words
might excusably infer that the arbitrator was convinced of the
Company's contention that the Sultans had had a long-cherished
wish to grant these concessions to Sir W. Mackinnon, and that the

wish had never been fulfilled because the capitalist had declined the offer. As a matter of fact, the arbitrator's award, in so far as it deals with the question at all, reveals facts which are completely inconsistent with the contentions of Sir W. Mackinnon and Mr. McDermott. We learn for instance that the proposal of 1877 for a cession of territory and sovereignty was not made by Seyyid Barghash to Sir William Mackinnon, but by Sir William Mackinnon to Seyyid Barghash.[1] The only evidence of this proposal produced was the draft of a contract, undated and unsigned, which was presented by the would-be concessionaires to the Sultan. Nothing further appears to have taken place until February 22, 1887, when the "Sultan Seyyid Barghash sent Mr. Mackinnon a telegram in which his Highness declared himself ready to grant him the Concession *which he (Mr. Mackinnon) had previously proposed* " (the italics are mine), and the Sultan then signed the formal concession which put the strip of coast between Wanga and Kipini in the hands of the British group of capitalists. Now Lamu was not included within the limits of this concession, and the Company's case was that the Sultan had nevertheless offered Lamu to Mackinnon in 1887 and that the offer had been accepted. The only evidence for this contention was the statement of " General " Mathews that he had been sent with a verbal message from the Sultan to Mackinnon's agent, Mackenzie, " authorising him to inform Mr. Mackinnon that all the territories to the north of the Kipini would be offered to him in preference, when they came to be leased or ceded." Baron Lambermont's opinion of this evidence is shown by his comment upon it: " . . . in the verbal message with which General Mathews was entrusted, whatever consideration his evidence may merit, one cannot find the elements of an actual and positive promise to grant a concession, whereof the essential conditions were sufficiently determined. And, as regards the reserved or anticipated acceptance of Mr. Mackinnon, it only forms the subject of a purely personal opinion on the part of the General." [2]
It appears that the memory of Sir W. Mackinnon and his brother

[1] The relevant passage in the award is as follows : " Whereas the contract of cession which should form the basis of these promises is represented only by a draft, which bears neither date nor signature ; Whereas, in that form, it can only be looked upon as a proposal made to Sultan Seyyid Barghash, without it being proved that such proposal was transformed into a Concession from his Highness to Mr. Mackinnon or into a general promise to cede the administration from the Sultanate to the English Company. . . ."

[2] It may be added that the actual finding of the arbitrator really amounted to this : (1) that neither the Germans nor the British had any legal or rightful claim to Lamu, (2) that there had been no concession or cession of Lamu to the Germans or to the British, (3) that the Sultan Seyyid Khalifa who had succeeded Barghash in 1888, after the Anglo-German treaty and the concession to the British Company, had expressed an intention of treating with the British with regard to Lamu, and (4) that therefore the Sultan Khalifa was perfectly at liberty to sign, if he so desired, an Agreement ceding Lamu to the British Company.

capitalists was at fault. A proposal of Sir William's to the Sultan Barghash in 1877, that he should grant a concession of all the sovereign rights over all his territories to a British Company, has been transformed in the rosy light of memory into an offer of this concession from the Sultan to Sir William. The impartial and cautious historian may therefore hazard the opinion that the Sultans of Zanzibar never had a desire—or a long-cherished wish—to give their kingdom or sovereignty away to any one. In 1877 Sir William Mackinnon, as an economic imperialist, was ahead of his times, and when he found that he did not get the support of the Foreign Office for his idea of acquiring the East Coast of Africa for the British Empire and the exploitation of British joint-stock companies, he dropped his proposal to the Sultan. In 1884 Germany, as we have seen, with some suddenness seized some of the territory of the Sultan. The Sultan immediately protested, not because he had a long-cherished wish to see his territories in the hands of English rather than German capitalists, but because he wished to see it in the hands of no one but himself. The German aggression came at the moment when the policy of ruthless partitioning of Africa among the European States was just getting into full swing. Sir William Mackinnon's old scheme was therefore revived, and this time he was to receive the support of the Foreign Office. The British and German Governments came to an understanding by which the East Coast of Africa was to be partitioned between them, and the territories handed over to the German and British Companies. We have seen the way in which this was accomplished. The Sultan of Zanzibar undoubtedly acquiesced in the arrangement—very much in the way in which a rabbit might be said to acquiesce in being swallowed by two pythons.

On April 18, 1888, the British East African Association became the Imperial British East Africa Company, and on September 3 the Company was granted a Royal Charter. This Charter authorized the Company to administer and exploit the territories for which it held, or should obtain, grants and concessions whether from the Sultan of Zanzibar or chiefs and tribes " with a view of promoting trade, commerce, and good government." Its position was, however, not altogether an easy one. As a joint-stock company it suddenly found itself in possession of some 200,000 square miles of territory and a population of perhaps 4,000,000 Africans. It had to earn dividends for its shareholders, and by the terms of its Charter it had undertaken to set up a form of administration and good government in its new possessions. Adjoining it upon the south was another immense block of territory handed over on the same conditions to a German Company. In neither place had any attempt been made either by Governments or capitalists to find out the wishes or attitude of the populations concerned, whether they were or were not willing to exchange the rule of the Sultan and chiefs for that of Dr. Peters' and Sir William Mackinnon's Companies. The vast majority of these peoples had scarcely heard of a European and had no experience of European States and administration. The whole territory had still to be occupied, and the whole of the new administration had to be built up from the beginning by Companies, controlled thousands of miles away in Berlin and London by Directors whose primary duty was to earn a dividend for their shareholders.

The difficulties and dangers did not end there. The operations of the two Companies were confined respectively to the two spheres of influence agreed to by their Governments. But the exact limits of those spheres had in the Government Agreement of 1886 not been defined; their actual delimitation was left for a future agreement. All that the Agreement of 1886 really did was to draw a line through the middle of the hinterland of the Sultan's strip of coast, and to provide that territory to the south should belong to Germany and to the north to Britain. Even the limits of the hinterland in the interior were left undefined. Here in itself was an almost certain source of future trouble. In the north was another source. The Sultan's concession to the German Company was confined to the coast between the Portuguese possessions in the south and Wanga in the north; his concession to the British Company was bounded by Wanga in the south and Kipini in the north. This arrangement left the coast north of Kipini unpartitioned, and it was understood that this piece of territory should be the subject of further negotiations.

The two Companies "took possession" of their kingdoms from the Sultan in 1888. They had some difficulty in making their possession effective. The peoples of Africa seemed to have a curious objection to be handed over to the rule of prominent European capitalists. When the Germans and their Company's chief Director attempted formally to occupy Pangani, they "were received with open hostility," Mr. McDermott tells us, ". . . they were fired on by the townspeople; the boats of a German war vessel were fired on at Tanga, and the vessel bombarded the town; even [1] the British flag was insulted in the excitement of the insurgents. . . . The whole coast burst into a flame of rebellion against European authority, and the people even threatened to renounce their allegiance to the Sultan of Zanzibar, if he attempted to re-establish the Germans." At this inopportune moment Mr. Mackenzie "arrived at Zanzibar with a small pioneer staff, to take over the coast leased under the concession to the Imperial British East Africa Company." The inhabitants of the "British sphere" were not more anxious

[1] The implication in "even" is amusing, and characteristic of the economic imperialist.

than those of the German to welcome European authority. Even before Mr. Mackenzie arrived, a disturbance had broken out at Mombasa. Mr. McDermott gives a description of the measures taken to overcome the resistance of the inhabitants which is very characteristic of patriotic history. The outbreak at Mombasa " was regarded as a backwash of the disturbance " in the German sphere : nevertheless it " was felt to be serious enough to call for an immediate display of repressive force." Two British warships and a body of the Sultan's (and " General " Mathews') troops "had the desired effect." "Quiet was restored" in the dominions of the Imperial British East Africa Company, just as quiet was once restored in Warsaw.

The troubles of the two groups of capitalists were not yet over. The British Company, warned by what happened to the German, did not attempt to hoist its flag or to change the native officials of the Sultan's administration. It adopted the wise course of biding its time and making itself inconspicuous. The Germans, who had less training and experience in this kind of imperialism, had made the mistake of being over-energetic. Their dominion was in open rebellion, and anarchy threatened the whole coast of East Africa. In these circumstances Germany and Britain decided to proclaim a blockade of the whole mainland which the Sultan had made over to the German and British Companies. The British Foreign Office in announcing the adoption of this blockade policy stated that it was directed against " the rebellion against his (the Sultan's) authority which has broken out in the mainland under the influence of the slave-dealers." Apparently the British Government had forgotten that, largely through its own influence, the Sultan had made over his authority on the mainland to the German and British capitalists, and that the rebellion was not against the Sultan's authority, but against that of the Companies.

The fact was that it had become evident that the Anglo-German Agreement of 1886 to partition East Africa and the complementary concessions of the Sultan to the Companies could not be made effective without force. There was great dissatisfaction and disappointment in Germany with the failure of these first imperialist adventures, and Bismarck was at first unwilling to use the forces of the State on behalf of the Company and doubtful whether in any case he would be able to get the consent of the Reichstag to expenditure for such a purpose. Eventually he decided that military operations might be taken to put down the risings under the pretext of suppressing the slave-trade.[1] The British Government fell in with his plan ; the Reichstag voted the money required for suppressing the slave-trade ; the blockade was proclaimed, and this, together with the military operations of Wissmann, succeeded by 1890 in inducing the Africans to accept European authority.

[1] See Zimmermann, *Geschichte des deutschen Kolonialpolitik*, pp. 140-158.

Before passing on to the final stage of the process by which the Sultan's sovereignty was taken from him by the two European States, a word must be said with regard to the nature of the German rule and colonization of East Africa. The reader has seen the methods by which Peters and his associates acquired their empire. They were similar to those by which all the Great Powers of Europe have acquired empire in Africa; but they were perhaps a little more brutally and cynically avowed than has been usual in other countries. The German Company had to be established by force, and that force was ruthlessly applied. The German Empire in Africa, like that of all other European States, Britain, France, Italy, Portugal, and Belgium, was founded upon the slaughter of its new subjects. The impartial historian will probably shrink from any attempt to estimate the relative degrees of savagery, blood-thirstiness, and brutality which the several nations of Europe imported into their task of spreading civilization and acquiring Empire. The deeper he goes into African history of the last forty years, the more painfully will he realize that no citizen of any of the Imperial States of Europe has the right to cast the first stone. He will know that the French have accused us of the same kind of massacres and atrocities of which we have accused them, and of which we now accuse the Germans. If he be an Englishman, he will certainly come to the conclusion that the dark spots in the record of Britain are less in number and degree than those of other countries. We must allow here for the bias of patriotism; but even when that allowance is made, there is reason for believing that there is a certain amount of truth in the conclusion. The Englishman has a long record as an imperialist : he was blooded in India generations before the German, the Belgian, and the Italian started on the hunt for Empire. The "blooding" was thorough and extensive. As early as 1772 the Indians had taught us the lesson—unfortunately at their, not our expense—that the pitiless exploitation of an "inferior" by a "superior" race is in the long run neither profitable nor possible.[1] Further, in the last quarter of the nineteenth century the traditions of English life were, on the whole, against brutality and the use of physical force, unless they could with some show of reason be called law or punitive expeditions. At the same time it would be wrong to under-estimate the influence of a political party which still retained some of the views and traditions of Bright, and which relied for power upon the votes of men who were the spiritual and intellectual descendants of the Anti-Slavery Abolitionists, Evangelicals, and Non-Conformists. All these factors combined to moderate the use of the "strong hand" and "strong government" by British soldiers, financiers, administrators, traders, and planters. The natural cruelty and

[1] See *Warren Hastings in Bengal*, 1772–74, by M. E. Monckton Jones, 1918.

savagery of the European, which is always liable to break out in the individual of any race when he finds himself among "uncivilized" peoples, was rarely condoned or allowed to become a principle of policy by those responsible for the administration of British possessions. Hence we are probably justified in maintaining, with shame and humility, that, as regards murder, robbery, savagery, and dishonesty in Africa, our record is better than that of any other State of Europe.

To judge the records of Germany and the other European nations fairly and accurately is extremely difficult. There is not the same tradition against brutality and the use of physical force among these peoples. There is no doubt that the German ruled East Africa and his other African colonies with a heavy hand. The German, as we have before had to remark, is ruthlessly logical, and prefers to call a spade a spade and imperialism imperialism. The logic with which he applied the beliefs and desires of economic imperialism to Africa was certainly ruthless, and he failed to deceive himself or other people as to what he was doing there. German rule and exploitation was therefore harsh and ugly, and there were also a large number of cases in which individuals were proved to have behaved with revolting brutality to the Africans. But all this does not help the impartial historian to weigh the record of Germany against that of France, Italy, Belgium, and Portugal. To apportion praise and blame would require a long and exhaustive enquiry which in this book would be out of place. We can here only give an opinion which is personal, but which, we believe, will be shared by most people who attempt to sift the evidence with an open mind. It is that the records of France and Italy are possibly less bad than Germany's, but that German administration in Africa was better than that of the Portuguese Colonies and the Belgian Congo. The reason for this opinion cannot adequately be given here, but in order that the reader may see that it is not irresponsible, I propose to quote opinions on German administration by two men who had every opportunity of judging it and comparing it with the British system of which they themselves formed a distinguished part. Writing in 1893 of our East African possessions, Captain (now Sir) F. D. Lugard was of opinion that the German administration in East Africa was in some respects an example which we ought to follow in the territory recently acquired by us, and the words used by him show that in his opinion even our methods with the natives were not very much superior to the German. "The endeavour," he wrote, "to create in East Africa a prosperity which may contrast in our favour with that of our German neighbours will be a worthy ambition for him to whom the administration may be entrusted. Hitherto they have set us an example in the thorough and practical way in which they have set about to develop their territories, though as regards tact with the natives, the advantage, perhaps, rests with us." [1] Two passages, written in 1899 by Sir Harry Johnston, who probably knows as much as any man living about the different European administrations in Africa, deserve to be quoted. Of East Africa he said : "The Arabs are becoming reconciled to German rule, while on the other hand the German officials are learning the art of dealing tactfully with subject races." And of the Cameroons he wrote : "Unfortunately as amongst some officials of the East African Company, so among a few of the Government servants in the Cameroons, there were instances of great cruelty committed about three years ago, cruelties which led to a serious revolt among the negro soldiery. Germany wisely did not hush up these affairs, but investigated them in open court and punished the guilty. I fancy when history takes a review of the foundation of these African states that the unmixed Teuton—Dutchman or German —is on first contact with subject races apt to be harsh and even brutal, but that he is no fool and wins the respect of the negro and the Asiatic, who admire brute force ; while his own good nature in time induces a softening of manners when the native has ceased to rebel and begun to cringe. There is this that is hopeful and wholesome about the Germans. They are quick to realize their own defects, and equally quick to amend them. As in commerce, so in government, they observe, learn and master the best principles. The politician would be very short-sighted who underrated the greatness of the German character, or reckoned on the evanescence of German dominion in strange lands." [2]

Before leaving this subject it is necessary to make what will almost certainly be a vain attempt to guard against misunderstanding and misinterpretation. As these pages are being written, a war is being fought in which a greater licence is being given to horrors and hatred than has ever been the case since mankind first claimed to be civilized. The war is being fought not only upon the battlefield : spiritually and intellectually also it is being carried on with all the machinery of modern civilization, the press, the platform, the pamphlet, and the poster. Every prejudice of

---

[1] F. D. Lugard, *The Rise of Our East African Empire*, 1893, vol. i. p. 402. Sir F. D. Lugard's view of the Germans in Africa may be seen from another passage in vol. ii. p. 86. The reader should remember that at the time he wrote it, the French and not the Germans seemed to him our chief rivals in Africa. Some French priests had hinted to him that the Germans were prepared to aid the natives of Uganda against the British. Sir F. D. Lugard quotes the comment on this which he wrote in his diary at the time : "I object also to the mean accusations against the honour of the Germans. This sticks in my throat dreadfully." And he adds : "I may note that a year later, when the war broke out, there were almost precisely the same innuendoes, and the Germans were, I believe, appealed to for aid, but my conception of German honour and good faith proved more correct than that of the Fathers."

[2] Sir H. H. Johnston, *A History of the Colonization of Africa by Alien Races*, 1899, p. 258.

patriotism is exploited for the purposes of this propaganda. Speeches are made and Blue Books published to show that the Germans alone among European peoples, by the brutality and barbarity of their administration, have shown themselves unfit for the white man's burden of Empire in Africa. In these circumstances it has seemed impossible to follow my inclination and say nothing about this subject. It is too intimately connected with economic imperialism and the events which we have had to deal with in this chapter. The preceding paragraphs were written immediately after reading the two Blue Books [1] issued by the British Government and containing information as to the treatment of the natives of South-West Africa by Germany. The publication of these documents is frankly part of a campaign for proving that Germany is unfit to administer African possessions, and that her colonies, captured during the war, should in the interest of the Africans be retained by the British Empire. To the historian who is accustomed to weigh evidence, and who tries to rise above the little tides and winds of political passions, momentary prejudices and cupidities, this fact will rouse suspicion, and his first instinct may perhaps be to dismiss these documents as a contemporary example of one of the commonest tricks of economic imperialism. His instinct would be wrong. The abominations inflicted by Germans upon the Herreros and other tribes of South-West Africa cannot be dismissed in this way by history. The only possible verdict upon these facts is, in my opinion, that the German State has proved itself absolutely unfit to own African colonies.

But the matter does not end there. The Blue Books contained no revelations for any one acquainted with the details of European rule in Africa. Ruthless slaughter of the natives, dignified by the official terms of wars or punitive expeditions, can be set down to the credit of every European State. The German extermination of the Herreros may have been more thorough and ruthless than has been practised or achieved by other Powers in "native wars," but the policy differed not in kind but in degree. As to the abominable cruelties inflicted by individuals upon natives, and the pitiless and dishonest economic exploitation of the inhabitants who were robbed of their land, their cattle, and their women, the records of Portuguese and Belgian administration equal, if indeed they do not surpass, that of Germany, while no European State, including the British Empire, can in these matters boast of a clean record. These documents prove that the German colonies should never be returned to Germany to rule on the old terms; they prove her to be absolutely unfit to own colonies; but they also prove, what

---

[1] "Report on the Natives of South-West Africa and their Treatment by Germany, 1918," Cd. 9146 : "Papers Relating to Certain Trials in German South-West Africa, 1916," Cd. 8371.

the whole of history has proved to a civilization which has always turned blind eyes to the proof of it, that all European States, in different degrees, have shown themselves absolutely unfit to own African colonies. It would be absurd to deny that European civilization, through the machinery of State and trade, has carried some considerable benefits into Africa ; but the autocratic dominion of European over African has been accompanied by such horrible cruelty, exploitation, and injustice, that it is difficult not to believe that the balance of good in the world would have been and would be infinitely greater, if the European and his State had never entered Africa. Slavery, drink, and rifles, and the bloodshed and degradation which capitalism, in its hunger for profits and dividends (the modern *auri sacra fames*), has carried into every bay and river and forest of Africa, can never be atoned for ; but that does not absolve Europe and its civilization from making in the twentieth century some amends to Africa for the crimes and cruelties of the nineteenth. That cannot be done by making a scapegoat of our enemies, by sending them out into the wilderness with all their and our own sins upon their backs, and by seizing the opportunity of dividing their " possessions " among ourselves. It can only be done if, in some way or other, both for Germany and ourselves and for the whole world of European States, we destroy the colonial system, founded upon economic imperialism, in Africa, and set up in its place some system of Government which will cease to make of Africa a mere farm—the live-stock human beings—for the stock-markets and marts and needy adventurers of Europe, which will assure to the Africans the rights and privileges of human beings, and which will cease to make colonies, from Cameroon to British East Africa, a mockery of our professions and our civilization.[1]

We must now return to the history of the British East Africa Company and its dealings with the territory which had once belonged to the Sultan of Zanzibar. The reader will remember that on September 3, 1888, the British Government granted a Royal Charter to the Company, and that about the same time the Company's Administrator-in-Chief, Mr. Mackenzie, arrived in East Africa " with a small pioneer staff " to take over the Company's territory. A word must be said with regard to the position and aims of Sir William Mackinnon and his associates. In after years, when the events which I am about to relate necessitated intervention by the State in the affairs and territory of the Company, the Directors claimed that the nation should recognize in a suitable manner— apparently financial—that their enterprise had been dictated rather by patriotic and philanthropic than by economic motives. " It is to be noted, however," wrote the Secretary of the Company, " as a factor exercising a very appreciable influence upon the course of

[1] I deal with the methods by which this may be done in Part III. Chapter II.

events, that the motives which inspired the founders of the Company were not by any means exclusively commercial. The Charter imposed obligations of an administrative character, but there was in the undertaking a considerable infusion of philanthropic and patriotic feeling which the Court of Directors adequately represented. Questions were not, therefore, always decided merely on their merits as matter of pure business; conceptions and obligations of a higher character frequently influenced the decisions of the Board." We shall have to enquire rather minutely into these conceptions of a higher nature which frequently influenced the decisions of the Directors: meanwhile the facts remain that in 1888 the enterprise was nothing more nor less than a joint-stock company, with a capital of £250,000, a distinguished Board of Directors described by the Secretary of State for Foreign Affairs as " some prominent British capitalists," and a number of shareholders who, we may assume, had been induced to subscribe capital not for philanthropic motives but for the ordinary purpose of earning unearned dividends. This joint-stock company had got possession of a vast extent of territory, lying on the east coast of Africa between Wanga and Kipini, ostensibly for the purpose of exploiting it commercially and thereby earning the dividends in the hope of which the shareholders had been induced to subscribe their capital. Further, they had purchased the prestige and support of the British Government in the Royal Charter by undertaking certain obligations of administration, etc.

That is not an unfair description of the position in 1888. It would be natural to expect that a Company in this position, whether its objects were commercial or philanthropic or both, would have proceeded at once to set up an administration and to undertake the commercial development of the enormous property which it had acquired. It is a remarkable fact that there is no evidence that the Company did anything of the sort. Five years later, when Sir Gerald Portal was sent out on a Special Commission by the Government to report upon " the best means of dealing with " part of the territory acquired by the Company, his first despatch to the Foreign Office was, to quote the Company's secretary, "a communication reflecting very seriously not only on the work of the Company, but on the personal character of the Directors." [1] His final report shows the reason why he formed this adverse opinion, and it led to the Company having to resign its Royal Charter and its ownership of all territory in Africa. The Company, as we have seen, left the administration of the few towns and villages of the coast practically as they found it: in the interior they made no attempt to establish any sort of Government or to develop the country. After five years the whole achievement of the Company, from this point of view, consisted in the establishment of two small posts, a fort at Kikuyu

[1] P. L. McDermott, *op. cit.* p. 286.

and a small station at Machakos. This is Sir Gerald Portal's comment: "... the only posts they (the Company) now hold in virtue of their Charter are (1) the fort at Kikuyu, where constant difficulties with the natives have hitherto prevented the introduction of any real administration, and (2) the smaller station at Machakos, at which an English employé is reported to have succeeded in organizing some trade in corn and cattle with the local tribesmen, and in establishing a growing influence. But neither of these places are of any commercial or political value except as stations on the road to Uganda and the Lake districts. In fact I have been given to understand, though with what justice I do not know, that the Company contemplate a retreat even from these, their last posts in the interior of Africa. But even assuming that they propose to retain their garrisons at these places, the question which now naturally arises is, whether the possession of these two small posts within 350 miles of the coast is a sufficient result for the five years which have elapsed since the Charter was granted to justify the Company in retaining that Charter any longer? So long as they retain it, they prevent any one else from undertaking the work which they have thrown down." [1]

[1] "Africa No. 2 (1894)." The Report is quoted in full in Appendix No. 13 in Mr. McDermott's book. The Directors' defence against Sir Gerald Portal's criticisms was as follows : "It were wholly unreasonable to expect that in a period of five years means should be found to police the country, to institute a judicial administration in the interior, and to construct tanks, to erect buildings, and form 700 or 800 miles of road " (quoted by Mr. McDermott, *op. cit.* p. 288). With regard to the particular paragraph in Sir G. Portal's final report, quoted above, the Directors made the following reply in a letter, dated April 11, 1894, addressed to the Secretary of State for Foreign Affairs : "It is also stated that the only posts held by the Company in the interior are the stations at Kikuyu and Machakos ; that neither of these places are (*sic*) of any commercial or political value except as stations on the road to Uganda, and it is asked whether the possession of these two posts ' is a sufficient result for the five years which have elapsed since the Charter was granted?' As to the value of Machakos and Kikuyu, the Commissioner's testimony in his despatch of May 24, pp. 2 and 3, hardly corresponds with his latter statement. 'The countries surrounding Machakos,' he says, 'are not only picturesque, but appear to be exceptionally fertile and capable of producing every sort of grain and vegetable with remarkable luxuriance. The people, too, are expert and diligent agriculturists, and have hitherto only been prevented by fear of the Masai raids from greatly extending the area of their cultivation. The climate is well adapted for Europeans, and I do not think it is an exaggeration to say that even European children would thrive in the district, which is, I believe, the case in none even of the best of the Indian Hill stations.' Of Kikuyu he speaks as a ' fertile and densely-populated country,' and the character of the country was already sufficiently established by all travellers who have visited it. As to whether the results of the Company's work are commensurate with the term of its existence, Sir G. Portal himself on p. 35 of the Blue Book bears different testimony to that just alluded to."

It will be seen that the Directors did not attempt to meet the real point of Sir G. Portal's criticism. The point was not that the Company had neglected to create a complete administration in five years, but that they had not begun to create any administration at all. Again the point was not that the two stations established by the Company at Machakos and Kikuyu were infertile or unhealthy, but that they were the only stations established by the Company in five years.

The Company not only failed to establish an administration and a government, as it had undertaken to do in accepting the Royal Charter, it also failed to pay dividends. At first sight, therefore, its economic imperialism may seem to have failed both economically and imperially. But that would be a superficial view. Its failure was in fact a triumph for economic imperialism, and the cause of it is to be found deep down in those beliefs and desires of economic imperialism which determined the actions and guided the policy of the Directors. The first fact which the reader must consider is this. In 1888 two great blocks of territory were handed over for administration and commercial exploitation to the German and British Companies. Both of them failed completely either to establish an administration or to exploit their possessions commercially. After three years the German Company, and after five years the British Company, were financially bankrupt, and their attempts to govern the country had been so disastrous that they had to be deprived of their Charters and their territories. Now the cause of this was in both cases the same. Instead of being content with the territory of which they had robbed the Sultan of Zanzibar, instead of proceeding step by step to establish an orderly government and administration and to develop means of communication and trade, they devoted their whole attention to an effort either to acquire or to establish claims to additional territory not included in their original " concessions."

This is a remarkable fact and one which explains all the difficulties into which Sir William Mackinnon landed his capitalist adventure. Mr. McDermott's book is, as I have said, an official *apologia* of the Company. One would have expected, therefore, that it would contain an account of the measures taken in the early years of its existence for carrying out the terms of the Royal Charter and for the commercial development of its domain. But there is nothing of the kind in the book. The chapters which deal with the three first critical years, 1888–90, are filled with an acrimonious account of a struggle between the German and British capitalists to acquire or to filch territory outside their original " concessions." Thus Chapter III. is devoted to "the Lamu Concession," and relates how Sir William Mackinnon and the " German Witu Company " engaged in 1889 in a bitter contest for a concession at Lamu, an island lying north of Kipini and outside the British concession.[1] Chapter IV. deals with a similar contest for the Belesoni Canal and the islands of Manda and Patta ; Chapter V. with a struggle for territories north of the Tana River, for the ownership of Witu and a further quarrel over Manda and Patta ;

---

[1] This contest was settled by the interference of the British and German Governments, which sent the dispute to arbitration. The dispute and the award of Baron Lambermont, the arbitrator, are referred to above, p. 260.

Chapter VI. with a dispute about the boundary line between the German and British concessions, and with Dr. Peters' Emin Pasha Relief Expedition which the British capitalists regarded—probably with justification—as merely a move in the great game between the German and British groups for acquiring more territory. Finally, in Chapter VIII. we reach the question of Uganda, which on a large scale was only another instance of this insatiable capitalist land hunger. Thus the first years of the economic imperialism of both groups were occupied not in development, but in a struggle for more territory, and this at a time when the combined navies of Germany and Great Britain had to be employed in order that the two Companies might maintain a foothold at all in the territories already belonging to them, when the whole effort of the adventurers ought to have been directed to establishing order and promoting prosperity in those territories, and when the capital of each Company available for this immense undertaking amounted to the absurdly inadequate sum of a few hundred thousand pounds.

The explanation of this extraordinary policy on the part of business men is simple. Their policy, like all policy whether of governments, prominent capitalists, or shopkeepers, was determined by beliefs and desires, and the beliefs and desires of these German and British financiers (together with their military and aristocratic associates) were those of economic imperialism. Their primal desire was to acquire control of territory either for themselves or for their Governments, and therefore to keep it out of the hands of the capitalists or Governments of other nations. This desire is the main content of those " philanthropic and patriotic " motives, those " conceptions and obligations of a higher character," which Mr. McDermott tells us influenced the decisions of the British Board of Directors and which formed the basis for his Company's claim to special privileges and treatment. Over and over again in his book when he comes to details of " philanthropic and patriotic " action by Sir William Mackinnon, we find that this action consisted merely, either in acquiring territory for the British Empire, or in preventing the acquisition of territory by some other Empire. The desire of these capitalists was for the ownership and control of territory in Africa ; their belief was that after they had acquired it they could make their ownership of it profitable. Their first object was therefore to acquire as much as they could possibly by any means lay hands on : they postponed for the moment a decision as to the methods by which they were to exploit it profitably.

I do not propose to analyse in detail the policy and actions of the British East Africa Company in all these disputes of its first years, partly because it would be too long a process, and partly because the proof of my statements will appear clearly in the history of its dealings with Uganda, which I shall investigate with some minuteness. I shall give only one example of this early policy, an example which illustrates admirably the operation and effect of the rival economic imperialisms of two groups of capitalists. Immediately to the north of Kipini, which was in 1888 the northern boundary of the British concession, lay a town called Witu. In 1885, from which year we must date the first partition of East Africa, Witu and its surrounding district was ruled by a " Sultan," Ahmet bin Sultan Komlut, surnamed Simba or the Lion. This man was of Arab descent and had spent most of his life fighting against the Sultan of Zanzibar for the possession of some islands. Driven out at last from the islands, he established himself in Witu. Simba claimed to rule Witu as an independent Sultan, but his claim was always denied by Zanzibar. The British took the part of Zanzibar in this quarrel, the Germans of Simba. To the British, therefore, Simba was naturally a bloodthirsty rebel, a slave-dealing sultan who made his territory a refuge for " malcontents, bankrupts and felons," and converted the surrounding country into a desert of plundered villages : in German accounts he appears as " a hero, struggling against Arab domination," an admirable ruler who was abolishing slavery and introducing order and civilization into a barbarous country. Matters reached a head in 1885, when the Sultan of Zanzibar prepared a force with which finally to reduce Simba, and made preparations to attack Witu from the neighbouring island of Lamu. The German Government intervened and informed Zanzibar that German forces would support Simba if he were attacked.[1]

This was the moment when negotiations were just beginning between the British and German Governments for the partition of the dominions of Zanzibar, and, pending a settlement, the Sultan Barghash was " advised " by Lord Granville and Sir John Kirk to discontinue his military expedition against Witu. The Anglo-German Delimitation Commission (see page 245) was then appointed, and the result was the Agreement of October 29–November 1, 1886. In that Agreement, however, nothing was said about Witu, and the question of its ownership remained undecided until 1887, when the Sultan of Zanzibar withdrew all his claims to the town and territory. Witu then became virtually a German protectorate. In the same year the German Witu Company was formed with the object of developing and exploiting commercially the German " protectorate." Such was the position in 1888, when the Imperial British East Africa Company entered into possession of its concession from Wanga to Kipini. The territory of Witu, the reader must remember, was just outside and to the north of the northern boundary of the British concession and sphere of influence. That was the significant fact in the situation both for the German and the British imperialists.

[1] See R. H. Lyne, *Zanzibar in Contemporary Times*, 1905, pp. 134 and 160 ; and McDermott, *op. cit.* pp. 34-36.

A German protectorate and exploiting company in Witu was a rampart against any possible expansion of the British Company and imperialists northwards. Hence the German action, and hence the energy with which the British Company proceeded to concern itself, not with the development of its territories, but with the affairs of Witu.

I have already had to mention the struggle between the British Company and the Germans for the island of Lamu, and the arbitration which finally settled that question. The struggle for Lamu was really only part of, and the first round in, the struggle for Witu. For Witu had no port of its own, and its commercial outlet was Lamu. That was why the Germans attempted to obtain a concession of this island, and that was also why the British Company immediately did the same, for the possession of Lamu would give to the British East Africa Company the power of throttling the trade of Witu. While the Lamu dispute was still proceeding, a new quarrel began. Herr O. Denhardt, the agent of the Witu Company, who was at the same time in the service of the Sultan of Witu, opened a customs-house in the Sultan's name at Chara on the Belesoni Canal, and began to levy customs dues on commerce of the Tana River which passed through the canal. The British Directors immediately acted with the greatest energy, overwhelming the Foreign Office with protests and complaints. Their attitude and their indignation are amusing when one remembers the position of the two Great Powers and the two Companies with regard to the dominions and sovereignty of the Sultan of Zanzibar. The Sultan of Witu was "a lawless ruler" who had committed "an outrage upon the territory and subjects of Zanzibar" by sending troops into the Sultan of Zanzibar's territory and by levying "arbitrary exactions from the commerce of the Tana." The "unfortunate people" of the district had appealed to the British Company to protect them against this "flagrant usurpation," and the British Company appealed to the British Government to "obtain the interference of the German Government to put an end to the oppressive aggressions of Witu." For the British Company "were unable to believe either that the German Government would continue to give its sanction to so flagrant a violation of territory, or that Her Majesty's Government would continue to acquiesce in a usurpation which violated the sovereign rights of the Sultan of Zanzibar—whose independence they were pledged to protect ; and the rights of the Company to which the Crown had granted the aegis of a Royal Charter." This was early in 1889, at a time when the British Government looked for and found its chief imperial difficulties and rival, not in Berlin, but in Paris, and when Downing Street was by no means willing to embroil itself with Germany in Africa. Lord Salisbury therefore gave Sir William Mackinnon a diplomatic answer, which to the British capitalist seemed to show an unaccountable "unwillingness to interfere with proceedings directed against what were now British interests."

The Company then decided to take matters into its own hands, and to vindicate by its own armed force "British interests" and the sovereign rights and independence of the Sultan of Zanzibar, for which it had acquired so sudden a concern. On July 17, 1889, Lord Salisbury was informed by Sir William Mackinnon that "the Company's representative would be forthwith instructed to despatch a body of troops to the Belesoni Canal to drive out the Witu soldiers and customs officials." An ultimatum was sent to Fumo Bakari, who had succeeded to the Sultanate of Witu, calling upon him to evacuate the Belesoni district, and a force of 150 men and a Maxim gun were "despatched by the Company from Mombasa to enforce the evacuation if necessary." The Sultan of Witu yielded to this show of force, and withdrew his forces and officials from the Belesoni district. His action, if Mr. McDermott's account is correct, was determined by advice or instructions from the German Government.

But the quarrels with the Germans over Witu did not end with the Belesoni Canal episode. Simultaneously a violent dispute broke out about the two islands of Manda and Patta, which lay outside the original concessions of 1888. It is not necessary to go into the details of this dispute : it is sufficient to say that the British Company claimed that the two islands belonged to Zanzibar and that the Sultan of Zanzibar had ceded them to the Company on August 31, 1889 ; while the Germans maintained that they belonged to Witu, which was under the protection of Germany and the German capitalists. The German capitalists were supported by their Government, and once more the British capitalists overwhelmed the Foreign Office with complaints and appeals. But negotiations were already proceeding between the British and German Governments with a view to a settlement of the whole question of territory on the east coast of Africa, and the Foreign Office was probably indisposed to prejudice the result by any hasty or provocative action with regard to the islands of Manda and Patta. Sir William Mackinnon was informed that "the question of the administration of the two islands by the Company must remain in abeyance pending discussion between Her Majesty's Government and the Government of Germany." To this the Company replied, that it had already hoisted its flag in the islands and taken over the administration. The Foreign Office replied that this action "in respect to a territory in the position of these islands must be held to have been taken without authority." This brought down upon the Government renewed protests from Sir William Mackinnon, but the Foreign Office was firm and, by a despatch of February 25, 1890, directed the Company to haul down its flag and withdraw its officers and troops from the islands. The Company obeyed, protesting vigorously. But the time was approaching when the quarrels between German and British capitalists in East Africa were to be suddenly and summarily ended by their Governments. On July 1, 1890, Britain and Germany signed an agreement by which the dominions of Zanzibar were finally partitioned between them, and their spheres definitely defined. German East Africa was ceded absolutely to Germany by the Sultan, and he himself and the remainder of his territories passed to Great Britain. At the same time by Article II. Germany withdrew " in favour of Great Britain her Protectorate over Witu." And now a curious example of international morality occurred with regard to the Sultanate of Witu. The Anglo-German treaty was signed on July 1. Towards the end of August, a German called Kuntzel, accompanied by a number of German workmen, set out for Witu with the intention of erecting a sawmill, felling trees, and engaging in the wood industry. The man was an adventurer of the worst type—" of a violent disposition," as the British Consul reported—who had posed in Germany as " Commander of the Bodyguard of the Sultan of Witu " and had landed in Witu dressed in a gorgeous uniform of his own design. He was warned by the British Consul in Lamu that it was unsafe for him to proceed to Witu " on account of the growing dislike evinced by the Witu people towards Europeans and Christians generally, and towards Germans in particular." Events showed that this dislike was not altogether unreasonable.

It must be remembered that the Sultan of Witu was an independent ruler, and although Germany, by the Agreement of July 1, had withdrawn her claims to his territory in favour of Britain (in reality the British Company, the Sultan's deadly enemy !), the Sultan himself was not consulted with regard to this arrangement. When Kuntzel landed, the Sultan refused to allow him to fell any trees, unless he brought a document of some sort from the British Consul. The Germans paid no attention and began to erect their sawmill. The Sultan retired to Witu and began to arm. This alarmed Kuntzel and his companions ; they prepared to fly, and as a preliminary Kuntzel shot down and killed a native. This act enraged the inhabitants, who fell upon the Germans, and killed Kuntzel and seven of his men.

. This is Mr. McDermott's comment upon the incident : " There was no doubt that, although the behaviour of M. Kuntzel and his companions was highly imprudent and unjustifiable, the massacre was perpetrated with at least the passive sanction of the Sultan of Witu, who made no attempt to save the lives of the Europeans who were being killed almost under his eye." The impartial historian will probably take a different view as to the culpability of the Sultan and the German. The German had no right to be where he was or to be acting as he was : he was armed and he was the aggressor in bloodshed. The reason why Mr. McDermott, as the apologist of the British Company, is so anxious to put the blame not on the German, but on the Sultan, is explained by subsequent events. The British Government, on the complaint of the German Government, decided to punish the "authors of the German murders." The "punishment" was the usual punishment meted out by Europeans to Africans. Admiral Fremantle with a force of 950 men, of whom 150 were the East African Company's troops, landed in Witu. The town of Witu was captured and burnt to the ground ; Fumo Bakari, the Sultan, who escaped, was declared an outlaw, and a price of 10,000 rupees was set upon his head ; the independence of Witu was abolished and martial law proclaimed. Thus was Herr Kuntzel avenged.[1]

On March 5, 1891, the British East Africa Company took over the administration of Witu, and gained that extension of territory to the north which they had been clearly working for ever since the original partition of 1886. The inhabitants of Witu, however, showed a curious aversion to exchanging the rule of their Sultans for that of British capitalists. All through 1891, " in spite of all the efforts of the Company, there was no peace ; trade and agriculture were at a standstill and anarchy prevailed." [2] In 1892 the Company determined to resort once more to force, and two unsuccessful expeditions were made against Jongeni, the headquarters of the rebellious inhabitants. Then, with the aid of a British man-of-war, a third and more successful attempt was made, and for the moment the chiefs and people were dispersed and subjugated. But in 1893 the insurrection against the Company broke out again, this time with such intensity that the Company finally decided to withdraw from Witu altogether. Witu was now placed under the Sultanate of Zanzibar, in other words it became directly a part of the British Empire. The result was that a considerable force of soldiers and blue-jackets was at once despatched to reduce the country to "law and order." There was some stiff fighting, a not unusual preliminary to the establishment of *Pax Britannica*, but the field-gun which accompanied the British forces was too much for the natives. Their strongholds, villages, and crops were taken, burnt, and destroyed. By 1894, to quote a British historian, "the reign of the Sons of Simba was for ever abolished, and the long lingering resistance to law and order disappeared." [3]

[1] For the facts connected with the Kuntzel affair see McDermott, pp. 147-152 ; Zimmermann, *Geschichte des deutsches Kolonialpolitik*, pp. 182-183 ; and Lyne, *Zanzibar in Contemporary Times*, pp. 161-162. According to Mr. McDermott and some other accounts, Kuntzel shot the native because he refused to allow him to leave the town.

[2] Lyne, *op. cit.* p. 165.　　　　　[3] Lyne, *op. cit.* p. 167.

Such is the history of how the Sultans of Witu lost their kingdom and their territory became part of the British Empire. One of the "claims" which the British Company put forward for special consideration at the hands of their Government and countrymen, consisted in their patriotic action in saving Witu for the Empire. The "claim" may be admitted. At the same time it should be noted that the Company could spend so much energy and employ expeditions of armed troops for the conquest of Witu during years when they admittedly had neither the men nor the money for the administration and development of the territories already acquired by them.

Sir William Mackinnon's Witu policy was, however, repeated in the far more important case of Uganda. Uganda was known to be one of the richest and most advanced kingdoms of Africa. The Anglo-German Agreement of 1886 gave no precise indication as to whether this country was included within the British or the German sphere of influence; and the future ownership of Uganda immediately became a question of great interest to the British and German imperialists. The British claimed that according to the hinterland theory Uganda certainly belonged to the British sphere, and from the point of view of geography there was much to be said for the contention : Uganda is undoubtedly the hinterland of the northern coast-line which the British Company obtained from the Sultan of Zanzibar rather than of the southern coast-line which fell to the German Company. Yet it is strange to find the German and British imperialists and statesmen invoking the hinterland theory with regard to this territory. They had themselves explicitly denied that the hinterland principle applied to it so far as the Sultan of Zanzibar was concerned. They had admitted that the sovereignty of the coast belonged to Zanzibar, and, therefore, if the hinterland theory was to be applied, the whole hinterland, including Uganda, belonged to Zanzibar. This they expressly denied, and forced the Sultan to adhere to an arrangement by which his sovereignty was limited to the coast-line. Then when they had got the Sultan to cede to themselves his sovereign rights over the coast-line territories, they claimed that the possession of these territories, which had given the Sultan no right to the hinterland, did give themselves a right to the hinterland. Such is the mysterious philosophy of economic imperialism.

The complete financial and administrative failure of the British East Africa Company was, on its own showing, largely, if not wholly, due to the fact that in its very first years, and with a capital of £250,000, it embarked upon the acquisition and conquest of the immense and distant kingdom of Uganda, before it had begun to develop the territories which lay between Uganda and the coast and which it had obtained from the Sultan of Zanzibar. Mr. McDermott, on behalf of the Company, contends that this action was forced upon it by public opinion in Britain, and that the Company was reluctantly compelled against its own interests and inclinations by this pressure of public opinion to go to Uganda and save it from falling into the hands of another Power. An examination of this contention reveals once more the curious interpretation which the economic imperialist will place upon historical facts.

According to Mr. McDermott, the interest of Europe and of the British Company in the future of Uganda began in the spring of 1890. It was then, he says, that it became " evident that the ' race for Uganda ' was about to take place in earnest." Two facts, he maintains, roused public opinion in England to the necessity of action if Uganda was to be saved from German hands, and it was this rousing of public opinion which forced the Company to despatch an expedition under Captain F. D. Lugard to Uganda. The two facts to which he alludes were the expedition of Emin Pasha from German East Africa into the interior, and the appearance of Dr. Karl Peters at the north of Lake Victoria Nyanza. The question of dates is here of the first importance. It was in February 1890 that Peters arrived in Uganda, and it was on March 31 that Emin Pasha finally decided to take service under Wissmann and the German Company and lead an expedition into the interior. And it was in March 1890 that, according to Mr. McDermott's account, Captain Lugard received instructions " to proceed with all despatch to Uganda to establish the Company's influence.

Let us first examine the nature of the pressure of public opinion which Sir William Mackinnon and his associates said was applied to them. "At this crisis," writes Mr. McDermott, referring to the spring of 1890, " the nation turned to the British East Africa Company as the agency whose duty it was to guard the national interests in Uganda. . . . The Company was subjected at this juncture to the pressure of a universal and strongly expressed opinion that it was bound by its Charter obligations to secure the interests of Great. Britain in the lake regions. Her Majesty's Government very clearly intimated that they looked to the Company to assert and maintain British rights in Africa, which were represented to depend on effective occupation. The fallacy underlying all the arguments and assumptions as to the responsibility of the British East Africa Company in these respects was that the immediate interests of the Company were identical with those of the nation. Nothing could be more specious, but none the less more groundless. It was far from the interest of the Company, with a small capital upon which the rivalry of foreigners, favoured by the diplomatic needs of British Imperial interests elsewhere, had already made serious demands, to embark upon expeditions in the remote interior which, whatever might be their eventual results, must immediately involve heavy and unproductive expenditure.

The importance of securing Uganda and the headwaters of the Nile within the sphere of British influence was certainly pressing, but to require a private company to undertake such onerous duties without State co-operation was illogical and unjust." [1]

Here the Company's account of the origin of their expedition to acquire Uganda is perfectly clear: unfortunately it is directly contradicted by dates and facts. First as to the statement that "Her Majesty's Government very clearly intimated that they looked to the Company to assert and maintain British rights in Africa, which were represented to depend on effective occupation." The implication in this statement is that the expedition to Uganda was despatched by the Company because of this intimation of the Government. The "intimation" referred to by the Company is apparently a passage [2] in a communication from the Foreign Office to the Directors. The passage does not, as a matter of fact, intimate that the Government looked to the Company to occupy Uganda; but that is unimportant because the communication from the Foreign Office was received by the Directors on April 2, while the Directors had already in the previous March given Captain Lugard instructions "to proceed with all despatch to Uganda to establish the Company's influence." The decision to send the expedition could not possibly have been influenced by the Government's "intimation," because the expedition had already received its instructions to start before the intimation was received.

[1] McDermott, *op. cit.* p. 116. Another passage on p. 123, in view of the facts which are given in the pages which follow, is worth quoting : "The influence exercised on the public mind by Mr. H. M. Stanley on his return from the interior must be counted as one of the most powerful factors which brought about the situation the Company had now (*i.e.* April 1890) to meet. The effect of his emphatic declarations of the importance of Uganda to Great Britain and of this country's rights to its permanent inclusion within the sphere of British interests, was such as to compel the Government to recognize the effective occupation of Uganda as a matter not to be postponed. Public opinion would brook no hesitation in the emergency, and to the force of this opinion, acting directly and through Her Majesty's Government, the Company had no choice but to yield. It may be admitted, without lessening the merit of the public enterprise thus undertaken at the expense of more personal interests, that the patriotic spirit of the Directors disposed them to accept the task without the justifiable protest that it exceeded the functions and obligations of the Company." Unfortunately for Mr. McDermott's accuracy, the patriotic Directors had, as we shall show, undertaken this enterprise on their own initiative and for their own objects several months before Mr. Stanley returned and before the Government or public opinion began to hear or to think of Uganda.

[2] The passage is as follows (see McDermott, p. 122) : "Information received from Colonel Euan-Smith shows that the state of affairs in Uganda is critical, and that Mwanga . . . may be disposed to accept overtures from the white men who may be first in the field. It is understood that the principal object which the East Africa Company has in view, after establishing its position on the coast, is to secure paramount influence in Uganda, and that steps have been taken for that object by the despatch of caravans. His lordship would be glad to learn the exact nature of these steps and the further measures which the Directors propose to take, in order that he may communicate the information to Colonel Euan-Smith in anticipation of the arrival at Zanzibar of a mission from Uganda said to be now on its way to the coast."

The plea of the Company and Sir William Mackinnon with regard to the pressure of public opinion also does not stand investigation. "The pressure of a universal and strongly expressed opinion," Mr. McDermott calls it; but the only example which he can quote is a leading article in *The Times* of April 3, 1890 (exactly one day after the Directors received the intimation of the Government!). This article expressed the opinion that the British East Africa Company should put its house in order and take "effective possession of whatever it hopes to keep on the shores of Victoria Nyanza." It will be noted first that the intimation to take "effective possession" of Uganda came not as the Company says from the Government, but from *The Times*. It is perhaps a coincidence that, throughout the Uganda affair, the leading articles in *The Times* newspaper supported and reflected not only the policy of the Company's Directors, but the actual words of its agents. In this leading article the Company, Mr. McDermott tells us, considered that *The Times* was "speaking as the mouthpiece of public opinion and of the Government"; and when two days later the same newspaper added that if the Company "can put Englishmen and English money into its territory upon any considerable scale, it need not doubt that due protection will be forthcoming," Sir William Mackinnon yielded to this "universal and strongly expressed opinion" and the expedition to Uganda was reluctantly started.

Once more, however, the ingenuous story of the badly treated, but patriotic, capitalist dissolves and fades away in the light of dates. *The Times* articles appeared in April 1890; the Directors had given their instructions for the despatch of the expedition in March; therefore the expression of public opinion through the mouthpiece of the newspaper could not possibly have influenced the Directors in their decision. Moreover, if *The Times* is to be taken as the mouthpiece of public opinion, a careful investigation of its files for the years 1889–91 shows that until April 1890 public opinion paid no attention at all to Uganda. The affairs of Uganda are hardly mentioned in this paper during 1889, and it is only after April 1890, and the leading article to which we have referred, that any attention is given to its future. Even in 1890 there are very few references to it and to its acquisition, and it is only in 1891 that the question receives prominence. It was therefore only after Sir William Mackinnon and his fellow capitalists had decided to send the expedition to Uganda that any mention of the necessity for doing so and for acquiring the country occurs in *The Times*; and if that paper represents public opinion, it would seem that the pressure of public opinion followed and did not precede Sir William Mackinnon's decision to acquire Uganda for his Company.

But the historian who goes for information to sources other than the official *apologia* of Sir William Mackinnon and his Company will discover a most extraordinary fact. The Company's story is that the Government and public opinion, roused in the spring of 1890 by the actions of the Germans, forced the Company to send an expedition to Uganda, and that the decision to send the expedition was taken in March of that year. The man chosen to lead this expedition was Captain F. D. Lugard. Now Captain Lugard in 1893 wrote two large and interesting volumes, *The Rise of Our East African Empire*, in which he told in great detail the story of the part played by him in the acquisition of Uganda by the British East Africa Company and the British Empire. Captain Lugard was one of those fortunate persons whose early life was chiefly occupied in killing things. An officer in the British army, he was employed at twenty-one in shooting Afghans in the Afghan War, at twenty-seven, Africans in the Sudan campaign, and at twenty-eight, Burmese in the Burma campaign. When not engaged on active service, he was passionately devoted to shooting wild beasts and, in particular, to big-game shooting. In 1887 these occupations had completely shattered his health, and, on the recommendation of a medical board, he was placed on half-pay. At that time, as he tells us, the Italians were "fighting against the Abyssinians, and smarting from their recent reverse at Dogali." Captain Lugard decided that the best cure for his shattered health would be for him to join the Italians in shooting Abyssinians in Abyssinia. He therefore sailed for Massowah, " with fifty sovereigns in my belt, and with practically no outfit at all except my favourite little ·450 rifle." But the Italians, for reasons which have appeared in a previous chapter, were in 1888 very jealous of the right to shoot Abyssinians, and they refused the co-operation of a captain in the British army. Captain Lugard had to leave Eritrea, and he set sail down the East Coast of Africa in quest of health and adventure. His boat put in at Mozambique, and there he heard that inland to the north of Lake Nyasa a war was proceeding between a British joint-stock company, the African Lakes Company, and the natives, who were "slave-raiders," and that an "expedition was being prepared to prosecute the war." "Here," he tells us, "I thought, is the very opportunity I have sought, of taking part in a good cause against the slave-raiders, ' in the place itself where the slaves are captured.' However, though eager to lend my services, I felt that it would be impossible for me to do so, unless the fighting was fully justified in my view." [1] Enquiries satisfied him that it would be as good a cause to shoot the slave-raiders of Lake Nyasa as the Abyssinians of Abyssinia, the Burmese of Burma, the Africans of the Sudan, or the Afghans of Afghanistan. For the next year Captain Lugard was employed in the war against the slave-raiders. The bad climate and a severe wound had not improved his shattered

[1] Lugard, *op. cit.* vol. i. p. 18.

health, and in November 1889, to quote his own words, " I gladly accepted a kind offer from Sir W. Mackinnon of a passage to Mombasa and back for my health in one of his ships."

Captain Lugard had as fellow-passengers on board his ship to Mombasa Sir Charles Euan-Smith, Consul-General at Zanzibar, and Mr. G. S. Mackenzie, who was going with a number of junior officers to "take up the duties of Administrator of the Imperial British East Africa Company." What happened on board the ship in November 1889 can best be told in Captain Lugard's own words :

We also heard news from Uganda. . . . Colonel Euan-Smith and Mr. Mackenzie were both strongly of opinion that an effort should be made to establish the Company's administration there; and Mr. Mackenzie at this early date (Nov. 1889) sounded me as to my willingness to command an expedition to Uganda. My interests were all in Nyasaland, but the task proposed to me offered as much scope as the one I had at first expected to undertake on Nyasa, but which now had been confided to another. I therefore readily accepted his proposal, with the proviso that if I should be required in Nyasaland—for as yet the Protectorate had not been declared, nor had Mr. Johnston been appointed, and I did not know whether I should be called upon to fulfil my obligations with Mr. Rhodes—I should be free to go there, provided the plans for Uganda had not taken definite shape, and provided, of course, that the War Office sanction was obtained. It had been decided—I do not know for what reason—to defer any immediate action ; perhaps news was expected from Mr. Jackson (who was in command of a large expedition in the interior) which might modify the views of the directors.[1]

This quotation shows that Mr. McDermott and the Company must by 1893 have forgotten the real facts with regard to the decision to send Captain Lugard to "establish the Company's administration" in Uganda. It was not the news of Emin Pasha and Dr. Peters in the spring of 1890, it was not the pressure of public opinion or the intimation of the Foreign Office in April 1890, which forced the Directors reluctantly to make that decision of March 1890. The decision had already been made in November 1889, for already in November 1889, five months before any of these events had happened, Captain Lugard had accepted the proposal of the Company's Administrator to command an expedition which should establish the Company's administration in Uganda. That is to say, only a year after the concession of 1888 had been made by the Sultan and the Company had been given its royal charter, "at this early date," as Captain Lugard himself says, when the officers of the Company were proceeding to Africa to establish an administration, the Directors had already decided and were making arrangements to acquire the kingdom of Uganda, which is somewhat larger than the whole of

[1] Lugard, op. cit. vol. i. p. 219.

the United Kindom, and which was separated by 800 miles of undeveloped country from the territory which they had just obtained upon the coast. They were supported in this decision by the British Consul-General in Zanzibar, the same Colonel Sir Charles Euan-Smith who later, as we have seen on page 207, was working with another group of British capitalists to gain control of the Abyssinian railways. We do not know whether the Foreign Office in London supported or even knew of this policy and action of their agent in Zanzibar; but in any case the incident is an instructive example of the way in which economic imperialism works behind the scenes.

After Captain Lugard had accepted the Company's proposal in November 1889 to command an expedition to Uganda, he was engaged until April 1890 in exploring the Sabakhi River, with the object "to open it up as a route into the interior," i.e. to Uganda.[1] He was doing this, and had already penetrated a considerable distance into the interior at Kibwezi, when on April 19 he received instructions from the Company's Administrator that he "should at once proceed to Uganda."[2] He immediately returned to the coast in order to prepare his expedition, but there various delays occurred, and it was not until August 6 that the expedition started.

The delays with regard to the despatch of Captain Lugard were due to the fact that in the interval " it was decided by the Court of Directors to give the proposed expedition a more imposing and authoritative character than was at first intended."[3] With this end in view Sir Francis de Winton, G.C.M.G., a Major-General who from 1884 to 1886 had been Administrator-General of the Belgian Congo, was induced to accept the post of Administrator of the Company's territory, and it was intended to make the expedition authoritative and imposing by substituting a Major-General and a G.C.M.G. for a simple captain as its leader. The Directors also proposed to turn the " expedition " into a miniature army, and to recruit for this purpose Sudanese in Egypt and Sikhs in India. The proposal to use Egypt and India as recruiting grounds for troops to be employed in the imperialist adventures of joint-stock companies in the interior of Africa met with considerable opposition from Sir Evelyn Baring (Lord Cromer) in Egypt and from the Indian Government. It is curious that if, as the Company claimed, they were reluctantly compelled by the Government and the public to undertake this expedition, Sir William Mackinnon protested strongly to the Foreign Office against the refusal of the Egyptian Government to allow him to recruit Sudanese for what he characteristically called " service as military police " in Uganda, and yet he failed to point out to the Foreign Office that the expedition for

[1] Lugard, op. cit. vol. i. p. 220. [2] Lugard, op. cit. vol. i. p. 288.
[3] McDermott, op. cit. p. 153.

which he required them had been forced upon him by the Foreign Office itself. In fact, he went out of his way to complain that the Government was not backing the Company's adventures, to draw a comparison between the British Government's attitude towards his company and that of the German Government towards the German company, and to point sorrowfully to the fact that his operations in East Africa were entirely a private enterprise.[1]

Major-General Sir Francis de Winton arrived in East Africa in June 1890 to take up his duties under the Company, and Captain Lugard resigned. In July Captain Lugard had withdrawn his resignation, and in August had started at the head of an expedition for Uganda. The reasons for these vacillations and changes are not stated either by Captain Lugard or by Mr. McDermott, but it is not difficult to guess what they were. A fortnight after Sir Francis de Winton arrived at Mombasa the British and German Governments signed the agreement of July 1, 1890, which, so far as the two Great Powers were concerned, partitioned East Africa finally between them. This agreement definitely placed Uganda within the British sphere of influence. Thus the position was suddenly and radically altered. The Company's pretext for an " imposing and authoritative " military expedition had been the necessity of forestalling Emin Pasha and Peters and the German Company in an attempt to convert Uganda into a German possession. The agreement of July 1 now made such an attempt impossible and the " imposing and authoritative " expedition unnecessary.[2] If Uganda was to be converted into a British possession, other pretexts and other methods were now necessary, and accordingly the Major-General once more made way for the simple captain.

[1] " The Court deem it hardly necessary in this connection to contrast the bloodless operations of the British Company with those of the German Government, nor to emphasise further the unequal conditions of a competition for administrative progress which is backed on the one side by the resources of an empire, and on the other is exclusively dependent on private enterprise." Letter of Sir William Mackinnon to the Secretary of State for Foreign Affairs. See McDermott, op. cit. pp. 154 and 155.

[2] It is a curious fact that two years later Sir William Mackinnon had completely forgotten the circumstances under which the advance into Uganda was actually made. In a letter to the Foreign Office, dated May 17, 1892 (Africa, No. 1 (1893), p. 3), he writes : " Her Majesty's Government will doubtless remember that the Imperial British East Africa Company was in a large measure compelled by the exigencies of the situation in East Africa while the spheres of influence of rival countries were in dispute in the early part of the year 1890, and by national sentiment as expressed both in the press and through the Government, to lose no time in securing for Great Britain the regions of the interior, without possession of which the then small sphere assigned to British influence, including less than 150 miles of coast-line, would have been shorn of most of its potential value, and the markets of the interior lost to British commerce." The only meaning of the passage is that Captain Lugard's expedition was despatched before the Anglo-German agreement of 1890 was signed ; but that is not true ; the expedition was despatched after the signing of the treaty, and when the spheres of influence of the rival countries were no longer in dispute.

Uganda was in a very few months converted into a British possession, and the pretexts and methods of this conversion deserve a short investigation. People sometimes forget that a treaty between two States binds only the parties to it. The agreement of July 1 bound only Germany and Britain : as between these two Powers it provided that Germany withdrew all claim to Uganda and would raise no opposition to its acquisition by Britain. This agreement gave no moral or legal title in Uganda to Great Britain. Neither Germany nor Britain had any title or rights in Uganda ; it " belonged " to neither ; it " belonged " to the people of Uganda and their king, Mwanga. For the British East Africa Company or the British Empire to acquire Uganda it was necessary for them to oust the legitimate sovereign and Government of the country ; and this Captain Lugard and his expedition proceeded very effectively and expeditiously to do.

Uganda was one of the most prosperous and advanced of African States. The British Commissioner, Sir Gerald Portal, in 1893 reported that it contained " a fertile soil," " a temperate climate," " a strategical position of great natural importance," and " a race of people of much higher intellectual development and civilization than any other Central or East African tribe." The government of the country was in the hands of a king, " nominally absolute and despotic, but actually shorn of " much of his authority, but there was still " an almost superstitious reverence on the part of a considerable proportion of the peasantry for the family and person of the King." The authority of the king was limited by the council of chiefs which was always summoned for consultation and advice in emergencies. Cultivation and native industries had reached a far higher level of development than was usual in Africa.

The country, however, had not escaped the miseries of political strife. When the capitalists of the British East Africa Company began to covet it, it had only just recovered from a violent upheaval. Politics in Uganda were inseparable from religion, and in order to understand the events connected with Captain Lugard's expedition it is necessary to know something of the previous politico-religious history of the country. The first attempts to open communications between Europeans and Uganda were religious, and took place in 1876 when the Church Missionary Society sent a mission under Lieutenant Smith, R.N. and Mr. O'Neill to the country. Its inhabitants, however, seem to have shared the views of King Theodore of Abyssinia regarding Christian missions (see page 145), and they promptly killed the two missionaries. The Christians of Europe were not, however, discouraged, and the C.M.S. soon succeeded in establishing missions in the country. They were followed in 1879 by a French Roman Catholic Mission. Both sects gained many converts, and the Protestants in 1884 considered that the time had come when Uganda should be endowed with an Anglican Bishop. Accordingly Mr. Hannington was consecrated Bishop of Uganda in that year, but this seems to have been too much for the inhabitants, and they killed their first bishop on his arrival in 1885 just as they had killed their first missionary on his arrival in 1876.

By 1885 religion and politics had already become inextricably confused. Mwanga had succeeded his father Mtesa as King of Uganda in 1884. He found two religions rapidly spreading through his country, the Christian and the Muhammadan. The two religions were competitors and rivals, and within the Christian community again were two rival and hostile sects, the Roman Catholic or French and the C.M.S. or English. The missionaries and capitalists who had to deal with Mwanga describe him as a cold-blooded, cruel, and savage despot. They accuse him of smoking bhang, and of still more unmentionable vices. Their accusations are probably true, but it must be remembered that this view of African rulers has always been taken by the citizens of European States engaged in the profitable task of seizing African territory. The French give a very different picture of Mwanga from that of the C.M.S. missionaries and the servants of the British East Africa Company ; but then the French were extremely angry that the C.M.S. and the Company brought about the inclusion of Uganda in the British Empire.

At any rate, Mwanga, as Captain Lugard says, very early in his reign came to the conclusion that both religions, " Mohammedan and Christian alike, . . . were disintegrating the country," and he proceeded to persecute them impartially. In 1888 Christians and Muhammadans combined to drive out Mwanga. The king fled to the south of Lake Victoria Nyanza, and his brother Kiwewa was chosen to rule in his stead. But the union between Muhammadans and Christians was short-lived, and in 1889 another civil war broke out, and the Christians were driven from Uganda. They turned to Mwanga and sent messages to him that they would reinstate him. The king accepted the invitation, and an attempt was made to overthrow the Muhammadans. Unfortunately dissension had already begun between the two Christian sects, the Protestant, which was now called " the English faction " (Wa-Ingleza) and the Catholics or " French faction " (Wa-Fransa). The quarrels led at first to the defeat of the Christians, and it was not until October 1889 that the Muhammadans were finally defeated and Mwanga reinstated as king.

The position, therefore, when Captain Lugard started for Uganda in August 1890 was this. The country was governed by its hereditary and independent ruler, Mwanga. A large number of the population were Christians : they were divided into two great factions, which called themselves respectively " English " and " French." Behind the " English " party stood the British missionaries of the C.M.S., and behind the "French" party the French missionaries of the Roman Catholic mission. The French missionaries already accused the British of using their religion and converts for political and imperialist ends, and the British made precisely the same accusations against the French. Into this already heated atmosphere there was suddenly launched an armed expedition, the aims and objects of which were obscure, by a British imperialist joint-stock company.

Neither Captain Lugard nor Mr. McDermott ever admits frankly that the object of this expedition was to deprive Mwanga of his kingdom and hand it over to the British East Africa Company. The reason presumably is that to admit this would be to admit that the whole business was a case of unabashed imperialist aggression. Sir William Mackinnon and Captain Lugard had no more right to deprive Mwanga and the Uganda chiefs of their territory and sovereignty than had Dr. Karl Peters to the territories out of which he swindled the chiefs of German East Africa. It is important, therefore, to examine the instructions which the Company gave to Captain Lugard with regard to the objects of his expedition. Luckily they have been recorded for us by Captain Lugard himself. "Mr. Mackenzie, the Administrator," he tells us, "left for England, after giving me an official letter in which I was directed to lose no opportunity of making treaties with the native chiefs on behalf of the Company, and of obtaining as much ivory as possible to recoup expenses. For the rest I was given an 'absolutely free hand,' and entrusted with the fullest powers, both as regards the formation of the expedition, its route and conduct in the interior, and the steps I should take on arrival in Uganda. Mr. Mackenzie simply said, 'As the credit of success will be yours, so will you have to bear the blame of failure,' and I was instructed (telegram, April 20, 1890) to assure Mwanga of our 'protection and powerful assistance.' " [1]

It will be seen that these strange instructions carefully refrain from stating to Captain Lugard the object of his expedition. He was to lead an armed force into the kingdom of an independent ruler, and when he got there, he was given "an absolutely free hand" to do—what? The instructions are silent. He was significantly told that, if he succeeded in doing whatever he was not told in the instructions to do, the credit would be his; and he would have to bear the blame of failure. Finally, he was to assure the independent ruler of our "protection and powerful assistance," but against what or whom he was to be protected and powerfully assisted is not explained either to Captain Lugard, to us, or, presumably, to Mwanga.

It may be said at once that Captain Lugard succeeded in the

[1] Lugard, *op. cit.* vol, i. p. 294,

object—whatever it was—of the expedition and gained the credit which his employers promised him. He became a Governor-General and a G.C.M.G. Mwanga, it is true, showed considerable reluctance to receive the Company's "protection and powerful assistance," but, after a civil war in which Captain Lugard's Maxim gun and armed forces were employed with great effect against the king and his supporters, and after the king and his armies, who had fled to an island, found themselves bombarded by the expedition which had come to protect and assist them, Mwanga was induced to reconsider his position and to accept the Company's protection. By 1894 Uganda had become a British Protectorate.

The story of the expedition need not be told in detail, but there are certain points connected with it which repay investigation. Captain Lugard tells us that he was determined to "assert my independence from the first," and with this object he crossed the Nile and marched his expedition into Uganda without asking the king—or, as he prefers to put it, "cringing to him"—for permission. His own view of his position can best be given in his own words : " As a result of international negotiation, Uganda and the countries round about had been ceded to the influence of Great Britain." (As I have pointed out before, this statement gives an inaccurate impression. Uganda had not been internationally ceded to Great Britain or to her influence : there was only an agreement between Germany and Britain by which Germany undertook not to stand in the way of Britain acquiring rights in Uganda. The agreement gave no legal or moral claim to Britain except *against Germany*.) " I myself, an officer of the army," he continues, " had been deputed, as the representative of a great chartered Company, to make a treaty with a semi-savage king noted for his cruelty and incapacity. I sought no unfair advantage, no acquisition of territory, no monopoly of trade,[1] no annexation of revenues. My task was to save the country from itself ; and for such a treaty as I proposed to make, I saw no need to stoop to bargaining by presents (of arms, a Maxim gun, etc., as had at first been suggested), and no cause for obeisance or deference." [2] Perhaps it is not strange that the king who saw his kingdom suddenly invaded by the armed expedition of a joint-stock company which boasted that it was " a great chartered Company " of a Great European Power, did not take quite the same view of things as the Company's representative, and that he hesitated to sign this treaty which Captain Lugard " proposed to make." Even a semi-savage king may hesitate to sign a treaty the object of which can only be described vaguely as " to save the country from itself."

---

[1] This is not true. See the terms of the treaty (given below, p. 282) which Lugard forced the king to sign.

[2] Lugard, *op. cit.* vol. ii. p. 20.

Captain Lugard arrived in the following way at the conclusion that he must save the country from itself. He had been " emphatically told " (he does not tell us by whom) " that the two Christian factions," the English and the French, " were animated by the most deadly hatred of each other, and that war had been imminent between them for some time." He had also been told with equal emphasis " that the Wa-Fransa and the Fathers were hostile to British influence, while the Wa-Ingleza and their missionaries were eager for it." He received instructions from Sir F. de Winton, Administrator-General of the Company, " to offer to Mwanga ' guarantees of peace in his kingdom,' and to ' impress him with a sense of the power of the Company,' with a view to securing ' a control of all white affairs in the country.' While exercising the strictest impartiality towards both factions, and assuring all of religious freedom and toleration, I was to ' consolidate the Protestant party ' if the others proved intractable."

The reader will notice that Captain Lugard went to Uganda with express instructions to exercise " the strictest impartiality " between two factions which were " animated by the most deadly hatred of each other," and at the same time " to consolidate the Protestant party." These two tasks, which the ordinary man might think to be incompatible, Captain Lugard always hotly maintained that he performed. He certainly " consolidated the Protestant " or English party, which, by a curious coincidence, happened to be " eager for " British influence and the influence of the great chartered Company.

On December 24, 1891, Captain Lugard presented a " treaty " to Mwanga at a full council of chiefs and asked him to sign it. Captain Lugard says that he insisted upon the king signing because the chiefs were ready to sign, " and in their hands the real executive power lay." He means presumably that the chiefs of the Protestant 'or " English " party were ready to sign, because he tells us at the same time that the king and the " French " party " of course " were " opposed to British influence." Later on in his book he defends his action in arming the Protestant party and aiding it in the civil war by pleading that it was the weaker party. Consequently he " insisted upon " the king signing because a minority of the chiefs were willing to sign. " Mwanga," he tells us, " shuffled and begged for delay. . . . The king was in a state of great excitement and fear, for he was under the absurd impression that if he signed he would become a mere slave." But Captain Lugard was " determined " ; he threatened to leave the country and go to Kabarega of Unyoro, who, as he tells us significantly, was " hostile to Uganda." Threatened in this way, Mwanga at last gave way, and said he would sign. There was at once a tremendous clamour (from a " set of bhang-smokers and rowdies," Captain

Lugard says), and threats to shoot the white men and those who signed. "I saw," writes Captain Lugard, "that it would be unwise to press the matter further at the moment, so I said that next day, being Christmas, we would do no work, but the day after I *must* have his reply."

Two days later the king signed "with a very bad grace." The terms of the treaty are summarized thus by Mr. McDermott:

Mwanga

acknowledged the suzerainty of the Company, placed his territories under its protection, engaged to fly no other flag, to make no treaties with, to grant no kind of concession whatever to, nor to allow to settle in the kingdom, acquire lands or hold offices of state, any European of whatever nationality, without the knowledge and consent of the Company's Resident, who was to exercise full authority over all Europeans resident in Uganda. The Resident was to be *ex officio* President of the Committee of Finance and Revenue, consisting of four members, elected (except the President) by the Council of State, whose duty it would be to assess, collect, and administer all the customs amd taxes. The revenue was to be applied (1) to the maintenance of the royal state, public salaries, etc. ; (2) to public works ; (3) to the maintenance of the army, which was to be organised and drilled by the Company's officers. Traders of all nations were to be free to come to Uganda, provided they did not import goods prohibited by agreement among the Powers. There should be free trade within the whole British sphere. The Company undertook to supply a staff of officials for the organization and administration of the country, all expenses of the Company not pertaining to its private trade to be borne from the public revenues. . . .[1]

The terms of this extraordinary treaty repay careful study. Its real effect would have been to give to a joint-stock company, as against other Europeans, whether British or foreigners, a complete monopolist power over the government, trade, and land of one of the richest and most advanced States of Africa, with an area equal to that of the United Kingdom and a population of $2\frac{1}{2}$ millions. It is true that the treaty seems to have provided for " free trade " and for freedom for traders of all nations to come to Uganda, but these clauses are completely nullified by the earlier provisions, which gave to the joint-stock company itself the right to say what Europeans should or should not be allowed to settle in the country, and complete control over the granting of commercial concessions and the sale or lease of lands. And yet Captain Lugard could say that he went to Uganda seeking no monopoly of trade !

The treaty was obtained admittedly by threats and against the will of the legitimate ruler and the majority of the population. Captain Lugard's defence of his action is curious. The king was a

[1] McDermott, p. 158.

semi-savage addicted to abominable cruelties ; he was a sodomite ; he was opposed to the idea of giving up his kingdom to Europeans, and " he would infinitely have preferred German or French domination " to British ; his " dreams were haunted by " the " spectres of vengeance " which he imagined that the British Government would exact for the late Bishop Hannington. " I regarded my mission," he explains, " as one for the reclamation and settlement of Uganda : surely I was right to refuse to be deterred from the course I had set myself to follow, by the opposition of such a king ? The treaty was certainly obtained against his will—I have never said the contrary. ' British prestige,' says Ashe, ' was at a discount, for the Waganda imagined that Englishmen might be killed with impunity in Africa.' This prestige it was my business to restore, and that I did restore it effectually before I left Uganda is indisputable." [1]

Captain Lugard in his book claims that he and his expedition, in restoring the prestige of Great Britain, " were the instruments of death to comparatively few—probably not a fraction of the number who have met their death elsewhere in Africa through the advent of other expeditions whose objects have been limited to exploration or to sport." [1] The claim may or may not be true. The slaughter of the inhabitants of Uganda which accompanied the restoration of British prestige after it had suffered so severely by the death of a single bishop was not inconsiderable, but Captain Lugard is correct in pointing out that European exploration, sport, and prestige have caused the death of immense numbers of Africans. If the late Bishop Hannington was avenged by the shooting of a few thousand Waganda, Captain Lugard's estimate of the proportionate value of an Anglican Bishop and of the inhabitants of Africa was probably moderate, as things went among imperialists in 1890.

Though Captain Lugard's main object was to restore Britain's prestige, it is remarkable that the terms of the treaty which he extorted from Mwanga dealt almost exclusively with monopolist rights and concessions which were secured for the Imperial British East Africa Company. The king "was under the absurd impression " that if he signed the treaty " he would become a slave." [2] But was the impression so absurd ? The treaty placed Mwanga, his government, and his power over the land and trade of Uganda entirely in the hands of Sir William Mackinnon's Company : all that the king received in return was a promise of the Company's " protection." The impression that " protection " was synonymous with slavery was shared by other African rulers, and was not quite so absurd as Captain Lugard would have us believe.

After the signing of this treaty there " was universal distrust

---

[1] Lugard, vol. ii. p. 41. [2] Lugard, vol. ii. p. 35.

and insecurity in the country." [1] Matters for a time improved a little, but " there was intense bitterness between the rival parties, daily threatening to break out in civil war." The king and the " French " party refused to fly the Company's flag : the " English " party accepted it. The chief cause of dispute between the factions was with regard to the ownership of land, and the king, who had now openly joined the Roman Catholics, gave judgment in favour of them. Captain Lugard took the side of the Protestants. I do not propose to enter into the complicated details of this dispute and the other quarrels, but one thing must be said in view of the ultimate outbreak of hostilities. Captain Lugard came to Uganda with instructions, as he tells us, " to consolidate the Protestant party " if he found that the Roman Catholics were opposed to the domination of the Company. He did find that the Roman Catholics were so opposed, and he did, in fact—whatever his intentions— consolidate the Protestants. And yet over and over again he pretends that he exercised strict impartiality between the two parties. As proof of this, he makes a great deal of the fact that at one moment the English C.M.S. missionaries complained that he was favouring the Roman Catholics. The complaint may of course have been founded on fact, but one cannot entirely overlook the fact that, in view of what subsequently occurred when Captain Lugard joined with the Protestants to destroy by armed force the Catholic party, the " complaint " was singularly useful as an argu- ment to prove that the Company's agents had exercised strict impartiality between the two rival religious parties. [2]

On March 31, 1891, Captain Lugard " with his own troops and the Uganda army marched out against the Muhammadan party, who were burning the villages within sight of the Uganda capital," Mengo. He defeated the Muhammadans, and then, after sending Captain Williams, R.A., with part of his force, back to Mengo, he himself proceeded on an expedition of exploration and conquest southwards to Lake Albert Edward. He was now at war with Kabarega, the powerful king of Unyoro, although, it will be remem- bered, it was by a threat to join Kabarega against Uganda that

---

[1] McDermott, *op. cit.* p. 158.

[2] The argument was in fact used at a most convenient moment. On March 24, 1892, two months after the outbreak of hostilities between the Company and the Roman Catholics (but apparently just before the news of the outbreak reached the coast) Mr. Portal wrote from Zanzibar to the Foreign Office as follows : " As Captain Lugard, and the English officers of the Company serving under him, thus appear to be attacked with equal violence by the leaders of each of the opposing factions in Uganda, the probability is that these officers are honestly striving to steer a middle course, and to favour neither party more than the other " (Africa, No. 1 (1893), p. 2). We must assume that when Mr. Portal wrote this he was unaware that Captain Lugard had received instructions to consolidate the Pro- testant party, and that he had already done so with the help of a Maxim gun and rifles.

he had induced Mwanga to sign the treaty. His march was through Unyoro and Toru, and between Lakes Albert and Albert Edward he constructed several military forts. Captain Lugard apparently laid claim to all the country through which he marched. This is shown by his curious treatment of the Manyuema tribe. North-east of Lake Albert Edward is a valuable salt lake. Captain Lugard chose to build a fort and leave a garrison at this point. He then informed the tribes in the neighbourhood that "they were welcome to go to the Salt Lake for salt, and that they would get a liberal supply from us : but that as we had to pay the garrison to protect it, and were even now engaged in maintaining it against the Manyuema, those who required salt must bring goods to barter for it. . . . We did not wish the Salt Lake to be closed to the surrounding tribes, but, on the contrary, to be more accessible than it had ever been before." [1] Captain Lugard claimed for the Company not only a monopoly of the salt, but also of all the ivory in this district. The argument is a strange one, particularly in the mouth of a man who had come to the country seeking " no monopoly of trade." He built a fort to protect the salt and ivory from the native tribes, and then argued that the presence of the fort was a reason for his claiming a monopoly of the salt and ivory. The Manyuema, however, claimed that the " ivory of the country was theirs and not ours," [2] and they objected strongly to being suddenly deprived of their right to take salt from the salt lake. In these circumstances the Manyuema threatened hostilities, and the instructions which Captain Lugard left with his lieutenant at the fort upon the salt lake are instructive. " If the Manyuema attack unprovokedly," he wrote, " you will of course do your best to give them a thorough lesson. . . . The paramount point for them to understand is, that they must not raid east of the Semliki, and that the ivory of this country is the property of the Company. Regarding the ivory from the far side of the Semliki [3] we have no claim on it whatever, but should not refuse to buy it if brought in for sale. They are, moreover, quite welcome to get salt from the lake provided they bring something in exchange. They must not come down in large armed parties to get it or trade. If more than eight guns come, they will be regarded as a war-party and fired on. . . ."

North of the salt lake, Captain Lugard crossed the Semliki

---

[1] Lugard, vol. ii. p. 271.   [2] *Ibid.*
[3] *I.e.* in the territory of the Belgian Congo. But the fact was that Captain Lugard had no real knowledge as to whether he had any right at all in any of this district, for he says in his instructions to his lieutenant : " Moreover, it is not certain how far these territories are in the Company's dominions, and though I should be glad to protect the natives up to the east of the Semliki, you must bear in mind that the *protection of the Salt Lake and our garrison there is the sole reason for which I have despatched this expedition.*"

River and entered the territory of the Congo Free State. At Kavalli's, due west of Lake Albert, he got into contact with a large body of Sudanese troops who had formed part of Emin Pasha's forces, but had found a free life in Central Africa so much to their liking that they had not followed their commander when he returned with Stanley to civilization. They now agreed to join Captain Lugard. According to Mr. McDermott, they consisted of "nearly 1000 soldiers armed with Remington rifles" and "many thousand followers, women and children." [1] Having obtained this very important addition to his armed forces, Captain Lugard made his way back to Uganda and its capital, Mengo.

Captain Lugard reached Mengo on December 31, 1891. The events which followed and the rapidity with which the crisis was precipitated are remarkable. On December 25, as he was approaching Mengo, he was met by his mails. Among his letters he found a despatch from the Directors ordering him immediately to evacuate Uganda, as the Company had decided to withdraw to the coast. The reason given was that the Company could no longer "keep up the expense of Uganda." The Company's policy behind these orders will be considered later; here I am only concerned with their servant, Captain Lugard. The prescience of their servant was almost uncanny, in view of the fact that the Directors were very soon to cancel their orders. For although Captain Lugard had been wandering for a year in Central Africa, completely cut off from all communication with his employers and ignorant of all events in the Company's office and the Foreign Office in London, as soon as he received these direct orders for the immediate evacuation of Uganda, he decided not to obey them. He not only did not obey them, but he "never breathed a word about them" to any other person except Captain Williams. They decided that one of them should stay in Uganda and that the other should go immediately to England "to make a buzz" [2] there against the policy of evacuation. Luckily the Directors themselves had already succeeded in making "a buzz" in London against their own policy, and on January 7, 1892, Captain Lugard received instructions reversing his previous orders.

Captain Lugard's reason for disobeying and suppressing the order to evacuate was that, if the Company withdrew, "the present state of peace" in Uganda would give place to anarchy and civil war. Seventeen days after he received orders to remain, Uganda was in a state of anarchy and civil war. The causes of the outbreak, as given by the Company and its agents, are extraordinary. They maintained that the war was due to an unprovoked attack of the king and the Roman Catholic or "French party," supported by the Roman Catholic French missionaries, upon the Protestant or

---

[1] McDermott, *op. cit.* p. 162. [2] Lugard, vol. ii. p. 293.

"English" faction, and that, as the "English" were numerically the weaker, Captain Lugard supported them with his arms and men. If this account be correct, the Roman Catholics and Mwanga, who had recently joined the Roman Catholic church, behaved in a manner almost inconceivably stupid. During the absence of Captain Lugard for a year they made no attempt to attack the "English" party, although the English Company was represented in Mengo only by Captain Williams and a very small force. Then in December 1891 Captain Lugard reappears out of the wilderness at the head not only of his own troops but also of nearly 1000 Sudanese soldiers armed with modern rifles. The Roman Catholic party were convinced that Captain Lugard was carrying out his orders to "consolidate the Protestant party," and that in case of an outbreak he would—as in fact he did—turn his guns upon the king and the Catholics. At the same time, according to Captain Lugard, the Roman Catholic priests began to spread the news that the Company had decided upon a withdrawal which would have placed the country completely in the hands of the Roman Catholics. And then, so we are asked to believe, at the very moment when their enemies had been heavily reinforced, at the very moment when with a little patience, if they had waited for the Company's withdrawal,[1] the country and their enemies would have been completely in their power, the "French" faction, with the connivance of the Roman Catholic fathers, made an unprovoked and hopeless attack upon the English party.

I do not propose to go into the accusations and counter-accusations connected with the "war" which followed in Uganda.[2] The

---

[1] Captain Lugard himself says (vol. ii. p. 288) that the first result of the Company's withdrawal would have been that "The 'English' party would leave Uganda for certain. The missionaries must follow, and there is a complete annihilation of the Protestant Uganda mission." Thus at the moment when the war began, Captain Lugard himself and the Company, who wished the British to remain in Uganda, and the Protestant missionaries and the "English" party, had everything to gain from an outbreak, because it not only meant the almost certain annihilation of the Catholics and French influence, but it also made withdrawal impossible: Mwanga and the Catholics and the French priests had everything to lose, and did actually lose everything, by the outbreak. And yet, according to the Company and its agents, the Catholics provoked the war within a week or two of Captain Lugard receiving his orders to evacuate Uganda!

[2] The reader who wishes to examine these for himself is referred to the following books and documents. The case against Captain Lugard, both for his action before the outbreak and his alleged "atrocities" (e.g. the massacres of Wa-Fransa, men, women, and children, which occurred in the islands) is contained in—1. *Notes on Uganda*, published by the Catholic Union of Great Britain, 1893. 2. Despatches from the French to the British Foreign Office contained in Parliamentary Paper, Africa, No. 1 (1893). 3. *L'Ouganda et les Agissements de la Compagnie East Africa*, published by La Procure des Missions d'Afrique, Paris, 1892. 4. Darcy, *Cent Années*, p. 363. The case for Captain Lugard will be found in—1. His own book, to which we have frequently referred. 2. McDermott, *op. cit.* 3. Captain Lugard's official reports published in the following Parliamentary Papers: Africa, No. 4 (1892), and Nos. 1 and 2 (1893). This question of Captain Lugard's actions is a

relevant facts are these. Captain Lugard, on the pretext that an outbreak was imminent, issued all the rifles in his possession to the " English " party. Immediately afterwards, on January 24, fighting began between the two factions. Captain Lugard joined the Protestants against the king and the Catholics. With the help of the Maxim and the Sudanese troops the Protestants utterly defeated the Catholics, who fled with Mwanga and the French missionaries from Mengo and established themselves on the island of Bulingugwe. Captain Lugard attacked the island, opening fire upon it with the Maxim ; once more the Wa-Fransa were badly beaten, although Mwanga escaped to the island of Sesse. Eventually the Catholics were induced to submit and the king returned to Mengo on March 30. On the same date he signed a treaty with Captain Lugard, as representative of the Company, which reproduced the terms of the treaty which had been presented to him when the expedition first arrived in Uganda.

On April 5 Captain Lugard divided the country of Uganda into three divisions in which the Protestants, the Catholics, and the Muhammadans were respectively to reside. The Protestants were left with the spoils of victory. The Roman Catholics were confined to the district of Buddu ; they were left without access to the capital, and the greater part of Uganda was handed over to their enemies, for whom Captain Lugard had fought on the pretext that they were numerically the smaller party ! The justice of this division is shown by the fact that, when a year later Sir Gerald

---

remarkable example of the bias of patriotic history. Every English historian represents his actions as marked by the nobility and humanity characteristic of British officers ; practically all French historians reproduce the following account of his " campaign," which will be found in Darcy, op. cit. p. 363 : " At the head of a considerable military force, Captain Lugard, of the British East Africa Company (Ibea), penetrated as far as Mengo, the residence of King Mwanga, and forced upon him a treaty of protectorate : then turning against the Catholics, he attacked them on some futile pretext, and drove them into a big island on Lake Victoria. There around the king and the French missionaries there had gathered for refuge a considerable multitude of men, women, and children. Against this harmless and defenceless population Captain Lugard turned his guns and Maxims. He exterminated a large number, and then, continuing his work of destruction, he gave full rein to his troops and adherents, who burnt all the villages and stations of the White Fathers, their churches, and their crops. To destroy the Catholics, that was the way to ruin French influence in Uganda ! The captain knew that, and he took good care to complete his work. After his expedition, there remained nothing of the work effected with so much labour by our countrymen." The important point is, perhaps, not whether the French or the British account is correct, but rather the unanimity with which the history and historians of each country accept a contradictory version. An amusing example has occurred within the last year. In October 1918 there appeared a book by a French Professor, Raymond Ronze, called La Question d'Afrique, in which the French author, accepting the French version of the actions of Captain Lugard, wrote of " la brutale conquête" of Uganda. The Times, in reviewing the book on October 31, 1918, naïvely protests and naïvely remarks that " the parts of the book which treat of the English in Africa ought to be thoroughly revised."

Portal came to Uganda as Government Commissioner, he set aside Captain Lugard's "settlement" and gave to the Catholics, in addition to Buddu, the province of Kaima, Sesse Island, the district of Lwekula, and the Shambas of Mwanika through the province of Mugema right up to the capital, Mengo.

Peace now reigned in Uganda,, and Captain Lugard decided that he must immediately return to England. He had two reasons for his hurried departure. The first may be given in his own words : "Moreover I anticipated that the French Fathers would give a version of the causes and events of the war which would not be in accordance with the facts as I knew them. . . . It therefore behoved me to go to England to explain and defend my action, though at this time, as I have said, I had no intimation at all of the charges in reality made against me by the French Fathers." His second reason was his determination to " make a buzz " in England against the proposal that Great Britain should evacuate Uganda. He left Mengo in June and arrived in London in October. He immediately began to "make a buzz " by writing letters to *The Times*, and by conducting a campaign of public speeches before geographical societies and commercial bodies up and down the country. And " in order to have a completely free hand and not be suspected of being merely the agent of an interested Company," he resigned his connection with the British East Africa Company before he began his campaign.

Captain Lugard was eminently successful in making his "buzz " in England. If the British Empire owed to him the original acquisition of Uganda, it also owed to him and his letters and speeches its subsequent retention. In order to complete this study of economic imperialism in Uganda, it is necessary to retrace our steps and briefly to examine the policy of the Directors of the Company and the course of public opinion in London during the time when Captain Lugard was operating in Uganda itself. Before doing so, however, something must be said with regard to Captain Lugard's personal position.

The view taken in these pages of Captain Lugard's actions will have been plain to the reader. Captain Lugard invaded Uganda without any moral or legal right. He went there with the intention of acquiring for a joint-stock company a kingdom to which neither he nor the Company had any right. He was prepared from the first to attain his ends by war and bloodshed.[1]

---

[1] Captain Lugard himself (vol. ii. p. 256) explains the necessity of war and bloodshed in such cases : " The introduction of law, order, and restraint into a savage country is necessarily accompanied at times by strong measures, involving perhaps war—as in the case of Kabarega, and later in Uganda—with its attendant suffering, to many who are not the principal offenders. . . ." And he goes on to defend himself against his critics by pointing out that he killed far fewer Africans in Uganda than General Gordon killed in the Sudan.

He set out with explicit instructions and with the explicit intention to consolidate one of two rival factions in the country, and the price which that faction paid for his support was their acceptance of the economic and political sovereignty of the Company. Despite this fact, he pretended that he remained absolutely impartial between the two factions. It is almost certain that, if he had chosen to do so, he could have prevented the anarchy and bloodshed of January 1892. If Captain Williams, with his small force, could keep the peace for the twelve months during which Captain Lugard was in the interior, Captain Lugard with his Sudanese troops could have prevented an outbreak, if he had wanted to make it perfectly clear that his arms and armed men would be placed not at the disposal of one of the two factions but at the disposal of impartial law and order. But such a course of action would have defeated the object with which he came to Uganda. His object was to acquire the country for his employers, and he could only acquire it by breaking the power of the king and the Catholics, who were opposed to the Company's domination, and by supporting the Protestants, who favoured it.

But though morally and legally Captain Lugard's actions were indefensible, there can be no doubt that he acted throughout from what he considered to be the highest and purest of motives. This is a psychological point which deserves some attention from the philosophic historian of economic imperialism. Captain Lugard and the majority of the soldiers and men of action who in Africa have actually been the agents of the acquisitive policy of economic imperialism have been genuinely moved by what to them have seemed the most noble and disinterested of ideals. You cannot read Captain Lugard's book without being immediately conscious of the genuineness of this idealism. Policy and men's action, as I have frequently insisted, are determined by men's beliefs and desires. Captain Lugard and the men, like him, who carried the sovereignty and economic exploitation of the European State into Africa, were only the last link in a chain of such beliefs and desires. They were in fact the blind agents of accumulated psychological forces which began in the stock markets and factories of Britain, France, and Germany. The primary communal beliefs and desires were evil, and their results in Europe and Africa were treachery, hostility, bloodshed, misery, and exploitation. But men, and particularly Englishmen, are quite unable to act from what they see to be evil motives or for ends which they see to be evil. If Captain Lugard had for one moment been able to see that the end of his actions in Uganda was merely the economic exploitation of the people of Uganda, through the power of the British State, and for the benefit of Sir William Mackinnon and his group of " some prominent British capitalists," there can be no doubt that he would have thrown up his job immediately and returned to his regiment, which was probably still shooting the Burmese in Burma. But the primary beliefs and desires which set in motion the actions of the joint-stock company in Uganda were by no means the same as the beliefs and desires of Captain Lugard, who was the ultimate tool of its policy in Africa. Captain Lugard's motives were, as I have said, of the very highest.

How does it come about that the agent of an evil policy can be so genuinely conscious of acting from noble motives ? The reason is very obvious in the case of Captain Lugard. Two facts enabled him to reconcile his passion for noble motives with the policy and results of economic imperialism. He suffered from two of the greatest curses of mankind, muddle-headedness and sentimentality. He was muddle-headed because he never attempted to be clear as to his own beliefs and desires, and to bring them into relation with his actions. He started with a belief that it was a good thing for the world that any particular spot on it should belong to the British Empire rather than to its inhabitants or to some other European State. He argued that it was the duty of a patriotic Englishman to do everything in his power to prevent the acquisition of territory by other European States and to forward its acquisition by Britain. He never examined the foundations of this belief ; he just accepted it in the same way in which King Mwanga accepted his belief that it was for the good of the world that Uganda should be ruled by King Mwanga, even though he were a semi-savage and a sodomite. It followed for Captain Lugard that practically any action was justified, provided that it made for the extension of British rule in Africa. His actions were therefore really determined by the highest and most disinterested ideals, patriotism and the love of his country, and solicitude for the good and happiness of the Waganda.

Psychologically there is no difference between Captain Lugard and the people in past centuries who burnt and tortured men and women from the highest of religious motives. In the seventeenth and eighteenth centuries there were literally thousands of people who were convinced that the salvation of the world depended upon inducing every one to believe that bread was flesh and not that flesh was bread, and their conviction was so intense and unquestioning that they considered themselves justified in taking any steps to impose their particular brand of God and dogma upon other people. In those days mankind had reached the stage of civilization at which they perceive that it is well that a hundred shall die on the rack and at the stake, if thereby you can induce a thousand to become members of the Holy Roman Church rather than the Church of Calvin, or to call themselves Jesuits rather than Jansenists. Captain Lugard and our own generation have now reached that

higher stage in civilization at which we perceive that it is well that
a hundred Africans should die before the rifles or the Maxim guns,
if thereby we can induce a thousand to become members of the
British rather than the French Empire, and call themselves Wa-
Ingleza rather than Wa-Fransa.[1]

But the analogy goes even deeper. Readers of eighteenth-
century literature will remember the extraordinary confusion of
mind and ideas in the religious controversialists and persecutors,
and how Voltaire and the Encyclopaedists were thus enabled to
attack and destroy their dogmas by wit, ridicule, and reason.
The persecutors, with perfect sincerity and from the highest of
motives, unconsciously confused their God with their Church or
their sect, and loyalty to and love of God was transformed into
loyalty to and love of a small clique of Jesuits and the Bull
Unigenitus. The same process is observable in Captain Lugard.
All through his book he confuses Sir William Mackinnon and the
joint-stock company with the British Empire. He was actually
in the service not of the Empire, but of the Company, and he
entered Uganda not to acquire it for the British people, but for
the Imperial British East Africa Company. But he himself seems
to be quite unconscious of these facts. The Company is for him
the Empire, and the loyalty and devotion to his " country " is by
a strange confusion transferred to a commercial enterprise whose
head office was in the City of London. Thus while the real object
of his expedition was to acquire Uganda for a group of some prominent British capitalists, he can honestly conceive of himself as
a patriot crusading in Africa for his country and for civilization.

To high principles and confused thinking Captain Lugard added
a curious form of sentimentality. Its nature and its effect can
best be shown by an example. One of his companions, a Mr. de
Winton, died of illness during the expedition. Captain Lugard's
comment is as follows : " One more life given to the work England
has undertaken in Africa—one more obligation upon those who
sent us, and who cannot turn back, having put their hands to the
plough. On our countrymen the greater shame if, having claimed
from us in Central Africa so hard a duty, our work should be all
in vain, and worse than useless." The sentimentality in this
passage will be apparent to the sensitive reader : the confusion
of mind to which we have already referred is also remarkably
obvious. Nobody really sent Mr. de Winton and Captain Lugard
to Uganda except themselves and Sir William Mackinnon : certainly
" England " and the English people did not, as he implies, send
them there. Not ten persons in England, as I have shown in the
previous pages, knew that the expedition was starting at the time

---

[1] As I write this sentence, November 11, 1918, the guns round London are
proclaiming the end of the Great War.

when Captain Lugard agreed to the Company's proposal to lead it. The obligation was that of Sir William Mackinnon and the Company to "England" and Uganda, and yet by a curious mixture of muddle-headedness and sentimentality this is transformed in Captain Lugard's mind into an obligation of "England" to the grave of De Winton and to the joint-stock company. And in Mr. McDermott's book you can see this obligation of England translated into a claim on behalf of the Company for payment in hard cash from the people of England.

We may admit, therefore, that Captain Lugard acted throughout on the highest principles and from the noblest of motives. But in confused minds, high principles and noble motives are the greatest of public dangers. The misery of the world and of Africa has not been caused by men who consciously pursue evil, but by men who do evil in the pursuit of what they imagine to be good.

We must now return to the policy of the Directors in London during the time that Captain Lugard was winning Uganda for them. At the end of 1890 Sir William Mackinnon addressed a letter to Lord Salisbury containing, as Mr. McDermott says, "the first categorical assertion by the Company of its claim to receive State co-operation." [1] The co-operation which the Company asked for was that the Government should guarantee interest on the capital which it was proposed to raise for building a railway from the coast into the interior. The suggestion, Sir William Mackinnon was careful to explain, was not of course made in the financial or commercial interests of the Company : " for itself, the Company asked nothing " : [2] no, it was only asking the Government to perform its obligations in helping to suppress the slave trade. " It was not disputed that advantage would be derived by the Company from the railway in the course of time " ; but that of course was not the object of the request, and Lord Salisbury was asked to note that the advantages would " accrue to commerce generally, and only remotely to the Company." And in order to make it absolutely clear to the British public that this was another purely altruistic scheme on the part of the prominent British capitalists, and not intended to benefit the British East Africa Company, it was to be understood that that Company should not, " except through such facilities as it might be in a position to afford, take any part in the construction of the railway, or exercise any control over it." [3] The railway Company was to be " an independent Company," and if subsequently it was found that the Directors of the one were also mainly the Directors of the other, well, these kinds of coincidences are bound to occur even in the most altruistic of financial families.

Lord Salisbury naturally consulted the Treasury. Sir William

<hr />

[1] McDermott, p. 175.   [2] *Ibid.* p. 178.   [3] *Ibid.* p. 180.

Mackinnon called at the Treasury, and the advantage of having a personage like the Marquis of Lorne upon your Board of Directors was shown by the fact that Sir William, when he called upon the Treasury officials, took with him the Marquis, in his character, we must presume, of financial expert rather than of son-in-law of Queen Victoria. The Marquis and Sir William seem to have been able to satisfy the Treasury of the necessity for bringing into existence yet another patriotic and philanthropic joint-stock company, and by March 1891 Lord Salisbury was able to inform the Directors that he was ready to settle the details of a grant in aid of the railway, which was to take the form of a Government guarantee of interest on a paid-up capital of £1,250,000.

But Lord Salisbury and the British East Africa Company had to proceed very warily. There was a not inconsiderable body of opinion which would look with great suspicion upon the subsidizing or guaranteeing by Government of any imperialistic joint-stock company, however altruistic its objects might be. Moreover, in Parliament, across the path of Lord Salisbury and Sir William and their "grant in aid," lay a watchful "Her Majesty's Opposition," a Liberal Party which, as long as it is not in office, is always anxious to examine the motives of economic imperialism. It was not, therefore, surprising that "the Government eventually came to the conclusion that the success of their policy might be prejudiced by introducing a bill to authorise the guarantee, in absence of an official survey certifying the practicability of the line and supplying an estimate of its probable cost."[1] So Parliament was not told of the proposed guarantee; it was asked in the first instance "merely for a small vote to cover the cost of a preliminary survey." But even this modest proposal roused the suspicion and opposition of Mr. Gladstone and his followers, and the Government was forced to withdraw the vote, though it pledged itself to the Company to re-introduce it in the following session.

When Lord Salisbury substituted the survey vote of £20,000 for the guarantee of interest on the capital of £1,250,000, Sir William and his co-directors were singularly disappointed, considering that their Company was not to benefit by or take any part in the construction of the railway. They immediately took action which amounted to the presentation of a pistol at the head of the Government. In view of the "financial position of the Company," they decided to withdraw all their establishments from Uganda, and orders were sent to Captain Lugard for immediate withdrawal. Captain Lugard, with singular perspicacity, did nothing of the sort; he disobeyed and concealed his instructions and thereby gave time for them to be cancelled—as in fact they very soon were—and for the great "force of public opinion" once more to come into play.

[1] McDermott, op. cit. p. 190.

The process by which public opinion became articulate was very remarkable. It began once more on September 28 in *The Times* with an article of one and a half columns from an anonymous "correspondent," who seemed to voice all the opinions of the Directors, and who, according to the Secretary of the Company, was "of evidently reliable authority." This correspondent informed the British public that "the probable and almost inevitable results" of a withdrawal "would be an immediate massacre of the native converts and European missionaries. . . . Indeed the consequences likely to result from our withdrawal might well assume the proportions of a national disaster." The article proceeded to give a tremendous testimonial to the work of the Company, and to point out that Uganda was a magnificent field both for British missionaries and British trade. The correspondent drew the conclusion that, instead of the Government allowing the evacuation of Uganda by the Company, it should immediately grant the subsidy for the railway which the Directors had proposed.

Between the previous outburst of public opinion in *The Times* in the spring of 1890 and the appearance of this article in September 1891 that newspaper had been curiously silent about Uganda. The earlier outburst, it will be remembered, was the pretext of the Company's entrance into the country; the later one was directed to keeping it there. The day after the appearance of the article of September 28, 1891, a Special General Committee of the Church Missionary Society was held. The Society's Treasurer, Sir T. Fowell Buxton, who happened also to be a Director of the British East Africa Company, was naturally present. There were also present two other Directors of the Company, Sir Arnold Kemball and Mr. G. S. Mackenzie, and Sir Charles Euan-Smith, whose hand we have so often found at work at the crises of imperialism. The result of this consultation was that the religious Society gave not only its moral, but its financial support to the Company. The Committee began by sending a memorial to Lord Salisbury deprecating evacuation. A few weeks later there was "an informal meeting" between some of the Directors of the Company and "the Secretaries and a few leading members" of the Church Missionary Society's Committee. At this meeting the Directors made the following extraordinary announcement to the C.M.S. : "that the Company would countermand the order (for withdrawal) by telegram and would delay the evacuation for twelve months, if £40,000, for a considerable part of which a few individual Directors would be responsible, could be guaranteed in the course of about a week." [1] Within a week the Society raised £11,000, and the order for evacuation was countermanded.

This incident is a wonderful example of the manufacture of

---

[1] Church Missionary Society, *Annual Report*, 1891–92.

"public opinion." Why did these prominent British capitalists go to a religious society, supported by voluntary contributions, for the paltry sum of £11,000 ? Is it conceivable for instance that Sir William Mackinnon, Chairman of the British India Steam Navigation Company, who had put £25,000 into the British East Africa Company at its birth, who together with the German bankers had helped to raise a capital of 15,000,000 francs for the Compagnie du Chemin de Fer in the Congo State, who, only six months before, had with Sir John Kirk, a co-director of the British East Africa Company, become a director of another Congo Company, the Compagnie du Katanga, with a capital of 3,000,000 francs—is it conceivable that this prominent British African international capitalist could not, if he had desired to save Uganda for the Empire, have put his hand in his pocket and found the necessary £11,000 there ? The answer of course is that public opinion would not have been formed or influenced if Sir William and his co-directors, or even Sir Charles Euan-Smith, had put an additional £11,000 into the British Company. But when all the good people who support the propagation of the Protestant religion in Africa showed their eagerness for also supporting the British East Africa Company there, the Directors were provided with a very effective stick to hold over the heads of any Government which might be disposed to allow them to evacuate Uganda.

It is untrue of course that, as so many French writers believe, the Church Missionary Society consciously acted as the agents of an Imperialist policy. The charges against English missionaries of this kind by Frenchmen have just as little truth in them as similar charges made by Englishmen against French missionaries. The religious Society and its supporters were undoubtedly thinking primarily of religion, and they were honestly convinced that the true faith could not be maintained in Uganda unless the Company's flag waved over the palace of King Mwanga. That does not alter the fact that they were in this matter unconsciously made the stalking-horse of economic imperialism. They provided £11,000, and promptly on November 2 a telegram was despatched to East Africa ordering Lugard to maintain his position, and hoping that he " will be able to secure large contributions from Mwanga." At the same time Lord Salisbury was informed by the Company that in consequence of the subscription [1] of these funds, it had been

---

[1] There seems to be a curious discrepancy with regard to the actual subscriptions. The C.M.S. were told by the Directors that the sum required to delay the evacuation for twelve months was £40,000, and that " a few individual Directors would be responsible" for " a considerable part" of this sum. The C.M.S. raised £11,000 in a week, and their subscription was eventually raised to £16,000. On November 2 the Directors telegraphed to Lugard to get a large contribution out of King Mwanga. On November 11 they informed Lord Salisbury that £25,000 out of the required £40,000 had been subscribed. On November 11, therefore, the part subscribed by the Directors could not have exceeded £9000. (Yet Captain

decided to prolong the occupation of Uganda until December 31, 1892.

Lord Salisbury expressed his satisfaction at hearing of the liberal contributions that had been made "for this important object." The hope of the Company that King Mwanga would make a large monetary contribution to the fund for maintaining the Company in his kingdom was not realized. In a few months Captain Lugard and the king were, as we have seen, fighting one another for the possession of Uganda. That fighting made a considerable difference in the general situation, and it was obviously very difficult after it to withdraw from the country. Nevertheless in May 1892 the Directors once more notified the Foreign Office that they were taking steps to evacuate Uganda at the end of the year. There followed an amusing little imperialist comedy. A Liberal Government was now in power, and the Liberal Party, when it had been in opposition, had attacked Lord Salisbury for his and the Company's imperialist policy in Uganda. Lord Rosebery, who was now at the Foreign Office, was in something of a difficulty : he was too good an imperialist to abandon Uganda, and yet he could hardly make his party take an immediate right-about-turn and annex the country out of hand. But the Foreign Office was equal to finding a way out of this difficulty. Lord Rosebery informed Sir William Mackinnon that he adhered "to the acceptance . . . of the principle of evacuation." But his representative in Zanzibar informed him that there were dangers which might arise "from immediate evacuation at the appointed time." Her Majesty's Government had therefore decided "to assist the Company by pecuniary contribution towards the prolongation of the occupation for three months," i.e. up to March 31, 1893. "It was, however, to be distinctly understood" that this financial help was given "solely with a view to facilitate the safe evacuation by the Company, which is rendered necessary by their financial position." [1]

This decision of the Government to postpone evacuation for three months was communicated to the Company on the last day of September 1892. In the beginning of October Captain Lugard arrived in England, and his arrival, as the Church Missionary Society's *Annual Report* remarks, was "exceedingly opportune." The postponement and his arrival allowed the voice of public opinion, starting once more in the columns of *The Times*, to assert itself. In other words, a tremendous campaign against evacuation

---

Lugard, vol. ii. p. 602, says that Sir William Mackinnon himself subscribed £10,000). Is this £9000 the part for which the Directors had undertaken responsibility, and if so, was it accurate to talk of £9000 as a considerable part of £40,000 ?

[1] See McDermott, *op. cit.* Appendix xi. p. 536.

was engineered in the country. Captain Lugard addressed his geographical and commercial bodies. In *The Times* leading articles and letters daily put forward pleas and arguments calculated to appeal to the hearts or the pockets of all the different classes in the country. Leading articles asked our imperialists to think of " the maintenance of our reputation in the eyes of the world," and our humanitarians not to " desert the natives," or to allow them " to fall under their own massacres, superstitions, etc." " Such a withdrawal would be nothing short of a national calamity." Philanthropists must remember that Uganda was necessary to the British Empire if the slave-trade was to be destroyed ; the City of London was asked to think of the trade of Central Africa, and even the British working-man was not forgotten, for he was assured that " we are not less bound in policy, since our hopes of new markets for our wares and employment for our workmen depend upon holding our ground in Uganda." [1] All blame was naturally placed upon the shoulders of the Liberal Government, and all praise showered upon the Company, which " must be identified for all practical purposes with national policy." Having thus identified Sir William Mackinnon with national policy, *The Times* was able logically to put forward and support the proposal which was in fact the main object of Captain Lugard's and the Company's campaign. " What the British East Africa Company needs to keep it going," said *The Times*, " is the construction of a railway from Mombasa to the shores of the Victoria Nyanza. . . . Capital would be forthcoming in abundance were the Government merely to guarantee a moderate dividend. . . . The Government guarantee would not only bring out capital to the railway ; but by convincing people that the Company must and will be supported, it would attract capital for the development of the interior." Captain Lugard's missionary work among " commercial bodies," aided by the voice of public opinion in *The Times*, was not without effect, and " the Chambers of Commerce of the United Kingdom . . . unanimously urged the retention of East Africa on commercial grounds." [2] At Folkestone the Archbishop of Canterbury appealed to the Church Congress

---

[1] See the leading articles especially of September 28, September 30, and October 21, 1892. Even in the heat of this campaign some people and papers saw the Company's action in a less rosy light. The *Economist* on October 8, 1892, criticized the Company for its sudden announcement of financial incapacity and of its intention to withdraw from Uganda : " With a cold self-interestedness, which it is not easy to characterize except by words like impudence . . . the Company claim the right, not of resigning their charter . . . but of picking and choosing among the territories committed to their care." The Company is to govern the productive lands, the Government to govern and accept responsibility for the jungle and desert lands. This paper goes on to speak of the callousness of the Company towards its natives in abandoning them to anarchy, and its cunning towards the Government which almost amounts to fraud.

[2] Lugard, *op. cit.* vol. i. p. 378.

"for emphatic prayer that, whatever the commercial difficulties, our country's course might be so shaped that Christian converts should not be abandoned to imminent destruction." [1]

The campaign at first had disappointing results. *The Times*, on October 21, had to admit that public opinion seemed very apathetic, and urged that it must be roused " to a more energetic survey of the case " by every possible means. It started on this good work in the same article by raising the bogey of French interference in Uganda, which, it said, was an imminent danger. But what probably turned the scale was the Archbishop's appeal " for emphatic prayer." It " met with a unanimous and hearty expression of interest. Diocesan conferences throughout the land, and meetings of friends of the S.P.G. and Universities' Mission, as well as the C.M.S., sent up to the Government memorials and resolutions. The Moderators and other dignitaries of the Church of Scotland, the Free Church, and the United Presbyterians sent a memorial urging that ' the advent of the British Government to Uganda, directly or by chartered company, has necessarily created an Imperial responsibility, and has so affected the position of the numerous native converts and of the missionaries themselves, as, in our opinion, to forbid withdrawal.' " [1] Captain Lugard, *The Times*, and all the Churches, when combined, were too much for public opinion. It had been very apathetic on October 21, but in December Mr. Bosworth Smith could write to *The Times* that " the country has made up its mind." The national calamity had been averted ; our good faith with the natives was to be maintained ; our pledge to King Mwanga to take his kingdom from him was not to be broken ; Uganda was to remain part of the British Empire. The workmen of Manchester and Birmingham breathed again at the knowledge that the retention of Uganda was to keep them in regular employment.

The exact process by which this result was obtained was simple and interesting. In the middle of December the Foreign Office approached Sir William Mackinnon " with regard to a continued occupation by the Company after the date fixed for withdrawal (March 31,1893)." Sir William consulted his Directors, and then proposed to Lord Rosebery that the Government should grant the Company £50,000 a year for three years, and that in exchange for this subsidy, which would cover the whole expense of administration, the Company would be good enough to retain Uganda. [2] This proposal was the logical conclusion of Captain Lugard's campaign and of the whole attitude of the Directors, who had always held that the Company could justly claim the same kind of support from the Foreign Office as the Governments of other countries gave to

[1] Church Missionary Society, *Annual Report*, 1892–93.
[2] McDermott, *op. cit.* pp. 279-282.

their subsidized imperialist companies.[1] But the proposal was too much even for the Liberal Imperialist Lord Rosebery : " he regarded it as putting an end ' to his project,' as he was convinced the ' Government will not, and indeed, should not agree to any such terms.' " Sir William then had some interviews with Lord Rosebery's private secretary, and eventually agreed to " place himself unreservedly in the hands of the Government." [2]

But on November 23 the Government suddenly " decided to send an independent Commissioner of our own, and not to interfere with the evacuation by the Company." I have already had to refer to Sir Gerald Portal's Commission of Enquiry in Uganda. Sir Gerald arrived in Mengo on March 17, 1893, and left on May 30. During his stay in the capital on April 1 the Company carried out its evacuation ; the Union Jack was hoisted, and the Company's rule in Uganda came to an end. But the Commissioner's Report (which was not published until after his death twelve months later) would in any case have made a continuance of the administration by the Company impossible. It contained severe criticism of the Company's methods. The Company had obtained access to these territories by signing treaties with native rulers, in which it " promised protection in return for certain commercial advantages." It had now withdrawn from these territories " without notifying to kings or chiefs of these countries any denunciation of the treaties made with them, . . . and without giving to Signatories of these treaties any warning of their approaching retreat." It had introduced into Uganda a large number of Sudanese soldiers, and on its withdrawal it had left them in the country without making any provision for their control. The Report speaks of " the hatred and terror inspired by these Sudanese ex-soldiers, and the deeds of cruelty practised upon native men and women by that portion of them who were left by the Company, unpaid and uncontrolled, on the western frontier of Uganda." The Report draws attention to the " great neglect, up to the present, of the road between Uganda and the east coast, and the failure of the Imperial British East Africa Company to effect any improvement in the means of transport of goods." Sir Gerald Portal summed up as follows: " Without wishing to criticise, and still less to blame, the Company's methods of government, the history of British East Africa for the last five years, and its present condition show us clearly that the experiment of combining administration and trade in the same hands has proved a failure, so far as this part of Africa is concerned ; and that the sooner this system is discontinued the better it will be for native races, for British commerce, for Zanzibar, and, as I believe, for the Company itself."

[1] Captain Lugard's arguments in favour of the government of Uganda by a subsidized private Company will be found in his second volume, pp. 604-611.
[2] McDermott, p. 283.

In June 1894 the decision of the Government was at last made known. It followed the lines of Sir Gerald Portal's recommendations. Uganda was to be declared a British Protectorate, and since, if the British Government was to undertake responsibility for administration in the interior, it was essential that it should also control the coast and intervening territory, it was necessary to oust the Company from the districts which were covered by the concession from the Sultan of Zanzibar. Lord Kimberley thought that this would raise " a question by no means without difficulty." He was right. The Government now proposed to buy up the rights of the Company both in the territories covered by the Sultan's concession and those in the interior. Each side accused the other of trying to make too good a bargain. The Company seems to have demanded £300,000 ; the Government considered the demand exorbitant, and spoke of cancelling the Company's Charter if a settlement could not be arrived at. Then once more *The Times* came to the support of the Company. " What an edifying spectacle for the world," it exclaimed, " an Imperial Government forcing a sale and buying in extensions of Empire at a knock-out where it is the sole bidder." It talked of "this miserable evasion of national duties and responsibilities "—the national duty being apparently to pay promptly the demand of the patriotic and prominent capitalists, who had made a rather bad speculation in economic imperialism. " This unmistakable expression of opinion," says Mr. McDermott, " produced an immediate effect." The Government made an offer which amounted to £200,000 for all the rights of the Company. But the haggling was not over. The Company endeavoured to screw another £50,000 out of the British public for " its private assets " : the Government resisted. *The Times* once more cracked its whip over the head of the Liberal Government. " The actual difference," it wrote, " between the two parties to the negotiation, although not inconsiderable from the point of view of shareholders trying to save what they can out of the wreck of their property, is absolutely paltry from that of a Government dealing not merely with commercial values, but with moral claims which honour forbids us to treat in the spirit of the huckster." And the vicious circle of economic imperialism is shown by the fact that it was *The Times* which had been the voice of public opinion instigating an advance to Uganda, which the Company had decided upon several months before, and it was *The Times* which now called upon the Government to pay up the £50,000 demanded by the Company, because it had acquired Uganda " on the instigation of the Press and the official representatives of the country."

The Times and the Company had their way. The British public met those " moral claims which honour forbids us to treat in the spirit of the huckster " ; the additional £50,000 was paid over to the Imperial British East Africa Company. Even then the patriotic shareholders were dissatisfied : they accepted the Government's offer, but passed a resolution that "having regard to the fact that the offer just accepted confessedly takes no account of the Company's outlay in acquiring and holding Uganda, the shareholders beg that the Directors will continue to urge that, in all the circumstances attending the effective occupation of Uganda in the national interest, and the special reasons for withdrawal, there exists a strong moral claim for compensation."

But the end of the Company and its work "in the national interest" had come. The Government refused to pay more than the £250,000. The Charter and the Concession were surrendered, and British East Africa and Uganda passed into the British Empire as Protectorates. The announcement of these Protectorates, said the Church Missionary Society's *Report*, "must be regarded as an answer to the Church's prayer."

CHAPTER VII

THE BELGIAN CONGO

In Chapter II. of this part of my book we entered upon a detailed investigation of the policy of European States and the effects of that policy in various geographical divisions of Africa. We have now accomplished at least a portion of this task in two divisions, Mediterranean and East Africa. I must confess that, when I started upon Part II., I had the intention of making the investigation complete, and of writing a complete history of policy, during the years 1880–1914, in the whole of the Continent. But it soon became clear that this would require not one, but three or four volumes. Such a history of imperialism in Africa would, I believe, be of some value; but for the purposes which I explained in Part I. the data already obtained are probably sufficient. I do not propose therefore to pursue the investigation into the divisions of South Africa and West Africa. It is true that conditions determining policy in those divisions have in some important respects differed from those which determined policy in the north and the east; but the differences are not vital; they would not invalidate conclusions drawn from the policy of the four Great Powers, Germany, Britain, France, and Italy, all of which we have been able to study in Mediterranean, Ethiopian, and Eastern Africa.

But there are two reasons which compel us to make an exception of one place on the West Coast, and to examine briefly the policy of European States which produced the Congo Free State. In the first place there is a very wide misunderstanding of the facts, and secondly, this misunderstanding has a most important bearing upon the problem of Africa, and proposals for its solution, which are being considered to-day.

As we shall see in the final chapter, many people who have studied this problem, and have become profoundly convinced of the evil effects of economic imperialism both upon Europe and Africa, look for the remedy in the substitution of some kind of international government, control, or trusteeship, for national imperialism and absolute individual sovereignty. These proposals

303

have been continually met by the objection that international government and the international solution have already been tried in the Belgian Congo, and that they proved a far worse failure than national imperialism. The statement upon which this argument relies—namely, that international government was tried in the Congo—has no foundation in fact; it is indeed in direct contradiction with the facts; but how widely the delusion is held is shown by a statement of so eminent and experienced an authority as Sir Harry Johnston (in the *Cambridge Magazine*, November 16, 1918): "So far as International Government is concerned, the ideal of the Labour Party for Tropical Africa, I condemn it uncompromisingly. We have seen what it was in the Khedival rule over the Sudan and the twenty-five years of the Independent State of the Congo."

I have given facts in another book, *The Future of Constantinople*, to show that international government was never really given a trial in Khedival Egypt, but there is at least some excuse for confusing the *condominium*, established in Egypt, with the system of international control discussed in the Labour Party's Memorandum on War Aims. There is no excuse at all for confusing the system established on the Congo with international government. No kind of international government or control was ever set up on the Congo, and the twenty-five years of the Independent State were years of the most unmitigated and ruthless economic imperialism and individual sovereignty which even Africa has ever known.

I shall prove this statement briefly, but conclusively. Before doing so, it is necessary to give the reader a word of warning and explanation. No one can touch the Congo question, even to-day, without finding that it is still warm with the heat of controversial passions. All kinds of extraneous prejudices have clustered about it, and around those who, in this country, performed an immense service to Europe and Africa by insisting upon an investigation into the facts. If I do not refer to, or use the books or evidence of, for instance, Mr. E. D. Morel, it is not that I do not recognize their value as evidence; it is simply that I wish to keep the whole investigation as far removed as possible from the atmosphere of temporary passion and prejudice. For the facts, which I shall place before the reader, I shall rely almost entirely upon official documents and treaties, and upon the evidence of Belgian writers.[1] The reader who wishes to study the evidence for himself will not have to go through any laborious course of reading: if he will study the "General Act of the Conference of Berlin," signed on February 26, 1885 (often called the "Berlin Act" or the "Congo Act"), and the

---

[1] After this chapter was in proof, *The Belgian Congo and the Berlin Act*, by Professor A. B. Keith, was published. It confirms the main contentions in this chapter.

various Declarations and Conventions in which the different states recognized the flag of the International Association of the Congo " as the flag of a friendly Government," and if he will read two books, *Droit et Administration de l'État Independant du Congo* by F. Cattier and *La Belgique et le Congo* by Emile Vandervelde, he will find himself in possession of all the relevant facts. In this chapter I shall only give those facts which bear upon the subject of economic imperialism and international government.

I have already given in the early chapters of this book some account of the events and policy which led to the creation of the Independent State of the Congo. King Leopold II. of Belgium first publicly showed his interest in Africa in 1876 when he founded The International African Association (L'Association international africaine) after the conference of explorers and geographers held at Brussels on September 12 of that year. The full title of this Association was " The International Association for the Exploration and Civilization of Central Africa " (L'Association internationale pour l'exploration et la civilisation de l'Afrique centrale). It was, in fact, an international scientific and philanthropic society of a well-known type. It proposed to create National Committees in the various countries, and the work of these Committees was to be directed and co-ordinated by a central Commission internationale in Brussels. During 1876 and 1877 National Committees were established in Belgium, Germany, Austria, Spain, Russia, Portugal, Switzerland, Holland, France, Italy, the United States, and Hungary : in fact Great Britain was almost the only country which did not establish a Committee (see Cattier, *op. cit.* p. 12). The Belgian Committee and some of the other National Committees carried out some explorations in Africa, principally on the east coast, between 1876 and 1879 : the return of Stanley from the Congo in 1878, as I have previously explained, gave a new direction and impulse to King Leopold's schemes. Stanley came to Brussels, a new Conference was held, the Comité d'Études du Haut-Congo was formed, and Stanley immediately began to make secret preparations for a new expedition to the Congo in the service of the Comité. It is important to note that, as M. Cattier points out (p. 16), although the Association and the Comité were ostensibly two distinct organizations, this was not really the case ; King Leopold and Colonel Strauch were the directing spirits in both.

In 1882, while Stanley was in Africa, the Comité was changed into " L'Association internationale du Congo." Stanley pursued his " explorations " on the Congo, and they resulted in the signature of the treaties in which the native chiefs and rulers handed over their sovereign rights to " L'Association internationale." Meanwhile there took place in Europe those negotiations between Portugal and Britain, and later France and Germany, described

in Part I. of this book, which led to the Berlin Conference, the
" Berlin Act," and the recognition of the Independent State of the
Congo. Those who, like Sir Harry Johnston, maintain that the
Belgian Congo was an experiment in International Government,
must mean that the Berlin Act and Conference in creating the
Independent State set up some form of international control or
government in the Congo. That is precisely what I deny : the
Berlin Conference created a new and independent State of the
Congo, but it was not subject to international control ; it was an
absolutely independent, sovereign State under the autocratic
Government of King Leopold who, in using his autocratic powers,
pursued the purest policy of economic imperialism.

Sir Harry Johnston and most of the world have been misled
because the word " international " occurs in the title of Leopold's
two Associations, the International African Association and the
International Association of the Congo. The International
African Association, when it was founded in 1876, was a
genuinely international and scientific organization. It was
controlled, at least nominally, by an international Committee,
although from the first all real power was in the hands of the King.
It is impossible to be certain as to the actual motives and intentions
of Leopold at this early date. M. Cattier and M. Vandervelde
both hold that in the days of the International African Association
his motives were genuinely scientific and philanthropic. There
is some reason to think that this view is correct, but it is quite
certain that at some moment the motives and intentions changed
completely and became economic and imperialist. M. Cattier, who
is by no means a hostile witness, dates the change from the return
of Stanley and the creation of the Comité d'Études. "It was
no longer now a question," he writes, " of carrying out humanitarian
and scientific plans. The object was narrowed and defined : the
desire was to share in the riches of the Congo basin and to convert
it into a commercial outlet."

After 1879 the whole enterprise ceased to be scientific, philanthropic, or international. It became a private venture of Leopold
with the object of obtaining African territory for economic exploitation. It is true that for a few years Leopold continued to maintain
a semblance of internationalism by employing Americans and
Englishmen, like Stanley and Sir F. de Winton, in responsible
posts ; but the nature of this internationalism is shown by the
circumstances under which the King in 1882 transformed the
Comité d'Études du Haut-Congo into the International Association
of the Congo. When, in 1879, the Comité was created, no attempt
was made to disguise its uninternational character. In 1882 the
Comité suddenly changed its name to that of " The International
Association of the Congo." " The reasons," says M. Cattier,

"which determined this change of name and the circumstances under which it was made are not fully known. One may, however, guess what they were. The King at this moment (1882) was well aware that his work could not be strong and lasting unless he obtained the recognition of it as a body corporate within the international community, *i.e.* as a State. It was useful from this point of view to introduce the word 'international' in the title of the Committee, and once more to put forward that pretence of internationalism with which the Association had already been surrounded."

Between 1882 and 1884 this "International Association" acquired in the Congo basin vast stretches of territory by means of "treaties" in exactly the same way and by the same methods as Britain, France, Germany, and their groups of financiers had employed for the founding of empires in other parts of Africa. Meanwhile in Europe Leopold, by adroit negotiations, obtained the consent of Bismarck and the French Government to his plan for converting these acquisitions into an "Independent State." Great Britain also agreed, with considerable reluctance, and the Conference of Berlin was summoned.

The Independent State of the Congo was founded at, but not by, the Conference of Berlin. It is important that the reader should understand this and what it means. The Conference was concerned with producing an International Convention, the "Berlin Act," "relative," to quote its preamble, "to the Development of Trade and Civilization in Africa; the free Navigation of the Rivers Congo, Niger, etc.; the suppression of the Slave Trade by Sea and Land; the occupation of Territory on the African Coasts, etc." This Treaty does not even mention either the International Association or the Independent State. The Independent State of the Congo was, in fact, founded by a number of International Conventions, most of which were signed during the Conference, between the various Governments and the International Association of the Congo. The formal recognition of its existence came when, at the last sitting of the Conference, permission was given to the representatives of the Association to sign the Final Act, as representatives of an independent State.

The International Association did not take the name of "The Independent State of the Congo" until some months after the Berlin Conference. Now, if that State was in any way subject to international control or government, such control or government must have been established either in the Conventions recognizing its existence, or in the Berlin Act, or in the actual Constitution of the State. I propose to examine each of these separately.

First, as to the Conventions; they were made with the various Powers separately, but they are all substantially the same. Let us take as an example the "Declarations exchanged between the Government of Her Britannic Majesty and the International Association of the Congo, Berlin, December 16, 1884." This instrument consists of seven short clauses. Clause I. declares that certain territories have been added to the International Association by "treaties with the legitimate Sovereigns in the basins of the Congo and of the Niadi-Kwilu." Clause II. declares that the administration "is vested in the Association"; Clause III. that the Association has adopted a flag, "a blue flag with a golden star in the centre"; Clause IV. relates to Customs duties; Clause V. to the rights of foreigners to religious liberty, etc.; Clause VI. to the slave-trade; and in the last Clause the British Government declares that it will "recognize the flag of the Association and of the Free States under its administration as the flag of a friendly Government." In this document, as the reader will observe, there is not one word about any kind of international government or control. On the contrary, the British Government by recognizing the flag of the Association as that of a friendly Government declared its intention of treating the Association as an independent, sovereign State. When the Association became The Independent State of the Congo, it was, so far as Britain and the other Powers which signed similar Conventions were concerned, in the position of an independent, sovereign, and national State.

The Berlin Act, too, established no kind of international control or government over the Belgian Congo. As I have said, this Convention does not even mention the Association or the Independent State. It merely defines certain regulations with regard to freedom of trade and navigation, the slave-trade, neutrality, and international relations, which the Signatory Powers agreed to apply to their possessions lying within certain boundaries in tropical Africa. This Act was signed and ratified by Austria-Hungary, Belgium, Denmark, Spain, France, Great Britain, Italy, Holland, Portugal, Russia, Norway and Sweden, and Turkey; and the Signatory Powers gave permission to the International Association to adhere to and sign its provisions. It follows that if this Act established any form of international control in the Belgian Congo, it also established it in the African possessions of the other Signatory States. All the provisions of the Berlin Act which applied to the Belgian Congo also applied to the British Nigeria, the German Cameroon, and the French Congo; yet neither Sir Harry Johnston nor any one else has ever suggested that International Government, "the ideal of the Labour Party for Tropical Africa," was established or tried in those colonies of the Great Powers. The fact really is that the Berlin Act was a failure very largely because it did not establish any kind of international control or government. It bound the Signatory Powers, and among them the Independent

State of the Congo, to undertake certain uniform obligations with regard to trade and administration in their African possessions; but it provided no kind of international control or organization for supervising the execution of the agreement or for seeing that the obligations were fulfilled. And so it came about that, when King Leopold was breaking both in spirit and letter the terms of his obligations, it was found that there was no method of controlling him internationally; he was the sovereign of an independent State, and he could defy the rest of the world to interfere on the Congo, precisely because there was no international control or government in Africa.

Lastly, we must examine the Constitution of this Independent State of the Congo. The Constitution is set out and analysed at great length, and with considerable ability, in M. Cattier's book to which I have already referred. M. Cattier naturally deals separately with the legislative, the executive, and the judicial powers exercised in the State. If there was any international control in this State, it would necessarily appear as a limitation upon the exercise of one or other of these powers. The Sovereign of the Independent State was King Leopold. No more autocratic Sovereign has ever existed in the world. Constitutionally the legislative, executive, and judicial powers were concentrated in his hands, and there was no limitation of any kind upon his exercise of them. The following facts will make this clear.

The legislative power was exercised by decrees. The power of issuing decrees was entirely in Leopold's hands. The laws for the whole of the Belgian Congo were made by the mere fact that Leopold signed a document beginning with the words: " We have decreed and decree that . . . " It was not even necessary that these laws or decrees should be published. The Government, i.e. Leopold, only published in the *Bulletin officiel* those decrees which it considered it to be in the public interest to publish (see Cattier, p. 185). Some of the most important decrees dealing with the rights of the natives were never published at all (see Cattier, p. 295, and Vandervelde, p. 55). Thus in this extraordinary State and Constitution not only was the power of making laws concentrated in the hands of a single man, but his subjects had no means of finding out what the laws were except through the actions of administrative officers. For instance, the decree of December 5, 1892, under which, as M. Vandervelde points out (p. 55), the Administration exacted forced labour from the natives and delegated to concessionary capitalist companies the right to enforce that labour, was never published. It was simply communicated, in the form of secret instructions, to Leopold's executive officers in Africa. It remained in force for ten years.

With regard to the legislative power only two other facts need be considered.   A limited power of making regulations or ordinances was given to the Governor-General, the chief executive officer in Africa.   This officer was appointed and dismissed by Leopold. He had the power of making "ordinances," but these ordinances, in order to become law, had to receive the approval of Leopold in the form of a decree.   As a matter of fact the Central Government of Leopold at Brussels exercised a constant control over the acts of the Governor in Africa.   Secondly, by a decree of April 16, 1889, Leopold created a *Conseil supérieur* sitting at Brussels.   The Council was, however, a mere figurehead.   Its members were appointed by the King, and its duty was merely to give advice when it was asked for.   It had no real power.

The executive and administrative functions of the Government were exercised by officers over whose appointment and dismissal Leopold always retained and exercised control.   The Secretary of State, the Governor-General, the District Commissioners, even many of the subordinates to the District Commissioners, were appointed from Brussels.   With regard to administration, says M. Cattier, " once more the complete centralization of the Government of the State is shown.   The will of the Sovereign finds no legislative or administrative obstruction; the Secretary of State under the King is all-powerful, and the Governor-General, while remaining in the most complete dependence on the Sovereign and the Secretary of State, exercises the powers of an autocrat in local administration."

As for the judicial powers, there was only one permanent Court of first instance in Africa, with its seat at Boma.   The judges were appointed and dismissed by decree of the King.   There was also an Appeal Court at Boma, of which the judges were appointed and dismissed in the same way.   Finally the *Conseil supérieur* had the power of sitting either as a *Cour de Cassation* or as a *Cour d'Appel.*   Thus the judiciary was appointed and dismissed by, and entirely subordinated to, King Leopold.

Such was the Constitution of the Independent State of the Congo.   There was no international and no constitutional check upon the absolute and autocratic powers of the Sovereign, King Leopold.   In exercising those powers, the King, with amazing persistence, ability, and ruthlessness, pursued a policy of economic imperialism.   M. Vandervelde seems to believe that for the first six years of the State's existence Leopold complied with his obligations and was still influenced by humanitarian motives, and that only in 1891 his policy changed to one of exploitation.   There is something to be said for this view.   But at any rate after 1891 the King's policy was to use his power and powers in Africa in his own economic interests and against the economic interests of other nations, while he subjected his African subjects to the most ruthless system of exploitation which even Africa has known.

Into the details of that system, and the incredible brutality with which it was applied, I do not propose to enter. They are on record and can be studied in British Blue Books and in such works as that of M. Vandervelde. It will be sufficient if I end this chapter by pointing out the chief methods by which this economic exploitation was achieved :

1. Leopold claimed to exercise his absolute powers of Sovereign to tax his subjects. Since he could not collect taxes in money, he argued that he would tax them either in kind or in labour.

2. He also claimed the right to demand from his native subjects the obligation of military service.

3. He claimed that the land was the property of the State and therefore of himself, the Sovereign of the State.

4. It was by exercising these " rights " and claims through decrees that he established his water-tight system of monopoly and exploitation. Thus since the land belonged to the State, the State by the decrees of 1891 and 1892 created a State monopoly of ivory and rubber, and over vast areas the natives were forbidden either to collect or to sell these products. But ivory and rubber were of no value to Leopold unless he had the labour to collect them and to bring them to the coast for transport to and sale in Europe. The labour was obtained by taxing in kind and in labour. First, under the decree of December 5, 1892, administrative officers were authorized to " take any steps judged useful or necessary for assuring the exploitation of the *Domaine privé* (Crown Land) " ; in effect this was an order to use the natives to collect rubber and ivory from the Crown land ; the collecting officers were paid a percentage upon the amount collected ; and under cover of the right to tax, a system of forced labour and slavery was established. For instance, an *impôt militaire* was levied. This tax was not fixed or constant ; the officer had the power of deciding what he would levy, of going to a native chief and informing him that he required so much in kind or so much in labour. The chief, informed of this " prestation," was obliged to produce either the men and women for labour or the tax in kind. Not only did the State, in the person of Leopold, use this forced labour for economic exploitation in the interests of the State, *i.e.* of King Leopold, but it actually delegated to private joint-stock companies the right to forced labour.

One other instance of the methods of economic imperialism in this State will suffice. King Leopold introduced conscription into his African possession. Every year he informed the Governor-General of the number of troops to be raised

by him. By the *impôt militaire* the Governor authorized
his subordinates to raise the required numbers. The native
troops, thus conscribed, were "subjected to military service
for twelve years. For twelve years they are deprived of
their liberty, removed from their surroundings, separated
from their villages " (Cattier, p. 269). The conscript passed
the first five years on active service, two years in the Reserve
of the Regular Army, and five years in the *Corps de Reserve.*
The *Corps de Reserve* was only another method of obtaining
labour for the purposes of economic exploitation. The
native, transferred to it, remained subject to military discipline
(Decree of January 18, 1898, and Cattier, p. 268); he was
paid £1 a year, and employed, under military discipline, in
cultivating Crown lands for the profit of the State and its
Sovereign, King Leopold.

The reader can now judge for himself whether the " experiment "
in the Belgian Congo was an experiment in international government or an experiment in economic imperialism.

PART III

REFLECTIONS AND CONCLUSIONS

CHAPTER I

THE EFFECTS OF ECONOMIC IMPERIALISM

THE reader was warned in the earlier chapters of this book that I proposed to plunge him into a maze of facts and details. If he has followed me with any closeness through the intervening pages, he may perhaps feel now, as we pause to take breath between Part II. and Part III., that we have often lost our sense of purpose and direction in the forest of facts through which we have wandered. I do not think that this charge can rightly be brought against us. We have been hunting together in those forests of history : we have been tracking, through the intricate policies and acts of States and individual men, certain beliefs and desires. I do not believe that I have escaped the ordinary perils and errors of those who hunt through history for cause and effect. I have often probably mistaken the trail. All kinds of preconceived ideas and prejudices—the distorting glasses through which every one is condemned to look at the world—have caused me to stray from the right path, to confuse beliefs, to mistake one desire for another, to impute wrong motives, to misrepresent acts and facts, to walk blindly through solid rocks, and to stumble over shadows. Such charges would undoubtedly be true : but I do not think that we have ever lost our sense either of purpose or of direction : we have never wandered from the trail to follow any other quarry than certain beliefs and desires shaping human policy and determining human action in Africa.

But the most difficult and dangerous part of our task remains. Hitherto we have been immersed in details and facts. We have been interpreting policies, unravelling beliefs and desires. We have some knowledge of what States and men aimed at and achieved in different parts of Africa. But now we have to enter a path which is undermined everywhere with the pitfalls of bias and prejudice. We have to look back and attempt to see, through the eye of God, this long and complicated procession of events, to see them not as isolated and particular actions and thoughts and motives, but as general movements of cause and effect.

The question which we have to answer is this : What has been the general effect of these beliefs and desires of economic imperialism which we have traced in Mediterranean Africa, in Abyssinia, in East Africa, and on the Congo ? The question and the answer will necessarily fall into two distinct parts. The beliefs and desires crystallize, as we have seen, in the form of policy, and that policy affects on the one side Europe, its States and its peoples, and on the other Africa and the Africans. I propose first to consider the political and social results of this policy upon Europe.

I. EUROPE

One has only to state the problem in this form to see how easy it is to slip at once into one of the commonest historical and political delusions. What we are considering is the effect of certain beliefs and desires, and it is natural for us to talk of their effects upon " Europe " and " Britain " and " France " and " Germany." But Europe and Britain and France and Germany—and Africa too— are only abstractions or metaphors. The beliefs and desires were within the heads and hearts not of States or " Powers," but of individual men and women, and their effects again were not upon abstractions and metaphors, but upon the lives of men and women. The anthropomorphic fallacy in religion, by which men create their God in the image of man, is well recognized : allowance is rarely made for a similar fallacy in history by which men attribute to States and nations and continents a human personality. It is impossible to exaggerate the amount of evil which has come into the world from this inveterate political confusion and super- stition, the personification of " States " and " Great Powers."

There are two senses in which the beliefs and desires of economic imperialism can reasonably be said to have affected " Europe " and the States of Europe. It is true that they have had an immense effect upon the personifications of those States in the minds of individual men. The reader will remember that we analysed Jules Ferry's desire that France should seize Tunis as " compensation " for Britain's seizure of Cyprus, and that we found that part of the compensation would undoubtedly consist in the fact that " any time in the last thirty-seven years any Frenchman might comfort and compensate himself with the reflection that if Englishmen ruled over Famagusta, Frenchmen ruled over Bizerta." We are dealing here not with States themselves, but with the images of States as they appear in the minds of men. Upon those images the beliefs and desires of economic imperialism have had an immense effect. The belief that the power of the State could be used in

Africa for the economic purposes of its citizens, and the desire so to use it, reacted naturally upon men's image of the State and their idea of its power and prestige. Those who aimed at using the State's power for their economic ends soon found that, in order to be able to use that power to its full effect, it was necessary that they, or the State, should acquire and control those territories and peoples which they wished to exploit. Hence the partition of Africa, which was the result of a determination in the great industrialized nations that the State should acquire African territory. Then by a natural association of ideas the possession and control of African territory was thought to add to the power and prestige of the State. Frenchmen talk of the conquest of Algeria or Tunis or the desert of Sahara as a glorious page in the history of the French State, and of the loss of the Nile Valley as a blow at French prestige, and Englishmen regard their African Empire as adding to the glory and the greatness of Britain.

In this sense economic imperialism has affected the European State : it has added to or dimmed its glory, greatness, and prestige. But, unless we are content politically to live in a world of unreason and superstition, it is necessary that we should be quite clear as to what this means. This glory and greatness and prestige are not objective qualities of States. A State is not a person, except metaphorically or in men's imagination. The qualities of power or wealth may attach themselves objectively to States either through the possession of armies and navies and munitions of war or through their treasuries ; but the qualities of greatness, glory, and prestige are applicable not to the State itself but to the image or personification of the State which exists only in the minds of its citizens, its allies, or its enemies. It is extremely doubtful whether the possession of an African Empire has added to the power of any European State : it is certain that it has in no case added to their wealth. It is possible that if the idea—adopted by France, and canvassed in Germany—of creating an immense army of Africans for employment in Europe and other parts of the earth were systematically carried out, the possession of an African empire would enormously increase the power of the European State. The alluring or appalling prospect—the choice of adjective must depend upon the reader's political prejudices—of Europe using the black hordes of Africa for fighting its battles and struggling for the glory and greatness which attach to " world-dominion," has not up to the present been realized. Only France has done anything to utilize the potential military power in her African possessions, and it is extremely doubtful whether, even in her case and in the Great War, she had in this respect a net gain or a net loss from her colonial empire. In the forty years before the war her empire undoubtedly weakened rather than strengthened her net military power. All other European States have been compelled to tie up or expend more military power in Africa than they got out of it.[1]

Thus while we must admit that it would be possible to increase the objective power of the European State by exploiting Africa as a recruiting ground, the conscience or incapacity of European man has so far prevented this. At the same time the objective wealth of the State, as distinguished from that of individual subjects or citizens of the State, has certainly not been increased by the possession of Empire. The budgets of all European States show that they have always, *qua* States, had an expenditure which exceeded the revenue in Africa. There remains then only the prestige or glory which attaches to the personification of States in the minds of men. Of this little more can usefully be said. Men have always worshipped images, sometimes of cats, sometimes of gods, sometimes of men, and now of States. They made strange sacrifices to their cats in Egypt and to their gods in Israel; and they make strange sacrifices to-day upon the altar of the State. In time men change their views as to what adds to or diminishes the glory of their idols. We have almost ceased to glorify God with such words as : " The Lord is a man of war : the Lord is his name. Thy right hand, O Lord, is become glorious in power : thy right hand, O Lord, hath dashed in pieces the enemy. Sing ye to the Lord, for he hath triumphed gloriously ; the horse and his rider hath he thrown into the sea." And the time perhaps may come when men will be astonished to read that their ancestors considered that the acquisition of Tunis and Uganda, by the means and methods which we have traced in the preceding pages, added to the glory of the French and British States.

There is a second way in which economic imperialism may correctly be said to have affected the European State. The primal motive power of the phenomena which I have tried to study in these pages is to be found in beliefs and desires. The most potent motive has been the belief that the power of the State can be and should be used to promote the economic interests of its citizens. This is the simple doctrine and faith of economic imperialism, and, just in so far as it has succeeded in translating itself into action, it has crystallized and become operative as the policy of European States. That means that the policy of European States has in Africa mainly been directed to promoting the economic interests of some of their citizens, and the power of the State has in fact been used there for economic ends. The history of Tunis and Tripoli, of Abyssinia and East Africa, has shown with some clearness how this result is attained ; but some words of warning and explana-

---

[1] The possession of naval bases in colonial possessions, of course, increases the naval power of States, *e.g.* of Britain, but principally with regard to the acquisition and holding of the colonial possessions themselves.

tion are necessary. Policy, particularly foreign and colonial policy, is determined by the beliefs and desires of a comparatively small number of men. The interference of the French, Italian, German, and British States in Tunis, Tripoli, Ethiopian Africa, and East Africa, was accomplished long before any one outside an extremely small circle in the various countries was aware that any action was even contemplated. The policy of interference is finally determined by an agent or two of the Governments in Africa—a M. Roustan or a Signor Pinna or a Sir Charles Euan-Smith—a few high officials in the Foreign and Colonial Offices, and a politician, a Secretary or Minister of State. These men are only the last levers which put in motion the power of the State : they are themselves set in motion by another small group of persons, the financiers, traders, and capitalists, who are seeking particular economic ends in Africa. It is extremely important that the relations between the small group of Government agents, officials, and statesmen, and the small group of capitalists and traders should not be misunderstood. The aim of the trading and financial group is always profit and personal profit ; but this motive rarely, if ever, influences the official and governing group. There is little, if indeed any, evidence of actual corruption of statesmen or government officials in the colonial adventures of European States. What happens is that the governing group is subjected to a persistent and powerful pressure from the small and influential profit-seeking group, and even when, as not unfrequently happens, it is actually opposed to the immediate aims of the financial and capitalist interests, it yields to the pressure. The way in which that pressure is applied will have become clear to the reader of the preceding pages. Frequently the agent of Government in Africa is in close contact with the agents of economic interests. There is no doubt, for instance, that M. Roustan in Tunis favoured the designs of the Paris financiers ; and we have seen that Sir Charles Euan-Smith was discussing with the agents of the British East Africa Company the expedition to Uganda and giving it his support long before any one in England had begun to think of Uganda. No suggestion of corrupt or improper action on the part of the Government agent is intended. Sir Charles Euan-Smith, like Captain Lugard, was certainly acting from the highest and most honourable motives : he supported the expedition to Uganda, not because it was in the interests of the British East Africa Company, but because he conceived it to be in the interests of the British Empire. That, however, does not alter the fact that thereby he accepted the doctrines of economic imperialism, and that he became an active agent in translating those doctrines into a policy of the British State. The position and outlook of the officials and statesmen in Europe are somewhat different. Occasionally, as with Ferry and Chamberlain, they consciously adopt the beliefs and desires of economic imperialism as the principles of national policy. More often they do this in a confused and unconscious manner, and their actions and policy are subjected to the constant pressure of the profit-seeking groups. The relations between the British Foreign Office and the British East Africa Company are most instructive from this point of view. The Government of Great Britain and its governing classes are certainly far less open to the *direct* influence of groups of financiers and capitalists than are those of France and Italy. There is clear evidence that our Foreign Office was not eager to support all Sir William Mackinnon's schemes and interests as fully as he himself considered that they deserved—" in the national interests." Yet our policy, whether under Lord Salisbury or Lord Rosebery or Lord Kimberley, was indisputably shaped by Sir William Mackinnon and his co-directors. This was possible because at need the Company could exert pressure from so many different sides upon the Government and the governing classes. Public opinion, as expressed in *The Times'* leading articles, was consistently behind Sir William Mackinnon. Wires, only waiting to be pulled, ran between the board room of the Company and the Archbishop of Canterbury and the Church of Scotland, wires which were as invisible to Lord Salisbury as they were to the Archbishop and "the Moderators and other dignitaries." The invisibility of wires, when pulled at crucial moments, adds to their effectiveness. Again, at crucial moments Sir William Mackinnon could walk round to the Foreign Office or the Treasury with the son-in-law of Queen Victoria as a certificate of his Company's character, a symbol of philanthropic patriotism, or an expert on finance. When we find *The Times*, the Archbishop, and the Marquis of Lorne uniting to support the policy of a group of " prominent British capitalists," it is hardly necessary to look farther for the reason why the policy of prominent capitalists is translated into the policy of British Governments.

This is the place at which a word must be said with regard to the personal position, the motives, beliefs, and desires, of the capitalists whose shadows have passed across the white sheet of these pages. It may seem to the reader that I have imputed evil motives to these men : and I cannot conceal the fact that in my opinion their actions, beliefs, and desires have had the most pernicious effects upon Africa and Europe. But I am not concerned with their personal beliefs, desires, and actions. I am concerned with them only as phenomena in the current of human history, and it is only because I conceive that history as made up of beliefs and desires, and their effects, that I have dealt with the psychology of, say, Sir William Mackinnon. Sir William, I am ready to believe, was a most patriotic and honourable gentleman and never acted from anything but what he believed to be the highest of motives.

It is extremely rare for human beings to pursue consciously ends which they know to be evil. Most people desire something and then automatically find reasons for believing it to be good. The capitalist imperialist is only a human being who has yielded to the tyranny of his own desires and of the social and economic system in which he blindly believes. The social and economic system allows him to regard personal profit-making as in itself a legitimate motive for either personal or political action. His desire is for profits to be made out of Africa, and the superstitions, the morality, the religion, the philosophy, the " civilization " of the age in which he lives, all allow him to make that profit by founding the British East Africa Company or the Congo Compagnie du Katanga, and still to regard himself as a philanthropic, patriotic, and most honourable gentleman. It is a mistake to exaggerate the personal responsibility or iniquity of these men. Their personal beliefs and desires and actions are only the smallest of wheels and levers in the great machine of social morality, superstition, and philosophy, unconsciously accepted by the vast majority of men and women, a machine which continually produces, with remarkable efficiency, a regular stream of unnecessary suffering in the world.

We must return, however, to States and their policy. I have shown how the beliefs and desires of economic imperialism have directly affected States in two ways. They have helped to create a peculiar image of the State in the minds of its citizens, and they have helped to form the " policy " of States. It is not necessary to emphasize the results of the imperialist policy upon the relations of European States in Europe. They are almost universally admitted to-day to have been disastrous. The use of the State's power in Africa to support the economic interests of its citizens and to acquire African territory has poisoned international relations at their source during the last forty years. We have seen in these pages something of the state of feeling which these hostilities and competitions have produced at different times between France and Britain, Italy and France, and Britain and Germany. The fact that this policy more than once brought the world to the verge of a European war, and was a very material cause in pushing it over the brink in 1914, is perhaps not the most important point. The important point is that so long as policy is dominated by this hostility and competition of economic imperialism, and the power of the State is controlled and directed by the profit-making desires, there can be internationally no stability or security, no real harmony or co-operation. European policy in Africa may not have been the immediate cause of the Great War, but you cannot have a policy such as Europe pursued in Africa between 1880 and 1914 without great wars.

In the realm of States and the policies of States men must

face the fact that they can have economic imperialism and war, or, if they do not want war, they must have a League of Nations and no economic imperialism. There can be no effective or lasting League, if States use their power in the undeveloped countries of the world *against* one another for economic ends. That statement has its proof written upon its surface. Under economic imperialism the policies and relations of European States in Africa are based upon the use or the potential use of power against one another : it is *Machtpolitik* in its purest form, and where the threat of force is the ultimate and main instrument of policy, there can never for a moment be security against two sides pushing the threat to the point at which the use of force becomes inevitable.

It is not necessary to labour this point. The most enthusiastic imperialist admits that the policy of Ferry and Chamberlain and Peters does not make for international friendliness and peace. There are certain things which men are prepared to purchase even at the price of a world of war ; and economic imperialism is believed in and defended because it is conceived as a necessary instrument for the acquisition and defence of these vital things. The German and the Frenchman and the Englishman each defends the system in Africa, which we have been studying, because, he says, it was and is the only method by which he can protect his vital national economic interests. It is necessary therefore that we should examine a little more closely the nature of these interests and the actual effects which the policy of economic imperialism has had upon them.

The first two Parts of this book have shown quite clearly the conception of those interests in the minds of the imperialist himself. The philosophy of imperialism is the same whether we examine it in the speeches of Mr. Chamberlain, Ferry, or Etienne, in the pages of Fabri, in the leading articles of *The Times,* or in the views of Crispi, General Luchino dal Verme, Captain Lugard, Karl Peters, Sir William Mackinnon, or Mr. McDermott. The interests which it is proposed to protect are economic interests, not of the personified State or of the " Government," but of the individuals who are the citizens of the State. The possession of or control over African territory is considered to be essential to the economic interests of the inhabitants of Manchester, Lille, Milan, or Hamburg. The reasoning upon which this belief is based can briefly be summarized. The very existence of the industrial populations of Europe, the argument runs, depends upon the possession of secure markets for their products and upon secure access to raw materials. In each country this security was threatened by the protectionist policy of other countries. By tariffs and other methods each State was trying to close its home European market against its rivals, and, if this system were extended to the colonial possessions of European States, and if any sudden seizure of undeveloped territories were made by some State or group of States, the inhabitants of less grasping or less far-sighted countries might wake up one morning to find themselves squeezed out of the world's markets and cut off from the supplies of tropical raw materials.   Consequently it was incumbent upon every State, if it was to protect the trade and industry of its citizens, if it was to ensure profits to its traders, manufacturers, and financiers and work to its working-classes, to forestall other predatory and hostile States in Asia and Africa by staking out "spheres of influence" or by seizing territory, to be reserved as reservoirs of raw material and markets for the products of the industry and commerce of its own citizens.   Thus Fabri, and the merchants of Hamburg and Bremen, and Dr. Karl Peters, and Zimmermann maintained that the policy of Britain, France, and Italy threatened the industrial and commercial future of Germans which could only be secured if the German flag waved over East Africa and West Africa and Cameroon and Togoland.   Ferry and Etienne and Lebon raised the alarm that the policy of Germany, Britain, and Italy was striking at the veins and arteries of French commerce and industry, and maintained that the French people could no longer exist unless the French flag protected the markets of Tunis, of the desert of Sahara, or of Timbuctoo.   Mr. Chamberlain, Lord Salisbury, Lord Rosebery, and Sir William Mackinnon urged that the policy of France, Germany, and Italy made a tropical Empire a necessity for Englishmen, and *The Times* and Captain Lugard succeeded in their campaign for the retention of Uganda by getting the Government or the public to believe that, if British factories were to be kept going and British workmen were to be kept in employment, the British flag must wave over Mengo.

It will be noticed that this is one of those vicious circles of beliefs and desires which are often set up in the minds of men and in their society.   The belief in the German that the power of the British State can and will be used in the economic interests of Britons and against those of Germans, creates for him the necessity of a policy of economic imperialism ; but the policy of economic imperialism is itself a crystallization of the belief that the power of the German State should be used in the economic interests of Germans and against those of Britons and Frenchmen.   Hence the German beliefs, desires, and policy, react and create for the Briton and the Frenchman the necessity of a policy of economic imperialism.   And so the human race goes plodding round the old vicious circle of its own beliefs and desires, the Frenchman following the German who follows the Englishman who follows the Frenchman, each driven along his path of policy by his fear of the other.   If they all agreed to work in co-operation instead of hostility and not to use the power of the State *against* the economic interests of one another, the original impulse of fear would be wanting, and the policy of a predatory imperialism would be unnecessary. But the beliefs of a capitalist society, the desire for gain, which is the motive power and religion of European civilization, are too strong to allow so simple a solution to be anything but utopian ; the whip cracks, the word of command is given, and man, noble in reason, plods on round his path of struggle and strife, of war and exploitation and slavery, his eyes fixed in fear and hatred upon the tail of the human sheep in front of him.

But no serious historian dare push the appeal to reason in dealing with national policy or the communal beliefs and desires of men. To expect policy to be rational, or to enquire too closely into facts, is the surest way to find oneself condemned as a visionary. The wise man, as the Greek pointed out many centuries ago, must accept the postulates of drunkenness and lunacy unless he wish to be thought drunk or mad. So we too, finding ourselves in the company of economic imperialists, must accept the postulates of economic imperialism ; the postulate, for instance, that Britain had to try and seize any piece of territory in Africa which its inhabitants were not strong enough to protect, in order to prevent France or Italy or Germany from seizing it ; that France had to try to seize it in order to prevent Britain, Germany, and Italy from seizing it ; and so on for all the Great Powers. We will not suggest that all this might have been avoided by none of these Great Powers attempting to seize it : we will accept this postulate of economic imperialism. And we will accept the further postulate that all this was necessary in order to protect the economic interests, the markets and the sources of raw materials, of the individual citizens of these Great Powers. But, having thus conformed to the divine law of drunkenness, lunacy, human nature, and international policy, we are still justified in asking a question : what, in fact, has been the result of this policy of imperialism, this seizure of African territory, upon the trade and industry and the economic interests of the citizens of European States ?

The answer to this question must be looked for in statistics. The statement is that the possession of African territory was necessary in order to serve as a market for the products, and a source of the raw materials of the industry, of the citizens of European States. The figures of foreign trade can alone show us how far Africa has proved a good customer and reservoir of raw material for the commerce and industry of the European States which partitioned her. If we wish to answer our question with any thoroughness, we must examine the figures from two points of view. We must take particular cases in which the seizure of territory was insisted upon by imperialists as essential to the economic interests of a particular nation, and investigate the actual effect of its seizure upon the commerce and industry of that nation ; further, we must examine the general or total commerce of the predatory nations in its relation to their total acquisition of territory in Africa.

I propose to take the particular enquiries first, and to examine the effects of the acquisition of the particular pieces of territory the history of which has been recorded in these pages, upon the trade and industry of the nations which acquired them.

A. ALGERIA, TUNIS, AND THE FRENCH AFRICAN EMPIRE

If economic imperialism can anywhere promote the economic interests of the citizens of the predatory European State, its effects should be observable in Algeria; for nowhere has the policy and its corollaries been applied more ruthlessly. The ring fence of protectionism against other nations has been drawn with amazing thoroughness by France around this country. The process began early, and the law of December 29, 1884, art. 10, enacted that " Foreign products imported into Algeria are subject to the same duties as if they were imported into France." [1] After that the tariff assimilation of Algeria to the mother country has been pro-gressively, and almost entirely, completed. The general tariff law of 1892 increased the protection of French products on the Algerian and of Algerian products on the French market, and duties were again raised in 1895. In 1893 the rule was finally established that " navigation between France and Algeria can be carried on only under the French flag."

" In short," as Professor Girault says, " both from the stand-point of navigation and from that of tariff, Algerian territory is treated to-day as national territory." France has, economically, treated Algeria as private property of her citizens as against the citizens of other European States, as an estate which is exclusively to furnish her manufacturers, financiers, shippers, and traders with a market for their goods and a source of raw materials. Let us first consider Algeria as a French private mine of raw materials.

In 1912 the value of the total Algerian exports was (excluding exports to French colonies) nearly 500,000,000 francs. They went to the following countries :

	Million Francs.
France	400
England	30
Belgium	15
Germany	12
Italy	9
Holland	8
Austria-Hungary	5
Russia	4
U.S.A.	2
Other countries	14

---

[1] For the facts in this section with regard to Algeria I have drawn largely on Professor Arthur Girault, *The Colonial Tariff Policy of France*, 1916.

These figures would appear to indicate that the policy of economic imperialism has largely succeeded, in so far as it aimed at converting Algeria into a reservoir of products for the inhabitants of France. Four-fifths of Algerian exports go to France; and England, the next country on the list, obtains only three-fiftieths. When, however, the nature of Algeria's exports are examined in detail, the effects of the policy are not quite so simple as these gross figures would lead one to suppose. The products of Algeria are almost entirely food, drink, and raw materials. The chief article of exportation is wine, and practically the whole supply is taken by France. The value of the wine exported to France in 1912 was 246 million francs. Next to wine come cereals, of which France in 1912 took a quantity of the value of 63 million francs. The value of live animals exported to France was 25 millions, and of olive oil 7 millions. In fact, about seven-eighths of the products which France derives from Algeria are made up of articles of food and drink.

But the chief claim of economic imperialism is that the possession of these African territories by the European State is necessary in order to reserve them as reservoirs of raw material for industry. Algeria produces a considerable amount of such raw materials for export, and it is a remarkable fact that although here the policy of economic imperialism has been pushed to its extreme logical limit, foreign countries have succeeded in getting an equal share of these raw materials with France. The facts are given in the following quotation from Professor Girault:

Let us pass to the crude materials of manufacture. Here the situation is quite different. Foreign countries buy extensively from Algeria as does France, and sometimes even more extensively. The exports of raw hides amount to ten millions; France takes two-thirds of them and foreign countries one-third. The foreign countries of the north of Europe buy from Algeria three times as much cork as does France (seven millions and a half against two millions and a half). The largest part of the vegetable horsehair (six millions) goes to Italy, Austria, and Germany. Almost all the alfa goes to England: that country buys eight millions of francs' worth of it. The chief part of the phosphates is sent to foreign countries. Germany buys to the amount of three and a half millions, Spain buys three millions, while France buys only one million. The exports of iron ore to foreign countries amount to about fifteen millions: England takes nine millions and a half, and the Low Countries more than four millions. The exports of zinc ore to foreign countries amount to 11,800,000 francs. Belgium takes nine millions.

It appears therefore that the most rigid system of economic imperialism has certainly affected the commercial relations of Algeria and France, and therefore the economic conditions of the

French. The acquisition of Algeria and the extreme protectionist policy adopted have undoubtedly combined to produce the conditions under which an extremely large proportion of Algerian products go to France and not to other countries. But it is not true that even here economic imperialism has succeeded in reserving for the use of French industry the raw materials of industry which Algeria produces. Germany and Spain, for instance, obtain six and a half times the amount of phosphates from Algeria that France obtains, and Britain and the Low Countries between them take nearly fourteen-fifteenths of the iron exported. The truth is that French industry and the working population of France benefit little if at all from the "reservoirs of raw materials" in this French "possession." The people who do benefit by it are the small number of concessionaires and capitalists who, because Algeria is a French possession, obtain the right to exploit these reservoirs. It is not the French public, but the small group of capitalists of the French Mokta-el-Hadid Company which exploits the Algerian iron mines and which supplies iron, not to French, but to British and Belgian industries. As far as French imports are concerned, the only effect of economic imperialism has been that France obtains from Algeria large quantities of wine, cereals, and other food, which she might perhaps under other circumstances have either produced herself or have purchased from other countries.

Almost exactly the same conditions are found in Tunis. It is true that tariff assimilation in Tunis has not gone nearly as far as in Algeria. Tunis is not from the economic point of view "treated to-day as national territory." Up to 1890 "the French market remained closed to the products of the colonists," and even since then, although most of the Tunisian agricultural products are admitted free into France, "other products" are "subjected to the lowest rates payable on similar foreign products." (See Girault, op. cit. p. 130.) But the results are much the same as in Algeria. In 1912 Tunisian exports were valued at 154,000,000 francs ; of these France obtained 67 millions, or 44 per cent. But this 44 per cent is made up almost entirely of agricultural products, and the greater part of the Tunisian raw materials goes to foreign countries. Thus 62 per cent of the phosphates go to foreign countries, nearly all the iron ore goes to Britain and Holland, most of the lead to Belgium, Italy, and Spain, and half the zinc to Belgium. Once more it is not French industry but the capitalists of the Compagnie des Phosphates and the two zinc-mining companies who benefit from the French "possession" of the phosphate and zinc in Tunis.

When we come to consider Algeria and Tunis as closed markets for the products of French industry, we find that the effects of economic imperialism are more obvious. In 1912 the total imports into Algeria were 670 million francs, and of these France supplied 568 million francs or about 87 per cent; the total imports into Tunis were 156 million francs, and of these France supplied 80,000,000 or about 51 per cent. There can in fact be no doubt that the protectionist policy of France in Algeria and Tunis succeeded to some extent in reserving those countries as partially closed markets for French goods. The fact that nearly nine-tenths of Algerian imports and over half of the Tunisian come from France might lead to a hasty conclusion that the policy of economic imperialism had entirely justified itself from the point of view of French economic interests, and was mainly responsible for providing Frenchmen with two large reserved markets for their goods. But there are certain facts which throw doubt on the validity of this conclusion. In the first place, it overlooks the fact that France is the nearest large industrial country to Algeria and Tunis, and that therefore under any circumstances the French would naturally have a great share of their import trade. Thus in 1885, when the existence of the Capitulations still prevented France from establishing a system of colonial preference with Tunis, she nevertheless supplied 50 per cent of the Tunisian imports. Similarly with Algeria. M. Girault points out that the tariff assimilation, which has been "a delusion" and "provokes bitter recriminations" in other French colonies, "raises no protests in Algeria." The reason is that in this case tariff assimilation "does not interfere with the natural course of commerce; on the contrary, it favours it." In other words, Algeria would, in any circumstances, be among the largest of France's customers, and *vice versa*; and economic imperialism, while it has increased the flow of trade between the two countries, has not, as it most certainly has in many French colonies, forced that trade into unnatural channels for the economic benefit of Frenchmen and to the economic detriment of the colonies.[1]

These conclusions are, for our purpose, not very satisfactory. What we want to know is the extent to which this policy of economic imperialism in the acquisition and subsequent handling of Tunis and Algeria has affected the economic interests of the inhabitants of France. Our figures and our facts give us a certain amount of information on the subject, but they do not enable us to give a very precise answer to the question. The evidence points to the conclusion that the policy has not succeeded in reserving for French industry any stores of African raw materials. The idea that any French workers would be out of employment if Britain or Italy had acquired Tunis instead of France—because iron and phosphate

---

[1] See Girault, *op. cit.* pp. 262 ff. Although M. Girault says that "Algeria profits more than she loses from our customs duties," he guards himself by adding: "This does not mean that the tariff is not excessive, or that it would not be preferable for France to adopt a more liberal commercial policy."

would thereby have been diverted to English or Italian and away from French industry—has proved a delusion. The raw materials of Algeria and Tunis have not benefited French manufacturers or workers but only a very small number of French capitalists—and that accounts for the fact that economic imperialism always receives greater support from finance than it does from either industry or labour. On the other hand, there is some reason for believing that the policy has increased the sales of French commodities in this African territory. To some extent economic imperialism has created here a market for French goods, and has therefore increased the profits of French industry and the employment of French workers. But to what extent? That after all is the real question; for the economic justification of economic imperialism—apart from its moral and political justification—must depend upon the number of manufacturers and workers whose economic interests have been actually affected by the French acquisition of Tunis and Algeria.

It is possible to furnish some answer to this question by considering the exports of France to Tunis and Algeria in relation to the total quantity of her exports to all countries. In 1912 France exported to Algeria and Tunis goods to the value of about 648 million francs; her total exports to all countries from 1906 to 1910 averaged in value 5527 million francs annually. If therefore economic imperialism could claim the credit for the whole of the French exports to these two possessions, it would have created a market for French goods which takes only 11 per cent of all the commodities exported by France. But such a claim on the part of economic imperialism would be, of course, absurd. Compare these figures with those for the early years of the decade 1880–1890, when economic imperialism had not yet been adopted as a policy. In 1885 French commodities exported to Algeria and Tunis were valued at 172 million francs, while the value of all exports of French product and manufacture in 1885 was 3088 million. Therefore the very highest which economic imperialists can claim is that their policy has in twenty years succeeded in creating a market in Algeria and Tunis for French goods which takes about 5½ per cent of all the commodities exported by France. When it is remembered that the value of French exports to Algeria and Tunis is about 2¼ times greater than the value of all French exports to the other French colonial possessions, it will be seen how extremely small the effect of economic imperialism must have been upon the volume of the foreign commerce of France, and therefore upon the economic interests of producers.

An examination of French commerce with French possessions on the continent of Africa points to the same conclusion. The following table shows for the year 1910 the total French exports to and imports from all French colonies and possessions in Africa:

French Exports to—							Francs.
Algeria	.	.	.	.	.	.	483,000,000
Tunis	.	.	.	.	.	.	58,000,000
Other French possessions in Africa		.	.	.	118,000,000

659,000,000

French Imports from—							Francs.
Algeria	.	.	.	.	.	.	401,000,000
Tunis	.	.	.	.	.	.	58,000,000
Other French possessions in Africa		.	.	.	135,000,000

594,000,000

Now compare these figures with the total commerce of France in the same year : the total of all French exports was 8,100,000,000 francs, and of all French imports 9,100,000,000 francs. Therefore in 1910 her African empire was responsible for less than 8 per cent of her export trade, and less than 7 per cent of her import trade. In the philosophy of economic imperialism the United Kingdom and Germany are economic enemies and rivals of France, while her African empire is a weapon to be used against those enemies and rivals. Truly a strange philosophy when we find that the United Kingdom and Germany are infinitely more important in the trade and commerce of France than the whole of this African empire. In 1910 France exported goods to the United Kingdom valued at 1230 million francs or about 100 per cent more than to her African empire, and to Germany goods valued at 764 million francs or 15 per cent more than to her African Empire, while her imports from these two countries together were nearly three times in value the imports from her African empire. Nothing could show more clearly that the economic beliefs behind economic imperialism are dreams and delusions.

B. BRITAIN AND EAST AFRICA

Sir William Mackinnon, Mr. Chamberlain, *The Times*, Captain Lugard, and Mr. McDermott all held the opinion that the acquisition and retention of British East Africa and Uganda were vital to British industry and commerce. They even went so far as to warn the British working-classes that, if a Liberal Government gave up Uganda, they would find themselves without employment, for the cotton goods and other commodities which they made for sale to the inhabitants of these territories would be made by Germans or Frenchmen, and the raw materials upon which British industry depended and which came from East Africa and Uganda would go to French or German factories. These prophecies were made in the 'eighties and early 'nineties : a quarter of a century has passed, and it is now possible to form some opinion upon the extent to which the prophecies have been fulfilled.

The table on the following page gives (1) the value of imports of East African products into the United Kingdom for periods of five years between 1884 and 1913; and (2) the average annual value of exports of the produce and manufactures of the United Kingdom to East Africa for the same periods. These statistics give some indication of the importance of these African territories as a market for British manufactures and as a source of supply of raw materials. The figures explain themselves : they reveal facts which are startling when compared with the statements of Mr. Chamberlain, *The Times*, and Captain Lugard.

The figures show quite clearly the importance which these territories have, in about a quarter of a century, attained in supplying raw materials to British industry. The exports from the whole of the East Coast of Africa to the United Kingdom consist almost entirely of food or raw materials. These exports have increased enormously between 1884 and 1913. From the whole coast (*i.e.* including Portuguese and German as well as British territory) the annual average between 1884 and 1888 was £115,000, while between 1909 and 1913 it was £1,427,000, an increase of 1140 per cent. Clearly the importance of the East Coast of Africa as a source of raw materials for British industries has materially increased since 1884. But its importance does not depend only upon the absolute increase in the exports between the two dates ; it also depends upon the relation between the raw materials supplied to British industries from this part of Africa and the raw materials supplied from the rest of the world. I have added statistics in the tabular statement which allow us to make this comparison. The annual average value of food and raw materials imported into the United Kingdom from all countries and British possessions between 1909 and 1913 was £526,743,000; the annual average of all imports (which are mainly food and raw materials) from the whole East Coast of Africa in the same period was £1,427,000. That means that to-day this part of Africa supplies 2 per cent of the food and raw materials required by British industry—in other words, a completely negligible quantity.

But so far we have been considering this coast of Africa as a whole and including in it Portuguese and German possessions. The whole case of the economic imperialist rests on the assertion that the possession of African territory by the European State is essential for the supply of raw materials for its industry. We must therefore exclude the German and Portuguese territory and examine the importance of the British territory alone. Of the total imports of £526,743,000 all the British possessions in East Africa together supplied £785,000, or ·1 per cent ; Uganda, which

ANNUAL AVERAGE IMPORTS INTO THE UNITED KINGDOM FROM EAST AFRICA (In £ Sterling)

Country Exporting.	1884-1888.	1889-1893.	Rate of Increase or Decrease.	1894-1898.	Rate of Increase or Decrease.	1909-1913.	Rate of Increase or Decrease.
Native States .	88,000	(29,000)		..		..	
British Possessions:							
Zanzibar and Pemba .	..	(188,000) } 285,000	+227%	191,000	+1% } −33%		
Other British Possessions .	..	(2,000)		2,000			
Zanzibar						180,200	−6%
East Africa						274,000	?
Uganda						218,500	?
Nyasaland						112,400	?
Total British East Africa Possessions						785,100	+306%
German East Africa .	27,000	36,000	+33%	200		89,100	+44,550%
Portuguese East Africa .				80,500	+120%	553,300	+587%
All East Africa .	115,000	321,000	+179%	273,700	−15%	1,427,500	+422%
Total food and raw materials from all Foreign Countries and British Possessions	?	?		?		526,748,700	

ANNUAL AVERAGE EXPORTS OF PRODUCE AND MANUFACTURES OF THE UNITED KINGDOM TO EAST AFRICA (In £ Sterling)

Country Importing.	1884-1888.	1889-1893.	Rate of Increase or Decrease.	1894-1898.	Rate of Increase or Decrease.	1909-1913.	Rate of Increase or Decrease.
Native States .	119,194	(142,205)[1]	+86%	..		..	
British Possessions:							
Zanzibar and Pemba .	..	(186,582)[2] } 162,957		86,404	−53%	97,605	+12%
Other British Possessions .	..	(12,443)[2]		107,801	+890%	East Africa 656,801 } +634%	
Uganda						39,680	
Nyasaland						90,410	
Total British East Africa Possessions				193,605	+19%	884,496	+358%
German East Africa .		1,036		13,470	+1200%	110,990	+746%
Portuguese East Africa .	80,556	204,756	+155%	877,709	+330%	1,813,070	+106%
All East Africa .	199,744	368,749	+84%	1,084,784	+194%	2,808,556	+159%
All Foreign Countries .	140,074,550	160,324,403	−14%	151,726,756	−6%	298,873,705	+94%
All British Possessions .	78,677,307	80,650,161	+2%	78,244,900	−3%	161,156,923	+106%
All Foreign Countries and British Possessions	222,751,857	240,974,564	+8%	229,971,656	−5%	453,030,628	+98%

[1] 1889–1891 ; after 1891 Native States are included in British Possessions.   [2] 1892–1893.

The Times and Captain Lugard said in 1891 was essential to the continued existence of British industries, supplied £218,000, or ·04 per cent.

Imperialists often assume that the mere fact of a piece of African teritory not being under the British flag implies that no raw materials produced by it are available for British industries. The absurdity of this hypothesis is shown by the statistics in the tabular statement. The increase of imports of raw material from East Africa into the United Kingdom between 1898 and 1913 rose by 422 per cent; those from British possessions in East Africa rose by only 306 per cent. The increase in the value of raw materials which British industries derived from German East Africa was immeasurably greater in this period than the increase in the value of raw materials which they derived from our own East African possessions, and greater even than the value of the materials derived from British East Africa and Uganda. The evidence of these figures is conclusive that German East Africa in German hands was no less valuable as a source of supply of raw materials for British industries than were British East Africa and Uganda in British hands.

If we turn to the second part of the table, we get a very good idea of the value of East Africa as a market for the products of British industry. Between 1884 and 1913 the rate of increase in the value of the produce and manufactures of the United Kingdom exported to the East Coast of Africa was almost the same as the rate of increase in the value of the raw materials from that part of the world imported into the United Kingdom, *i.e.* about 1200 per cent. Yet by 1913 this part of the world still took a minute and negligible quantity of the products of British industries. For the years 1909–1913 it took on an average goods to the value of just over 2¾ million pounds, while the total annual value of all produce and manufactures of the United Kingdom exported to foreign countries and British possessions was 455 million. Thus the whole coast, including German and Portuguese possessions, furnished a market for about ·6 per cent of the total exports of British industries. But the figures are even more startling if we examine only those which relate to the British possessions on this coast. In the first place the rate of increase in the exports to the British possessions has actually been less than that in the exports to German East Africa. The significance of this fact is obvious when it is remembered that Mr. Chamberlain and the economic imperialists of the British East Africa Company argued that the main reason why Britain should seize and retain Uganda and British East Africa was in order to keep the Germans out and prevent them from closing these territories to the products of British industry. Twenty-five years have revealed the falseness of this argument and of the terrible picture drawn by them of the unemployment which would fall upon the British worker if Sir William Mackinnon and his fellow-capitalists were not allowed and encouraged to acquire Uganda. According to these figures, the number of workers in Britain to which German East Africa has afforded employment by taking the products of British industry has increased at a higher rate between 1890 and 1913 than has the number to which Uganda and British East Africa has afforded employment.

Secondly, it is necessary to consider the relative importance of the British possessions on the East Coast of Africa as a market for British products. The annual average value of British produce and manufactures exported to these countries during the period 1909–1913 was £884,000 ; that of British produce and manufactures exported to all foreign countries and British possessions was £455,000,000. Therefore all these British possessions on the East Coast only take ·1 per cent of the exports of British industry. Uganda, that country which was to save the British workman from unemployment, actually takes no more than ·006 per cent of the total exports of British industries. It is clear that the incorporation of Uganda in the British Empire has had no more and no less effect upon British trade, industry, and employment, than if it had been sunk in the Indian Ocean and blotted off the map of the world.

It is unnecessary to pursue our investigations into these figures. They tell their own tale. The prophecies of the economic imperialist with regard to the East Coast of Africa have proved completely false. British possessions there are of negligible importance to British industry, whether as sources of supply for raw material or as markets for manufactures. The use of the State's power in these regions has affected the economic interests of very few of its citizens. A few hundred Englishmen, capitalists and planters, who directly exploit the territories by the purchase of land and mining rights and the flotation of joint-stock companies, have made—and sometimes lost—money. But trade, industry, and labour, generally, have reaped no advantages. It is not difficult to discover the reasons for this. Economic imperialism in this part of Africa was founded upon two economic delusions. " By seizing this territory," said Sir William Mackinnon and Mr. Chamberlain, " we shall reserve it as a reservoir of raw materials for British industry." But this could only be accomplished in one way, namely, by preventing, through tariffs or other methods, the manufacturers of other European countries from purchasing the raw materials produced in East Africa, and so reserving them at low prices for British manufacturers. Now this is only possible where, as in the case of palm-kernels on the West Coast of Africa, the raw materials are produced by natives. Where, as in East Africa, the raw materials are produced by British capitalists, planters, and joint-stock companies, these European subjects of the European State take good care to see that they are not prevented from selling their products in the dearest market : if that market be Britain, they will sell to British industry ; but if it be Germany or France, they will sell to German or French industry. The Colonial Office is able to reserve the palm-kernels on the West Coast for British industry and to keep down the price paid for them to the West Coast native, because the native is powerless and inarticulate ; but it has never attempted—it knows it would be impossible—to apply the same system to the raw materials produced by the white man in East Africa. And what is true of British colonial policy in this respect, is true of the policy of the other European States. Neither Germany nor France has succeeded in effectually reserving the raw materials in their African possessions for their own industries and industrialists. The reason is that the raw materials are mainly exploited by European capital, and European capital is always strong enough to protect its own interests. Its own interests are not to provide patriotically raw materials for the national industries, but to sell them to the highest bidder. Hence in practice the English manufacturer finds no difficulty in obtaining raw materials from the French capitalist in Tunis or the German capitalist in German East Africa ; and the French or German manufacturer finds no difficulty in getting his supplies from the English capitalist in the British possessions. Once more we see that it is national financiers, not traders or industrialists, who benefit from the acquisition of territory by Britain, France, or Germany.

The other delusion of the economic imperialist has to do with the importance of these African territories as a market for European manufactures. " We must acquire Uganda and British East Africa for the British Empire," said *The Times* and Captain Lugard, " in order to reserve these rich and populous districts as a market for British exports, and so keep the wolf of unemployment from the door of the simple, British working-man." But these imperial economists forgot the law of economics that supply must depend upon demand. The rich and populous markets upon which they turned covetous eyes consist of a few hundred white men and several million Africans. The importance of these territories as a market for British industries depends therefore upon the demand of the Africans. Now the African is, according to European standards, wretchedly poor, and he is accustomed to invest such wealth as he has, not in the products of British industries, but in cattle. If a free man, he lives upon what he himself produces in a Native Reserve ; if he works, he works for a white man who pays him at the rate of about 4s. a month. It is obvious that a population where wages work out at between £2 and £3 a year will never provide a very rich market for the products of European industry. Is it very surprising, in these circumstances, that Captain Lugard's hopes have not been fulfilled, and that British manufacturers are only able to sell goods to the people of Uganda of the annual value of £39,000 ?

C. German East Africa and the German Colonial Empire

It is unnecessary to discuss at length the effects of German economic imperialism upon the economic interests of the German people. If facts and reason had any influence at all upon men's political judgments, no one could remain under the common delusion about the importance of colonial possessions, for it would be universally recognized that the German policy of economic imperialism had been a complete failure, and that, despite that fact, the German people had surpassed all the other nations of the world in the rapidity of industrial and commercial improvement.

In 1912 the value of German exports to German East Africa was £870,000, and of imports from German East Africa £780,000.[1] The total value of German exports in that year was £484,000,000, and of imports £578,000,000. Those figures alone show that this possession has practically no importance for German industry and trade. As a matter of fact the British possession of West Africa is of far greater value to German industry and trade than the German possession of East Africa. In 1910 German imports from British West Africa were valued at 108 million marks as against 12 million marks from German East Africa : that is to say, that a British possession in Africa was nine times more import- ant as a source of raw materials for German industries than the most valuable of Germany's African colonies ! Even as a market for German products British West Africa very nearly equalled German East Africa, for German exports to the British colony in 1910 were valued at 15 million marks, and to the German colony at 19 million marks.

Finally the general effects of the policy of economic imperialism upon German industry and commerce can be estimated from the following figures. In 1909 the total imports from *all* German colonies and possessions into Germany were £1,865,000 or ·4 per cent of the total German imports, the German exports to *all* German colonies and possessions were £2,025,000 or ·5 per cent of the total German exports. It is a curious commentary upon the doctrines and policy which we have been examining in these pages, and in which the Germans were among the most fervent believers, that

---

[1] The figures are taken from Zimmermann, *Geschichte der Deutschen Kolonial-politik*, p. 264 ; they are lower than those given in some English books, *e.g. The Statesman's Year-book.*

in 1909 the trade of Germany with her colonies was just equal to her trade with the British possession of the Malay States ; it was one-twelfth of her trade with British India !

II. Africa

We have now examined the results of economic imperialism in so far as they affect Europeans in Europe : we still have to attempt to obtain some idea of the conditions of life which this policy has created for the Africans in Africa. I propose to state the facts from this point of view with regard only to British East Africa. I have chosen British East Africa from among all the territories whose history I have examined in these pages for the following reasons. I wish to obtain and to give the most favourable view possible of modern imperialism as a civilizing agent. Experience and temperament have made the rule of the British over non-adult races an example of everything that is best in modern imperialism. If we examined the administration of German, Portuguese, or Belgian possessions, we might discover defects in the treatment of and attitude towards the natives which are perhaps due to the defects in the temperament or character of the European rulers. Even the French and the Italians are notoriously lacking in some of the qualities which have made the Briton born to empire. Therefore, if in any part of Africa we are to find economic imperialism justifying itself as a governmental system for Africans, it must be in a British possession like British East Africa ; and if there are any defects in the administration of the natives of British East Africa by Europeans, we may be certain that those defects are ten and a hundred times greater in the African Empires of Germany, Portugal, Belgium, France, and Italy.

The population of British East Africa consists of about four million natives and a few hundred Europeans. The Europeans are either Government servants or planters and farmers. These planters or farmers again either own or lease land themselves or are the employees of joint-stock companies. Land exploited by Europeans is either devoted to cattle or sheep farming, or to the production of grain, pulse, rubber, coffee, sisal, etc. The government of the country is entirely in the hands of the Europeans. The Governor and the Civil Service are appointed by the Crown from England and are under the Colonial Office ; the Legislative and Executive Council are composed entirely of Europeans. The question which we have to consider is how the Government, and the few hundred Europeans, regard their relationship, their rights and obligations, to the four million natives.

East Africa is an agricultural country, and therefore the question of the land is of the most vital importance to the condition of its inhabitants. As we have seen in a former chapter, it is only some thirty years ago that Sir William Mackinnon and the British East Africa Company "acquired" the country. At that time the land was undoubtedly in the occupation and possession of the natives. The British Government has succeeded to the inheritance of Sir William Mackinnon's Company, and it now claims possession and ownership of all the land of British East Africa. How does the Government treat the Africans with regard to the land of Africa? The Government alienates from 300,000 to 600,000 acres of land annually, but it is a remarkable fact that not one single acre of this land is either leased or sold to the native inhabitants of the country. Government either sells the freehold of these hundreds of thousands of acres, or leases them on leaseholds of, usually, ninety-nine years. The sales or leases are confined to Europeans and to British Indian subjects. The result is that no native of Africa has a legal title to a single acre of the soil of British East Africa. The exploitation of the soil of this "possession" is reserved for the British inhabitants.

But we must examine the position of the natives a little more closely. The majority of them live in tribes, and to these tribes the Government has allocated Reserves. The land within a Reserve is reserved for the use of the tribe, and is not alienated by the Government. No native, however, has any legal title to land within the Reserve, and there is no security of tenure of such land even for the tribe. Only one tribe, the Masai, has had a Reserve assigned to it by a treaty, and that case will have to be referred to again. A Reserve can at any moment be cut down or abolished by the Government, and neither the tribe nor the individual native would have any legal claim or title to the land from which they were ousted.

The circumstances connected with the Masai tribe, their land and treaty, will make the whole position of the native and the European plain. The Masai is a pastoral tribe and its entire wealth consists in its flocks. When we first came to East Africa we found this tribe living by grazing its flocks upon communal land and by raiding from time to time the wealth of other tribes. It has some curious customs, among which a circumcision festival, held once in eight years, caused considerable unrest among the Masai themselves and much moral distress to the English settlers. Mr. Jackson, a Government administrator, noted, however, in an official Report (Blue Book, Africa, No. 8 (1904), Cd. 2099) that the stories with regard to the unrest and religious ceremonies had been greatly exaggerated, and "were made the most of by those settlers who can see no good in the Masai and are keenly desirous of appropriating the best of their grazing grounds at Naivasha."

The process of "appropriating the best of the Masai grazing grounds" for white settlers began in 1902. The best grazing grounds of this tribe unfortunately lay on both sides of the railway which had been built through British East Africa to Uganda. Naturally land alongside the railway was just the land which would be most suitable for exploitation by Europeans. And so in 1902 a British joint-stock company, the East Africa Syndicate, applied for a large grant of land on both sides of the railway at Gilgil in the grazing grounds of the Masai. The application was made to the Foreign Office (East Africa was at that time a "Protectorate" under the Foreign Office) and was "accepted in principle." The British Commissioner, Sir Charles Eliot, was directed to decide the terms of the lease according to his own discretion, although he was warned that the fullest consideration should be given to all native rights. The Syndicate applied for 500 square miles of land. The Sub-Commissioner called a meeting of the elders of the Masai tribe and explained what was wanted. The elders pointed out that the " area embraced the pick of their grazing ground, (but) agreed to raise no further objections provided the remainder might be left to them." Sir Charles Eliot soon after visited the district, and informed the elders that no further grants between Naivasha and Nakuru (*i.e.* in their grazing grounds) would be considered. (See Mr. Jackson's Memorandum of February 22, 1904, in Blue Book, Africa, No. 8 (1904), Cd. 2099). 320,000 acres were then leased to the Syndicate. According to the terms of the lease, it was to run for twenty-five years, the Syndicate paying a rent of one peppercorn for the first seven years and thereafter a yearly rent of £500 ; the Syndicate also had the right of purchasing the land at any time during the lease for the sum of £50,000 (see Form of Lease in Africa, No. 9 (1904), Cd. 2100, p. 24).

But other people besides the East Africa Syndicate were " keenly desirous of appropriating the best of the Masai grazing grounds at Naivasha." During 1903 Sir Charles Eliot reported to the Foreign Office that 650,000 acres of land had been applied for by Messrs. Bowker, Chamberlain, & Flemmer, in the name of Mr. Pullinger, a wealthy Johannesburg capitalist. The facts connected with this application form one of the most curious incidents in British colonial administration. Sir Charles Eliot, the Commissioner, " reserved " a certain area to be granted to Messrs. Flemmer and Chamberlain. Mr. Jackson, a Deputy-Commissioner, and Mr. Bagge, a Sub-Commissioner, two of Sir Charles Eliot's subordinates in the East African administration, happened to be in England in 1904. They reported strongly to the Foreign Office against these grants. Mr. Jackson, in a Memorandum, pointed out that the applications covered 75 per cent of the grazing grounds in the valley and on the plateau, which he had assured the Masai in the name of the Government would be kept for them (see Jackson's Memorandum and Lansdowne's telegram of February 27 to Eliot in Blue Book, Africa, No. 8 of 1904). "The settlers," he stated in another Memorandum, "think they can stake out huge claims wherever they like, in the best areas, regardless of the established claims of the Masai." The Masai are in every way very well behaved, friendly and orderly ; and ought not to be unjustly treated because they do not happen to cultivate or trade in stock. Mr. Jackson suggested that the only solution was to create a Reserve for the Masai out of their grazing grounds, and maintained that such a Reserve "is not an acre too much." As for the European applicants, since they "appear to think that there is such a brilliant future and fortune before them in wool and frozen mutton . . . they will no doubt easily find other areas, . . . though perhaps not quite as suitable for sheep as those . . . that have been grazed for generations by the Masai flocks."

Acting on these reports, the Foreign Office telegraphed to the Commissioner that the Secretary of State could not sanction the grants. Sir Charles Eliot replied that he would reduce the area granted to Chamberlain and Flemmer, but " I am unable to stultify myself by withdrawing the grant. . . . To do so is tantamount to saying that a huge area may be given to a Syndicate who do not even pay rent, but that respectable private applicants may not have available land by paying for it. Sooner than let this be done . . . I will resign Government service." The Foreign Office then gave Sir Charles the option of either resigning or of withdrawing his instructions with regard to the grant. Sir Charles chose to resign, but his despatches throw an interesting light upon his position and that of the settlers whose interests he was defending. He stated that if the Masai are allowed to keep the best land, there will be danger of a "Jameson" raid by the whites. None but Europeans have a right to the best parts of the land. "The Masai and many other tribes must go under. It is a prospect which I view with equanimity and a clear conscience . . . Masaidom . . . is a beastly, bloody system, founded on raiding and immorality." Sir Charles Eliot's resignation was accepted.[1]

But the matter did not end here. In 1904 the Government signed a formal treaty with the Masai chiefs by which it was agreed that certain territories should be "reserved" for the tribe. In signing the agreement the chiefs appended a note asking that " the settlement now arrived at shall be enduring so long as the Masai . . . shall exist, and that European . . . settlers shall not be allowed to take up land in the settlements." The arrangement was a curious one : the reserved area was in two parts, one to the

---

[1] He has lately been appointed to represent the British Government in Siberia and to act as intermediary between it and the Russian people.

south and the other to the north of the railway, and the Government
agreed to keep a right of road with access to water between the
two Reserves, so that the Masai could drive their cattle from one
to the other. What was the object of this agreement? It is
clearly shown in the agreement itself : it is there stated that the
Masai " by this removal vacate the whole of the Rift Valley, to be
used by Government for purposes of European settlement." Now
an East African official, Mr. Hollis, Secretary for Native Affairs, in
an official report to Government in 1910 (Blue Book, Africa, No. 11,
Cd. 5584), states that " from the first the white settlers regarded
the highlands of East Africa, with their salubrious climate and
exhilarating breezes, as a white man's country, and envious eyes
were cast on the vast grazing areas . . . in the Rift Valley lying
astride of the railway." The treaty of 1904 therefore was in the
interests of the white settlers : it pushed the Masai back from their
lands astride the railway and from the Rift Valley, and it "reserved"
the land astride the railway and in the valley for the white settlers.

   But the white settlers were not satisfied. The best part of
the land in the north reserved for the Masai by the agreement of
1904 was the Laikipia grazing grounds. Within four years of the
signing of the agreement suggestions began to be made for removing
the Masai entirely from the north to the south of the railway.
The Government official, Mr. Hollis, once more gives us the reason
for these suggestions ; they were, he writes, " without doubt made
solely in the interests of the settlers . . . envious eyes were being
cast on the Laikipia grazing grounds." This reason was, however,
naturally not stated at the time ; the reason given was a strange
one. The northern Masai had become, since the agreement of 1904,
completely separated from the southern part of the tribe. " This,"
to quote Mr. Hollis, " was entirely due to the Government not
keeping their promises. . . . Instead of giving them a road half a
mile broad between the two Reserves, . . . it had been reduced to
such an extent that it was practically useless for cattle, and the
land on either side had been leased to Europeans ; then (in August
1908) the movement of cattle from one Reserve to another had
been prohibited altogether owing to quarantine regulations." This
separation of the tribe into two parts, which was solely due to the
Government not fulfilling its agreement, was made the excuse for
proposing to remove the northern Masai from Laikipia and for in-
corporating them in the southern Reserve. Lenana, the chief of the
southern Reserve, naturally favoured the proposal, for it would
increase his power. But the northern Masai were unwilling. The
Government proposed to increase the southern Reserve by adding
a new area to it on the west, so as to make room for the northern
Masai. The northern chiefs sent men to inspect this proposed new
area, and they reported that it " was too small, that there was

an insufficiency of water, and that the Sotik would steal their cattle." The Governor was in favour of the proposal, and urged that "the gravest reason for the movement is that the Paramount Chief is losing his power by our having broken treaty some years ago (which was) absolutely necessary (for) quarantine purposes and owing to impossibility to permit Masai to wander over half-mile road through sixty miles of European farms." But the Secretary of State was against it, and on February 4, 1911, he telegraphed to the Governor, "It has been decided that Masai shall not be moved from Northern Reserve."

Exactly two months afterwards the Governor succeeded in getting the decision reversed. The *East African Standard*, in narrating these events, remarked that "the white settlers who had ousted the Masai from the rich pastures of the Rift Valley insistently looked with longing eyes on Laikipia, and Sir Percy Girouard, true to his role as the Settler's Governor, was found zealous to assist in the consummation of their desires." On April 3 the Governor held a meeting of the northern chiefs, and, according to his report, those chiefs who a few months before had been against the move, and who had expressed the opinion that the proposed new area in the south was too small and had insufficient water, now said that "it was their own wish that they might be allowed to move to the new area." They not only made the request but signed an agreement with the Governor, and on May 29 the Colonial Office approved the agreement.

The Masai were removed from the northern Reserve. The white settlers had thus become possessed of all the best grazing grounds both of the Rift Valley and Laikipia, and the Masai had been permanently and legally, and apparently at their own request, ousted from all their best land bordering the railway. The results are significant. Within a short time of this removal the *East African Standard* wrote : "That the Masai have been seething with unrest is a fact only too well known, yet officialdom resorts to bluff in order to keep the settlers ' in the dark.' Rumours of possible risings among the Masai have for many months been rife from the lakes to the Coast." The reason for this unrest soon became clear. The Masai, who according to the Governor had voluntarily asked for the agreement of 1904 to be set aside, within eighteen months were appealing to it and against the agreement of 1911. The tribe in 1913 brought a suit against the Government for breach of agreement. The sequel is illuminating with regard to the rights of natives in Africa when once the power of the imperialist European State has entered their territory. The High Court, Nairobi, ruled that it had no jurisdiction to try the case. It upheld the Attorney-General who, on behalf of the British administration, pleaded that " since the agreement between the Government and the chiefs of the Masai, resulting in the now famous 'move,' constituted an Act of State, the trial could not be heard in the local Court. Further, the Masai were not subjects of the Crown since they did not own allegiance to the Crown, and that accordingly the Treaty was made as between one independent sovereign and another."

It may perhaps be some consolation to the Masai, now that they have lost their lands to the British settlers, to remember that they are not British subjects but an independent sovereign. The actual results of these events are, however, obvious. All their best grazing lands have been taken from the Masai and sold or leased to British settlers. Those British settlers have been given a legal title, and the Courts of the Empire will protect them in the ownership or possession of the land. The Masai have no legal title, and, according to the Attorney-General and the High Court at Nairobi, could under no circumstances whatever acquire any legal title which the Courts of the Empire would uphold to any land in British East Africa. Their only method left to them for defending their land is, as in the case of every independent sovereign, force of arms, and if they attempted to use that method, they would have to contend with the armed force of the whole British Empire. It is no exaggeration to say that the Government and the law have been placed at the disposal of the white settlers in order to enable them, under the cover of formal legality, to rob this tribe of its land. We must assume with Sir Charles Eliot that the result is one which is to be viewed with equanimity and a clear conscience, for no punishment can be too much for a "beastly bloody system founded on raiding and immorality."

The Masai, in their occupation of the Reserve, were "protected" by a written agreement or treaty. No other tribe in East Africa holds a Reserve on a written document. The security of their tenure is therefore, if possible, less than was the Masai's. The situation is therefore that in East Africa the natives are relegated to Reserves, consisting of the least fertile and least valuable land, that they are not allowed to buy or lease land outside the Reserves, and that they have no legal title at all to the land within the Reserves. Meanwhile the best land is sold at extremely low prices or leased for very low rents to white settlers.

The effect of this system upon the social condition of the native is disastrous. East Africa is an agricultural country. The only methods by which the native can support himself are by cultivating land himself, or by cattle and sheep farming, or by working on the Europeans' land for a wage. I shall have to consider the last alternative at some length later. If the European State in East Africa had as its object the promotion of the interests of the natives, it would obviously make it its first business to encourage agriculture or cattle and sheep farming on right lines by the natives. It is only necessary to look at the budget of this colony to see that the British Government does not attempt to do this. For the year 1909–1910 the total revenue was £636,000 and the total expenditure was £669,000. The total sum which the British Government expended on education for the 4,000,000 inhabitants was £1835. The expenditure on the Post Office alone which serves the white settlers' interests was 1400 per cent more (£26,700) than that on education. The Government spent the sum of £21,764 on agriculture, but in the section of the Administration Report which deals with the expenditure of the money (Colonial Report, No. 669, Cd. 5467, pp. 15-19) there is no evidence that any of this money is spent on native agriculture or stock raising; the only persons whose interests are mentioned are white settlers. For instance, a Government which could only find £1800 for the education of its 4,000,000 native subjects was yet able to find the money for importing "the Hunter Improvement Society stallion, 'Royal Fox.'"

It is no exaggeration to say that the revenue of British East Africa is spent almost entirely upon the interests of the few hundred European settlers and upon "law and order." This is all the more remarkable when it is remembered that the only property tax, the hut tax, is levied on the natives. The white settlers, who are the property owners of the country, are extraordinarily lightly taxed, for they only pay a poll tax of £1 and their share of import duties.

But the white settlers and the European Government are not content with having ousted the natives from the best land of the country and with having relegated them to Reserves where no attempt is made to introduce them to the "blessings of civilization." The land is useless to the European unless he can get the expropriated native to work for him. But the native shows a marked disinclination to work for the European and the wages offered to him; and, if anything shows the system of economic exploitation which results from economic imperialism, it is the attitude of the white settlers and the Government towards this "labour problem." I propose to end this section by giving some facts with regard to this attitude, drawn from an official document.

In 1912 the complaints of the European landowners and farmers with regard to the shortage of labour induced the Government of British East Africa to appoint a "Native Labour Commission" to enquire and report on the subject. The Commission consisted of a Judge, two Civil Servants, the Chief Engineer of the Uganda Railway, four persons representing the European community, and two European missionaries. The Report together with the evidence was published in British East Africa, but not in this country. A large number of European planters and farmers gave evidence.

They all complained of the difficulty of obtaining native labour. Their evidence was confirmed by the Secretary for Native Affairs. The native would not work voluntarily for a wage, but only if he was forced out of the Reserves to work. "It was, generally speaking, not the really able-bodied, but the old and young who were forced out to work." The method of forcing the native out to work was described by this Government official. The white settlers go to an Agent who undertakes to supply native labour from the Reserves. A native who leaves the Reserve to labour has to be registered with the District Commissioner. "There was no doubt at the present time," said Mr. Hollis, "that whenever an Agent wanted labour, he went to the chiefs and bribed them, with the result that a number of men were brought to the Commissioner to be registered. If these men were asked if they wanted to go, they often said : 'No.' . . . One could not call this voluntary labour."

The evidence of a chief, Muturi, shows how this system of forced labour actually works in the Reserve. "If," he said (p. 238), "word came through the District Commissioner that a European previously unknown to him wanted labour, he would summon a large number of men, and ask who wanted to go. If the number fell short of that asked for, he would report to the Government Officer, and if informed that he must make the number complete, he would order certain men to go. A spearman would be sent to arrest any man who refused to go, and he would be taken before the Native Council at headquarters, by which he would be fined three goats for disobeying the chief ; the goats would be slaughtered and eaten by the Council. The Council would then order him to go to work, an order which he could not escape obeying." The white farm-owners are very much against any District Commissioner who does not lend himself to this system of forced labour. Mr. Owen Grant, of the East African Estates Company, Limited, said (p. 10) : "Every possible assistance had been given him by District Commissioners, but he considered that they were very much hampered by rules and regulations. It was wrong, however, that District Commissioners should ask natives who were brought before them to be registered whether they wished to go out and work. The native would naturally always say 'No.'"

Such native labour as is obtained by the white settler is, therefore, on the evidence of the Secretary for Native Affairs, forced labour. Let us examine the conditions of employment which are offered and refused by voluntary, and imposed upon forced labour. The evidence of the planters and farmers shows that the wages paid by them vary from Rs.3 per month (4s. a month, or a little over a penny a day) to Rs.7 per month (9s. 4d. a month, or a little over threepence a day). One planter said that methods of indenturing young native labour appeared to him to be excellent. "He himself had had splendid results from utilizing child labour on his farm, both boys and girls of about fourteen years of age. . . . Children were paid at the rate of R.1 (1s. 4d.) for fourteen days' actual work, without food."

It is perhaps natural that an employer should consider that results are excellent when he can obtain children of fourteen years of age to work for him for one penny a day, and able-bodied men for threepence a day, the hours of labour varying from eleven to nine (with one to two hours' break at mid-day). It is perhaps also natural that even East African natives will not work for these employers unless they are forced to do so. The disinclination of the native to work on the white man's farm becomes even more intelligible when one enquires into the way in which he is treated. When the labour recruiting agent has bribed the chief and the chief has made his forced levy on the tribe and registered his victims before the District Commissioner, the labourers have to be removed from the Reserve to the white man's farm. The Commissioners reported that the disinclination of the natives to go and work on these farms was in part due to the method in which this removal was conducted on the railway. The conditions are thus described by the Commissioners (p. 325) :

It is an acknowledged fact that native labourers are packed tight into the ordinary third-class coaches and even iron-covered goods vans during their journeys, which may extend to three consecutive days and nights, if they are travelling the whole length of the line, as they are not conveyed by the ordinary passenger train, and are liable to be side-tracked to allow other trains to take precedence of them. The heat during the day, owing to the want of ventilation, and the cramping for several hours at a stretch must be well-nigh intolerable. Combined with this is the custom of locking the doors for long periods during the journey, with the natural result that the coaches become fouled, adding to the already inhuman crowding an unspeakable insanitary condition. In addition, water can only be obtained now at such places where the doors are unlocked, in accordance with existing railway regulations.

Under such conditions the British Government and the English settlers have found it impossible to inculcate in the native mind the dignity of human labour. Perhaps we should at this point say with Montesquieu, " If I had to prove our right to make the negroes slaves, I would say : the people in question are black from head to foot ; their noses are so flat that it is impossible to pity them. One cannot believe that God, who is a very wise Being, has placed a soul, at any rate a good soul, in a body which is completely black."

At any rate, even with these inducements in the rate of wages and the amenities of railway travel, and with the system of unofficial compulsion described above, the English settlers cannot induce the natives to work for them. The planters and farmers who gave evidence before the Government Commission were practically unanimous in their demands for a solution of this labour problem. Their solution was a simple one. They asked the Government to cut down the native Reserves so that they would be unable to maintain the native population, and to increase the hut tax to Rs.10 for those natives who did not work on a European farm, while reducing it for those who did work. At the same time many of them asked Government to fix by law a standard wage of Rs.4 (5s. 4d.) a month.

It will be seen that this is a demand for slavery pure and simple. The reader who is not familiar with the psychology of economic imperialism may, perhaps, be disposed to think that I have misunderstood or exaggerated the demands of these Englishmen. I have not. Nearly every white settler who gave evidence before the Commission was in favour of these proposals. I will quote at random from their evidence. Mr. H. Scott of Limoru said (p. 5) :

In his opinion the free movement of natives from one locality to another should be done away with. This would go a long way to solve the labour difficulty. . . . His idea was that the natives resident in any one District should supply the labour for that District. . . . A standard wage of Rs.4 should, he thought, be established. . . . Increased taxation would, he thought, increase the labour supply, not so much, however, near towns, as in such cases the natives would be able to obtain the necessary money by raising and selling of additional produce. Boys who worked for a certain number of months in the year should pay less than those who did not work at all. The tax, therefore, should be raised to Rs.10 for boys who did not work, and reduced to Rs.3 for those who worked.

Mr. Fletcher of Kyambu said (p. 7) :

In his opinion the only way to obtain more labour would be through increasing the cost of the natives' living by means of additional taxation. He was in favour of a fairly heavy Poll Tax, with a remission proportionate to the number of months a native had worked for a European farmer. The farmer would grant a certificate to all natives working for him showing the length of time he had been employed. A certificate from Indians should not be accepted. . . . The Reserves were a great deal too large. . . . If the Reserves were cut down sufficiently, it would undoubtedly have the effect of turning off a large number of natives, who would be made to work for their living.

Mr. P. E. Watcham of Ruaraka said (p. 9) :

Reserves, he thought, should be cut down so as to force the natives to take up their residence on European farms.

These quotations, which are typical of the proposals in the 300 pages of evidence which the Report contains, show clearly enough the attitude of the English settlers. In their opinion the native has no right to land and no right to live his life for himself; he should be compelled to work on the white man's land for a wage fixed at twopence per day by law by the white man. They propose to use the power of the State to cut down the land, in occupation by the natives, until it is unable to support the native population. The native will thus be faced by the alternatives of starvation or of working for the settler on the settler's terms. And in order to make the result still more certain, the cost of the natives' living is to be increased by taxation, so that they will be compelled to work for the white man in order to earn sufficient money to pay the taxes. It may be added that in British Nyasaland this system had already been adopted, and there the native who cannot prove that he has worked has to pay double taxes.

The white settlers, it will be observed, repeatedly in their evidence stated that the native Reserves were much "too large." But Dr. Norman Leys, Government Medical Officer, Mombasa, stated (p. 274):

> The inadequacy of the Reserve in the Fort Hall and Nyeri districts for future development is patent. There is little unused land except what is necessary for pasture and fallow. There is a constant movement down into the poorer land on the plains (Crown land) from pressure behind. . . . *The Reserves are thus below the standard demanded by Sir Edward Grey from the Congo Free State, namely, land adequate for the development of two generations.*

The views of the English settlers which we have given above are merely a reflection of the beliefs and desires of economic imperialism. The Government, they hold, should see that the land and peoples of British East Africa perform the function destined for them, namely, to promote the economic interests of the white settlers. The attitude of the Commission in its Report and recommendations towards these demands is very curious. For instance, on the question of Reserves the Commission held that it had "insufficient information before it to decide whether the demarcated Reserves are too large, though there seems to be a general opinion in the country that this is the case." This was, it should be remembered, a Government Commission, and yet it states that it cannot obtain information as to whether the Reserves are or are not sufficient to maintain the native population. There is nothing in the evidence recorded to show that it attempted to get the information. It quotes a "general opinion in the country" that the Reserves are too large; but that general opinion to which it refers was the opinion only of white settlers, who frankly stated that the Reserves ought to be cut down until they could not support the native population. The Commission in its recommendations, in effect, adopted the white settlers' demand and proposal, though it did not state them quite so baldly. It recommended that all natives living outside the Reserves be removed within them, and that the Reserve should then be re-demarcated and cut down "with a view to reserving sufficient land for the present population only." The effect would therefore be that any increase of native population would immediately make the Reserves insufficient to maintain the population, and natives would be forced out of the Reserves to work on the white man's land.

But the recommendation of the Commission with regard to taxation is still more significant. It started by stating that "it is recognized that . . . taxation does bring natives into the labour market, but that to increase taxation . . . with a view to increasing the supply of labour is unjustifiable." In the very next sentence, however, the Commission expresses its opinion "that increased taxation should be imposed upon natives to meet the expenses of its recommendations, and that owing to their wealth they are well able to pay higher taxes upon property." The casuistry of the Jesuit is famous, but, surely, it was never equalled by this casuistry of imperialism. For the recommendations of the Commission are not intended to promote the interests of the natives ; the re-demarcation of the Reserves, etc., are recommended as means of increasing the labour supply, of promoting the economic interests of the white settler. The Commission admits that increased taxation will "bring natives into the labour market" ; it holds that increased taxation in order to bring natives into the labour market is unjustifiable ; and then it finally recommends increased taxation (which will bring natives into the labour market) not in order to bring them into the market, but in order to pay for other recommendations the whole object of which is to bring natives into the labour market !

The white settlers of British East Africa and the Government Commission have, of course, good authority for their views. On August 6, 1901, Mr. Joseph Chamberlain in the House of Commons dealt with this question of native labour and taxation which had cropped up in another part of Africa. He thus explained the philosophy of economic imperialism :

In the interests of the natives themselves all over Africa we have to teach them to work. . . . Suggestions have been made in the debate that it would be wrong to tax the natives. I do not agree at all. It would not for a moment be considered wrong to tax them on the ground that they were receiving benefits for which they pay their share of the cost. It is only suggested that it is wrong when there is the ulterior result that the native will have to work to obtain the money to pay the tax. Why should that which is right in itself be wrong because incidentally it will have a result which I venture to say is also right ? For if by these indirect means, we can get the native to undertake industry, we shall have done the best for them as well as for ourselves.

And on March 24, 1903, Mr. Chamberlain, in another speech in the House of Commons, explained his views still further. He said that the capitalists in Africa who asked for taxation to compel the native to work for them at a wage were very much hurt at its being said that they wanted forced labour. Mr. Chamberlain sympathized with them. He explained that it was wrong to call this " forced labour." Forced labour was labour forced to work by physical means ; but if you compelled a native to work by taxing him so much that he was compelled to work for the European and the wage offered by the European, this was not forced labour, but moral suasion. " The progress of the native," he said in a fine peroration, " in civilization will not be secured until he has been convinced of the necessity and the dignity of labour. Therefore I think that anything we reasonably can do to induce the native to labour is a desirable thing."

Men's beliefs and desires are a kind of iron shutter which descends across their eyes and minds. The philosophic historian does not delude himself into believing that any facts or arguments can pierce it. Those who share the beliefs and desires of Mr. Chamberlain and the gentlemen who gave evidence before or sat upon the British East African Commission will continue to desire what they desire and to believe what they believe. And the lives of millions of Africans will be moulded by those beliefs and desires. The white settler has taken the best land from the native. The Reserves are to be cut down until they are unable to support the native population : thus the native will be forced out of the Reserve, and in order to escape starvation will be compelled to work upon the white man's land for the wage offered to him. And in order to make the process quicker and more sure, the native is to be taxed, so that he will be compelled to adopt the only means of obtaining the money with which to pay the tax, the wages of the white man. And when the white man has got his cheap labour on a legal maximum or standard wage, tied to his land or his mine by the power of the European State and by the law—not forced labour because the labourer is not forced by the lash or iron, but only by taxation, law, and starvation—when we have obtained all this, and the happy African, expropriated from all the best land of Africa, is working nine hours a day for twopence a day upon his master's land, and his children of fourteen years are producing " excellent results " at one penny a day (without food), then we Europeans are to congratulate ourselves because, as Mr. Chamberlain explained, we are not only doing good to ourselves by getting cheap labour, but also doing good to the natives by convincing them " of the necessity and dignity of labour " at twopence a day.

We may end this chapter by noticing two curious facts. If any one had suggested to Mr. Chamberlain that all persons in Great Britain who lived on " unearned increment " should be taxed 30s. in the £ in order to compel them to work and convince them of the necessity and dignity of labour, Mr. Chamberlain would have probably replied that what applies to the natives of East Africa does not apply to the natives of Park Lane. Moreover, many of the imperialists who agree to-day with Mr. Chamberlain are horrified and enraged by what is happening under Bolshevik rule in Russia. The Bolshevik Government is presenting all its subjects with the alternative of labour or starvation. The only difference between Mr. Chamberlain and Lenin is that Mr. Chamberlain said to the natives of Africa, " You must work for the white mine-owner or white land-owner (for twopence a day if that is what the white man offers) or we shall see that you starve "; while Lenin says, " You must all work for the community for an equal wage paid by the community, or the community will see that you starve." It is curious that what is barbarism in Russia should be civilization in Africa.

CHAPTER II

If the view of history and of historical cause and effect put forward in this book be correct, the life of man, in so far as it is politically determined, is determined by communal beliefs and desires. How far and how deeply men's lives are affected by political causes under their own control is an interesting question which we cannot here pause to investigate. The facts examined in this book at any rate warrant the conclusion that Africa and the lives of its inhabitants, as we know them to-day, have been moulded very largely by the communal beliefs and desires to which we have given the name economic imperialism. One peculiar thing in this situation is that the political good and evil fortune of this continent and of its millions of inhabitants has been determined, during the last thirty years, mainly from outside, by the social and economic ideals and philosophy of alien white men. It is true of course that the communal beliefs and desires of the Africans are part cause of their present political and economic condition; if they had had the psychology of European civilization instead of African savages, they would never have fallen under the dominion of Europeans. But the psychology of the African has been only the passive agent in the making of his life and history; the active agent has been the beliefs and desires of Europeans.

In the last chapter I have attempted to trace the general effects of European policy in Africa. In my judgment those effects have been almost wholly evil. The European went into Africa about forty years ago desiring to exploit it and its inhabitants for his own economic advantage, and he rapidly acquired the belief that the power of his State should be used in Africa to promote his own economic interests. Once this belief was accepted, it destroyed the idea of individual moral responsibility. The State, enthroned in its impersonality and a glamour of patriotism, can always make a wilderness and call it peace, or make a conquest and call it civilization. The right of Europe to civilize became synonymous with the right of Europe to rob or to exploit the uncivilized. The power of each European State was applied ruthlessly in Africa. In bitter competition with one another, they partitioned territory which belonged to none of them. By fraud or by force the native chiefs and rulers were swindled or robbed of their dominions. Any resistance by the inhabitants to the encroachments either of individual Europeans or of European States was treated as " rebellion," and followed by massacres known as wars or punitive expeditions. In this process tribe was used against tribe and race against race, and wherever any native administration existed it was destroyed.

This work was accomplished by men who were not more rapacious or evil than the ordinary man ; it was accomplished by men often of ideals and great devotion, but who accepted a political dogma, namely, that their actions were justified by the right and duty of the European State to use its power in Africa for the economic interests of its European subjects. Just in the same way those who burnt and tortured heretics were probably no more cruel or evil than the majority of their fellows ; they were men of ideals and great devotion who accepted the religious dogma that it was the right and duty of the Church to torture men's bodies for the sake of their souls.

The dogma of economic imperialism prevailed with the aid of modern rifle and gun. The slaughter of the most warlike Africans encouraged the survivors to submit, and peace descended upon the greater part of Africa. The first stage of economic imperialism was accomplished, and the European looked round and openly proclaimed that the work he had done was good. The reason which he gave and gives for this opinion is interesting and deserves a little examination. The policy of conquest and partition which we have described is usually defended on two grounds : first, that it was inevitable ; and secondly, that it eventually substituted a system of law and order for one of lawless barbarism.

It is true that if men believe and desire certain things, and then translate their beliefs and desires into actions, effects inevitably follow. But it is difficult to see why the inevitability of these effects justifies either the beliefs, the desires, or the actions. If the ruling classes believe that it is their duty to burn heretics and desire to burn heretics, heretics will inevitably be burnt ; and if irresponsible traders armed with European rifles conceive that it is their right and duty to exploit Africans armed with assegais, Africans will inevitably either be shot or exploited. This no doubt raises a difficult problem for the European State. If it does not interfere to regularize the exploitation and regulate it under the name of conquest, the ferocity and cupidity of the European are themselves unregulated, and the native is either exterminated or enslaved. There is no doubt that non-adult races like the Africans suffer worse things when they are left under "independent" rulers to deal with white traders and financiers, than when the white man's State intervenes and conquers the African's country. Such intervention has, in fact, always proved to be inevitable. But the final situation is created by the beliefs and desires of the European traders and financiers, and neither those beliefs nor desires, nor the conquest and the methods by which the conquest is made, are justified because the last stage in this process follows inevitably from the first.

The second argument is that this last stage in the process is actually better than the first, that the inhabitants of East Africa under British rule, and of Algeria and Tunis under French rule, are better off and happier than they were before the European State entered Africa. Put in this way, the statement is not easy to prove or disprove. It is, however, quite certain that those who have been disgusted by the effects of the rapacious and bloodthirsty European exploitation of Africa, and who by a natural reaction have looked back to a Golden Age of peace and innocence before the European came there, are wrong. There have been no Golden Ages of uncivilized peace and innocence in the world's history, least of all in the continent which was scourged by the slave trade. The African was a savage with all the vices of savagery. Like all human beings, the natives of Africa, not satisfied with the perpetual and unavoidable sufferings which Providence inflicts upon their species, contrived to make their own and their neighbours' lives as miserable as possible. Their methods, when compared with those of our own, were crude ; they consisted in war, religion, cannibalism, and cruelty. But the savage has not that organized and intelligent persistence in making his neighbour's life unbearable which is so characteristic of Western civilization. His efforts are spasmodic, often ill-contrived and inconsistent. For example, the warlike tribes of East Africa were in the habit, until quite recent times, of raiding their neighbours' lands and villages for cattle and women : but it was a custom, universally observed, that the victims should be given twenty-four hours' notice of the attack ; so that, in practice, the cattle and such women as their owners did not desire to see carried off, were removed to a place of safety, and bloodshed was reduced to the minimum compatible with human pugnacity.

Life in Africa during the first fifty years of the nineteenth century was undoubtedly ugly and cruel and bloody. But its misery was not, like that of civilization, organized or continual. This fact accounts for the contradictory descriptions and estimates of it which we find in the works of travellers and missionaries. The villages and country of the Congo, which the civilization introduced by King Leopold subsequently converted into a desert, seemed to Coquilhat when he visited them in 1883 to be idyllic, the inhabitants prosperous, peaceful, and happy. On the other hand, men like Grenfell, who knew and denounced the atrocities perpetrated by European economic imperialism in the Belgian Congo, furnish evidence of the horrors of barbarism which preceded them.

It is, however, for our purpose unnecessary to attempt any accurate comparison between the misery of African savagery and the misery of European exploitation. Even if we admit that the atrocities of the first far outweigh the atrocities of the second, and that Europe has given to Africa the inestimable gift of law and order, this is no justification of the system of conquest, partition, and economic exploitation which we have examined. When Europeans are forced to defend the evil that they have done in Africa by pleading that the evil has been less than that done by the savage rulers and the Arab slave traders whom they have destroyed, their case must be a singularly weak one. Economic imperialism stands self-condemned if the only thing which it can say for itself is that the present conditions in British East Africa, for instance, are rather better than they were when Captain Lugard led his expedition into Uganda.

The past and the present of Africa are dark pages in the world's record. What of its future ? The European is here faced by a problem with which his own future, and that of his civilization, are inevitably bound up. He can, if he will, continue to follow the path of those beliefs and desires which we have examined, and the public policy of European States will be the policy of economic imperialism. But in that case we must not delude ourselves with the belief that we can escape from the consequences of our actions, or that the political sins of one generation are not visited upon the next. The African question has not been settled either for white man or black man by the partition of Africa among four or five European States. If the same economic beliefs and desires continue to govern our policy and shape our actions as they have done in the past, the social results within Africa, and the international results outside it, can be predicted with considerable certainty. The States which possess territory there will attempt to reserve it for economic exploitation by their own subjects. The tariff, the differential export duty, the subsidy, the manipulation of railway rates, and the concession, will continue to be used as economic weapons. The concessionaires and small groups of prominent capitalists in the possessory States will make fortunes, and Labour will be induced to believe that it is guaranteed against unemployment by making goods of the annual value of £30,000 for a few million natives under the national flag, although it makes goods of the annual value of hundreds of millions of pounds for purchase by those peoples who are represented to be its enemies and rivals. Meanwhile the citizens of non-possessing States who see themselves apparently shut out of rich markets and denied access to the stores of raw materials will, as in the past, refuse to believe that God has chosen only four or five peoples to bear the white man's burden of lucrative imperialism, and will determine to take the first opportunity of upsetting the *status quo*. International relations will again, unconsciously perhaps, be firmly established on a foundation of rivalry, cupidity, aggression, fear of aggression, and force. The land-owning nation, knowing that it won and holds what it owns solely by the right of force, will also know that the landless nation will, when the opportunity presents itself, challenge that ownership by appealing once more to force. The peace of the world will depend upon a shifting balance of power, or rather upon the calculations of a few statesmen and soldiers as to whether the balance has at last shifted to their side. For if anything is certain in international politics, it is that you cannot base international relations in one quarter of the world upon right and law and co-operation, and in another quarter upon economic hostility and force. You cannot combine the ideal of a League of Nations in Europe and America with the ideals of economic imperialism and *Machtpolitik* in Africa and Asia. If the power of the European State is to be used to promote the economic interests of its citizens and to damage the economic interests of those who are not its citizens, the final test of power or force will not be made in Africa and Asia, but upon the old graves in the battlefields of Europe.

Such must be the inevitable international effects outside Africa of economic imperialism. Within the continent the policy must proceed to its logical conclusion. The millions of Africans, who belong to the black non-adult races, will remain subject to the autocratic government of alien white men. The belief that the economic development of the country should be the first duty of the administration in order that it may fit into and serve the economic—the industrial and financial—system of Europe will be the main principle of government. The acceptance of the principle that the power of the European State should be used in Africa to promote the economic interests of European citizens will subject the Colonial Offices and Colonial Governments to the irresistible pressure of the handful of white men who have economic interests in Africa. If those interests require that the native shall not be educated, he will not be educated; if they require that he shall be demoralized and poisoned by gin, gin will be sold to him; if they require that the native shall be forced to work on the white man's land for a penny a day, taxation or starvation will furnish the necessary inducement; if they require that land occupied by natives shall be sold to Europeans, the natives will be removed into Reserves, and the Reserves will then be cut down until the native is forced to return to work for a penny a day on the land from which the European expropriated him. In this process of what Mr. Chamberlain called " convincing the native of the necessity and dignity of labour," the whole tribal organization, and the bonds which bound together the fabric of native social life, will necessarily be destroyed. The Government will be powerless to substitute, whether by education or otherwise, anything in their place ; for any real education will unfit the native to take his place as a docile labourer on a penny a day in the scheme of economic imperialism. Thus the natives will receive an ever larger measure of the blessings of law and order, and the European an ever increasing measure of cheap labour. The exploitation of Africa by Europe internally as well as externally will be based upon force, the primitive right of the stronger to enslave the weaker. At the worst this right will be enforced with the cruelties and atrocities which Europe associates with the Belgian Congo and the German and Portuguese Colonies ; at the best the right will be enforced by the milder, more respectable, and no less efficacious British method of legislative enactment.

Such must inevitably be the future of Africa if it be shaped, like the past and the present, by the desires, beliefs, and policy of economic imperialism. The conditions necessary, if the evils are to be turned into blessings and the professions of our civilization made good, are not really so obscure or complicated as the economic imperialist would have us believe. Africa is a continent inhabited by a population which belongs almost entirely to non-adult races. It is true that for Europe to withdraw to-day from Africa and to leave these non-adult races to manage their own affairs is impossible. For generations Europe has exploited Africa for economic ends, at first by the slave trade, and later by commerce, agriculture, mining, and finance. No change for the better would be brought about by the European State withdrawing its control. Economic imperialism has itself created conditions in which that control must inevitably continue. We are thus faced with a curious position in Africa. Primitive peoples are suddenly confronted with a highly complex alien civilization in which social policy is mainly directed towards safeguarding its most cherished principles, the sacred rights of property and the even more sacred right (and duty) of selling in the dearest and buying in the cheapest market. In all the relations of organized political, economic, and social life the primitive peoples are unable to hold their own with the civilized. Only the sun, malaria, and sleeping sickness have saved and will continue to save the African from extermination at the hands of the white man. The white man is inferior to the native only in this inability to exist and propagate in the greater part of Africa. Thus millions of Africans must continue to co-exist with European civilization. But the ideals of Europe, the economic principles upon which our society is based, inevitably result in the political subjection and the economic exploitation of Africans by Europeans. The European State, if it remains in Africa, is necessarily an instrument of that exploitation; if it withdraws, it merely hands over the native to the more cruel exploitation of irresponsible white men.

The question then is, how the European State can be changed from an instrument of economic exploitation into an instrument of good government and progress, not for a few hundred white men, but for the millions of Africans. Many answers have been given to this question, but a careful investigation of them will show that they nearly all fall into one or other of two classes. Some people when they look at the African problem see very clearly the disastrous effect which the imperialist side of the policy of economic imperialism has had both upon Africa and upon Europe. The struggle of State against State, in order to acquire and to retain African territory, seems to them the root of the evil. The use of the State's power against other States for economic ends has been the cause of international hostility in Europe, and of the expropriation, exploitation, and extermination of natives in Africa. "Abolish," they say, "this international or inter-state system, with its political principle of aggression, domination, and empire, and its economic principle of protection and exploitation, and you will have removed the causes which have poisoned both the relations between European States and the relations between Europe and Africa." This diagnosis finds the disease to be one of international relations or politics: its adherents naturally recommend political remedies. They would seek through a League of Nations to base the relations of European States in non-adult countries upon a foundation of co-operation rather than of hostility. Such States would renounce the policy and the right to use their power in Africa against the citizens of other States and to promote the interests of their own citizens: they would accept instead President Wilson's principle of "the removal . . . of all economic barriers and the establishment of an equality of trade conditions among all the nations." And it is only a step for the more adventurous spirits along this line of thought to arrive at the conception of substituting for national possession, ownership, or exploitation, some form of international control or administration. The ultimate vision in this direction is that of the imperial government of African possessions in the interests of particular European nations giving place to international government in the interests of the Africans themselves.

But if economic imperialism is imperial, it is also economic and this fact has led some observers and reformers to a different diagnosis. The disease to them is not so much political as social and economic. The imperialist policies of Germany, France, and Britain, the hostility and competition of these States, the seizure of territory, the ruthless conquest and massacres of natives, are, no less than the subsequent exploitation of the lands and lives of the inhabitants, merely symptoms. These thinkers find the ultimate cause of the problem in those economic beliefs and desires of Europeans to which I have had so often to refer in these pages. Those Europeans, they argue, who ever think about Africa, regard it in the light only of a potentially profitable estate. The relations between Africa and Europe are neither political nor social nor moral, but economic. The main object of a civilized European's life is to earn his living or to make profits, and of every hundred Europeans who have relations with Africa ninety-nine are concerned only with earning a living or making profits out of the Africans. Translate these social beliefs, desires, and philosophy into the facts of history and actual life, and you get first the preliminary political struggle for African territory in which profits may be earned, and secondly the exploitation of the land and inhabitants of Africa by those Europeans who are wise enough to make use of the opportunity.

Those who take this view of the situation naturally look for little improvement from any political remedy such as a new international system or international administration and control. They are world physicians who move in a stratum of thought rather different from, and certainly more virginally scientific than, that of the internationalist: for them society is fashioned by men's social philosophy, a philosophy to which conscious reason contributes as much as it does to the social philosophy of a well-fed kitten who kills a mouse. On this hypothesis, if the relations of Europe to Africa are to change, the beliefs and desires of Europeans in Africa and with regard to Africans must change. Hence when this class of thinker or reformer makes concrete proposals, they take the form, not of a change from imperialism to internationalism, but of a change in the social and economic relations between the African and the European. The "native" is no longer to be regarded as the "live-stock" on Europe's African estate, as the market for the shoddy of our factories and our cheap gin, or as the "cheap labour" by means of which the concessionaire may supply Europe with rubber and ivory and himself with a fortune, but as a human being with a right to his own land and his own life, with a right even to be educated and to determine his own destiny, to be considered, in that fantastic scheme of human government which men have woven over the world, an end in himself rather than an instrument to other people's ends.

Thus among those who desire to see a change in Europe's treatment of what I have called non-adult races there are two distinct schools of thought. If any one join either of them, he must be prepared to be set aside by all practical men, and particularly by "those who know Africa," as a doctrinaire, a visionary, and a crank. He will also find himself opposed by many of the few people who desire the same end as he does himself, but who belong to the other school of thought. I therefore confess, with some hesitation, that I belong to both schools, for I thus lay myself open to attack, on both flanks and from the rear, by friend and foe alike. I propose, however, to take my courage in both hands, and to burn my boats at the end of this book by giving my reasons.

Much of the criticism of the international solution of the problem of Africa seems to me justified. The ultimate beliefs and desires which create that problem are economic and social. They are part of that system upon which European society is now based, and which we call for short the capitalist system. The capitalist system is not the creation, nor does it consist, of "capitalists." It is created by and consists of the beliefs and desires, the subconscious social philosophy, of the millions who are born and die in European cities and villages. We who are part of those millions accept our knowledge and our ideals as instinctively and automatically as the mouse-hunting cat; but, being human beings, we thereby in the process create a society and social philosophy whose effects are felt far beyond the boundaries of Europe. It is dangerous to attempt to define in a sentence or two anything so complicated and subconscious as this social philosophy. But its essence undoubtedly consists in the domination of men and their society by economic ideals. Whatever be the cause, it is certain that at no time in the history of the world has there existed a society of human beings dominated by such a universal economic passion as ours is. It is the passion of buying cheap and selling dear. The commodities which we desire to sell dear and to buy cheap differ from person to person : some of us deal in wheat and cotton goods, others in labour, others in the product of the intellect or imagination. But in all these transactions, which fill nine-tenths of our lives, we accept unconsciously the same principle, ideal, and even obligation : to make a profit out of cotton goods or labour or stocks and shares or works of art or historical investigation, by selling in the dearest and buying in the cheapest market.

The application of this principle to the relations of Europeans to Africans is undoubtedly the fundamental cause of the African problem. Europe has treated the African and his land simply as something to make a profit out of, something which it could buy very cheap and sell very dear. In the process different parts of Europe and different Europeans have struggled and fought and swindled one another for possession of this valuable prize. But merely to stop this economic struggle in so far as it is carried on by groups organized in nations will not change Europe's relations with Africa, which are based upon economic exploitation. You may substitute international control for national imperialism, and you will still find, if the economic beliefs and desires of Europe continue the same, that the struggle for the economic exploitation of the African is now carried on by international instead of national groups.

Thus we are forced to the conclusion that if the European State is to become an instrument for good rather than of evil in Africa, the economic beliefs and desires of Europeans must suffer a change. This no doubt is a terrible confession of failure for any philosophical historian to make at the end of his book. For we are demanding not only the social revolution, but, as most people will think, a change in human nature. Immediately all the copy-book maxims and truisms—the Gospels of human delusions and superstitions—rise up and bear witness against us, for a writer might as well write himself down a fool on his title-page as to ask in his last chapter for a change in human nature.

I am content to say with St. Paul to the world of critics who will rise up against me at this point : " I speak as a fool : for ye suffer fools gladly, seeing ye yourselves are wise." All I ask is that the critics will not misrepresent my folly. It is a common habit among critics, when a writer argues that some evil in the world will never be extirpated unless men change their beliefs and desires, to turn upon him and say : " You speak as a fool : you say that men are going to change their beliefs and desires, the beliefs and desires which form the very fabric of human nature : you say that human nature itself will change, that wars will cease, that the leopard will lie down with the lamb, the strong men bow themselves, desire fail, and the Kingdom of God will be upon earth. You speak as a fool, for human nature, that perfect and immutable flower which has given to the world the heritage of Adam and of Cain, murder and theft, the struggle for existence, cannibalism, war, idolatry, the Holy Inquisition, prostitution, wife-beating, and marriage, slavery, circumcision, drink, the sweating system, capitalism, and economic imperialism—this human nature remains everywhere and always beautifully the same. Expellas furca, tamen usque recurret."

But I do not say that human nature *will* change, that the economic beliefs and desires which have moulded European society into its industrial and capitalist form *will* give way to other beliefs and ideals. What I do say is, that as long as the social philosophy of capitalism and competition, the ideal of profit-making and buying cheap and selling dear, dominates our society, the effects will show themselves in such political and social conditions as those which we have traced in Africa. In other words, the capitalist system in Europe produces the exploitation of Africa, and the struggle to exploit Africa, politically and economically, will continue as long as the economic beliefs and desires of Europeans continue to produce the capitalist system in Europe. The African will never obtain peace, prosperity, and progress until the European ceases to regard Africa as a place in which he may earn dividends, sell his cotton and his gin, obtain land, rubber and metals, and buy cheap labour. The reader must answer for himself the question whether this change in the psychology of the European would require a greater change in human nature than that which appears to have converted a peculiarly savage variety of ape into a Plato, a Shakespeare, and a Christ.

Those who find a solution of the African problem in a change in the social and economic relations of Europe to Africa are justified. It is even not difficult to trace the lines which the revolution would have to take. The European State would, as we have seen, have to continue in Africa. But the belief that the State should use its power to promote the economic interests of Europeans would have to give place to the belief that its position was merely that of trustee for the native population and that its only duty was to promote the interests, political, social and economic, of the Africans. The position of trustee would entail a definite political programme which no European State has attempted to carry out in Africa. I propose to enumerate briefly some of the more important measures and principles which would be essential in this programme :

1. The land in Africa should be reserved for the natives. Where natives are not able to develop the land, it should be developed by the State, any profits from such development being devoted to the training of the natives in order that they may eventually be able themselves to make the best use of the land.

2. Systematic education of the natives with a view to training them (a) to take a part in, and eventually to control, the Government of the country, and (b) to make the best use of their land and its mineral and other resources. This would entail the deliberate discouragement of the European wage- and labour-system in Africa and of the exploitation of the country by private planters, capitalists, and joint-stock companies.

3. A corollary of these measures would be the gradual expropriation of all Europeans and their capitalist enter- prises. It should be remembered that in most parts of Africa a system of private or individual ownership of immovable property did not exist before Europeans came to the country : communism in land is the natural and native system in Africa.

Most of the economic, and many of the social, evils afflicting that continent are due to the fact that the stronger and politically dominant race is forcing its capitalistic system of society upon the native population, to whom the system is distasteful, unsuitable, and often unintelligible. Europe is certainly strong enough to fasten its landlordism and capitalism securely and permanently upon Africa ; but if it does, while a few men reap a fine harvest of profits, the world as a whole will reap a finer harvest of misery and degradation. The only hope for Africa lies in a return to the communal system, developed, improved, and organized by the European States. This will be the real test of whether Africa is going to be administered in the interests of its own peoples or in the interests of Europeans. If the European State is to care for the interests of the natives, it must treat the land as a trust, and must seek by every possible means to teach the native to develop his land himself and to reap the full economic advantages from it. But such a system never would grow up or work side by side with European landlords and lessees, concessionaires, and capitalist companies, exploiting land and people, and clamouring for " cheap labour."

4. The application of all revenue raised in Africa to the development of the country and the education, health, etc., of the native inhabitants.

5. Absolute prohibition of alcohol.

6. Complete neutralization of Africa, *i.e.* in no case shall any military operations between European States be allowed in Africa ; no recruiting of native troops ; military forces to be reduced everywhere to the minimum required for police duties and maintaining order, the dismantling of all fortifications and naval bases, and the prohibition of all submarines in African waters.

These proposals will, of course, appear Utopian, a demand for a change in human nature. They are Utopian, but only in the sense that they assume that a Christian and European civilization shall act in accordance with its professions. How many times has it been asserted by the most practical of imperialists that we are only in Africa to promote the interests of Africans ? If the assertion were true, there would be nothing to object to in these six proposals.

Economic imperialism will never disappear out of the world unless the beliefs and desires of economic imperialism change to other ideals. But, as I have tried to show, those beliefs and desires are part of a larger complex, the complex of capitalism. It is ridiculous to imagine that Europe can or will rule the forests of Africa in accordance with the maxims of Christ and the Sermon on the Mount and at the same time apply to Paris, London, and Berlin the doctrines of Machiavelli and Bismarck and the ideals of the market and the Stock Exchange. Those who buy cheap and sell dear in Europe will not buy dear and sell cheap in Africa, and a world which slaves for its profits in Europe will enslave for profits in Africa. That is why it is impossible to believe that any mere change in the political or administrative system will ever build upon the ruins of imperialism " that city of which the pattern is laid up in Heaven for him who desires to see it."

But while internationalization is by itself no solution of the African problem, the ideas behind it would have a large place in any scheme of reform. We have seen that an essential part of that solution would be the substitution of the idea of trusteeship for that of ownership and exploitation. The white man must cease to seek his own economic interests in Africa, and must become the trustee for the interests of Africans. Now this conception of the part which Europe should play in Africa has always been the basis of internationalist proposals. The substitution of any form of international control for national ownership would be the sign and symbol that the notion of ownership and exploitation had given place to that of trusteeship. We may go even further and say that, so long as the absolute right of ownership of African territory is reserved to individual States, that right will continue to be used to promote the economic interests of the citizens of the possessing State, against the interests both of the citizens of other States and of the native inhabitants. Economic imperialism can only be destroyed by a social revolution, a revolution in men's beliefs and desires ; but the revolution itself requires for its success the acceptance of the ideal and the system of international trusteeship.

The whole question of internationalization and international control has lately been altered by the rapid growth of the idea of a League of Nations. It is widely held that if the white man's burden is the burden of a trustee for non-adult races, then the ultimate trusteeship should be vested in the League of Nations. Proposals take one of two forms : either that individual States shall continue to administer particular pieces of territory, but shall do so as mandataries of the League ; or that the League itself shall as the international trustee make itself responsible for administration.

Most people believe that the latter proposal is impossible and Utopian. The failure of international government is a commonplace, though it is a curious fact that even Sir Harry Johnston is compelled in order to prove this failure to quote as an example the Belgian Congo, in which, as I have shown, the experiment was an extreme form of economic imperialism and there was never a vestige of international government. And to those who sadly shake their heads over the terrible failures of international government in the New Hebrides and Samoa it is fair to say : " And what about national government in Africa ?   After reading the facts in this book, can you honestly say that national government has proved itself any more successful ? "

The truth is that international government of non-adult races has never been tried either in Africa or anywhere else, and has therefore never failed. It has never been tried, partly because people do not wish to try it—for it might succeed—and partly because those who do not wish it to be tried or to succeed, have induced the rest of the world to believe that it has been tried and has failed. It will not be tried until a sufficient number of people want it to succeed—and it will then succeed. That is the usual history of political experiments and of human progress.

If Europeans were genuine in their professions with regard to non-adult races, the internationalization of Africa under the League of Nations would come to-morrow. The sovereignty over Africa would be vested in the League, which would delegate its powers of administration under a written constitution to International Commissions in precisely the same way as the European Powers, with marked success, delegated their powers of administration over the Danube and its navigation to the Danube Commission ; the International Constitution for Africa would embody the six principles which I have indicated above, and the International Commissions, acting within the limits of their constitutional powers, would administer the territories entrusted to them with one single aim, namely, the interests of the Africans and their education in self-government ; the economic interests of Europeans and European States would be disregarded, except that absolute equality of commercial conditions would be guaranteed within Africa.

Such a system of international government would, if it were established, work admirably in Africa—but upon one condition, namely, that the white races believed that they were the trustees of the non-adult races and desired to fulfil that trust. The Danube Commission was established and succeeded, as a form of international government, because the Powers and peoples realized that the community of European nations were the trustees of the general interests concerned with the navigation of the Danube, and that the selfish interests of individuals and individual States should be subordinated to that of the community. Those interests were committed to the International Commission as a trust, and the machinery of internationalism worked, because the power which moved it was these new beliefs and desires. The Commission became a living trustee of international interests.

The League of Nations will not, in our lifetime, succeed to the empire, or empires, of Africa ; economic imperialism will not yield to internationalism; and international commissions will not create a new age and a new generation of men in the darkest of the dark continents. The reason is not that international government is a failure, impossible, Utopian, but that the Western world has no belief in or desire for its trusteeship. Europe will continue to pursue its own economic interests, and not the interests of the natives, in Africa, until the inevitable Nemesis overtakes it and history will record one more failure of national government. Then some poor fool will again propose the international solution, and all the wise men will shake their heads and laugh at him, and point out the immaculate record of man's past under national government, the complete success of everything that is sufficiently old to be dead and rotten, and the impossibility of anything which had not proved already out of date and a failure in the time of our fathers and fathers' fathers. There are, it is quite true, no Utopias in the world, but that is because the world does not desire Utopias.

There remains the other solution, the proposal that the League shall formally declare its trusteeship of non-adult races, and then proceed to hand them over to particular States as its mandataries. The great advantage of this proposal lies in the fact that it will enable the world in appearance to introduce a new and noble system, and in reality to leave everything exactly as it was before. As I write, the Peace Conference in Paris is discussing this question of mandataries, and *The Times*, in a leading article, discusses the same question with its admirable lucidity. It points out that any system of a " trust " depends entirely upon the obligations imposed upon the trustee or mandatary. And then it goes on to explain what the mandatory system under a League of Nations would " rightly " mean. " Rightly defined," it says, " this system ought to mean nothing more hampering than the imposition upon the trustee of an obligation to give the beneficiary good government. It should bind them to the civilized world to administer subject peoples in the interests of the governed; in fact, it should bind them in formal fashion to do exactly what, of their own accord, just nations do already."

The reader who has followed and weighed the facts recorded in these pages must decide for himself whether he will be satisfied to see the League of Nations bind in formal fashion Great Britain, France, Italy, Belgium, and Portugal, to do exactly what, of their own accord, they have done already in Africa. Personally I believe these nations to be just nations, but I hesitate to accept this mandatory system just because it may be so easily used to throw a cloak of pseudo-internationalism over the kind of acts which these just nations have committed in Africa. Nations are just, because they are composed of individuals who are on the whole, and within the limitations of human nature, just. States are unjust and cruel largely because the economic and political theories of our age, the economic and political beliefs and desires which make empires and policies, deprive the individuals of their sense of responsibility for imperial acts of States. The mandatory system, as accepted by *The Times*, would only provide one more method of soothing to sleep the unquiet conscience of just nations and just men.

There are probably few of those optimists left who believed that the League of Nations would be the beginning of a new era in international relations. We shall find a few new, fine names with which to clothe the nakedness of ancient evils ; we shall call exploitation trusteeship, slavery labour, and profit-making patriotism. The world, as Reland noted two hundred years ago, wishes to be deceived. Its latest method of self-deception is probably correctly indicated in *The Times'* leading article. Economic imperialists will rebaptize themselves in the waters of internationalism and put on the white garments of a League of Nations. The League will formally declare itself the guardian of non-adult races, and then hand them over to their mandataries, the good and unselfish Powers of Europe. Evil Powers, like Germany, Holland, Norway, Sweden, and Denmark, will be excluded from Africa, and the good Powers, like Portugal, which have shown their capacity for " ruling natives," will reluctantly consent to shoulder the burden of trusteeship. But it is improbable that the trustee will find itself particularly " hampered " by its obligations or mandate. It will merely bind itself in formal fashion to do exactly what, of its own accord, it has done already.

The old system will thus probably continue to operate under a new name, until its accumulated evils bring its own destruction. That destruction may come, sooner than some people expect, by a tremendous catastrophe, perhaps a revolt of the " beneficiaries " against their guardians and benefactors. When it does come, we shall certainly be told that it is one more failure of international government.

For these reasons it is difficult to feel any great enthusiasm for this new mandatory system of the League of Nations. It is, however, arguable that it would be at least an improvement upon the old system. It might be some advantage to have a formal recognition of the principle that the European State is in Africa a mandatary of the world of nations, that it has no mandate to promote the interests of a small number of its European subjects, and that its first duty and obligation are to its African subjects. But the principle will only be effective if the League itself is an effective force. It may be stated with absolute certainty that the League will have no effective force at all unless the following conditions are fulfilled :

1. The obligations of the mandatary both to the non-adult races

and to other States must be defined in the treaty, and guaranteed by the League.

2. The League must have some organ authorized to watch over and supervise the fulfilment of the trust and the execution of treaty obligations. This organ would be ineffective unless it had very considerable powers of enquiry and inspection. It would have to be a permanent Commission of the League to which would be delegated the duty of entertaining, enquiring into, and reporting on any complaints from subject races or from States with regard to the non-fulfilment of its obligation by a mandatary.

3. The League would have to guarantee absolute equality of commercial opportunity, by means of free trade and the open door, in all African territory committed to its trust.

4. The League would have to possess and to use the power of revoking a mandate upon a report from its permanent Commission that a mandatary was not complying with its obligations either towards its subjects or towards other States.

Every one of these conditions is shown to be essential by the whole history of international relations, and in particular by the history of the Congo Act. It is useless to set up an elaborate system of international obligations, if no means are provided for seeing that the obligations are fulfilled. And here once more we come back to those sources of human action and human history, men's beliefs and desires. As soon as you come to providing the means for carrying out the general statements and fine sentiments which it is so easy to embody in international declarations and leading articles, you come up against men's beliefs and desires. The current of no man's life will be affected by a League which publicly declares that it is the trustee of the interests of Africans in Africa and that it has entrusted five unselfish European States with the duty of governing and promoting the interests of its wards ; but a League which goes on to create means for seeing that the mandatary fulfils its obligations will immediately touch the desires and actions of many men. We test men not by what they say but by what they do, and we should test nations and Leagues of Nations not by their declarations, but by their actions. Only we must remember that it is the beliefs and desires of individual men which govern the actions of men and nations, of Powers, of States, and of Leagues ; for man, as I said in my first chapter, is a rational animal, and controls his destiny in Europe—and in Africa.

INDEX

Abdulla, Emir of Harrar, 161, 162
Aberdeen, Lord, 77, 79, 116
Abyssinia, 33, 54, 138-227
  and Egypt, 151, 152, 155, 156
  and the Nile, 138, 155, 183, 196-203
  future of, 219, 220
  government of, 140
  policy of European States in, 203
  position in Africa of, 140
  under Theodore, 140-151
Adowa, battle of, 173, 178
Africa—
  economic imperialism in, Part II.
    Chap. I., 315-351
  future of, 352-368
  geographical divisions of, 69
  in 1815, 1880, and 1914, 55, 56
  Mediterranean, 69-137
  partition of, 55-68
Algeria, 22, 26, 28, 57, 69-78, 79, 89,
  98, 325-330
Assab Bay, 153, 154

Baori, the, 74
Banning, E., *Le Partage politique de
  l'Afrique*, 44
Benadir Company, 175
Bérard, Victor, 24
Berlin (Congo) Conference, 42, 43, 307
Berlin, Congress of, 1878, 94 ff.
Bieberstein, Baron Marschall von, 129
Bismarck, 58, 121, 122
  and East Africa, 237, 240, 254
  and Leopold I., 42, 307
  and Samoa, 32, 33
  and Tunis, 94, 95
  colonial policy of, 34-36, 43
Bizerta, 117-120
Bleichröder, von, 32, 35
Bône-Guelma Railway Company, 97 ff.,
  107, 108
Botmiliau, French Consul, Tunis, 88, 91
Bourne, H. R. Fox, *Civilisation in
  Congoland*, 240
Bright, John, 14, 16
Britain, Great—
  and Ethiopian Africa, 152 ff.

Britain, Great (*contd.*)—
  and France in Nile Valley, 187-201
  and Harrar, 157 ff., 166-168
  and Italy in Abyssinia, 159-173, 185,
    221-227
  and Johannes VI. of Abyssinia, 164
  and partition of Africa, 42
  and Portuguese colonies, 39 ff.
  and slave trade, 229-233
  and Theodore of Abyssinia, 145-151
  and treaties with native chiefs, 237-
    240
  and Tripoli, 129 ff.
  and Tunis, 93, 102, 118 ff., 126
  and Zanzibar, 175, 229-235, 244-254
  Congo Treaty with Portugal, 1884, 38
  economic imperialism of, 25-27, 203,
    330-336
  economic results of imperialism in
    Africa, 330-336
  struggle with France in Abyssinia,
    178-220
  treaty with Belgian Congo, 1894, 185
British East Africa, 241-276, 330-336
  native reserves in, 340-351
  treatment of natives in, 337-351
British East Africa Company, 32, 33,
  183, 242-302
  administration and aims of, 260-269,
    300
  and compensation, 301, 302
  and Uganda, 269-302
  and Witu, 264-269
  method of acquiring British East
    Africa, 245-254
  request for subsidy, 293-295
  threatens to evacuate Uganda, 294-
    301
British South Africa Company, and
  Portuguese colonies, 39
Brown, Dr. George, *Autobiography*, 33
Burke, E., 15, 16
Busch, *Bismarck*, 34
Bussidon, Charles, *Abyssinie et Angleterre*, 144

Cam, Diogo, 38

Cameroons, 34, 35
Cape to Cairo scheme, 181-185, 202
Capitalism, 358-364
Caprivi, 129
Castlereagh, Lord, 73, 231
Cattier, F., 305, 306, 309, 310, 312
Chad, Lake, and French imperialism, 124 ff.
Chamberlain, Joseph, 7-9, 13-15, 17, 18, 25, 57, 179, 180, 193-195, 203, 241, 319, 322, 323, 330, 331, 333, 334, 349-351, 357
Charles X. of France, 71, 72, 75-77, 79-81, 116
Chefneux, M., 198
Chesterfield, Lord, 208-210, 214, 243
China, 23, 26, 54
Chirol, Sir Valentine, 131
Church Missionary Society, 295-299, 302
Clemenceau, M., 106-108, 110
Clermont-Tonnerre, M. de, 76
Cobden, R., 14-16
Compagnie Impériale des Chemins de Fer Éthiopiens, 31, 33, 198, 205-218
Concessions, economic—
  in Abyssinia, 198, 199, 204-219
  in East Africa, 246-254
  in Tunis, 84 ff., 88, 93, 94, 97 ff.
Congo, Belgian, 303-312
  administration in, 310-312
  Association Internationale du Congo, 37, 41, 306
  Berlin Conference and Act, 38, 42, 307-309
  Comité d'Études du Haut Congo, 37, 305, 306
  constitution of, 309, 310
  conventions establishing, 307, 308
  economic imperialism in, 311, 312
  internationalism and, 304, 306-312
  method of acquisition, 239, 240
  treatment of natives in, 256, 310-312
Crispi, Francesco, 97, 121, 322
  and Ethiopian Africa, 169, 170, 172-174, 178, 203
  and Tripoli, 122-137
Cromer, Lord, 139, 189, 190, 203, 275
Curtis, Lionel, 15
Curzon, Lord, 197
Cyprus, 95

Dahomey, 54
dal Verme, General Luchino, 127-129, 132
Darcy, Jean, 27, 39, 40, 41, 71, 73, 83, 88, 89, 96, 102, 155, 160, 168, 186, 188, 189, 210, 212, 222, 287, 288
Debidour, M., Histoire Diplomatique, 160, 168, 222, 224
de Brazza, S., 41, 42, 43, 239

Decharme, P., 178, 236, 237, 238
Delcassé, M., 58, 119, 135, 136, 186, 192, 193, 216
Delonole, F., 170, 186, 212, 221
Democracy, 5, 6, 10
D'Estournelles de Constant, La Politique française en Tunisie, 82, 83-85, 87, 91, 92, 94, 96, 98, 102, 105-107
Deutsch - Ostafrikanische - Gesellschaft. See German East Africa Company
de Winton, Sir Francis, 243, 276, 281, 306
Dilke, Sir C., 24, 167, 223
Disraeli, B., 24
Djibuti, 166, 173, 204-218
Dongarita, struggle for, 158, 159, 200
Driault, M. Edouard, 134

East Africa. See Britain, British East Africa, British East Africa Company, German East Africa Company, Uganda, Zanzibar
Economic penetration, 73 ff., 205-218
Egypt. See also the Nile
  and Britain, 193-195
  and Tunis, 96, 102
  economic imperialism and, 115
  international control in, 91
Eliot, Sir Charles, 339, 340
Empire and Commerce, 18, 26, 116, 241, 322 ff.
Entente cordiale, 215-218
Eritrea, Italian colony of, 170, 173, 204
Ethiopian Africa (see also Abyssinia, Eritrea, Somalilands), 138, 139
Etienne, M., 134, 160, 174, 185, 186, 195, 241, 322, 323
Euan-Smith, Sir Charles, 207, 243, 271, 274, 275, 295, 296, 319
Exmouth, Lord, 72

Fabri, Herr, 31, 33-36, 241, 322, 323
Fallot, M. E., 25, 28, 70, 135
Farre, General, 99, 108, 109, 113
Fashoda, 119, 190-195
Feillet, M., 28
Ferry, Jules, 25, 26, 42, 57, 95, 98, 99, 101, 102, 104-113, 116, 117, 119, 121, 128, 241, 319, 322, 323
  speech on economic imperialism, 46
Filonardi, Signor, 174-177
Filonardi Company, 175
Fletcher, C. B., The New Pacific, 33
France—
  and Algeria, 22, 69-78, 79-81, 325-330
  and Ethiopian Africa, 152 ff.
  and Harrar, 157 ff., 166-168
  and Italy in Abyssinia, 159-173, 221-224
  and Menelik of Abyssinia, 172, 173, 196-201

France (contd.)—
and partition of Africa, 42
and Saharan empire, 120, 133-135
and slave trade, 233
and Tripoli, 123-137
and Tunis, 82-113, 116-122, 126, 327-330
economic imperialism of, 24 ff., 31 ff., 134, 203, 325-330
in Nile Valley, 187-201
struggle with Britain in Abyssinia, 178-220
surplus population and, 27-30
French Revolution, 5
Frere, Sir Bartle, 41, 233
Freycinet, M. de, 99
Freytag, Gustav, 34

Gambetta, 25, 108
Gering, Max, 16
German East Africa, 34, 35, 228, 236-241, 244-249, 336
German East Africa Company, 33-35, 236-241, 245-249, 262
German South-West Africa, 258
Germany—
and Abyssinia, 217
and partition of Africa, 43
and Portuguese colonies, 40
and Tripoli, 128 ff.
and Witu, 264-269
and Zanzibar, 175, 235-242, 244-249, 252-259
colonial administration of, 255-259
economic imperialism of, 25 ff., 34 ff., 42 ff., 255-259, 336
surplus population and, 30
Ghadames and Ghat, 124 ff.
Gibbons, The New Map of Europe, 135
Gilmour, T. Lennox, 205, 212, 213, 215, 216, 217, 218
Girault, Professor A., The Colonial Tariff Policy of France, 325, 326, 328
Girouard, Sir P., 343
Gladstone, W. H., 24, 40, 154, 155, 204
Godeffroy, J. C. and Son, 31-33
Granville, Lord, 40, 241, 264
Greenwood, Arthur, 16, 17
Grey, Sir Edward (Lord), 58, 187, 189, 192, 222
Grogan, E. S., The Cape to Cairo, 182
Grunzel, J., 14
Guyot, Yves, 26, 28, 83, 107

Hamilton, Angus, Somaliland, 175, 178
Hanotaux, G., 117-120, 134, 136, 137, 171, 172, 185, 193
Hansemann, von, 32, 35, 37
Hansing & Co., 35, 235, 236, 237
Harrar, 151-154, 157 ff., 161, 162, 165-169, 171, 204, 209, 213

Harrington, Colonel Sir John, 202, 203, 212, 214, 215, 217
Hatzfeld, Count, 130, 131
Hertslet, The Map of Africa by Treaty, 122, 171, 174, 222, 226, 241
Hewett, Admiral, 162
Hinterland principle, 123, 124
in East Africa, 247, 248, 269
in Sahara, 133
in Tripoli and Tunis, 124 ff.
Hohenlohe, Prince, 34, 35
Holstein, Baron, 131
Hussein, Bey of Algeria, 74 ff.

Ilg, M., 187, 197-199, 205, 212, 219
Imperialism, economic, 19; Part I., Chap. III., 44 ff.
and acquisition of territory, 263 ff.
and capital, 116, 327, 355
and capitalism, 358-364
and chartered or concessionary companies, 175-178
and concessions, 84 ff., 88, 97 ff., 198, 199, 208-219, 246-254, 282, 283, 355
and finance, 73 ff., 83, 84, 86, 87, 89, 98, 100, 104, 208-218, 248 ff.
and international government, 304, 358-368
and Jingoism, 24
and maps, 132, 171
and public opinion, 71, 108-113, 270, 271, 295-300
and strategy, 76 ff., 80-82, 93, 105, 108, 114, 117-120, 198
and tariffs, 322-330
and the Churches, 295-302
and treatment of natives, 255-259
British, 24 ff., 256
economic effects of, 325-337
effects of in Africa, 337-351, 352-358
effects of in Europe, 310-337, 355, 356
French, 24 ff., 46, 123, 124, 126, 256
German, 24 ff., 33 ff., 255-259
in Africa, 53 ff.
in Asia, 53 ff.
Italian, 93, 96 ff., 103, 114-137, 256
results of, for natives, 337-351
taxation of natives under, 347-351
India, 22, 23, 139, 229, 255
Industrialism, 5-6
International Ethiopian Trust and Construction Company, 208-218, 242
International Financial Commission, Tunis, 90 ff.
International Government, 91, 304, 306-310, 358-368
Italy—
acquires Benadir Coast, 175
acquires Somaliland, 173-178

Italy (contd.)—
  and Ethiopian Africa, 152 ff., 174
  and France, 103, 120-137, 159
  and Menelik of Abyssinia, 168-170,
    196
  and Tripoli, 122-137
  defeat at Dogali, 164
  Imperialist policy in Abyssinia, 159-
    173, 177, 196, 203, 220
  Imperialist policy in Tunis, 93, 96 ff.,
    103, 120-122
  occupies Massowah, 159, 160, 163,
    164

Jameson, Dr., 180
Jingoism, 24
Johannes VI. of Abyssinia, 151, 152,
    162-166
Johnston, Sir H. H., 40, 41, 56, 245,
    257, 274, 304, 305, 306, 308, 364
Jonquière, C. de la, Les Italiens en
    Erythrée, 152, 153, 154

Keith, A. B., The Belgian Congo and
    the Berlin Act, 304
Keltie, J. Scott, 28, 55, 56
Kirk, Sir John, 234, 235, 243, 264, 296
Kitchener, Lord, 188, 190-192, 196
Kolonialverein, 33, 34
Kusserow, von, 32, 35, 37

Labour, native, 344-351
Lagarde, M., Governor of Djibuti, 190,
    191, 196-198, 201, 203
Lambermont, Baron, 250, 251
Lamu, 250, 251, 265
Lavisse, M. E., 167, 168, 171, 222-224
League of Nations, 322, 358-361, 363-
    368
Lebon, A., 184, 190, 196, 323
Lejean, M., French Consul in Abyssinia,
    142, 143, 145
Le Marchand, M., L'Europe et la Con-
    quête d'Alger, 71
Lémonon, M., L'Europe et la Paix
    Britannique, 40, 102, 160, 168, 171,
    192, 212, 217, 219, 222-224
Leontieff, Count, 198-200
Leopold I., of Belgium—
  and Bismarck, 42, 307
  early policy in Congo, 41, 305
  influence on economic imperialism,
    37 ff., 43
  motives of, 306, 310
  powers of, in Congo, 309-312
Leys, Dr. Norman, 348
Lichnowsky, Prince, 40
"Logic of facts," 74, 79 ff., 82, 83, 87,
    104
Lorne, Marquis of, 243, 294, 320
Louis-Philippe, 76, 79
Lüderitz, Herr, 34, 35, 37, 43

Lugard, Sir F. D., 26, 183, 244
  and King Mwanga, 280-289
  economic beliefs of, 330, 331, 335
  expedition to Uganda, 270, 273-289
  instructions to, 279-281
  motives of, 330, 331, 335
  opinion of, on German Colonial Ad-
    ministration, 256, 257
  Propaganda of, in England, 289, 297,
    298
  relations of, with missionaries, 287
Lyne, R. N., Zanzibar in Contemporary
    Times, 233, 264, 268
Lyons, Lord, 101, 102

Maccio, Signor, 97
McDermott, P. L., British East Africa,
    234, 244, 249, 250, 251, 253, 254,
    260-264, 266-272, 274-276, 282,
    284, 286, 287, 293, 294, 297, 299,
    300, 301, 322
Mackenzie, E. N., 250, 253, 254, 259,
    279
Mackinnon, Sir William, 234, 235, 243,
    249-253, 259, 262, 263, 265, 266,
    269, 270, 272, 274-276, 279, 283,
    290, 292-294, 296-300, 320, 322,
    323, 330, 334
Mahdi, the, 158-160, 162, 163, 165
Maltzan, von, 33-36
Marchand, Captain, 190-196, 200, 201
Markham, Sir Clements F., A History
    of the Abyssinian Expedition, 141,
    146, 147, 148, 149
Masai, the, 338-343
Mathews, Sir Lloyd, 234, 235, 250, 251
Mediterranean Question, the, 22, 57,
    72 ff., 79 ff., 93, 105, 114, 116, 128,
    136
Menabrea, General, 130, 132, 136, 137
Menelik, Emperor of Abyssinia, 32
  agreement of, with Britain, 1902, 201-
    203, 213
  and Nile Valley, 196-203
  becomes emperor, 166
  occupies Harrar, 165
  peace with Italy, 178
  receives arms from France, 172
  receives arms from Italy, 163 ff.
  Treaty of Uccialli with Italy, 1889,
    165, 168-170
  Treaty with France, 1897, 197
  Treaty with Italy, 1888, 165
  war with Italy, 172, 173
  and internationalization of railway,
    215
  quarrels with France, 211 ff.
Mercantilism, 14, 16
Michell, Sir L., Life of Rhodes, 179, 181
Missionaries—
  in Abyssinia, 143 ff.
  in Uganda, 277-289

" Mittel-Afrika," 135, 174, 181-185, 195
Morel, E. D., 304
Morié, L. J., *Histoire de l'Éthiopie*, 150, 152, 165, 170, 200, 201
Morocco Question, the, 58, 218
Mustapha khaznadar, 86
Mwanga, 271, 277-289

Napier, Sir Robert, 144, 146-148, 151
Napoleonic Wars, 5, 22, 230-231
Nationalism, 5, 6, 10
New African Company, 208 ff.
New Caledonia, 27, 28
New Egyptian Company, 208 ff.
Newton, Lord, 94-96
Nile, the, 138, 155, 187-201

Obock, 152-154, 157, 204
Oceana Consolidated, 208 ff.

Palmerston, Lord, 150
Patriotism and history, 11, 12
Paulitschke, Dr. P., *Harar*, 158, 161
Pervinquière, M. Léon, 137
Peters, Dr. Karl, 34, 35, 236-241, 253, 254, 263, 270, 274, 276, 279
Pinna, Signor, 88, 90, 91, 93, 94, 319
Pinon, M. R., *L'Empire de la Méditerranée*, 136
Piracy in Mediterranean, 72 ff.
Policy—
    and commerce, 9-11, Chapter II.
    (Part I.), 26, 318-324
    definition of, 5, 13
Polignac, Prince de, 57, 58, 79, 93, 116
Population and empire, 27 ff.
Portal, Sir Gerald, 260, 261, 277, 284, 289, 300, 301
Portugal—
    and Britain, 39
    and Mittel-Afrika, 174, 182
    claim to Congo, 39
    Congo Treaty with Britain, 1884, 38 ff.
Pottinger, Sir Henry, 23
Protectionism, 19

Rambaud, A., *Jules Ferry*, 42, 46, 107, 108
Rassam, Hormuzd, *Narrative of the British Mission to Theodore*, 141, 146-148
Reland, 11
Rhodes, Cecil, 57, 274
    and Portuguese colonies, 39
    and the Chartered Company, 185
    Cape to Cairo scheme, 174, 179-185
Ribot, M., 131, 137, 189
Rochefort, M., 111, 112
Roches, M. Léon, 84, 88
Rodd, Sir Rennell, 196, 197

Ronze, Raymond, *La Question d'Afrique*, 288
Rose, J. Holland, *The Development of the European Nations*, 38
Rosebery, Lord, 25, 186, 188, 297, 299, 300, 320, 323
Roustan, M., 88, 98, 107, 111-113, 319
Rubattino Company, 97, 98, 153
Russell, Earl (Secretary of State for Foreign Affairs), 145, 146, 150

Sahara, French policy in, 125 ff.
Saint-Hilaire, B., 25, 99, 101, 108, 111, 112, 113
Salisbury, Lord, 94, 95, 97, 126, 127, 129, 130, 131, 167, 174, 190, 192, 245, 265, 266, 293, 294, 296, 297, 320, 323
Samoa and Germany, 31
Sargent, A. J,. 23
Schimper, Herr, 141, 148
Seyyid Barghash, 229, 233, 234, 235, 249, 251, 252, 264
Seyyid Khalifa, 251
Seyyid Majid, 229, 235
Seyyid Said, 229, 232, 235, 249
Sidgwick, Henry, 6
Sidi-Saddok, 86, 87, 91, 101
Singer, *Geschichte des Dreibundes*, 121
Slave trade, 229-233
Somaliland, British, 150, 209 ff.
Somaliland, French, 153, 208-218
Somaliland, Italian, 173-178, 228, 238
Soult, Marshal, 71, 72
Stanley, Sir H. M., 37, 38, 41, 42, 239, 271, 305, 306
State, the, 4-11, 22, 316-318
    and commerce, 5 ff., 10, Chapter II.
    (Part I.), 318-324
Stevenson, R. L., 33
Strachey, St. Loe, 96, 102
Sudan Expedition, 189-195
Suez Canal, 139

Talleyrand, 71
Tariffs, 322-324
Theodore of Abyssinia, 140-151
    and Europeans, 142-146
    and missionaries, 143 ff.
Times, The, 77, 203, 288
    and colonial mandates, 306
    and Uganda, 272, 289, 295, 297-299, 301, 323, 330, 333, 335
    influence of correspondent of, 131
    on Fashoda, 192
    on Tunis, 112, 113
Togoland, 34, 35
Tonkin Expedition, 25
Treaties—
    Anglo-French regarding Harrar, 1888, 167-168, 221-224

Treaties (contd.)—
  Anglo-French Declarations, August 5, 1890 (Zanzibar and Madagascar), 126
  Anglo-French regarding Nile Valley, 1899, 195
  Anglo - French - Italian regarding Abyssinia, 1906, 218
  Anglo-German regarding Zanzibar, 1886 and 1890, 175, 245-254, 267, 276, 277, 280
  Anglo-Italian regarding Ethiopia, 1891 and 1894, 161, 170, 171, 172, 221-227
  Anglo-Portuguese regarding Congo, 1884, 38
  Bardo or Casr Said, 1881, 100, 120-122
  Berlin Congo Act, 1884, 38, 307-309
  Franco - Italian on Tripoli and Morocco, 136
  Ucoialli, 1889, 165, 168-170, 172, 178
Tripoli, 122-137
  conquest of, 135
  population of, 123
  trade of, 124, 125, 137
Tunis, 82-113, 114, 327-330
  and Tripoli, 114-137
Turkey, 9, 70, 74
  and Tripoli, 128 ff.
  and Tunis, 88, 89

Uganda, 33, 54, 183, 185, 228, 242, 269-302, 330-336

Vandervelde, Émile, La Belgique et le Congo, 305, 306, 309-311
Vienna Congress and slave trade, 231

Waddington, M., 94, 95, 97, 111
Waldeck-Rousseau, M., 210
Weber, Theodor, 33
Wellington, Duke of, 22, 57, 58, 77, 79, 80, 93, 116, 128
Whately, 15, 16
Witu, 240, 264-269
Woermann, C., 33-37, 57, 235
Wood, British Consul, Tunis, 84, 88-91, 94, 97
Woolf, Leonard, The Future of Constantinople, 91
Wylde, A. B., Modern Abyssinia, 152, 163-166, 173, 199, 201

Zanzibar, 174, 175, 228-312
  and Benadir Coast, 174
  and slave trade, 232, 233
  partition of, 244 ff.
Zimmermann, Alfred, 32, 33, 34, 36, 236, 237, 254, 268, 336

THE END

Printed by R. & R. CLARK, LIMITED, Edinburgh.

For Product Safety Concerns and Information please contact our EU
representative GPSR@taylorandfrancis.com Taylor & Francis Verlag GmbH,
Kaufingerstraße 24, 80331 München, Germany

Printed and bound by CPI Group (UK) Ltd, Croydon, CR0 4YY
08/05/2025
01864391-0008